Praise for *Out of Mao's Shadow*

"Compelling. . . . It is Mr. Pan's achievement in *Out of Mao's Shadow* that he makes the dark side of China's glittering economic growth palpably real to the reader by showing the fallout of these changes on the lives of individual citizens, just as he shows the potent effect that a few brave individuals—speaking up on behalf of civil liberties, freedom of the press and government accountability—can have on the party's conduct of day-to-day business. Fluent in Chinese, Mr. Pan . . . interviewed artists, workers, peasants, journalists and entrepreneurs, and his portraits of these people possess both the immediacy of first-rate reportage and the emotional depth of field of a novel."

—Michiko Kakutani, *The New York Times*

"One of the most revealing books about China since it opened up to the outside world in the 1970s."

—Richard Bernstein, *The New York Review of Books*

"A model work of investigative political journalism."

—Jeffrey Wasserstrom, *The Guardian*

"A fascinating read."

—Jon Stewart, *The Daily Show*

"A dark, sober, but highly important look at the struggle against repression in China."

—Lori Valigra, *The Christian Science Monitor*

"Pan has chosen his subjects well, lets them speak, and delivers a fascinating portrait of New China."

—Gordon Chang, *New York Sun*

"A number of foreign correspondents have returned from China in the past 20 years and written books attempting to put a human face on the giant. Many of these books are good, but for readers interested in fundamental political questions, *Out of Mao's Shadow* stands out. Philip P. Pan . . . has put together human stories with a political meaning."

—Bruce Ramsey, *The Seattle Times*

"Required reading."

—Billy Heller, *New York Post*

"A privileged inside look at China's populace with the secrecy veil lifted, showing how their struggles for personal freedom are slowly building a more tolerant and open democracy. . . . Pan's stories about key players in China show how far the country has come in recent years because of the efforts of many brave people."

—Verna Noel Jones, *Rocky Mountain News*

"Pan focuses these 11 profiles on China's lonely dissidents. . . . These narratives show China's social and political tensions playing out through personal enmities, petty bribery and subtle moral compromises. Pan's stirring reportage shows that, even in China, the individual can make a difference—at a price."

—*Publishers Weekly* (starred review)

"As the former Beijing bureau chief for the *Washington Post*, Pan has had a front-row seat to what he calls the 'struggle for China's soul' between capitalism and authoritarianism. But, unlike many books in this genre, Pan brings the battle alive through vivid portraits of everyday people including entrepreneurs. This is a dense and complex story, but one that is masterfully told."

—Amy Haimerl, *Fortune*

"Books on China are being published at an alarming rate, but one seems to stand out because it is written by a veteran foreign correspondent who seems to understand the country's soul. Plus, he speaks the language fluently. Philip P. Pan's *Out of Mao's Shadow* is a vivid look inside China through the eyes of its political and intellectual leaders."

—Steve Bennett, *San Antonio Express-News*

"For seven years, Pan, former Beijing bureau chief for the *Washington Post*, traveled China and talked to officials, journalists, artists, entrepreneurs, and ordinary citizens to get a portrait of an extraordinary time in that nation's—and the world's—history."

—*Booklist*

"Phil Pan is one of the finest American correspondents to have worked in China, a penetrating reporter who works from the ground up. This is an extraordinarily important book about China's unfinished politics."

—Steve Coll, *The Bin Ladens: An Arabian Family in the American Century*

"*Out of Mao's Shadow* is a stunningly researched and crafted book, filled with tales of individual heroism, triumph and heartbreak. Pan shares his subjects' relentless curiosity and drive to find truth; the result is a book that's immediate, moving, and ultimately thrilling."

—Rachel DeWoskin, author of *Foreign Babes in Beijing: Behind the Scenes of a New China*

"As correspondent for the *Washington Post*, Philip Pan covered China like no one else, using his fluency in the language to penetrate Chinese society. He goes beyond his newspaper reporting to tell the story of Chinese people pressing unsuccessfully for political change. Pan's book gives the lie to the notion that China is inevitably heading towards democratization."

—James Mann, author of *Rise of the Vulcans: The History of Bush's War Cabinet*

"Philip Pan, a journalist blessed with fluent Chinese and an intrepid curiosity, tells a heartbreaking story of good people abused and their revolutionary sacrifices forgotten."

—Christopher Wren, author of *The End of the Line: The Failure of Communism in the Soviet Union and China*

"Philip Pan has brought great patience and a rare sensitivity to political reporting in China. This is the story of how power actually works in China."

—Peter Hessler, author of *Oracle Bones: A Journey Through Time in China*

"Philip Pan's book is a masterpiece of reportage, revealing the layers of dirt and pain that lurk just beneath the shiny surface of modern China. Weaving the past and the present into one seamless narrative, Pan beautifully relates the stories of extraordinary Chinese individuals as they struggle to reclaim their nation's soul."

—Rob Gifford, NPR correspondent and author of *China Road: A Journey into the Future of a Rising Power*

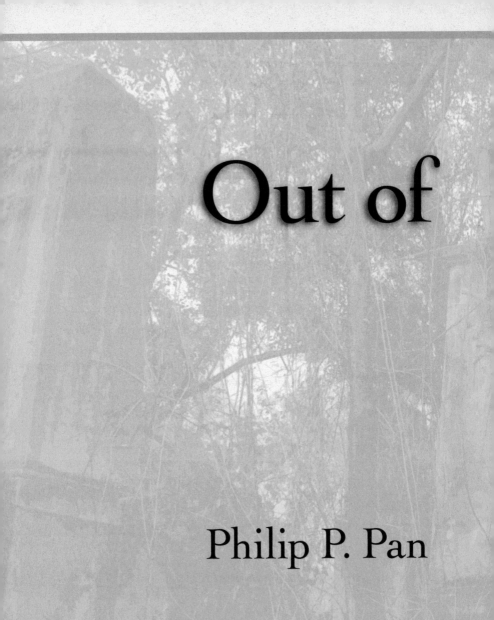

Out of

Philip P. Pan

Mao's Shadow

The Struggle for the
Soul of a New China

SIMON & SCHUSTER PAPERBACKS

NEW YORK   LONDON   TORONTO   SYDNEY

For Sarah and Mookie,
and for my parents

ILLUSTRATION CREDITS
Philip P. Pan: title page, 80, 294; AFP / Getty Images: 2; Courtesy of Hu Jie: 22, 48;
Peter Parks / AFP / Getty Images: 112; Ji Guoqiang / ImagineChina: 148;
Gao Zhan: 176 (both photos), 268, 273; Taozi: 198; He Longsheng: 236

Simon & Schuster Paperbacks
A Division of Simon & Schuster, Inc.
1230 Avenue of the Americas
New York, NY 10020

First Simon & Schuster trade paperback edition June 2009

SIMON & SCHUSTER PAPERBACKS and colophon are
registered trademarks of Simon & Schuster, Inc.

For information about special discounts for bulk purchases,
please contact Simon & Schuster Special Sales at
1-866-506-1949 or business@simonandschuster.com.

The Simon & Schuster Speakers Bureau can bring authors to
your live event. For more information or to book an event, contact
the Simon & Schuster Speakers Bureau at 1-866-248-3049 or visit
our website at www.simonspeakers.com.

Designed by Level C

Manufactured in the United States of America

10 9 8 7 6 5 4 3 2 1

The Library of Congress has cataloged the hardcover edition as follows:

Pan, Philip P.
   Out of Mao's shadow / Philip P. Pan.
      p. cm.
Includes bibliographical references and index.
   1. China—Social conditions—1976–2000.   2. China—Social conditions—
2000–   3. China—History—1949–   I. Title.
   HN733.5.P36   2008
   306.20951'09045—dc22   2008011550

   ISBN: 978-1-4165-3705-2
   ISBN: 978-1-4165-3706-9 (pbk)

CONTENTS

Part III
STRUGGLE SESSIONS

Out of Mao's Shadow

INTRODUCTION

On a warm Friday night in the summer of 2001, I stood amid hundreds of thousands of young Chinese pouring into Tiananmen Square in a joyous and largely spontaneous celebration of Beijing's successful bid to host the Summer Olympics in 2008. As fireworks lit the sky and blasts from car horns echoed across the city, the exultant crowd pushed through lines of riot police, filling the square and its surrounding boulevards. "Beijing! Beijing!" the revelers chanted, many of them waving little red Chinese flags. "Long live the motherland! Long live the motherland!" University students shimmied up traffic lamps, singing the national anthem and patriotic hymns such as "Without the Communist Party, There Would Be No New China." Shirtless young men ran laps around the square, trailing red and green banners and shouting obscenities in jubilation. Bicycles, motorbikes, pedicabs, and cars packed the streets, the giddy people on board flashing victory signs. From atop the Gate of Heavenly Peace, where Mao Zedong proclaimed the establishment of the People's Republic of China in 1949 and where his portrait still hangs, the men at the helm of the Communist Party looked out on the masses and basked in the outpouring of national pride.

I had arrived in Beijing only months earlier, a new China correspondent for the *Washington Post*, and the collective outburst of joy in the political heart of the nation took me by surprise. Not since the pro-democracy demonstrations in 1989 had so many people converged on Tiananmen, and the contrast was inescapable and jarring. Back then, the multitudes of young people who filled the square were protesting the corruption of the Communist government and calling for demo-cratic reform. The army crushed those protests, and in the early 1990s, when I was studying Mandarin in Beijing, the memory of the massa-cre still darkened university campuses. But now people seemed to have forgotten the party's violent suppression of the democracy move-ment, and the crowds in Tiananmen were cheering the government. What had happened to the demands for political change? How had the party regained its footing? And how long could it hold on to power?

Over the next seven years, I searched for answers to these ques-tions, a quest that took me to cities, towns, and villages across China. What I found was a government engaged in the largest and perhaps most successful experiment in authoritarianism in the world. The West has assumed that capitalism must lead to democracy, that free markets inevitably result in free societies. But by embracing market reforms while continuing to restrict political freedom, China's Com-munist leaders have presided over an economic revolution without surrendering power. Prosperity allowed the government to reinvent itself, to win friends and buy allies, and to forestall demands for demo-cratic change. It was a remarkable feat, all the more so because the regime had inflicted so much misery on the nation over the past half century. But as I examined the party's success, I also saw something else extraordinary—a people recovering from the trauma of Commu-nist rule, asserting themselves against the state and demanding greater control of their lives. They are survivors, whose families endured one of the world's deadliest famines during the Great Leap Forward, whose idealism was exploited during the madness of the Cultural Revolution, and whose values have been tested by the booming econ-omy and the rush to get rich. The young men and women who filled Tiananmen Square in the spring of 1989 saw their hopes for a demo-cratic China crushed in a massacre, but as older, more pragmatic adults, many continue to pursue political change in different ways.

In the three decades since Mao Zedong's death, China has undergone a dizzying transformation. A backwater economy has become a powerhouse of manufacturing and trade, with growth rates that are the envy of the world. Skyscrapers have sprouted from rice paddies, gleaming cities from fishing villages. Infant mortality is down, and incomes and life expectancy are up. With economic change has come political progress, too. The terror campaigns that Mao favored, the mass denunciation meetings, the frenzied crowds of youngsters waving little red books—they are all things of the past. People enjoy greater prosperity but also greater personal freedom and access to information than ever before under Communist rule. By almost any measure, the country's last twenty-five years have been the best in its five-thousand-year history. But the Chinese people have not yet escaped Mao's shadow. A momentous struggle is under way for the soul of the world's most populous nation. On one side is the venal party-state, an entrenched elite fighting to preserve the country's authoritarian political system and its privileged place within it. On the other is a ragtag collection of lawyers, journalists, entrepreneurs, artists, hustlers, and dreamers striving to build a more tolerant, open, and democratic China.

The outcome of this struggle is important not only because half of the planet's population without basic political freedoms lives in China, or because other governments around the world are already copying the Chinese model to curb demands for democratic change by their own peoples. It is also important because what kind of country China becomes—democracy, dictatorship, or something in between—will help answer one of the pressing questions of our time: How will the rise of China affect the rest of the world? In other words, the future of the Chinese political system could define how China behaves as an emerging global power, how it interacts with its neighbors in Asia and with that nation watching it so closely on the other side of the globe, the United States.

This book is an attempt to describe the battle for China's future through the eyes of a handful of men and women. I begin in Part I with the efforts of individuals to unearth and preserve the nation's tragic recent history. The party's ability to rewrite the past is critical to its grip on the present and the future, and it has tried to maintain a sanitized account of events that serves to justify its rule. But, from the violent beginnings of Chinese communism to the Tiananmen Square massacre, society is beginning to recover the truth. Part II explores how the party evolved after Mao's death and adapted to survive. The totalitarian, socialist state that Mao built is no more. In its place is a more cynical, stable, and nimble bureaucracy, one that values self-preservation above all else and relies on an often corrupt and predatory form of capitalism to survive. This section tells the stories of miners and factory workers left behind and the apparatchiks and tycoons who thrived. I conclude in Part III with four ordinary people who tried to push the limits of what is permissible in China just as a new party leadership raised hopes of democratic progress. Thrust into the national spotlight, they are forced to make difficult decisions about when to fight and when to back down, and to weigh the consequences of their choices for their families and their nation.

Having tasted freedom, having learned something about the rule of law, having seen on television and in the movies and on the Internet how other societies elect their own leaders, the Chinese people are pushing every day for a more responsive and just political system. The party has struggled to adapt and sometimes retreated in the face of such popular pressure, but it has not yet surrendered, not even close. Its leaders, and its millions of functionaries and beneficiaries, continue to cling to power, marshalling their considerable resources in a determined and often obsessive effort to maintain control over an increasingly vibrant society. Many people who care about China tell themselves that democratization is inevitable, that the people will eventually prevail and the one-party state will fail. I certainly hope so. But I have seen that there is nothing automatic about political change. It is a difficult, messy, and often heartbreaking process, and it happens—when it happens at all—because of imperfect individuals who fight, take risks, and sacrifice for it. They can be noble, courageous, selfless, stubborn, vain, naive, calculating, and reckless, and I was fortunate to meet so many of them during my time in China. Their stories inspired this book.

Part I

REMEMBERING

Zhao Ziyang in Tiananmen Square with a bullhorn in 1989. Wen Jiabao, his aide then and the Chinese premier now, stands facing straight ahead to his left.

1

THE PUBLIC FUNERAL

They came from the walled compounds of the Communist Party elite and the shantytowns of the disgruntled and dispossessed, from universities and office towers, from booming cities and dirt-poor villages across China. They came by the thousands, citizens of a nation on the rise, defying the lessons drilled into them by state propaganda and the caution taught them by a century of bitter experience. On a cold January morning, in sleek sedans and battered taxicabs, on bicycle and on foot, they made their way past security checkpoints, refusing to turn back even when police snapped photos and recorded their names for the state's secret files. Slowly, they converged on a vast cemetery on the western outskirts of Beijing. There, in a small memorial hall, on a dais surrounded by evergreen leaves, lay the man whose death they had come to mourn, a man the party had told them to forget.

They last saw him more than fifteen years ago, with a bullhorn in his hands and tears in his eyes, standing in Tiananmen Square amid the students who were demanding democratic reform in the spring of 1989. Zhao Ziyang was general secretary of the Communist Party then, only the third man to hold the party's top post after Mao's death, so it was a surprise when he suddenly appeared before dawn that May morning and waded into the crowd of young protesters. He was a grandfatherly figure in a gray tunic suit, already seventy years old with white hair and large round glasses. As the television cameras rolled, he told the students he sympathized with their cause and accepted their criticism, and he urged them to go home. But his voice trembled with emotion, and there was a hint of the tragedy to come in his words. "We have come too late, too late," he said, choking up, his face drawn with exhaustion. And then he was gone. It was not until much later, after the tanks had entered the capital and the soldiers opened fire, killing hundreds, perhaps thousands, that the world learned Zhao had been ousted by party elders just before coming to the square. He had sided with the students, refusing to order the military to crush the demonstrations.

The party put Zhao under house arrest and set about erasing him from public memory. He was airbrushed from photographs, deleted from textbooks, and any mention of his name in the media was forbidden. It was as if the Communist leader who came closer than anyone else to bringing democratic change to the country simply ceased to exist. As he languished in custody, the state spun its own version of history: The bloodshed in Tiananmen was necessary to restore order. China was too big, too poor, too uneducated for democracy, which would lead to chaos and civil war. Only one-party rule could ensure stability in the world's most populous nation, and only stability could guarantee the economic growth needed to make the country strong. The propagandists promoted these arguments tirelessly, and the censors buried competing views. With repetition and the passage of time—and the help of an economy that soared—many Chinese came to accept this view of their nation, and the world welcomed China back into the ranks of respectable powers. But all the while, the party continued to confine Zhao to his traditional courtyard home in Beijing. He was a symbol of another vision for China, one that still resonated with the public despite the party's efforts to wipe it out. The men who held power knew this, and they were afraid.

When Zhao died on January 17, 2005, after suffering a series of strokes at the age of eighty-five, the party's leaders convened a series of emergency meetings to prepare a response that would prevent his death from triggering a new debate about the Tiananmen massacre or fresh demonstrations for democratic reform. Though Zhao had served as premier for seven years and party chief for three, pioneering the market reforms in the 1980s that would transform the Chinese economy, his successors ordered state television and radio not to announce his death. The very few granted permission to report the story were told to use a one-sentence dispatch that referred to him only as "comrade" and to make no mention of his past leadership posts. The *Beijing Evening News* buried the item on page sixteen, under a brief about the Golden Globe awards ceremony in the United States.

But the party's control of information had weakened in the years since Tiananmen. Word of Comrade Zhao's death spread quickly across the nation he once led via home satellite dishes and cell phones, e-mail and instant messaging. Within hours, citizens posted thousands of notes of sorrow and remembrance on Internet bulletin boards, then watched as the censors tried to delete them. "Can't we grieve when someone has died?" wrote one user in frustration on the Web site of the *People's Daily*, the party's flagship newspaper. In the following days, as it became clear the leadership had decided to deny Zhao the honor of a state funeral, people began sending flowers to his home; soon there were enough to fill several rooms. Then mourners started showing up at the house. Hundreds came to pay their respects, and when police tried to stop them, they waited outside in the cold. Some refused to leave and were dragged away.

Zhao's death revealed a scar on the nation's conscience. For years, people had tried to put Tiananmen behind them. Friends avoided the subject, and parents told their children not to ask about it. Many of those who had been part of the democracy movement threw themselves into making money, claiming they no longer cared about their country's political fate. The pain of remembering, the guilt of giving up and moving on—for many, it was too much to bear, and looking away seemed the only way to live. But when Zhao died, people allowed themselves a moment to reflect again on those young men and women killed in 1989, and to ask whether their sacrifice had meant anything. They examined what had become of their country in the years since the massacre, and let themselves wonder what might have been had the students moderated their demands and prevailed. They considered the failings of the party's marriage of authoritarian politics with capitalist economics. Yes, China had grown more prosperous and gained international prestige. But the boom had also left many behind, and the nation's troubles were obvious to anyone willing to see: the stifling limits on political and religious freedoms, the abuse of power by privileged officials, the sweatshop conditions in the factories, the persistent poverty in the countryside, the degradation of the environment, the moral drift of a cynical society.

Zhao had been a party activist since he was a teenager, but when Politburo hard-liners pressured him to crush the demonstrations in Tiananmen Square, he refused. And when the nation's paramount leader, Deng Xiaoping, ordered troops into the capital, he tendered his resignation. Years later, when Deng offered to reinstate him if only he would admit he was wrong and endorse the crackdown, Zhao again said no. Zhao made it clear that there was a line he would not cross. How many others could say the same? How many had signed statements repeating the party's lies about Tiananmen to save themselves in the crackdown that followed? How many continued to curry favor with the party to further their careers or gain an edge in business? How many could really say their hands were clean?

WANG JUNXIU HAD just arrived in his Beijing office, and was bypassing the government's Internet controls and checking the news on overseas Web sites. As he clicked, he spotted the item: Zhao Ziyang, former Chinese Communist Party chief, dead at eighty-five. So it really happened, he thought. The old man finally passed away.

A stocky fellow in his mid-thirties with a rough, pudgy face, Wang was the cofounder and chief executive officer of China's most popular blog-hosting Web site, Bokee.com. For weeks government censors had been warning him to prevent rumors about Zhao's failing health from being posted on the site. Zhao could die at any moment, they said, and if he did, they didn't want Wang's five million users reading about it or discussing it. As usual, Wang assured them he would comply. But he also knew there was really no need for the warning. His company had long ago programmed its software to block people from mentioning Zhao's name in their blogs.

Wang felt a dull sadness. Until the censors started calling, he had not thought about Zhao in years. For most of the past decade and a half, Wang had been immersing himself in books about memory chips and programming languages, and building a comfortable life for himself and his wife, complete with a two-bedroom apartment in the suburbs. But Zhao's death brought back memories from another life, one in which he dared to fight for principles like freedom of speech. It stirred up feelings that had been gnawing at his conscience and doubts about the choices he had made. It made him wonder what had become of the young idealist he once was.

It felt as if a lifetime had passed since he participated in the protests in Tiananmen Square, but now he remembered the exhilaration of marching through the city as part of a crowd of hundreds of thousands; the cry of students chanting slogans for freedom and democracy; the conviction that he could make a difference and help steer his nation toward a better future. He was a junior at the China University of Politics and Law then, a shy kid from the countryside who gained self-confidence in the student movement. As the demonstrations grew and spread across the country that spring, Wang set up a loudspeaker station on his campus so classmates could broadcast news and speeches. He often spent his days in the square and his nights at the loudspeaker station, sleeping only a few hours at a time and living off the adrenalin rush of idealism. He was at the station on the night the army opened fire, reading out the reports of violence as they came in, but he kept thinking that there must be a mistake, that the military couldn't have done this, that people weren't really dying. When the bodies of four students killed in the shooting were brought back to the university, he put down the microphone and wept.

Later that morning, teachers and classmates urged Wang to flee the capital: he had attracted attention to himself, and they feared the authorities would be looking to arrest him. Rushing to the rail station, Wang saw the smoking wrecks of cars and buses that residents had tried to use to block the army's attack. He caught the first train out, and eventually made his way to his hometown in rural Shanxi Province, where he listened to the reports of student arrests and waited for word of his own fate. Several tense weeks later, the university summoned him back to campus—he would be allowed to return to school and graduate if he confessed. Wang felt he had no choice. The teachers assigned to his case let him get away with describing only his own actions and never pressed him to name others who took part in the demonstrations. But like many students in his situation, Wang had to endorse the military crackdown and write that he had been "tricked" into supporting the democracy movement. It was a lie, but at the time he was just relieved to be getting off easy.

After earning his law degree, Wang returned to his hometown and struggled to find work because no one wanted to hire someone tainted by participation in the Tiananmen protests. As the government pushed ahead with market reforms, though, the emerging private sector began to overtake the state economy, creating opportunities even for political outcasts. A fellow law student and Tiananmen protester named Pu Zhiqiang helped Wang get a job at an advertising firm in Beijing. The company was hired to produce a regular feature page about computers for a state newspaper, and Wang was assigned to edit it. He threw himself into work, learning as much as he could about the computer industry. One job led to another, and within a few years he had gained enough experience and expertise to start a tech consulting firm with a friend. Suddenly he was a member of Beijing's growing middle class.

Each year, Wang let go of the past a little more. It hurt to dwell on the tragedy, to think of the lives lost and the fact that no one would ever be held accountable, to wonder how China might be different if the party had set the nation on a path of gradual political reform. The Communist Party maintained a tight grip on power, and as far as Wang could tell, there was nothing he could do about it. So, like almost everyone else, he moved on. He focused on his own problems instead of the country's, on work instead of politics, on money instead of justice.

Wang worked so hard that his health suffered. In 2000, he was forced to take a medical leave and while recuperating at home, he found himself exploring the World Wide Web. The Internet was still relatively new to China, and the government had not yet started blocking access to politically objectionable Web sites. Bored and restless, Wang came across the vast array of material available online about the Tiananmen Square demonstrations—essays, memoirs, reports, even videos. He was quickly drawn in, spending entire days in front of his computer, scrolling through one compelling document after another. A novel he found online left a particularly deep impression. It was based on the experiences of a group of friends who agonized over whether to help a democracy activist wanted by police after the massacre; in the end, they tried to smuggle him out of the country but were betrayed by one of their own, and they all ended up in prison. It was during this break from his hectic career that Wang began to think about the potential of the Internet; he would help start Bokee.com three years later. It was also during the medical leave that Wang first read at length about Zhao Ziyang. In the final days of the democracy movement, he had seen a poster on campus calling on students to "protect" Zhao, and he recalled reading a number of reports about political reform written by think tanks under Zhao's control. But the party's efforts to erase Zhao from history had been so effective that Wang never appreciated who Zhao was and what he had done until he read about him on the Web. It was only then that he learned Zhao was still alive and being held under house arrest.

After Zhao's death, Wang felt compelled to examine his own life, to ask himself if he had strayed too far from his principles in the years since Tiananmen. Yes, he marked the anniversary of the movement every year by visiting the square with a few old friends. Yes, he once signed an open letter urging the government to apologize for the massacre. But could he have done more? His company had challenged the state's monopoly of the media by giving millions of Chinese a place to publish on the Web. But given his compliance with the party's Internet censors, was that enough?

The more Wang thought, the more he knew he had to pay tribute to Zhao. At home that evening, he sat in front of his computer and composed a eulogy:

Your death will be in our hearts forever, never to be forgotten. We will always remember that you once used your body to block the bullets that gunned down our nation's glorious future. You calmly endured 16 years of life without freedom. You never bowed your head. You stood up for justice. You displayed the utmost in political courage. Because of you, there was a rare bit of color in the gloom of politics. And yet the cowardly souls you tried to redeem repaid you with cruel confinement. For 16 years, you as a common citizen frightened those destroying our nation, shamed those who are fainthearted, and inspired people of integrity and ideals. All patriotic people who cherish justice, whether they are old or young, from north or south, followed you closely, praying for you and hoping that one day they might fight for the nation's future with you. We shared the same willingness to act regardless of what might happen to us, the same love of our country, the same desire to pursue justice and freedom. But now, before we could realize our dreams, the heavens have taken you from us. How could we not grieve deeply?

Wang signed the essay "The 1989 Generation," and sent copies to some friends.

The next day, he read online that people were visiting Zhao's home to pay their respects to his family, and he decided that he would also go. He skipped work a few days later. Together with a few friends, he bought some flowers and located Zhao's house using an address he found on the Internet. No one tried to stop them as they walked down a narrow alley to the house, but inside past the large red doors, Wang noticed several men who appeared to be state security agents. Some had cameras and snapped photos, but he was no longer frightened. He signed his name in a guest book on a table near the entrance and left his phone number, too.

The house was of a traditional design, with rooms positioned around two small courtyards. The family had set up a memorial shrine in a small study located to the left, and it was full of wreaths of white and yellow chrysanthemums graced with black and white ribbons carrying messages of condolence. A portrait of Zhao wearing a light blue shirt hung on the center of the main wall. Nearby was a funeral scroll: "To be your children is the honor of our lives. To support your decision is our unchanging choice."

What Wang found most striking about Zhao's house was how ordinary and run-down it was. The walls were dirty, the ceilings were low, and the study was furnished only with a shabby sofa, an old desk, and a small collection of books, among them the translated memoirs of a few U.S. and Soviet leaders and a recent exposé of rural corruption, *An Investigation of China's Peasantry*. It occurred to Wang that the house was not much bigger or better than his parents' simple home in the countryside. So this was where a great man had been confined in old age, left to die all but forgotten by the world.

Wang expressed his sympathies to Zhao's relatives, who were dressed in dark blue cotton coats, and he gave them copies of the eulogy he'd written. One of Zhao's grandchildren, a teenage girl, started to cry as she read the tribute, and as he watched her, Wang found himself wiping away tears, too.

• • •

FUNERALS FOR POPULAR Chinese leaders can be politically sensitive affairs. In 1976, Mao tried to restrict public mourning for his long-time deputy, Premier Zhou Enlai, the man who engineered the rapprochement with the United States and was viewed as a voice of restraint during the insanity of the Cultural Revolution. But a million people lined his funeral route, and tens of thousands later staged protests in Tiananmen Square and clashed with police. The 1989 demonstrations in Tiananmen were also triggered by the death of a popular leader, the reformist party chief Hu Yaobang, who had been ousted by hard-liners two years earlier. So in 2005, the leadership approached Zhao's funeral with particular caution. It wanted a memorial service that would help the nation forget Zhao's life, not celebrate it.

The task seemed easy enough, for it had never been very difficult to persuade people to forget Zhao. Western governments stopped asking about him almost as soon as he fell from power, and kept his name off the lists of political prisoners they inquired about. Many analysts at the time considered Zhao an authoritarian leader who sided with the students as part of a power struggle, not a genuine democrat. His critics argued that he never showed much interest in democratic reform before the Tiananmen movement, and accused him of helping the party's hard-liners topple his liberal predecessor. Zhao backed the prodemocracy demonstrations, they said, only because he was an opportunist making a power play against the paramount leader Deng Xiaoping. This was the cynic's interpretation of Zhao's decision to oppose the military assault in 1989, and Deng and the men he picked to replace Zhao were more than happy to let it stand. The last thing they wanted people to believe was the alternative, that Zhao was that rare exception in the history of Chinese Communist Party leaders: a man who could no longer go along with evil.

But in time, that's what the evidence showed he was. In internal documents smuggled out of China and memoirs written by people who worked with him, a picture emerged of Zhao that challenged the party's caricature. Not only was he a bold advocate of capitalist-style economic reforms at a time when party conservatives were fighting such policies as ideological heresy, he also was a proponent of political reform who favored a democratic transition in China, albeit a gradual one. During his three years in power, Zhao promoted discussion of changes in the party's ossified political structure to reduce corruption, including the introduction of competitive elections and increased autonomy for local and national parliaments. He told one aide he hoped provincial-level elections could be held within a decade. Another recalled that during Zhao's tenure, neither the Politburo nor its powerful Standing Committee ever discussed a single case involving a "political crime." And when officials sought his instructions about a new film about the Cultural Revolution, Zhao suggested the party stop interfering in the arts. "I don't investigate movies, I watch them," he said. "If I have to issue instructions for every movie I see, I think I'll stop watching movies."

When the students filled Tiananmen Square, Zhao encouraged dialogue and calm, cautioned his colleagues against heavy-handed measures, and appeared to sympathize with the protesters' demands. "Democracy is a worldwide trend," he told the Politburo on May 1, two weeks after the demonstrations began and months before the fall of the Berlin Wall. "If the party does not hold up the banner of democracy in our country, someone else will, and we will lose out. I think we should grab the lead on this and not be pushed along grudgingly." A few weeks later, Zhao discussed the subject with the Soviet reformer Mikhail Gorbachev, who had come to Beijing at the height of the student protests for a previously scheduled summit meeting. "Can a one-party system ensure the development of democracy?" Zhao asked his Soviet counterpart. "Can it implement effective control over negative phenomena and fight the corruption in party and government institutions?" Gorbachev recalled the conversation in his memoirs:

> From Zhao's arguments, it followed that the Chinese leadership was prepared to follow the path of political reform by giving the masses a chance to enjoy broad democratic rights under one-party rule. He concluded that if this did not work out, the issue of a multi-party system would inevitably arise. In addition, he emphasized the need to strengthen citizens' constitutional rights and create an optimal correlation between democracy and law. Law must be based on democracy, and democracy must be based on law. . . . To be frank, the openness demonstrated at my meeting with [Zhao] amazed me. . . . Here he was, faced with a dem-

ocratic challenge from the student masses. Zhao Ziyang had to know that many were demanding the imposition of order, since the student demonstrations had taken on the character of civil disobedience. But most of these demonstrators were people who had followed him, after all, or at least who had been inspired by ideas he himself shared. Herein lay his drama.

The drama reached its climax the day after Zhao's meeting with Gorbachev. In an expanded session of the Politburo Standing Committee, Deng proposed the imposition of martial law to clear the square and end the protests. Zhao objected, and when he was overruled, he tendered his resignation.

After the bloodshed, Zhao submitted to life under house arrest. From his home at No. 6 Fuqiang Hutong, he watched in frustration as the party blamed him for the student "turmoil" and then set out to make sure the country forgot him. He tried to resist. In the late 1990s, two letters he wrote demanding a reassessment of the Tiananmen protests were leaked to the public. And later, in interviews secretly conducted by various friends in the years before his death, he managed to present his views for the historical record. He explained his plans for gradual democratic reform, answering critics who accused him of moving too slowly as well as those who said he had moved too fast, and he faulted Deng for failing to grasp the need to adapt the political system to the new economy he was building. He denied trying to push out his predecessor, and criticized his successors—China's current leaders—for lacking vision and forbidding even talk of political reform. He worried about rampant corruption and rising discontent with the party's rule, and wondered whether those who benefited most from China's one-party market economy—party hacks and their cronies—were already too powerful and entrenched for any leader to introduce democracy. But most of all, he denounced the Tiananmen Square massacre. "There was an argument that the suppression was the last resort, as there was no alternative. This argument is wrong," he said. "We had many chances that would have made a solution without bloodshed possible."

Zhao lived under constant surveillance, and security remained tight even as he lay on his deathbed in the hospital. Some party officials resorted to putting on white lab coats and pretending to be doctors so they could keep a closer eye on him. When Li Rui, the eighty-eight-year-old former government minister who once served as an aide to Mao, attempted to visit Zhao in late December, security agents blocked his way for nearly an hour before a supervisor intervened. Days before Zhao's death, the seventy-five-year-old former Politburo member Tian Jiyun was permitted to see his former colleague for the first time in more than fifteen years, but security agents insisted on staying in the room to monitor their brief conversation. After Zhao died of lung failure, Tian returned to the hospital. "Now that he has gone," he told Zhao's children, "we don't have to be afraid any more of people saying we are plotting some so-called hidden scheme!" Zhao's only daughter, Wang Yannan, announced her father's death in a text message to friends with her cell phone: "He left quietly this morning. He is free at last!"

But even after Zhao's death, the security apparatus didn't back off. His children began having trouble making and receiving calls with their cell phones, and the calls that did go through were often cut off. Police set up checkpoints around his house, blocking friends trying to visit to express their sympathies. They also detained a large group of petitioners, ordinary citizens from around the country who had traveled to Beijing with grievances against the abuse of power by local officials, and who unfurled a banner "in memory of our good leader." When Bao Tong, the seventy-two-year-old former aide to Zhao who was the highest-ranking official arrested in the Tiananmen crackdown, attempted to leave his apartment building to pay his respects, a team of plainclothes security agents shoved him back inside and into an elevator. His seventy-three-year-old wife was knocked to the ground in the scuffle and hospitalized for weeks with a fractured vertebra. Bao sprained his wrist and a finger, but the agents wouldn't let him see a doctor unless he removed a white flower pinned to his shirt and a black armband he was wearing, traditional symbols of mourning. He refused and endured the pain instead.

Meanwhile, Zhao's children began negotiating their father's memorial arrangements with senior party officials assigned to handle the funeral. The family wanted to host the service and open it to the public, but the party insisted that it be allowed to take control and restrict attendance. Another point of dispute was the content of an official obituary evaluating Zhao's life. Such obituaries are standard protocol for senior officials, but Zhao's family objected because the party's draft accused him of making a "serious mistake" in 1989 and played down his role in promoting the market reforms that transformed the economy. They argued that if any "mistake" was mentioned, the party should be specific about what their father had done wrong, and note that he spent the last years of his life under house arrest for it. There was also disagreement over what would happen to Zhao's ashes. The party agreed to place them in the Babaoshan Revolutionary Cemetery, the nation's main resting place for revolutionary heroes and high government officials, but selected a small memorial hall that the family complained held only the ashes of lower-level officials. Later, the family inquired about purchasing a plot in the section of the cemetery open to the public. Party officials lied and told them it was sold out, apparently because they worried the tomb might become a gathering place for the party's opponents in the future.

After sixteen rounds of negotiations in little more than a week, the party finally told the family it intended to organize a modest, invitation-only funeral and refrain from publishing an official evaluation of Zhao's life. The family would be allowed to submit a list of guests and take his ashes home. Zhao's children reluctantly agreed, but outlined their concerns in a letter to party authorities. They noted that their father had been held under illegal house arrest for nearly sixteen years, and urged the party to give people who had been prevented from seeing him for so long a chance to attend the funeral and say good-bye. They said their father never changed his position on the Tiananmen Square movement, and neither would they. The party was just wrong, they wrote, and no matter what it said about him now, "history would draw the correct conclusion."

ABOUT A WEEK after Wang Junxiu visited Zhao's house, the family arranged for him to get an invitation to the funeral. Wang knew that attending the service would be a political statement, and that there could be consequences. Perhaps the secret police would put his name on some blacklist, or scrutinize his company's finances, or put pressure on his business partners. Anything could happen, or nothing could happen. The uncertainty had the effect of magnifying fear, and the party used fear to discourage people from concerning themselves with politics or public affairs. It preferred that they focus on their narrow self-interests, because that made it easier to keep them divided and prevent them from coming together to challenge its rule. It preferred that people skip Zhao's funeral. Wang recognized that there was no benefit to attending the service, only risks and costs. But he decided almost immediately that he would go. His conscience demanded it. As a member of the Tiananmen generation and one of the many students that Zhao had tried to defend, he felt it was the least he could do.

Wang woke before dawn on the morning of the memorial service. The Babaoshan Revolutionary Cemetery was on the other side of the city, and he had arranged to meet a few friends and share a ride. It was a frigid winter day, and brisk winds had cleared away the pollution that usually choked Beijing, revealing a cloudless blue sky. Despite the cold, Wang dressed lightly, just a sweater and a leather jacket. He took a cab to a nearby light rail station, passing the headquarters of the army's 2nd Artillery Division, the offices of the computer manufacturer Lenovo, and a vast construction site where yet another luxury apartment complex was going up. The train took him from the suburbs to a subway station in the city, where his friends picked him up in a jeep. There were three others in the car with him: Xue Ye, an environmental activist; Mo Zhaohui, a book publisher; and a driver employed by Mo's publishing house. Both Xue and Mo had participated in the 1989 demonstrations, and the three of them had been friends for years.

Sitting in the back with Xue, Wang noticed three large bundles of white cloth on the floor of the jeep. In the days before, he and his friends had decided to carry banners in honor of Zhao to the service, and Mo had paid a company to make them. "You are free at last!" read one. "Our memories will not fade, your ideals will never die!" read another. The third said, "You inspired awe by maintaining justice, and that will not diminish with time!" Each was signed "The 1989 Generation." Wang had felt strongly about bringing the banners. He knew that most of the leaders of the Tiananmen movement had been exiled, and that others who participated had been detained in recent days to prevent them from attending the funeral. He thought the banners would speak on their behalf. He also wanted other people, especially those younger than them, to know that his generation had not been silenced and had not forgotten what happened. But as he examined the bundles of cloth in the car, Wang realized there was a problem. They were too big and too heavy. At least two people would be required to carry each one, even if they were not unfurled. After some discussion, Mo and Xue said they would carry one in first, and if no one stopped them, Wang would recruit friends to help him bring in the other two.

As they drove toward the cemetery, Wang noticed more and more police taking up positions on the streets, men in dark blue uniforms with motorcycles, cruisers, and vans. The vast deployment seemed intended to crush any attempt to stage demonstrations in the city. Some of the officers were setting up checkpoints and roadblocks, and Wang began to worry they might be stopped and prevented from going to the funeral. Xue wondered aloud if the police might try to seize the banners and get rough with them. He scribbled a few names and numbers on a scrap of paper, then handed it to Wang along with his house keys. "If anything happens," he said, "call these people and give them my keys." Wang looked at his friend, and it suddenly occurred to him that they were not young anymore. The 1989 generation had grown up. As they approached the cemetery, it was almost 9 A.M.

The memorial activities had begun four hours earlier, in the hospital where Zhao died. The authorities had prohibited Bao Tong, his chief political aide, from attending the funeral, but at the family's insistence, the party agreed to let him pay his respects in a private ceremony at the hospital. He arrived in a police motorcade under armed guard at 5 A.M. and walked into the room with his hand still bandaged from the scuffle two weeks earlier. Bao looked thin and frail, the white flower still pinned on his shirt, and as a funeral dirge played, he bowed his head before Zhao's body. It was the first time since Bao's arrest in May 1989 that he had been permitted to see his old colleague. "You are the only person now with a clear understanding of some things," one of Zhao's sons said to him, referring to the party's secret deliberations before the crackdown. "It's clear to everyone now," Bao replied. "Everyone knows what happened. The people all know." After the ceremony, he posed for a photograph with Zhao's extended family. But as soon as Zhao's daughter took out her camera, party officials objected and tried to take it from her. Her brothers came to her defense, and there was yelling and chaos. "If you are human, leave us alone!" Bao shouted. It was only after the family threatened to cancel the funeral that the officials finally backed off and let them take the picture.

The funeral motorcade departed the hospital soon afterward. It was still dark out, and police stopped traffic at every intersection on the route to the cemetery. The motorcade sped through the sleeping city, almost racing, as if the authorities were worried someone might wake and catch a glimpse of it going by. Zhao's family urged the police to show some respect and slow down, but they were ignored.

At the cemetery, there was a dispute over a funeral scroll the family had prepared. "You advocated democracy and stood by your conscience. Your children are proud of you," it said. "In the Western heavens, you finally won your freedom. Your grace remains with us forever." A party official objected. "Democracy, hmph! Freedom, hmph! You can't put these up during a funeral hosted by the organization." Zhao's family refused to back down and threatened to walk out if the scroll were not put up. But at 8:10 A.M., twenty minutes before the funeral was scheduled to begin, the family was asked to take their positions for a practice run of the ceremony. Instead of a rehearsal, though, the party started the actual service. Without a warning to the family and without the funeral scroll going up, an orchestral dirge started playing, and the first guests, members of the party's senior leadership, walked into the hall.

Zhao's successors—the retired party chief, Jiang Zemin, and the new president, Hu Jintao—didn't bother to show up. Neither did Premier Wen Jiabao, who once served as an aide to Zhao and accompanied him on his last desperate visit with the students in Tiananmen Square. Instead, the government was represented by Jia Qinglin, a man many considered one of the Politburo's most corrupt members, precisely the kind of figure Zhao had hoped his political reforms would prevent from rising to power. Jia and the few other party bigwigs who came were whisked away before other guests were allowed to enter.

Neither the time nor the location of the memorial service had been announced to the public. But outside, thousands of people from across the country were converging on the cemetery. Hundreds were already waiting at the gate. The family had submitted a list of nearly three thousand guests to the party, including almost everyone who had visited their home or contacted them after Zhao's death. But it was clear that many more had come hoping to pay their respects to Zhao. Uniformed and plainclothes police were everywhere, trying to stop those without invitations while letting the others through. One group of mourners hoisted a banner that said "Zhao Ziyang's spirit lives forever," and then police tackled them. Others tried to break through the police cordon and were dragged away.

Wang's companions dropped him off in the crowd, then took the jeep to the parking lot, where they were going to try to bring their banners in through a different gate. He got in line, and began making his way toward the cemetery through the police checkpoints. Along the way, he ran into one old friend after another, and marveled at the number of people who had decided to come. At one gate, a small crowd had gathered around officers who had stopped an elderly woman because she didn't have an invitation. She was in her eighties and could walk only with the help of her granddaughter, who did have an invitation. Several of the guests were arguing with the officers, urging them to show compassion and let the old woman in. Later, inside the cemetery, Wang saw another small crowd gathered around the police, and then realized that his friends Mo and Xue were at the center of the group. The police had taken the banner from them. After a brief delay, they let them continue inside without it.

Wang and his friends fell in behind the crowd of mourners waiting to enter the memorial hall. They stood in a row of four, talking quietly as they stepped inside. Fifty funeral wreaths were placed along the walls, and the photo of Zhao in the blue denim shirt was displayed at the front of the small room. Zhao's pale and gaunt body lay on a dais, dressed in a traditional, high-collared jacket and covered by the red-and-white Communist Party flag. As loudspeakers played the dirge, Wang and his friends bowed three times before Zhao's body. Then they each shook hands with Zhao's relatives, who stood along a wall to the left. But no one was allowed to linger. Plainclothes officers briskly ushered Wang and his companions out as others behind them repeated the ceremony.

As he left the building, Wang felt an intense anger welling up inside him, and he wept in frustration. It was not just the scaled-down memorial service, which he considered an unacceptable substitute for the full state funeral Zhao deserved. Nor was it only the disrespectful behavior of the police and the huge security presence, which he found insulting to Zhao's memory and his legacy. (How could the authorities send an armored antiriot vehicle to the funeral of the man who refused to order troops into Tiananmen Square?) Rather, he felt a deep despair over what had become of his nation since Zhao's death. Leaning on a wall outside the memorial hall with tears in his eyes and a police officer barking at him to keep moving, Wang was overcome by the magnitude of the country's problems—the rampant corruption and abuse of power, the rising inequality and injustice, the moral decay of society.

And then he noticed the people around him. The mourners represented a remarkable cross section of China's emerging civil society. Wang had met some of them before. Others he knew only by reputation. There were environmentalists and journalists, businessmen and bloggers, and a generation of students too young to remember the prodemocracy movement of 1989 yet still inspired by its ideals. Wealthy entrepreneurs and well-known scholars stood shoulder to shoulder with humble farmers and laid-off factory workers. There was the labor activist Lu Kun, whose husband was in prison for starting a study group to discuss democratic reform, and the young AIDS activist Li Dan, who had clashed with the authorities to expose a hidden epidemic caused by local blood banks. There was Li Heping, one of several self-taught lawyers at the forefront of a campaign to protect the rights of ordinary citizens and force the party to obey its own laws. Wang remembered the missing faces, too, people whom the police had detained in recent days to prevent them from attending the funeral, including his old classmate Pu Zhiqiang, now a prominent freedom-of-speech lawyer, and the historian Ding Zilin, who lost a son in the massacre and was working with a group of mothers to compile a list of all those killed in Tiananmen.

Zhao's death marked the end of an era in China. If the nation were ever to undergo the democratic transition he envisioned, it wouldn't be because of one of Zhao's timid successors in the Communist Party leadership. It would be because of these people who had come to his funeral—people who refused to forget the past and dared to work for a different future. Despite the pain of decades of violent political turmoil and the temptations of a flourishing and freewheeling economy— or perhaps precisely because of both—these people had not given up on Zhao's vision of a more democratic China. On a day of mourning, Wang saw in them a glimmer of hope.

2

SEARCHING FOR
LIN ZHAO'S SOUL

On the afternoon he lost his last steady job, Hu Jie bicycled aimlessly through the smog and traffic of Nanjing, brooding over the mystery of his abrupt dismissal. It was a sweltering Tuesday in the summer of 1999, and his shirt clung to his back with sweat as he navigated the alleyways of a bustling district not far from the Yangtze River. In the sky above, dark clouds threatened a downpour. But Hu kept pedaling, unsure where he was going or what he should do. His mind was racing, disturbed by the past, troubled by the future, returning again and again to the same question: Had the authorities discovered his obsession with the dead woman?

He was a lean, imposing man, with broad shoulders and intense eyes, and he looked younger than his forty-one years. For much of his life, Hu had been a soldier. He served in the air force as a fighter jet mechanic, then as an officer and a political instructor, and there was still something of the soldier in the way he walked and talked, even in the way he sat: watchful, on edge, ready to snap to attention. But there was a bohemian quality about him, too. The plain dark t-shirts he favored and the beard covering his square jaw hinted at his life after the military, when he moved into an artists' ghetto and tried to reinvent

Hu Jie

himself as an oil painter, then as a documentary filmmaker. It was only years later, as he surrendered to middle age, that Hu took his latest, most conventional job, as cameraman and producer for Xinhua, the government's official news agency. There he put together video reports for private screening by party officials across the country. It was a comfortable post, with all the benefits and privileges associated with a position near the top of the state's propaganda apparatus, and it allowed him to provide a stable home for his wife and son.

Yet Hu knew he didn't really fit in at the agency. Xinhua paid the bills, opened doors, and gave him access to equipment and resources, but Hu always saw himself as an independent filmmaker first and an employee of the state second. Between assignments, he continued working on his documentaries, examining poverty in the countryside, the status of rural women, and other subjects the news agency routinely ignored. His films were not truly subversive, but they cast a critical eye on Chinese society, and that was usually enough to alarm the high priests of the propaganda ministry, who labored to project a sunny image of the party's rule and quash anything that might cast doubt on that ideal. Hu knew the censors would never approve his documentaries for release in theaters or dissemination through other official channels, so he distributed them himself on videodiscs. He also knew it was only a matter of time before someone at Xinhua noticed what he was doing and decided a fellow like him didn't belong there.

Now, after two years on the job, it seemed that day had finally come. Earlier that humid afternoon, Hu's boss had called him into his office and fired him. The man didn't say much. He just mumbled a weak apology that he "couldn't resist the pressure from above." Hu was furious, but he went quietly. He didn't press for an explanation; he knew he wouldn't get a straight answer. He signed a resignation letter, cleaned out his desk, and collected the last of his wages.

As he bicycled through the traffic of Nanjing, along boulevards lined with poplar trees, past office towers gleaming with mirrored glass and apartment blocks adorned with damp laundry, Hu considered his sudden unemployment. He felt uneasy, almost nauseous, certainly worse than he had expected. Searching for the source of his anxiety, he recalled his latest project, a subject he had come across only a month earlier, while doing a favor for a friend. He had been helping her move furniture for an old classmate of her parents, and during a break from the heavy lifting, she had mentioned that her parents also went to school with someone named Lin Zhao.

"Lin Zhao? Who's that?" Hu remembered asking.

His friend hesitated a moment before answering. Lin Zhao was a young woman who attended Peking University in the 1950s, she said, a talented poet and writer who grew up not far from Nanjing, in the ancient canal city of Suzhou. Of all the students at the university, she was the only one who refused to write a political confession during Mao's Anti-Rightist Campaign. Her intransigence was rewarded with a prison term, and later, during the Cultural Revolution, with a death sentence. But she left behind a secret legacy: she had continued writing in prison, using her own blood as ink.

Hu was stunned. He considered himself a well-informed and educated person, but he had never heard a story like this, never imagined that anything like it could happen in China, even during Mao's rule. His head was swimming with questions: Why was Lin Zhao executed? What did she do? And what about her prison writings? He knew there was a tradition in ancient China of government ministers and military commanders sending urgent messages to the emperor in their own blood. But what would drive a young woman, living just a few decades ago, in a city not far from his own, to cut her flesh and write in blood? Surely, Hu suggested, she must have scrawled out only a few words. But his friend said no, apparently she had written hundreds of pages.

Hu wanted to hear more. He had been searching for a new subject for a documentary, and this seemed to have potential. When he asked his friend for help, she agreed to go to her parents for more information. In the weeks that followed, Hu began looking into Lin Zhao's story, and he was quickly drawn in. It was as if he had stumbled upon a lost and precious piece of history, a mystery waiting to be unraveled. If he had been merely curious at first, soon he found himself thinking about the dead woman at all hours, at work, during meals, as he lay in bed trying to sleep. The more he learned, the more questions he had. He knew he was poking around where the authorities didn't want him, and his instincts told him that what he was doing might be dangerous. But he pressed ahead, because despite the passage of time, what happened to Lin Zhao felt urgent and relevant to him, while the risks of pursuing the story seemed vague and uncertain.

But the risks were coming into focus now. Would his wife lose her job at the bank? Could they be evicted from their apartment? Would his teenage son be denied admission to university? He suspected the Ministry of State Security was behind his firing, and if the secret police was involved, anything was possible, even arrest and imprisonment. The thought made him nervous, and angry. It seemed ridiculous that that could still happen in China, which had come so far and changed so much in his lifetime. He just wanted to make a documentary, about something that had happened long ago, and now he was out of a job and worried about going to jail.

Hu knew the safe thing to do would be to abandon the Lin Zhao research. He knew his firing from Xinhua was a warning. Still, he could not shake a feeling that he was meant to uncover what happened to that young woman so many years ago and record it for the future. Now that he was unemployed, he had the time to focus on the project, but he wondered if he had the courage. Years later, when he described the moment for me, Hu said a passage written by the ancient Confucian philosopher Mencius came to mind as he wandered the city on his bicycle:

So it is that whenever Heaven invests a person with great responsibilities, it first tries his resolve, exhausts his muscles and bones, starves his body, leaves him destitute, and confounds his every endeavor. In this way, his patience and endurance are developed, and his weaknesses are overcome.

"I just kept thinking about her story, and how it might be lost forever," Hu told me. "And I thought, if I didn't preserve it, who would?" By the time he got off his bicycle, he had made up his mind.

THERE WAS LITTLE in Hu's background to suggest he would press ahead with the Lin Zhao project, much less devote the next five years of his life to it. He had no formal training in history, or journalism, or even filmmaking. His parents had been factory workers, and like most Chinese of his generation, his schooling had been haphazard, disrupted by Mao's final and most destructive political movement, the Cultural Revolution. He was eight when the campaigns began, and he stopped going to regular classes soon afterward. Instead of high school, he worked in a machinery factory. At age nineteen, a few months after Mao's death, he enlisted in the military.

What little Hu did pick up about his country's recent history was limited to the rosy version of events promulgated by the party. In these accounts, Mao was "the Great Teacher, the Great Leader, the Great Commander, the Great Helmsman," "the reddest of red suns," and "the greatest genius and teacher of revolution in the present age." The Communist Party was "the mightiest, most glorious, most correct, most lovely party," "the great emancipator of the toiling masses of the Chinese nation," and even "our dear father and mother." In newspapers and on the radio, in textbooks and in speeches, the economy was always setting new records and the waves of political purges ordered by Mao were described, if they were mentioned at all, as victories against "reactionaries," "counterrevolutionaries," or other enemies allied with the forces of "international capitalism" and the "American imperialists." It was history scrubbed clean, an elaborate fiction designed to sustain the party's rule. Fabricating and controlling history was so important to the party that it devoted a vast bureaucracy to the task, an army of propagandists, ideologues, and censors who labored to deceive the masses in the name of serving them. By some estimates, the party employed one propaganda officer for every hundred citizens. The result was a complex tapestry of truth and lies intended to bury unpleasant memories and obscure inconvenient facts. Those who built and served this official history twisted even the Chinese language to their purpose: blessing certain phrases with the approval of the state, stripping others of meaning or legitimacy—trying to manipulate not only how people talked but also what they thought. Those who challenged the official truth did so at their peril.

But after Mao's death in 1976, things began to change. The trauma of the Cultural Revolution damaged the party's authority, and its control over history weakened. In the 1980s, with the government in retreat, a wave of freethinking swept the country, and prohibited material—literature, films, music—suddenly became available. The old orthodoxies—Marxism, Leninism, "Mao Zedong Thought"—had been discredited, and people were searching for new answers. At the height of this intellectual fervor, the military pulled Hu from his duties repairing jets and sent him for training as an officer who would be responsible for the indoctrination of troops in party ideology. Yet even the Air Force Political Institute in Shanghai was not immune to the changes taking hold in the nation. A liberal-minded general there suspended almost all classes in the tired socialist canon, replacing them with lessons in market economics, Western political theory, and Freudian psychology. History was still largely off-limits, but Hu began to question what he knew. Later, as the party tried to reassert control, it sent Hu materials condemning books and other writings that it had banned, so he could better indoctrinate the soldiers under his command. But Hu found himself more interested in the prohibited works than in the party's critiques of them. He read the investigative reports on party corruption by the journalist Liu Binyan, the underground verse of the soldier-poet Ye Wenfu, even a Chinese translation of Aleksandr Solzhenitsyn's *The Gulag Archipelago*.

After the 1989 Tiananmen Square massacre, the party clamped down again and redoubled its efforts to shape the public's understanding of events. Mao's cult of personality had collapsed, the ruling ideology had been exposed as a terrible mistake, and now the state had ordered soldiers to kill students in the heart of the capital. The party's ability to define history—to suppress memories and guard its secrets—was more important than ever to its grip on power. The propaganda machine pressed harder. Newspapers and magazines were "rectified." Scholars and journalists were purged or silenced. But the party could no longer dominate popular consciousness as it once did. Too much had happened. Too much had changed. Too many people refused to forget.

Until he heard the story about Lin Zhao, Hu had never given much thought to his country's recent history. But he knew that what he had been taught was incomplete, that there were gaps and blank spots, facts that had been hidden and people who had been erased. He knew just enough to make him curious.

THE MONDAY MORNING after he lost his job, Hu was standing in the crowded lot of Nanjing's central bus station, video camera in hand. Throngs of travelers, most of them migrant workers laden with bundles of goods to be sold in the countryside, jostled for position around a fleet of mud-splattered buses. In the chaos, Hu focused his camera on an elderly woman waiting to board a bus headed for Hefei, a provincial capital a few hours to the southwest. She was in her late six-ties, small and frail, with graying hair and a slight shuffle to her step, but there was something about her that projected strength. Hu zoomed in on her wrinkled hands, which were clenched around a small brown bag. Inside the bag, he knew, was a bundle of papers: poems, letters, essays, and other tributes to Lin Zhao written by people who had known her. The old woman had spent years collecting them, and now she gripped them tightly, as if worried they could be scattered by a breeze and lost forever. Those papers—and her own fading memories—were all she had left of an old friend.

The timing of Ni Jinxiong's visit to Nanjing was a lucky coinci-dence for Hu; she was passing through the city the week he lost his job. A mutual friend arranged for the two to meet, and when Hu ex-plained his plan to make a documentary about Lin Zhao, the woman agreed to help. Half a century had passed since Ni and Lin Zhao first met as teenagers. The nation was in turmoil then, torn by civil war and teetering on the brink of revolution. Lin Zhao had run away from home to enroll in a journalism school sympathetic to the Communist cause. Ni was a student there, and she befriended the runaway. Now, in her twilight years, she was traveling the country, searching for peo-ple who knew her classmate and gathering their remembrances of her, which she hoped to publish in a book. Hu planned to follow Ni on her journey and build the documentary around her. He could tell her story, and slowly, through her, he could tell Lin Zhao's story as well.

Hu had started shooting documentaries only four years earlier, at the suggestion of a friend. He was struggling to make it as an oil painter at the time, indulging a longtime interest in art after an honor-able discharge from the air force. He had seen enough of China as a soldier to understand the punishing poverty that many people still lived with, but whenever he tried to portray their lives on canvas, crit-ics attacked his work as inaccurate and insulting to the Chinese peo-ple, or dismissed it as excessively faithful to reality and therefore lacking in creativity. Documentaries, Hu decided, might be a better fit for him. Though the state had always produced propaganda films, independent documentary moviemaking was a relatively new field, emerging as the party's control of the media weakened, and cameras, computers, and other tools became more affordable. Those who pio-neered the form in China favored a simple, observational style, and

Hu's first films adopted the same approach. They were all set in the present, focusing on ordinary people such as coal miners or farmers, shot using a handheld camera, with few sit-down interviews and little narration. But the Lin Zhao project presented a new challenge. Hu wanted to read what she had written with her blood in prison. He knew that was critical, that it would be the heart of the film. But he had no idea how he would find the writings.

Meeting Ni was Hu's first big break, and she lifted his spirits as well as his confidence. She was his strongest lead, but just as important, she was also the first sign that he was not alone in his quest. So many of his friends wanted only to look toward the future, which seemed so bright, and they chided him for his fascination with such a dark corner of their nation's history. They felt the past was better left alone, that it was best not to pick at old scars. Hu could sense their discomfort whenever he talked about his project, so he forced himself to stop bringing it up. Even his wife and his son disapproved. So Ni's commitment to recording Lin Zhao's story comforted him and gave him strength. Listening to her stories, going through the material she had gathered from across the country, Hu realized there must be many others out there who refused to bury their memories. It reminded him that while it was common to forget, it was also normal to want to remember.

As he sat with Ni on that first bus trip, watching the old woman doze and the countryside rushing by, Hu felt as if they were making a forbidden journey into a secret past. At the time, he was unsure how much Ni knew of Lin Zhao's story. He could sense that she was still nervous about talking to him, that she did not trust him entirely. He understood her apprehension. It made sense, given the times she had lived through, and his own background with the military and Xinhua. Why, after all, would a stranger with the credentials of a party loyalist take an interest in her efforts to publish a book about Lin Zhao? So Hu didn't push. In their first meetings, he didn't even take out his camera. He just let her talk, and he resisted the urge to ask all the questions he had. Slowly, though, on that first trip, and in the weeks that followed, Ni opened up, and what she knew about Lin Zhao's life began to come out.

Lin Zhao was actually born Peng Lingzhao in 1932, the eldest child of a prominent family in Suzhou. Her father was a university

graduate who had studied in England and written his thesis on the
Irish constitution. Two years out of college, he took the civil service
exam and was appointed a county magistrate in Suzhou. Her mother
was a successful entrepreneur, a banker who sat on the board of a bus
company. At the time, the Nationalists and the Communists were
fighting a civil war, and Japan had seized control of northeastern
China and established a puppet state. Closer to home, Shanghai had
been carved into concessions controlled by France, Britain, the
United States, and Japan. It was a time of violent political passions,
and the nation's divisions strained the Peng family. Lin Zhao's father
served the corrupt and failing Nationalist government, but her mother
favored the Communist rebels, who vowed to do more to fight the
Japanese. She secretly funneled money to the Communists, established an underground radio station, and was once arrested by Japanese forces. The couple often fought, and their arguments sometimes
focused on their daughter and what political values she should be
taught.

She was a delicate child, prone to illness, but a voracious reader
and a gifted writer. She was also headstrong, and by age sixteen, she
had made up her own mind about her loyalties. She joined an underground Communist cell, began writing articles criticizing government corruption using the pen name Lin Zhao, and earned a spot on a
blacklist maintained by the Nationalist military authorities in the region. Both of her parents were alarmed—one of Lin Zhao's uncles had
already been executed as a Communist—and after their daughter
graduated from high school, they tried to send her to university overseas to wait out the civil war. But the teenager wouldn't leave. She was
caught up in the fervor of the times, and wanted instead to attend a
journalism school run by the Communists in territory they controlled
nearby. When her parents refused to let her go, she packed a bag and
left on her own, promising never to return. Three months later, on October 1, 1949, the Communists completed their revolution and established the People's Republic of China.

When Ni met her at the journalism school, Peng Lingzhao had already started introducing herself as Lin Zhao, giving up her surname
to distance herself from her family. She was pretty and still girlish,
a slender young woman who wore white blouses under tailored
workman's overalls and braided her hair in long pigtails with ribbons

tied on the end. She was as devoted to the Communist Party and its cause as anyone in her class, and she developed a reputation at the school for her graceful poetry, her quick wit, and her sharp tongue.

Like her classmates, Lin Zhao was assigned in the summer of 1950 to travel the countryside as a member of a land reform work team, one of thousands the party dispatched to dismantle the unequal system of land ownership, abusive rents, and high taxes that had trapped the nation's peasants in misery for generations. The work teams moved from village to village, redistributing farmland from landlords to the peasants who once toiled for them. To succeed, the work teams needed to reassure a rural populace uncertain the Communists would last and still fearful of the influential elites who had held sway in their villages for so long. It was not an easy task, and in much of the country the teams resorted to violence. Mass meetings were organized in which peasants were encouraged to "speak bitterness" about their past suffering while landlords were dragged out and humiliated and tortured. Mao told the work teams not to intervene when peasants lashed out at these "class enemies," and in almost every village, at least one and sometimes several landlords or their relatives were beaten to death or executed. By 1952, the death toll had climbed as high as two million. The landlord class, which had dominated rural society since the Han Dynasty more than two thousand years ago, was all but wiped out, and nearly half the nation's arable land was confiscated, divided into small plots and given to peasants, including for the first time women. With land reform, the party proved itself capable of providing a better life for ordinary people in the countryside—and established itself as a force to be feared.

If Lin Zhao had any misgivings about the use of such brutality to achieve the party's goals, she never expressed them to her classmate. "We all understand that land reform is an important step in strengthening our motherland," she wrote in a letter to Ni at the time. "Our posts are combat posts. When I think of this, I must work hard, otherwise I will never live up to the expectations of the party and the people." In another letter, she added: "My hatred for the landlords is the same as my love of the country. This kind of love and hate—they are both forces pushing me forward." With Ni's help, Hu tracked down the leader of Lin Zhao's work team, now a retired civil servant. The three of them traveled together to Bali Village, a hamlet near

Shanghai where Lin Zhao had been stationed. Standing amid the lush green rice fields, the man recalled how Lin Zhao had once ordered a landlord placed in a vat of freezing water overnight. Later, she told her comrades that his screams made her feel "cruel happiness" because residents of the village at last would no longer be afraid of the man.

"A few days ago in town, the 'May 1' team executed more than ten people," Lin Zhao wrote in another letter. "Among them was a traitorous, despotic landlord whom I was responsible for. From collecting materials, to organizing the denunciation, all the way to applying for a public trial, I had worked to decide his fate. After the execution, some people didn't have the courage to look, but I did. One by one, I looked at each of those enemies who had been shot, especially that local despot. Seeing them die this way, I felt as proud and happy as the people who had directly suffered under them."

Despite her dedication to the party, Lin Zhao's comrades sometimes criticized her for being "petit bourgeois," because of the books she read, or the poems she wrote, or most often, because of the blunt way she pointed out the faults of others. Though she had condemned her parents, and had not seen them for three years, her privileged background and her father's service in the Nationalist government made her an easy target. Once, when her parents wrote to her, she was moved to reply in a letter that they should confess their "misconduct and guilt." But even that was not enough for the party. "I was naive in the way I read my parents' recent letter, which didn't sound as backward as in the past and seemed quite progressive," she wrote to Ni. "Just because of that, I was sure that they were not counterrevolutionaries. But with my comrades' help and teaching, I realized that to perform duties for the illegitimate government was a crime in itself. I also realized that my political consciousness and class awareness are far below the party's standards." Her loyalty to the party was total, and as the government built up Mao's cult of personality, Lin Zhao began referring to him as Father. "My feelings for my family have lessened a great deal. I have only a red star in my heart now," she wrote to Ni. "I know I am here, and he is in Beijing or Moscow. Whenever I think of him, I feel so excited."

Hu did not find Lin Zhao's devotion unusual. He knew such faith in Mao was common in the early days of the party's rule. He himself had waved a little red book of the Chairman's sayings as a child during the Cultural Revolution. Even the ugly violence of the land reform campaign did not surprise him, because he could understand the need for extreme measures to topple such an entrenched and unjust economic system. But as Hu listened to Ni Jinxiong's stories and read Lin Zhao's letters, what perplexed him was how such a fervent believer in Mao and his rule found herself just a decade later in prison, and then facing execution. Hu and Ni visited a retired professor who described for them how he, Lin Zhao, and several others were arrested in 1960 for publishing an underground magazine. But the professor couldn't answer the most pressing question on Hu's mind: Why did Lin Zhao turn against the party she loved? Or was it the party that turned against her?

After the trip, Hu accompanied Ni back to Shanghai, where she was living in retirement, and where Lin Zhao had spent the last years of her life in prison. Ni introduced him to several other people there who knew Lin Zhao, and she took him to see an old building where Lin Zhao's family had once lived in a second-floor apartment. Hu had been waiting to film the place, because it had figured prominently in a story told by Lin Zhao's sister that Ni had shared with him. The date was May 1, 1968, and Lin Zhao had been incarcerated in Shanghai for several years. Their father had committed suicide, and the sister was living with their mother in the apartment. That afternoon, they heard a commotion below their window, and a man's voice asking for relatives of Lin Zhao. Then there was a knock on the door. When they answered it, a police officer was standing outside.

"Who is Xu Xianmin?" he asked.

"I am," Lin's mother replied.

"You are Lin Zhao's mother? Your daughter has been suppressed. Pay the five-*fen* bullet fee."

The older woman was confused. The police officer spoke again, his voice rising: "Hurry and pay the five-*fen* bullet fee. Your daughter has been executed by gunshot."

As her mother stood stunned in the doorway, Lin's sister rushed into another room, fumbled through a drawer for five *fen*—the equivalent of less than a penny—then returned and gave it to the officer. It was not until the man left that her mother realized what had just transpired. Suddenly, she collapsed on the floor in grief, sobbing and crying that if she had been an ordinary housewife, her daughter never would have had such a life of suffering. At the time of her execution, Lin Zhao was thirty-six.

Hu's research proceeded quickly at first. Almost every week, Ni would track down a classmate or another acquaintance of Lin Zhao's and call Hu, and he would get on a train and meet her in Shanghai. She would introduce him and persuade people to speak to him on camera. Everything was going smoothly, and Hu was certain he would be able to finish the documentary within a year. After a few months, though, the calls from Ni became less frequent, and then they stopped altogether. She was running out of leads, yet Hu was far from understanding what had happened to Lin Zhao.

There was another problem, too. He was out of money. Since losing his job, Hu had depleted his savings to fund the project, to pay for the videotapes, train tickets, and other expenses. His wife was still working at a bank, but they had agreed he would spend only his own money on the documentary. They needed her modest salary to cover their household expenses, and to raise their son. They had also agreed he would never borrow money from her for the film. Maybe the rules could be bent, but Hu knew the Lin Zhao movie had already put a strain on his marriage. He had met his wife when he was still in the military, and she had been patient with him through his various career changes over the years. She stood by him when he quit the boring civil service job that the air force had arranged for him after he was demobilized, and she supported him when he tried painting, and also when he switched to documentaries. But getting fired by Xinhua was different. She had pressured him to find that job, part of a push for him to settle down and take greater responsibility for supporting his family. Now that he had left Xinhua, she worried he was backsliding on his promises to her, that he was putting his family second again. She complained that he felt he owed more to society than to his own wife and son, and that it would be difficult for them to make ends meet on her wages alone.

So they agreed that if Hu needed money to make a trip for an interview, he would have to earn it first. Usually he did it by hiring himself out as a wedding videographer. It was exhausting and often tedious work, a full day and night on his feet filming a couple getting married, and another day editing the material into a movie. Hu tried to make the most of it, treating each wedding like a documentary subject and taking care to edit each movie differently, often experimenting with different techniques and styles. For all his efforts, though, he could earn only two hundred yuan per wedding, or about twenty-five dollars. His wife sometimes needled him, joking that he was getting cheated by being paid so little for the best wedding films in China.

As the calls from Ni grew scarce, Hu broadened his search for information. But he couldn't just go to a library and read about this period in history. Even when he was at Xinhua, he didn't have access to party archives on the era. The only way for him to find out what happened to Lin Zhao was to locate people who knew her. After graduating from the journalism academy, Lin Zhao was assigned to work at a party newspaper in the city of Changzhou, on the southern bank of the Yangtze between Nanjing and Shanghai. Then she took the national college entrance exam in 1954 and, after receiving the highest score in Jiangsu Province, she was admitted to the prestigious Chinese literature department at Peking University. Whatever caused the falling-out between her and the party, it happened while she was a student there. So Hu turned the focus of his research north and called everyone he knew in Beijing, where he had been stationed with the air force for several years and where he had lived in the artists' commune. He also went back to Ni and the people he had met through her, and asked them to help him locate Lin Zhao's classmates in Beijing.

He took the train on his trips to and from Beijing, sitting for fourteen hours each way in the cheap hard-seat cars, and he usually stayed with his sister, a photographer who had an apartment on the city's east side. Slowly, he began locating and interviewing people who knew Lin Zhao, and as he did, he started to form a picture of her as a student at Peking University, commonly known by its abbreviated Chinese name, Beida. Lin Zhao was one of the youngest members of her class, he learned, and one of the most popular. The young men on campus, especially, took an interest in her, not because she was the prettiest or the smartest of their classmates, but because she seemed different from the other women. She was a bit more stylish in the way she dressed, and a bit more daring in her behavior. She had a delicate

constitution and often suffered bouts of illness, as she did in childhood, but she liked to drink and dance, and she more than held her
own in witty back-and-forth with others. She could be blunt and even
cutting in arguments about literature and politics, because she never
toned down her comments to conform to some traditional Chinese notion of femininity. She was also an excellent student, one of the
faculty's favorites. As a sophomore, she became editor of a campus
poetry journal, and the next year she was named poetry editor of the
university literary magazine.

Early on, Hu tracked down one of several men he heard had
courted Lin Zhao at Beida. As a student, Zhang Yuanxun worked
alongside her as an editor at the literary magazine. Now he was a
scholar of Chinese literature in Qufu, the city in eastern China known
as the birthplace of the philosopher Confucius. Zhang had every reason to refuse to speak to Hu. As a professor at the local university,
and also a successful businessman—he owned the supermarket on
campus—he had much to lose and little to gain by discussing a past
that the authorities had sought to erase. He was intimately familiar
with the potential consequences of crossing the party. After the Anti-
Rightist Campaign, he spent more than two decades in the labor
camps. Hu knew this because a well-known newspaper in Guangzhou, *Southern Weekend*, managed to circumvent the censors in 1998
and publish an interview with Zhang that broached the taboo subject.
The article included a brief section about Lin Zhao, and it had spread
quickly among her old classmates. It referred to Lin Zhao as "a hero
who 40 years ago insisted on the truth without fear of those with
power," and Hu found it heartening. Here was proof he was not alone
in his efforts to preserve this piece of history. It was perhaps the first
time Lin Zhao's name had been mentioned in a Chinese newspaper in
almost two decades, and Hu knew it couldn't have been easy for the
editors at *Southern Weekend* to slip it in. He was encouraged by the article for another reason, too. If Zhang had agreed to risk an interview
about his experiences with *Southern Weekend*, perhaps he would also
help Hu with his documentary.

So with the meager profit from another wedding film, Hu bought a
train ticket to Qufu. He didn't make an appointment or call ahead, he
just went to see Zhang unannounced, because he didn't want to give
him a chance to say no. In the end, there was no need for concern. Of

all the people Hu had interviewed thus far, Zhang was the most immediately forthcoming. He was a feisty old man, with a thick shock of gray hair and large, thick-rimmed glasses. He exuded confidence, and he spoke without fear or hesitation, often gesturing excitedly with his hands. At first Hu thought the reason Zhang was unafraid was that he had survived so much already, and so there was little more the party could do to intimidate him. But as he listened to him speak, Hu realized there was more to it than that. He noticed a sadness about the older man, and he realized that Zhang was speaking to him out of a sense of personal duty, too. Zhang eventually told him he had made a promise to Lin Zhao, and he intended to keep it.

His story began in the spring of 1957. The Communist Party had consolidated its control of the nation, establishing its dominance over the cities with mass political campaigns as violent as land reform had been in the countryside. Its drive to build a socialist economy was nearly complete, with almost all private businesses nationalized and the farmland that had been distributed to peasants taken back and organized into cooperatives. After decades of war, China was at peace, having fought the United States to a stalemate on the Korean peninsula. But from his perch inside a walled estate on the grounds of the old Forbidden City, Mao was not satisfied. The party's tight grip on almost all aspects of life had alienated and stifled the nation's most educated citizens, and he knew it would be difficult to modernize China without the help of its scientists, scholars, and thinkers. Perhaps even more troubling, the party seemed to be drifting away from the masses and had begun to calcify into a privileged elite not unlike the one it had overthrown. Uprisings in Poland and Hungary in 1956 had shown what could happen when Communists lost touch with the people. Mao's solution, at least the one he put forward in public, was a bold invitation to intellectuals and others outside the party to criticize Communist rule and offer suggestions for improvements. "Let a hundred flowers bloom, let a hundred schools contend," he declared. Though his colleagues in the leadership were nervous about opening the party up to attack, Mao seemed confident the public had been won over and predicted its criticisms would be like a "gentle breeze or mild rain" that would help keep the party in line.

The Hundred Flowers Movement began slowly at first, as local cadres dragged their feet and intellectuals conditioned by the party's violent record hesitated to stick their necks out. Then in the spring of 1957, Mao embarked on a tour of eastern China to jump-start the movement with assurances he was serious about letting people vent their dissatisfaction with the regime. By mid-April, scholars, writers, artists, businessmen, members of the minor political parties allied with the Communists, and others mustered their courage and began to speak out, often after being persuaded to do so by party officials under pressure to make sure the movement was a success. The "mild rain" that Mao had forecast quickly became a typhoon as long-suppressed frustrations with the party were suddenly unleashed. By mid-May, the storm had spread to Peking University, and Zhang was standing at the center of it.

For weeks, party authorities on campus had been holding meetings of teachers and professors, encouraging them to join the campaign. But it was not until May 19 that the "blooming and contending" began in full at Beida. At dusk that day, Zhang and another classmate, Shen Zeyi, wrote a poem in large black characters on a sheet of red poster paper and affixed it to a wall outside the main student cafeteria. "It Is Time!" they declared, urging their classmates to answer the party's call for criticism and advice.

It is time, young people, to free our throats and sing,

To write of both our pain and love on paper.

Do not suffer in private, do not be indignant in private, do not grieve in private,

Reveal the joys and sorrows inside our hearts, expose them to the daylight,

For even if criticism and censure fall upon our heads like a sudden and heavy rain,

Fresh sprouts have never feared the light of the sun.

"At the time, this was very shocking speech," Zhang told Hu. "In our China, no one said anything like this. We all said the same thing, that the Communist Party was good. Good, good, good. Yes, yes, yes. Then suddenly this other sound came out, so it got people's attention."

News of the poster spread quickly and a crowd of students soon gathered around, reading it by flashlight. Some copied the poem into their notebooks, and others snapped photos of it. Zhang noticed more lamps burning in the dormitories than usual that evening, as students gathered in small groups, debating the party's shortcomings late into the night. When he returned to the cafeteria the next morning, his poster was surrounded by dozens of others. Over the following week, thousands more went up on the "Democracy Wall," and on buildings across campus. One of the first posters criticized the party's interference in university affairs, and urged party officials to withdraw from campus and allow Beida to be run more democratically. Many of the posters complained that opportunities to study abroad, teaching posts, and the best jobs after graduation were given to party members or other students deemed "ideologically reliable" rather than to those with the best grades. Several ridiculed the Soviet teaching materials used on campus, including texts in literature classes that ignored Western authors and science books that claimed all major discoveries were made by Russians. Others demanded that the party's secret personnel files on students be destroyed, and an end to the tedious, mandatory lessons in political ideology. But students didn't limit their criticism to education issues. Echoing opinions expressed by intellectuals across the country, they also attacked the arrogance of party officials and the privileges they enjoyed, and called for democratic reforms and sweeping guarantees of freedom of speech, press, assembly, and association. There were also calls for a review of the abuses committed by the party and its security forces during earlier political campaigns, and at least one student questioned Mao's cult of personality. Even Khrushchev's secret speech exposing Stalin's crimes was translated from a text in an English-language newspaper and distributed, undercutting the party's version of Soviet history and, by extension, raising questions about Mao's fallibility.

For every poster that found fault with the Communists, though, there were others that voiced support for the party and attacked its critics. As the debate gained intensity, students began delivering speeches in a plaza on campus near their dormitories, often addressing crowds of thousands and engaging in debate with audience members. Standing on a dais erected there, a young woman from nearby People's University who called herself Lin Xiling gained national attention by condemning socialism in China as a sham because it was undemocratic. Students held secret meetings and established new organizations, and they began making connections with their compatriots at other universities across the country. Zhang joined one particularly outspoken group at Beida, the Hundred Flowers Society, and was elected chief editor of its magazine, *Public Square*. Shen Zeyi, his friend and poster coauthor, was named deputy editor.

Lin Zhao knew both men well from the literary magazine. In fact, they had both been competing for her attention. When she saw the posters attacking their poem, she was moved to write and put up a verse of her own defending them. She was still a loyal Communist; she had recently written a series of poems glorifying the party. But by the spring of 1957, there were signs she was beginning to question some of the party's actions, especially a recent campaign against independent thinking that resulted in numerous suicides in literary and academic circles. So naturally, she was excited by the Hundred Flowers Movement, which she believed meant the party was acknowledging its mistakes and asking the public to help set it straight. "On a spring day like this, everywhere people are discussing the rectification campaign, and we are full of excitement, just waiting," she wrote at the time.

What Lin Zhao and her friends didn't know, and couldn't have known, was that Mao was already having second thoughts about the campaign he had launched. The intensity and depth of public anger exposed by the Hundred Flowers Movement surprised him and threatened to undermine the party's authority. On May 15, before Zhang even put up his poster at Beida, Mao sent a secret memo to party officials of Central Committee rank and above. For the first time, he used the term "Rightist" to describe those who admired bourgeois democracy and rejected the party's leadership, and he blamed them for "the current spate of wild attacks." On Mao's instructions, the party did not announce his change of heart. "We shall let the Rightists run amok for a time and let them reach their climax," he wrote. "Now that large numbers of fish have come to the surface themselves, there is no need to bait the hook."

Looking back, Zhang said, the first hint at Beida of Mao's reversal may have come on May 22. It was a hot, muggy night, and Zhang was standing at the center of a large crowd that stretched into the darkness outside the cafeteria. Three exciting days had passed since he and Shen had posted their poetic call to arms, and the debate that evening seemed to begin like many that had unfolded on campus. But then it took an ugly turn. One student after another stood on a cafeteria table that had been dragged outside and began denouncing Zhang in unforgiving ideological terms. Some accused him of "inciting counterrevolution," perhaps the most serious of political crimes in China. They were all party members, they had surrounded him, and they were taking turns berating him.

Suddenly, someone else leapt onto the table. It was nearly pitch-dark, and few in the crowd could see who it was. But a woman's voice—clear and melodious, with a soft southern accent—rose up over the din of the shouting male students. The clamorous audience hushed, as if enchanted. In the dim light of the night, Zhang could barely make out Lin Zhao's face. But her words were burned into his memory.

She said, "Aren't we calling on people outside the party to offer suggestions? When they didn't, we pushed them again and again to speak up! So when they finally do, why do we fly into a rage? Take Zhang Yuanxun. He isn't a party member, or even a member of the Youth League. He wrote that poem, but is that enough for these people to get so angry and rise up like this to attack him?

"What kind of meeting are we having tonight?" she said. "Is it a meeting for speeches or a struggle session? It shouldn't be a struggle session, because we don't need to denounce anyone. Who are we denouncing? Zhang Yuanxun? Why should we denounce him? You, sirs, who spoke just now, I know all of you. You are all party members in the Chinese literature department."

Zhang grew animated as he described the scene to Hu, gesturing with his hands and nearly jumping out of his seat as he spoke. "And just like that, she silenced them!" he said. "You see how bold she was?"

Lin Zhao continued speaking, he recalled, and began describing what she called a "contradiction" between the demands of one's conscience and the demands of "the organization," by which she meant the party. But someone in the back of the audience interrupted her. "Who are you?" he barked. "What's your name?" Without hesitating, Lin Zhao shot back: "Who are you? Who are you to question me? Are you a police officer, prosecutor, or court official? A plainclothes agent?

"It's okay, I'll tell you. My name is Lin, the character with two trees in it. Zhao, the character with the sword over the mouth next to the sun," she said. She paused for a moment, then added: "Whether the sword is over the mouth, or the sword is over the head, I don't care. Since I'm standing here, I don't care where the sword is!"

Word of Lin Zhao's eloquence spread quickly across campus, and the next day, posters appeared that attacked her by name. But as others rushed to her defense, Lin Zhao herself went missing. A friend found her passed out in bed, her pillow soaked with red wine. On her desk was a piece of paper with three lines of poetry in her handwriting:

> *The heavens have wronged me,*
> *If I cannot endure it,*
> *Who will bear this responsibility?*

Lin Zhao would never take the spotlight again in the Hundred Flowers Movement. After that night, Zhang said, she refused to participate anymore in the "blooming and contending" and instead withdrew to the rare books collection of the university library. It was as if she sensed the danger approaching and was struggling to reconcile the conflict she had described between her conscience and her loyalty to the party.

The debates on campus continued without her. But as the days passed, the party began to isolate its critics and reassert control. "Any word or deed at variance with socialism is completely wrong," Mao declared, and the statement was painted in large white characters on the side of a building on campus. At the end of the month, the editors of the campus literary magazine convened a meeting to expel Zhang. This time, Lin Zhao stood with his accusers. She was still trying to make sense of the events of the past few weeks, and had not yet abandoned her faith in the party. Now that the party had labeled him a Rightist, she believed it. She was truly angry, Zhang recalled, and felt he had betrayed her. "I feel I have been deceived," she said.

Mao formally launched the Anti-Rightist Campaign with an editorial in the *People's Daily* about a week later. "Certain people," it said, were using the Hundred Flowers Movement as a pretext to "over-throw the Communist Party and the working class, and to topple the great cause of socialism." His original speech inviting public criticism of the party was published in state newspapers, but Mao rewrote history and added a new section setting limits on what could be criticized—words he had never uttered at the start of the Hundred Flowers Movement. After months of promising people they would not be punished for speaking out, the party began to do just that.

At Beida and elsewhere, the optimism and excitement of the spring gave way to a summer of fear, suspicion, and mistrust. As Mao turned from cultivating "blooming flowers" to rooting out "poisonous weeds," the party began a witch hunt. One by one, those who had voiced "Rightist" opinions were identified and summoned to self-criticism meetings, where they were told to confess their crimes, implicate colleagues, and renounce friends. Many students, still loyal to the party and convinced they had really lost their way, did what the party asked. Others believed they had done no wrong but tried to figure out how they could save themselves. As tensions on campus grew and the campaign got uglier, Lin Zhao found it increasingly difficult to ignore her own doubts about the party. "No sound at this time is better than any sound," she wrote in a note to a friend, in a frank warning indicating she no longer trusted the authorities. Her friend promptly turned the note over to party officials.

Shen Zeyi, who had coauthored the big-character poster with Zhang, was one of the first prominent student activists to confess. Before a full meeting of students and faculty, he renounced all ties with Zhang. Later, state newspapers published an essay he wrote titled "I Apologize to the People." Over the following months, others who had spoken out came under growing pressure to capitulate in struggle sessions. Security agents shadowed the most vocal students. The lively campus debates over ideas became denunciation meetings, and at times they got physical, with students shoved to the ground and forced to bow their heads. Some held out longer than others, but eventually, almost everyone targeted in the campaign gave in. A handful of students fled to their hometowns in the provinces or attempted to seek refuge in foreign embassies, but they could not escape the party's grasp. In the end, it made little difference if you confessed or not. Once you had been labeled a Rightist, you were doomed.

As others were falling in line, though, Lin Zhao was moving in the opposite direction. She found the the Anti-Rightist Campaign sickening. She was upset by the personal attacks, and distraught over the lives that were being ruined, and she saw the party's behavior as a betrayal of those who had trusted it most. The Hundred Flowers Movement was over, criticism of the party was no longer welcome, but Lin Zhao decided to get more involved, not less, as if her conscience had finally triumphed over her feelings for "the organization" and she wanted to make up for lost time. She tried to help Zhang publish one last issue of the magazine of the Hundred Flowers Society, and she wrote a bitter poem under a pen name, describing the denunciations of classmates as a "saber cutting my young heart, leaving it scarred and marked." At times she was openly defiant, reading aloud on campus from the Lu Xun short story "Diary of a Madman," in which the protagonist is convinced the people around him are practicing cannibalism and pleads with the reader to "save the children."

Lin Zhao could have chosen a different path, Zhang said. Her own participation in the Hundred Flowers Movement had been limited, and if she had stayed quiet, she might have escaped punishment. But at the self-criticism meetings, she refused to admit wrongdoing or express remorse. Instead, she surprised those in the room by talking back to her accusers. As a classmate recalled, when one of the party members asked her to describe her views, Lin Zhao replied, "My view is that all people are equal, and should live in freedom, harmony, and peace. We shouldn't attack people like this. If you must do this, then do it. But what good is a society like this? It's no good at all." She said the party's invitation to the public to help correct its faults had been "insincere," and that it didn't care now whether those who took up its offer lived or died. She refused to renounce Zhang and other friends who had been labeled Rightists. When the party members continued to criticize her, she retorted that they were dancing on her body and wiping blood from the bottom of their shoes on her face. As the weeks passed, the pressure to confess was intense. Lin Zhao's friends pleaded with her to get it over with, to protect herself and say what the party wanted to hear, as everyone else had. Instead, Lin Zhao swallowed an overdose of sleeping pills. Classmates found her and saved her, but party officials later said the suicide attempt was a sign of her "vile attitude," another offense against the people.

By autumn, the worst of the Anti-Rightist Campaign seemed to have passed. The Rightists had been humiliated and silenced. They were outcasts on campus, shunned by their classmates and subject to arbitrary harassment. But the struggle sessions were over, and a semblance of normalcy returned to the university. People were exhausted, drained emotionally, and ready for a break from the political drama. Zhang went back to work on his thesis after confessing, hopeful he would be allowed to graduate. Lin Zhao, however, suspected the party was not yet finished with them.

One Saturday night in late December, Zhang happened to run into her at a bookstore off campus. Her face was wrapped in a white scarf, and their eyes met across a table of paperbacks and magazines. It was dangerous for two Rightists to be seen talking to each other, and it had been months since he had seen her. Without saying a word, she left the store, and Zhang followed her into the cold. They ducked down a dark alley lit only by the stars, and walked until they reached an open field where they could be sure they were alone. "The situation is getting worse. We should prepare to be arrested," Lin Zhao said. "Remember my family's address. No matter how long we suffer, we can't lose touch." They traded addresses, but wrote nothing down and memorized them instead. A scrap of paper with an address was just the kind of thing the party could use as evidence of a Rightist conspiracy.

The police came for Zhang just four days later, on Christmas morning. He was labeled an "ultra-Rightist" and sentenced to eight years of reeducation through labor at a prison farm south of Beijing, the beginning of a twenty-two-year ordeal. Lin Zhao was sentenced to three years of labor "under observation." Nearly 1,500 others at Beida were punished as well, almost a fifth of the eight thousand students and teachers at the university. Some were allowed to remain at the school, but many lost their jobs, were expelled or worse. Shen Zeyi, who wrote the poster with Zhang, was sent to a labor camp in northern Shaanxi Province. A math lecturer who helped translate the Khrushchev speech was sentenced to life in prison. The founders of the Hundred Flowers Society all received long sentences, too.

Across the country, more than half a million people were shipped off to labor camps or exiled to toil in the countryside. In many places, party bosses ordered that at least 5 percent of people in each work unit be unveiled as Rightists, and as a result even people who didn't criticize the party were punished so officials could meet their quotas. Mao justified the crackdown by accusing two of his ministers, leaders of one of the small coalition parties, of organizing a Rightist plot to overthrow the socialist system. He was contradicting himself, of course, accusing people of crimes when they had only done what he asked. But now the party said it was because the Hundred Flowers policy had been designed all along to "lure the snake out of its hole."

Eight years later, in 1966, Zhang completed his sentence but the labor camp ordered him to undergo "continuing reform." The only change was that he could go home once a year. Zhang had another trip in mind. He had not forgotten Lin Zhao's family's address, and he was determined to see Lin Zhao again. She was already in prison by then, but her mother persuaded the authorities to let him visit her by telling them he was her fiancé. Lin Zhao was still refusing to confess to any crime, and the prison wanted him to persuade her to "reform her thinking." Zhang had the same goal; he was worried about her health and thought she should give in, so she could be released sooner.

He saw her in May 1966, two years before her execution. He had sneaked away to Shanghai during one of his trips home, and now he was waiting in the visiting room at the Tilanqiao Prison. Two dozen armed guards and other prison officials entered the room first, then Lin Zhao finally shuffled in with the help of a woman in a medical coat. Lin Zhao's face was pale and gaunt, her clothes worn and ragged, and much of her hair had turned gray. Tied around her forehead was a white cloth on which she had scrawled a large character in fresh blood: *Injustice*. But she smiled when she saw her old friend. To Zhang, it was as if the stylish young woman with pigtails tied with white silk ribbons was standing there again. The prison officers were surprised; later, they said they had never seen her smile before.

The officers remained in the room for the meeting, but Lin Zhao didn't care. She told Zhang she was being tortured, that the prison encouraged the other inmates to beat her every day in "struggle sessions," that she feared she would be raped. One of the officials interjected, telling Zhang not to believe her because she had mental problems. But Lin Zhao challenged him: "What kind of country treats the words of a mentally ill person as a crime? When you convicted me of counterrevolution, why didn't you say I was mentally ill then?" Zhang tried to change the subject, urging Lin Zhao to cooperate so she could be released. But she replied that the authorities had already decided to execute her. She coughed as she spoke, spitting blood into tissues that she crumpled up and tossed on the floor. "I could be killed at any moment, but I'm sure history will bring a day when people will speak of today's suffering," she told Zhang. "I hope you will tell people in the future about this suffering." She asked him to gather her poems, essays, and letters and publish them, and to look after her mother and her younger siblings after her death. And then she wept. The room was quiet. The prison officers said they had never seen her cry before, either.

Later, Lin Zhao reminded Zhang of what she had said long ago during the Hundred Flowers Movement about feeling deceived by him. "What I hate most is deception," she told him now. "I finally understood later, we really were deceived. Hundreds of thousands of people were deceived."

They were almost out of time. Lin Zhao asked Zhang to come closer, and he walked around the table and sat at her side. She said she had a gift for him, and she reached into a cloth bundle she had with her, and dug around for a moment. Zhang was curious what it could be. Lin Zhao pulled something small out, and he couldn't see what it was at first. Then she placed it in his open palm: a tiny sailboat, folded from a cellophane candy wrapper.

Lin Zhao

3

BLOOD AND LOVE

Hu Jie stared at the small boat in his hand. It was a fragile wisp of a thing. For more than thirty years, Zhang had kept it safe, guarding it like a secret treasure, and now he was giving it to the filmmaker. He said he was getting old, and was worried it would be lost when he passed away.

Zhang never saw Lin Zhao again after that prison visit. Instead, the officials at his labor camp put him in solitary confinement. His tiny cell was an oppressive, mosquito-infested room without windows or light, and they let him out only for interrogation by officers who suspected his meeting with Lin Zhao was part of some plot against the party. It was during one of these sessions, in the summer of 1968, that he was told Lin Zhao had been executed. "What's your opinion?" the reeducation officer snapped. Utterly defeated, Zhang replied, "I have no opinion." He remained in the cell for 138 days, then spent a decade toiling in prison farms and coal mines. During the terror of the Cultural Revolution, he and his family destroyed almost everything that could be used against them—old letters, magazines, photographs. But he held on to Lin Zhao's little sailboat, wrapping it in paper and hiding it away, for who would suspect it was more than just a scrap of folded cellophane?

Now he wanted Hu to take it. He wanted to pass it on to someone who knew what it was, who understood where it came from and what it meant to him. Hu accepted the gift quietly, and said he would look after it. He felt as if he were also accepting Zhang's burden, that he was agreeing to preserve Lin Zhao's memory and tell her story, fulfilling the promise that Zhang made to her during that prison visit so many years ago.

The two men had been talking for five days straight, sometimes on camera, sometimes off camera, taking breaks when they were tired or hungry. Zhang was a terrific storyteller, and Hu was mesmerized by his tale, almost all of which was new to him. He had only the vaguest impression of the Anti-Rightist Campaign before. He knew it was something bad, and that it was somehow associated with Mao, but until Zhang explained it to him, he didn't know exactly what had happened. Now he could see the scale and significance of the event. It was a turning point in Chinese history, he thought, the moment when the party reneged on its promise to allow a more democratic political process, a promise that had helped it win support and take power. It was the moment when it became clear the government would not tolerate even loyal dissent. Hu was surprised by the scope and fervor of the Hundred Flowers Movement, and by the ruthlessness of the Anti-Rightist Campaign. But what he found most astonishing was that it had all been erased so completely from the public's memory. How could events of such magnitude, he wondered, have been forgotten so quickly? What did it mean for a nation to know more about emperors and dynasties hundreds of years in its past than about people and events a few decades ago? It wasn't normal or healthy for a society to go through a cataclysm like the Anti-Rightist Campaign and never discuss it, Hu decided. He wondered if the absence of historical knowledge hindered social progress, if this ignorance of the past had prevented people from building on the experiences and arguments of Lin Zhao and her classmates. How might the Tiananmen Square democracy movement have been different if the students had been familiar with the ideas of their predecessors in the Hundred Flowers Movement, for example? Something else bothered him, too. If he and others his age were unaware of events as momentous as these, how would the knowledge be passed to the next generation?

On the train back to Nanjing, Hu decided to change the focus of his film. He couldn't just build the documentary around Ni. The story was too big for that. He needed a broader framework, one that would let him explore Lin Zhao's life but also convey the drama of the times she lived in. He wanted to force people to reconsider their understanding of the past and the lessons it held for the present. Like many people his age, Hu had concluded long ago that communism was a failure, and it was obvious to him that the party, despite its rhetoric, had embraced capitalism as the path to a brighter future. But listening to Zhang gave Hu a new perspective on China's experience with communism. It was not just a mistaken ideology or economic theory, he realized, but also an extraordinary event in the development of mankind, an attempt to build a perfect society that inspired a nation but resulted in cruelty on an almost unimaginable scale. It was a great experiment in human affairs that ended in great human tragedy, and Hu marveled at how absurd it all seemed in retrospect. How could it have happened? How could people follow Mao through something like the Anti-Rightist Campaign, and then into a disaster like the Cultural Revolution? And how could the party remain in power through it all? He wanted to make a documentary that raised such questions by putting Lin Zhao's life in historical context, and he couldn't do that by following someone else around. He would have to abandon the observational style of his earlier films and take a more active role, becoming the central character of the film himself. He wanted to find and interview more people who knew Lin Zhao, as well as others who had lived through the era. It meant more research, more time, and more money, but Hu was convinced it would be worth the effort. He assured his worried wife that the result would be something special, his best film yet.

It was slow and difficult work. One after another, Hu tracked down interview subjects and tried to persuade them to speak with him about Lin Zhao. Again and again, they rebuffed him. Some people were rude, others apologetic, but if there was a common theme to their responses, it was fear. Hu could hear it in their voices when he called, and see it in their eyes and body language when he showed up at their doors unannounced and explained what he was doing. One couple Hu visited was so traumatized by the Cultural Revolution that they still kept everything in their home wrapped in newspaper, to make it easier to pack up and flee. Many of those Hu wanted to interview were former Rightists, and their tragic experiences had taught them caution. They had been "rehabilitated" and given new jobs after Mao's death, but the party that persecuted them was still in power, and the labor camps they toiled in were still open. They understood there

could be consequences to speaking out, and Hu understood their re-
luctance to talk. They had lost so much of their lives already, and they
wanted to enjoy the rest of their years in peace. It was not that they
had forgotten the past. It was that they remembered too well.

But for every person who declined to be interviewed, there were
others who opened up. Most were wary at first. They too had suffered, and they were also afraid. But once they overcame that initial
hesitation and started talking, they often couldn't stop. They had been
through so much, and they had bottled up their feelings and suppressed their memories for so long, that when they began talking
about Lin Zhao, it was like opening a floodgate. The past came rushing back, and they would talk for hours without interruption. At times
it seemed as if they were using the interviews as a form of therapy, and
Hu often left the sessions drained and exhausted. Many of these people had never shared their experiences with anyone else before, not
even with their own families. Several asked to be interviewed away
from home, so their children wouldn't learn of the misery they had endured. They told Hu they were speaking out for Lin Zhao, but he
sensed they were also doing it for themselves. They had taken part in
historic events that the party had buried, and because the party denied what they had been through, it was as if the fact of their existence
were being erased, too. The country was moving on, looking forward,
and no one seemed interested in what had happened to them. Neither
journalists nor historians came to interview them, and they never saw
anything about their experiences in books or magazines or on television, except occasionally in a publication or video smuggled in from
overseas. As they got older, they wondered what, if anything, people
would remember of the Hundred Flowers Movement and the Anti-
Rightist Campaign after they died. Then, out of nowhere, a filmmaker
showed up, and asked to hear their stories and record their memories.
The urge to bear witness suddenly triumphed over the instinct to stay
silent. By talking to Hu, they were refusing to let history forget them.

One man broke down in tears as soon as he opened his door to Hu.
Lu Fuwei was seventy, a retired reporter for Xinhua, but once he had
been Lin Zhao's party branch secretary at Peking University, a classmate in the literature department who had gone along with the decision to label her a Rightist. He sat on his sofa sobbing for several
minutes before collecting himself and speaking to Hu. "What Lin
Zhao said at the time was just common sense. It wasn't that she saw

things others didn't, it was just common sense," he said. "But because we were at a low point in history, common sense was counterrevolutionary." After Mao's death, Lu managed to slip in a sentence about Lin Zhao's execution in an essay about the Cultural Revolution, and he helped organize a quiet memorial service for her. Next to her photograph at the ceremony were red ribbons on which Lu had written just two characters instead of a traditional elegiac couplet. One was a question mark, and the other an exclamation point.

In each interview, Hu gathered more information about Lin Zhao. He learned that after being labeled a Rightist, she was supposed to undergo labor reform at a coal mine, but a professor concerned about her health intervened and arranged for her to carry out her sentence at an orchard on campus instead. There she had a brief romance with Tan Tianrong, the most prominent student Rightist at Beida and one of the founders of the Hundred Flowers Society. Hu tracked him down in the port city of Qingdao, where he had been appointed a college professor after being released from the labor camps. Tan refused to be interviewed at first, even after Hu pleaded with him in a letter and sent him a photo of Lin Zhao. Later, Hu traveled to Qingdao to see him in person. Standing inside the doorway to his apartment, Tan demurred again, but Hu wouldn't let him shut the door. He kept saying how important it was to record this part of history, and argued that the least he could do was talk to him off camera. After almost forty minutes, Tan finally relented. "If you hadn't come so far for Lin Zhao," he said, "I wouldn't have let you in." After a while, he agreed to speak on camera, too. He described the short time he and Lin Zhao enjoyed together before he was sent to a labor camp, and recalled a conversation they had in the summer of 1958 after spending a day on campus trying to kill mosquitoes on the party's orders. "She said to me, 'I was laughing in my heart the whole time, laughing at the party's insanity,' " he recalled. "Back then, I only felt suffering. I wasn't like her. It never occurred to me the party had gone insane."

Near the end of 1959, Lin Zhao was allowed to return home on medical parole. Her parents had separated by then; her mother was living in Shanghai and her father in Suzhou. She reconciled with both of them, and apologized for her denunciations of them as a teenager enthralled by the party. A year later, after she was arrested, her anguished father committed suicide.

During his first trip with Ni Jinxiong, Hu had interviewed a retired professor who told him Lin Zhao was arrested in 1960 for help-ing publish an underground magazine critical of the party. Now Hu could put her participation in the magazine in perspective. She had escaped with a relatively light sentence in the Anti-Rightist Cam-paign, and she had been allowed to go home for medical treatment. If she had refrained from further political activity, that might have been the worst of it for her. But instead of lying low, she made contact with a group of graduate students in physics at a university a thousand miles away in the frontier city of Lanzhou, in Gansu Province. Many of them had attended college in Beijing and some were natives of Shanghai, but the party had sent them west to be closer to the remote labs and test sites where the army was trying to build an atomic bomb. They were some of the brightest young minds in China, but because they were outsiders in Gansu, local cadres targeted them during the Anti-Rightist Campaign and sent them to labor in the countryside. A few of the students happened to meet Lin Zhao during a visit home, and she was quickly drawn into their plans to publish a magazine crit-icizing the party's policies. They managed to print only one issue on a mimeograph machine before the authorities caught them. In Septem-ber 1960, police arrested about forty students and teachers in Lan-zhou in connection with the publication, as well as a local party chief and dozens of local residents who sympathized with them. A few weeks later, police in Suzhou arrested Lin Zhao, too.

Hu searched for a copy of the magazine, and for people who could explain what might have driven Lin Zhao to participate in such a risky endeavor. Eventually, he found the answer in another hidden chapter of the party's history. Hu had heard stories of a famine that swept the nation between 1958 and 1961, but he had always accepted the explanation that it had been limited in scale and the result of "three difficult years" of natural disasters. Now, as his research into Lin Zhao's life deepened, he learned the truth. There was indeed a famine, but it was neither limited nor caused by natural disasters. In reality, some thirty million people—and perhaps as many as fifty million—starved to death in a catastrophe that was the direct result of party policies, specifically a campaign known as the Great Leap Forward. Launched in 1958, the Leap was Mao's attempt to catapult China into a state of utopian communism by mobilizing the public into a frenzy of accelerated economic production. Across the countryside, huge communes were set up in which peasants were forced to pool their land and possessions, meals were served in mass dining halls, and wages were replaced with "work points." At the same time, the party announced a series of absurdly ambitious economic targets as Mao vowed to overtake Britain and the United States in steel production within fifteen years. Millions of people were diverted from the fields for worthless industrial schemes, the most notable of which were "backyard furnaces," primitive smelters in which villagers tried to turn all their metal belongings—cookware, bicycles, tools—into steel. Peasants were told to spend less time in the fields and more time on such foolish projects, and encouraged to eat more in the new dining halls, because the Great Leap Forward was supposed to be a success. As officials sent in false reports of bumper crops to flatter Mao and protect their jobs, the stage was set for the deadliest man-made disaster ever visited upon China.

When the famine struck, those who had been punished as Rightists witnessed it up close. There were serious food shortages in the cities, but conditions were most severe in the countryside, where many of them had been sent for reeducation through labor. They told Hu how the old and the young died first, how the strong survived by eating bark, insects, and even dirt, how people in the most desperate parts of the country resorted to cannibalism. These were the most difficult interviews Hu had done yet, and he often teared up behind the camera as he recorded the stories. Huang Zhen, a Rightist and veteran of the Korean War who had befriended Lin Zhao in Suzhou, told Hu of his duties at a labor camp in a once-bountiful region not far from the Yangtze:

> In the winter of 1961, every morning on the farm, we carried the corpses out to be buried. It wasn't just one or two each day. . . . We would wrap them in their blankets and tie both ends with a straw rope. Then we used two other ropes, one to tie around the neck and the other around the feet. Two of us would use a long bamboo pole, about this thick, and carry the body for a mile to the Xizhi River. We dug a pit and buried the bodies. Then we marked the grave.
>
> Okay, so we buried them. But the local residents saw the graves—one, two, three, four, five, six, seven, eight, nine, ten,

twenty, thirty, forty graves. After we left, they would dig up the bodies we had just buried. What did they want from the dead? They wanted clothes and blankets. The people were so poor that they had no blankets. The next day, we came and saw the mess they made with the graves. . . . We had to treat the corpses well. They were naked, but what could we do? We just covered them with dirt.

As the famine spread, only one senior party official mustered the courage to point out the obvious. Peng Dehuai, the minister of defense and a hero of both the Revolution and the Korean War, sent a private letter to Mao that criticized the Great Leap Forward and described the dire conditions he had seen on a recent tour of the countryside near his hometown. Mao responded by distributing the letter at a party plenum in July 1959 and launching a vehement attack against Peng as a Rightist who was plotting against the party. It was a ridiculous charge, but in an effective bit of political theater, Mao threatened to quit and lead the peasants in a new revolution against the government if other party leaders didn't back him. The showdown was over almost as soon as it began. Never again would a member of the Politburo dare to openly challenge the Chairman. Peng was humiliated and stripped of power, and Mao launched another purge of party ranks that eclipsed the Anti-Rightist Campaign, with as many as six million people punished. To prove that Peng was wrong, the party accelerated the Great Leap Forward instead of slowing it down, and millions more across the nation died of hunger.

Lin Zhao had been skeptical of the Leap from the start. The effort to kill mosquitoes that she mocked as "insanity" was one of the early phases of the campaign. But if she laughed at the party's crusade against the "Four Pests"—rats, sparrows, and flies were also targeted—she was angered by the reports of mass starvation in the countryside that followed, and by what she saw as the stubborn refusal of party officials to do anything about it. This was what moved her to risk imprisonment and publish the underground magazine with the physics students in Gansu Province, where starvation was especially widespread. "We were certain we would be punished for doing it," one of the students, Gu Yan, told Hu. "But we felt we had to do it. Somebody had to stand up. If nobody dared to speak out, there would be no hope for the nation."

As Hu located and interviewed people involved in the magazine, he discovered that Lin Zhao and her friends also used the mimeograph machine to print an open letter to party leaders criticizing the Great Leap Forward and protesting Peng Dehuai's ouster. But none of the people he interviewed had copies of the letter or of the magazine. The materials had all been seized by the police when Lin Zhao and the others were arrested.

Hu was always looking for examples of Lin Zhao's writing. He wanted to hear her describe in her own words what she had been through, and he asked everyone he interviewed if they had saved any letters, essays, or poems, anything that might offer some insight into her thoughts at the time. Most said they had destroyed everything like that to prevent the authorities from using it against them. But occasionally he would come across an old letter, or a poem scribbled on the back of a photograph. Several people told Hu that Lin Zhao routinely made copies of writing that she considered important, and gave them to friends for safekeeping. It was as if she knew that her words were in danger of being lost, and that some day, someone might try to recover them. Before her arrest, for example, Lin Zhao asked a university dean she respected to hold a stack of her writing for safekeeping. The dean, however, burned the collection during the Cultural Revolution.

Hu learned that Lin Zhao was released from prison on medical parole for several months in 1962, and that during that time she wrote a series of political essays and letters, including one to the president of Peking University. After finishing each piece, she sent a copy to the police, and another copy to the prison authorities. But she also gave a copy to an old classmate, someone who was not politically active and who escaped scrutiny by the party. Hu tracked down the classmate, and made arrangements to go see her. But before he could make the trip, he received a phone call from her son. The woman had passed away. Hu asked the man if his mother had said anything about Lin Zhao before her death, or if she had perhaps left a package for him. The man said he would check, but a few days later he called back and said he had found nothing.

Such disappointments were common in the course of Hu's research. But he took heart that Lin Zhao had been thinking ahead and trying to hide copies of her writing. He was sure that there was a stash out there somewhere, just waiting to be discovered, and he was determined to find it. He was less certain about how he might obtain her prison writings, the material she had penned with her blood. But he was confident that he would find those, too. He had already unearthed so much of the buried past, and he had come to believe that the party could not keep such things hidden forever.

HU OFTEN WENT back to see the people he interviewed. At first he was being thorough, keeping in touch in case they had come across new material or located someone else for him to talk to. But then he found himself visiting them just for the company. He worked alone on the documentary for the most part. He had no colleagues, and other than his sister and a handful of others, he had no one to talk to about the film. Most of his friends weren't interested and couldn't understand his obsession with a woman long since dead. But the old Rightists he interviewed, men and women in their sixties and seventies, appreciated what he was doing. They shared his commitment to documenting Lin Zhao's life, and they recognized the importance of recording this piece of history that they had lived through. Hu felt comfortable around them, and they welcomed him into their lives, too, for they understood loneliness.

One of the people Hu befriended was a retired librarian in Beijing named Gan Cui. He was an unassuming man in his late sixties, with thinning white hair, piercing dark eyes, and a smoker's stained teeth. As a Rightist, he had spent much of his life doing hard labor in the desert province of Xinjiang, and the experience left him with a roughness that never completely disappeared, even after he was rehabilitated and sent to work at a literary research institute in Beijing. He dressed plainly, sometimes carelessly, with little regard for fashion; a typical outfit might include a ragged sweatshirt and green camouflage trousers, or a jacket with only the top buttons fastened. When they first arranged to meet, Hu walked by Gan twice without spotting him, because he looked more like an aging roughneck than a literary scholar. But Gan knew how to tell a story, and Hu went to see him whenever he made the trip to Beijing. He enjoyed sitting in Gan's cramped apartment, sharing a pot of tea with the old man as his two pet macaws chirped in Chinese, "Hello, miss! Hello, miss!" And every time Hu visited, Gan shared a little more of his past.

As a young man, Gan was a journalism student at People's University, a new school established by the party near Beida to train officials after the Revolution. During the Hundred Flowers Movement, he admired those who spoke out about the party's shortcomings, but was shrewd enough never to make any speeches or put up any posters himself. His record was spotless, and he might have made it through the Anti-Rightist Campaign unscathed were it not for an incident at the start of the crackdown. At the time, the most prominent critic of the party on campus was a young woman in the law department named Lin Xiling. In a series of bold speeches at Beida, she rebuked the party as undemocratic, bolstering her arguments with details obtained from a boyfriend who worked for a senior party official. She described the party's suppression of independent thinking as Stalinism, at a time when Stalin was still considered a hero, and she even challenged Mao himself. "Chairman Mao's statements aren't golden rules. Why can't they be opposed?" she asked. Such daring won her a following on campuses across the country, but it also made her a target. When the Anti-Rightist Campaign began, party officials prepared an ambush. As an officer of the campus student association, Gan was told to invite Lin Xiling to a public debate but to make sure it turned into a denunciation session. He did as he was told. The first seven speakers he called followed the party's script, delivering speeches condemning her. Then Lin asked if she had a right to speak. Without thinking, Gan said yes and gave her the floor. She was only able to say a few words before party loyalists shouted her down and seized the microphone from her. In the heat of the moment, Gan scolded the students who had disrupted his meeting: "Does it make sense to let only you speak but not to let her?" The outburst would cost him twenty-two years of his life. When the university failed to find enough Rightists to meet the party's quota, it accused Gan of "supporting and sympathizing with Lin Xiling" and added him to the list.

At first he received the lightest possible sentence, a form of probation that allowed him to stay in school. He was told to report for work at the journalism department's reference library, and it was there that he met Lin Zhao. She was twenty-six then, and had been sent to work in the library after her stint at the orchard at Beida. They were the only ones working in the library, and their job was to read through and catalogue its collection of old newspapers. But their supervisor was a kindly woman, and she let them have access to the library's vast collection of old books. Gan found a rare block-printed edition of *The Plum in the Golden Vase*, the famed Ming Dynasty erotic novel, and spent most of his time studying that. Lin Zhao preferred more high-brow fare, novels from the Qing Dynasty written in classical Chinese. When she saw what Gan was reading, she laughed, and found another book for him: a translation of *The Decameron*, the collection of bawdy novellas by the fourteenth-century Italian author Giovanni Boccaccio.

As Rightists, they were both outcasts on campus, and naturally, they became friends. When Lin Zhao came down with tuberculosis in the winter and stopped coming to work, Gan visited her daily and tried to nurse her back to health. He moved a stove into her cold dorm room and made sure she had enough coal and firewood, and he brought her breakfast and lunch. When she lost her appetite for the dull fare from the cafeteria, he woke every morning at five to take a bus to a downtown hotel so he could bring her back a bowl of its tasty Cantonese porridge. As Lin Zhao began to recover, party officials noticed how much time the two spent together, and summoned Gan to a meeting, where he was warned that they were not permitted to date. Annoyed, he returned to Lin Zhao's room and told her of the party's latest commandment. She laughed, and asked if he was afraid. He said no, and she said, "Let's go for a stroll." And then the two began walking on campus holding hands, openly defying the party.

"It wasn't that we developed what you would call a romantic relationship on our own," Gan explained to Hu. "It was the organization that kept putting pressure on us about it. . . . The more they tried to prevent us from dating, with her personality and my personality, the more we dated, just to show them."

Gan and Lin Zhao often went on long evening walks together, and on Saturday nights they might go dancing or take in a play if they could get free tickets. He learned to play the *erhu*, a classical Chinese string instrument, and serenaded her under the window of her second-floor dorm room. She put on a colorful *qipao*, a body-hugging traditional dress, when everyone else was wearing drab Mao suits, and took him to the restaurant of an expensive hotel. They ordered a single dish, the cheapest, fish head braised in soy sauce. As a child, Lin Zhao had attended a school run by Christian missionaries, and now she started going to church again, bringing Gan along. He watched in awe as she practiced English with the foreign diplomats who attended the service; like most other students, the only foreign language Gan could speak was Russian.

The two of them often talked about literature, and she showed him what she was writing, plays and long poems that contained thinly veiled criticisms of the party's rule. Gan admired her writing; he could see she was more talented than he. But he urged her to be more careful and more realistic, arguing that it was useless to challenge the party. He said she was like an egg trying to smash a rock, adding that even if she had an army of a hundred thousand troops, the party could still crush her. But Lin Zhao refused to give in. She said it might take thousands, or tens of thousands, or even millions of eggs, but the rock could be broken. With steady effort and time, the political system could be changed. Even dripping water, she said, could split a stone.

As graduation approached in the spring of 1959, Gan asked their party branch secretary for permission to marry Lin Zhao. The man immediately rejected the request, adding with contempt that two Rightists could never wed. Soon afterward, the party ordered Gan to report for labor reform in Xinjiang, the desolate province bordering Kazakhstan in China's far west. He was being punished for his forbidden romance with Lin Zhao, who was being sent to Shanghai on medical parole. They tried to enjoy what was left of their time together, but the summer was fleeting, and in late September, Gan accompanied Lin Zhao to the city's central train station. He promised to come find her as soon as he could, and he asked her to wait for him. Then they embraced on the platform and wept. She left on an overnight train heading south, and the next morning, Gan began his five-day trip west.

He spent the next twenty years on a military work crew in Xinjiang, digging up grass and other vegetation from the hard soil for use in cough syrup and other medicine. At first he wrote Lin Zhao a letter every week, but after six months she stopped writing back. A soldier returning home to Shanghai checked on her for him and sent a letter saying she was ill and in the hospital. But something about his choice of words led Gan to conclude she was really in prison. For years, he kept photos of her at his bedside, and she sometimes appeared in his dreams after the long days of backbreaking labor. Eventually, Gan gave up hope that he would ever be allowed to leave Xinjiang. He convinced himself that Lin Zhao had been more fortunate and had gotten married. It was not until 1979, after he was rehabilitated and allowed to return to Beijing, that he learned she had been executed.

Upon returning to Beijing, Gan moved on with his life. He married, divorced, and married again, and he had a son. But he told Hu he often found himself thinking about Lin Zhao. Sometimes he wondered how things might have been different if he and Lin Zhao had been allowed to marry. Perhaps, he said, he could have persuaded her to compromise and do what was necessary to survive. Perhaps, if they had settled down and started a family, she would have been more careful. Perhaps she would still be alive today. Once, when his wife was in the other room, Gan even told Hu that he had loved Lin Zhao more than he ever loved his wife.

But it was not until more than a year after Hu met him that Gan revealed to the filmmaker the depth of his devotion. Hu was in Beijing again, staying with his sister, when Gan called and asked if he could help him sell an antique book. Hu said he would drop by and take a look, but Gan insisted on bringing it to him instead. Later, Hu realized that Gan wanted to make sure he was telling the truth about where he was staying, a final precaution before placing his trust in him completely. He must have been reassured by meeting Hu's sister and seeing her apartment, because then he told Hu his secret: He had a collection of Lin Zhao's prison writings, nearly 140,000 words of it. Hu was dumbstruck. Was he hearing correctly? Could it be true? The disappointment would be unbearable if it wasn't, and he didn't want to get his hopes up. How could the old man have obtained such material, he wondered, and why did he hide it from him for so long? Gan wanted to show it to him, so they went back to his apartment, where he retrieved an old blue Adidas gym bag. From the bag he pulled out a thick stack of paper, bound with string and packed in brown wrapping paper. There were nearly five hundred yellowing pages, each full of writing in black ink, and he was willing to let Hu read it.

Later, Gan explained where the pages came from. After the Cultural Revolution, he had been fortunate enough to receive a letter from an old friend telling him to flee his prison crew and rush back to Beijing because the political winds had shifted and the Rightists were being rehabilitated. His escape and early return to the capital meant he was able to get permission to live and work in Beijing while most

Rightists were assigned jobs near the labor camps where they had been held. Gan was given a position in the library of the Institute of Literature, a research center in the Chinese Academy of Social Sciences. The director of the institute, Xu Juemin, was married to a former classmate of Gan's, and the couple often invited him to their home for dinner. On one such evening three years after he returned to Beijing, Gan walked in and saw a woman who looked just like Lin Zhao—it was her sister, Peng Lingfan. As it turned out, the institute director happened to be a distant cousin of Lin Zhao's. The four of them spoke of little but Lin Zhao that evening. Gan thought it was as if fate had intervened to keep her in his life.

A few years later, Peng immigrated to the United States, and she gave the institute director a package of papers, photocopies of a portion of Lin Zhao's prison writings. When the party was rehabilitating Rightists, Peng had fought to clear her sister's name posthumously. A court eventually agreed but it didn't provide any details of her case nor did it disclose the whereabouts of her remains. One afternoon, though, Peng was summoned to an office of the Shanghai public security bureau located on the Bund, the avenue of majestic European buildings on the Huangpu River. The official who met with her didn't give his name, and instead of asking questions, he offered some answers. He said the city's public security apparatus had long been divided about how to handle Lin Zhao, and even now, long after her death, the question of her rehabilitation remained a matter of intense dispute. Many people had been punished for trying to protect her, he said, and some had died for it. Her execution, he said, was approved by higher levels, and those who had argued for it continued to hold important posts. The official appeared nervous. "I hear you have an excellent memory, but there is no need to remember our conversation," Peng later quoted him as saying. Then he gave Peng a bundle of papers. She recognized Lin Zhao's handwriting immediately.

Gan knew nothing of the documents until long after Peng had moved to the United States. The institute director finally showed them to him and asked for his help. Both he and the director had retired by then, and the director's eyesight was failing. He couldn't read Lin Zhao's handwriting, and hoped Gan might be able to decipher it. Gan took the papers home and kept them hidden. At the time, he was working as a volunteer in the guard booth at his apartment complex. Each morning before breakfast, he sat in the booth studying Lin

Zhao's writing, trying to make out the tiny, faded characters she scribbled so long ago in prison. The material was written in ink, but Lin Zhao indicated in the text that she had written almost all of it in blood first, then copied it after prison authorities gave her pen and paper. Now, slowly, Gan copied her words again, sentence by sentence, page by page. He worked on it at least an hour a day. Sometimes, in the privacy of the guard booth, he cried while reading her words and committing them to paper again. When he finished, the final product totaled 469 pages. And now it was in Hu's hands. Gan told the filmmaker he could borrow it for three days.

Hu read feverishly deep into the night, driven by the excitement of discovery. Nearly two years had passed since he first heard Lin Zhao's name and set out to find her prison writings, and he could scarcely believe they were finally in his possession. He had been looking for them for so long, and he had heard so much about Lin Zhao's literary talent, that it seemed unlikely these pages could meet his expectations. And yet they did. He was mesmerized by the material, blown away by the passion and intensity of her words. He was reading a copy of a copy of a copy, but the writing was so fierce that it made sense to Hu that it had originally been written in blood.

The document was ostensibly a letter to the editors of the *People's Daily*, the party's official newspaper, but it was unlike any letter Hu had ever seen. The main text was 438 pages long, and there were eight appendices of material. Lin Zhao appeared to have composed the letter over a period of several months when she was thirty-two; in the first paragraph, she wrote that it was Bastille Day, July 14, but by the time she signed and dated the letter, it was December 5, 1965. The main body was a stream of thoughts, arguments, and accounts of prison experiences presented in a long, meandering text without any clear structure. Some parts read like a diary, other parts like a manifesto, and occasionally it deteriorated into an incoherent rant, but every page was brimming with emotion and defiance.

"The Anti-Rightist Campaign—that miserable reign of terror in 1957 left a mark and a void in the lives of many people, and in the life of this young person," Lin Zhao wrote near the top of the letter.

Of course, this was the Communist Party's fault! It was not only wrong, it was outrageously wrong! Whenever I think of that miserable year, 1957, my gut aches and I cringe! Truly, whenever this particular year is mentioned, whenever I see it or hear it, it is as if I have been conditioned to feel pain! Until then, the intellectuals of China still retained some sense of justice, but after that year, it was almost completely destroyed, wiped out! Your respected newspaper, gentlemen, once again fostered violence and reeked of blood!

Lin Zhao sprinkled the text with allusions to literature and history. When she accused prison authorities of depriving her of pen and paper, she recalled that a czar had used the same tactic in trying to silence the dissident poet Rainis. "But it may not work so well on this young rebel!" she declared, noting that she had already written two other letters in blood to the *People's Daily*. She often referred to herself in the third person, as "the young rebel," and described herself as a "freedom fighter" and a "soldier of Christianity." She wrote that she fully understood the terrible cost of challenging the party's rule, but that she had no choice, because her conscience demanded that she do so. She accused the party of taking advantage of the idealism of her generation, and asked whether political change could be achieved peacefully rather than through violence. She also described how difficult it was to write in blood, how she would prick her finger and use a hairpin as a pen. Sometimes the blood dried too quickly and it would take her an entire afternoon to write a few words, and sometimes she would bleed too much and it would make her dizzy. Blood was a recurring image throughout the letter.

Is this not blood? Our innocence, naivete, and righteousness were insidiously exploited, and our kindhearted nature and ardent temperaments were misused. As we grew up and began to realize the absurd cruelty of the truth and demand the democratic rights that we deserved, we were persecuted, tortured, and oppressed in vicious and unprecedented fashion. Is this not blood? Our youth, love, friendship, studies, careers, ambitions, ideals, happiness, freedom . . . all that we live for, all that a human being has, were almost completely destroyed and buried by the foul, evil rule of this totalitarian system. Is this not blood? This evil regime, which has stained the history of this nation as well as of human civilization, was established, strengthened, and sustained by blood.

Lin Zhao wrote of the abuse she suffered in prison, of being beaten and tortured, of her fear of sexual assault, of guards who handcuffed her in painful positions and force-fed her through her nostrils. When she could not bear the torment, she wrote, she tried to commit suicide by swallowing soap or cutting her wrist with glass. She said she struggled to retain her sanity in the face of such agony.

I wrote a few lines in blood on the concrete wall: "No, no! God will not let me go mad, as long as I live another day. She must keep me sane and preserve my memory!" But under such persistent, sinister, and endless harassment and pressure, it seems I really have gone mad! God, God, help me! I have almost been driven mad! But I must not lose my mind, and I don't want to lose my mind!

At times, Lin Zhao's writing grew so muddled and confused that Hu wondered if she had indeed suffered a mental breakdown. But for every rambling passage, there were others that were as clear and articulate as anything he had ever read. Perhaps the sharpest writing appeared in the supplemental material appended to the letter: four pieces of poetry, one of which was a satire of a well-known poem by Mao; three short essays; a statement by Lin Zhao upon her conviction in 1965; and an annotated copy of her December 1964 indictment. Lin Zhao copied the indictment word for word and embedded her own comments in the text. Hu found it striking not only because it was the first detailed account of Lin Zhao's alleged crimes he had seen but also because her remarks were so unyieldingly defiant and scornful.

Lin Zhao, the prime culprit of the "China Free Youth Fighters' Alliance" counter-revolutionary clique, has been arrested under the law by public security organs and an investigation has been completed. The case has been transferred to this agency for examination and prosecution. The investigation confirms that: The defendant, Lin Zhao, originally named Peng Lingzhao, also known as Xu Ping and Lu Ming, female, 32, *(Note: It should be 30),* native of Suzhou, Jiangsu Province, with a bureaucratic capitalist class family background, *(Note: I don't know what you are trying to say)* is an adult student with some university education *(Note: It was the persecution of your notorious, so-called Anti-Rightist Campaign of 1957 that interrupted my studies!)*. . . . In 1957, because she opposed the party and opposed socialism, she was reduced to a Rightist *(Note: The hypocritical language that totalitarian rulers are accustomed to using mixes truth with lies and confuses the public to the extreme! This sentence, properly written, should say: In 1957, inspired and driven by the ardor of youth and a conscience that had not entirely expired, she became an activist of the May 19th democratic anti-tyranny movement at Beida!)* and was given a punishment of labor under observation while retaining her status as a student. *(Note: Thank you for showing mercy and leniency! But it was also because you didn't know about all of Lin Zhao's activities at the time!)* In 1959, she came to Shanghai to recuperate from an illness. On Oct. 14, 1960, she was arrested.

When the indictment said her father had committed suicide because he feared punishment as a counterrevolutionary, Lin Zhao retorted, "We've heard this all before: Everyone who commits suicide does it because they 'fear punishment' for their crimes." When the indictment said she wrote in a "hunger strike letter" that she would sit in prison for the rest of her life and never change her views, Lin Zhao replied, "It's true. Share it with the heavens and the earth!" When the indictment accused her of "opposing socialism," she wrote, "If this so-called 'socialism' means tyrannizing, persecuting, and humiliating people, then there is absolutely no shame in 'opposing socialism' or attacking 'socialism'!" And when it accused her of "putting up a last-ditch struggle" against the party in prison, she suggested her comments on the indictment might be a fine example of that. On the indictment's last page, the prosecutors noted they had collected eight volumes of her writings and of witness testimony as evidence against her. Lin Zhao interjected again: "According to the principles of Marxism-Leninism, the 'law' is merely the 'will of the ruler'! Resistance is a crime, struggling for freedom is a crime, demanding human rights is even more of a crime, so what need is there for 'evidence and witnesses'?"

Lin Zhao also appended to her *People's Daily* letter a statement she penned after the court sentenced her to twenty years in prison. "This is an extremely reprehensible and shameful judgment, but as a rebel I also take pride in this highest honor," she wrote, adding that she would "work harder" to live up to the sentence. "Just watch! The court of history will proclaim a verdict for future generations," she concluded. "You totalitarian rulers and treacherous scoundrels, shameless usurpers of state power and traitors who have brought disaster upon the people, you will become not only the true defendants but also the prosecuted criminals! Justice will prevail! Long live freedom!"

When Hu finished reading the document, the winter sun had begun to rise over the hazy city. From the window of his sister's apartment, he watched as the first rays of dawn struck the construction cranes scattered across the skyline and the traffic began to build on the capital's intersecting roadways. Years later, when I asked Hu how he felt that morning, he replied that it was as if he had been exposed to "a level of thinking" he had never encountered before and never imagined existed in his country. He said he felt invigorated, and proud. "I stood at the window, watching the eastern sky get brighter," he recalled, "and I thought it was extraordinary that a great woman like Lin Zhao once lived in China. . . . I thought she was a national treasure."

NOT LONG AFTER Hu located the Lin Zhao documents, a friend called with some disturbing news: an agent of the Ministry of State Security had come around asking questions about him. Ever since he lost his job at Xinhua, Hu had assumed the secret police were keeping tabs on him, and he sometimes suspected they were following him or tapping his phone. But now he knew for sure that they were doing . . . something. It was unnerving, knowing that these shadowy men were making inquiries about him, but having no idea what they planned to do or when they were going to do it. Hu likened it to swallowing an insect and wondering what it was doing inside his body. It was an uncomfortable, sickening feeling. A while later, other friends reported that state security agents had approached them, too, and Hu began to worry he might be arrested at any moment. But it was not prison that frightened him most. It was the possibility that he might not be allowed to finish the documentary, that he would never be able to tell Lin Zhao's story. He had worked so hard and for so long on the film. He felt like an artist who had finished a lengthy apprenticeship but was told he would die before he could complete his masterpiece. Hu was sure that no one else was doing this research, and he worried that if he were stopped, all the information he had uncovered would be buried again, maybe forever.

The prospect of arrest drove him to work harder and faster. After returning the papers to Gan, Hu had persuaded him to introduce him to Lin Zhao's cousin, the retired director of the literary institute, and the man gave him the version of the letter that was in Lin Zhao's handwriting. For months Hu pored over the text, double-checking Gan's work and trying to recognize words that Gan had been unable to read. The documents were full of new information and new leads, and Hu stepped up and expanded his search for interview subjects. He felt as if he was racing against the police, trying to finish his film before they completed their investigation and took him away. It was nerve-racking but also energizing, and it spurred him on. As he worked on the film, he tried to deepen his understanding of history and political theory, reading as much as he could because he thought that each book he read would be one less volume he would have to take to prison. He told his friends to tell the state security agents to come speak to him directly, and he treated each week that passed without a knock on his door from them as a reprieve, another chance to gather more material and make the documentary better.

Hu also sensed that a natural deadline was approaching. Lin Zhao's contemporaries were getting old, their memories were fading, and some of the people he wanted to interview had already died or fallen seriously ill. As that generation passed from the scene, their stories, experiences, and insights would be lost, too. Hu believed he was rescuing that history before it was too late. Lin Zhao's letter reminded him of how much he still didn't know about her life, and how much he might never know. Did she really ask a foreigner named Arnold to smuggle her writings out of the country, as the indictment alleged? Did she compile a list of senior party leaders to whom she planned to send a protest letter? What else did she write in prison? And why was her sentence changed from twenty years to death?

One of the most intriguing questions raised by the letter was re-

lated to a rumor Hu had heard early in his research—that Mao himself had visited Lin Zhao in prison. Hu had dismissed the idea at first,
because it seemed so unlikely. But as he studied Lin Zhao's letter, he
noticed passages in which she described interacting with someone she
called "the autocrat."

> These words are typical of his personality. A young person can
> detect the odor of the autocrat's words as easily as reading his
> writing, whether directly or indirectly, whether he makes an ap-
> pearance or shrinks away. "I refuse to believe I can't subdue you
> stupid little girl!" "Should I listen to you, or should you listen to
> me?"

Hu assumed Lin Zhao was quoting one of the prison officials until he
discovered many other passages in which she clearly used "the autocrat" or "your autocrat" to mean Mao, because she also used his title
as chairman of the party's Central Committee and cited his poetry.
She attacked the cruelty of his rule, and wrote of his "horrible, cold,
ruthless, mean soul." Perhaps, Hu thought, Lin Zhao used "the autocrat" to refer to Mao in some places and a prison official in others. But
there were also a few sections in which she seemed to merge the two,
writing that "the autocrat" was both the chairman of the Central
Committee and director of the prison.

> He never considers the consequences of his actions, or if he does,
> he only considers one side. It's very clear from that quick-
> tempered, headstrong, arrogantly rude and maniacal statement
> of his, "I refuse to believe I can't subdue you stupid little girl!"
> Indeed, I'm afraid that's just how the autocrat thinks. He de-
> feated rivers and oceans, and utterly routed Chiang Kai-shek's
> troops, so how can it be that "I" cannot subdue "you witless little
> girl"? He truly does "refuse to believe" it! Given the autocrat's
> mistaken and absurd way of thinking, that is entirely natural
> and inevitable.

Hu knew that Lin Zhao's mind was not completely sound when she
was writing the letter, but the possibility his heroine had faced down
Mao was too interesting to ignore. Even if she had suffered a break-

down, Hu reasoned, that didn't necessarily mean Mao had never toured her prison. Hu consulted scholars who confirmed that Mao often visited Shanghai while Lin Zhao was in prison, and they also noted the Chairman's notorious predilection for young women. But so much about Mao's life remained shrouded in official secrecy, and none of them could say for sure if Mao ever toured his prisons.

Hu never solved the mystery and he left it out of his film, but he did uncover one more clue. In the summer of 2001, Ni Jinxiong arranged for him to meet Lin Zhao's sister, Peng Lingfan. She had returned to Shanghai from the United States for a visit, and though she was nearly seventy, Hu immediately saw the resemblance to the young Lin Zhao he had seen in photos. He explained to Peng that he was making a documentary about her sister, and presented her with a gift, a volume of Lin Zhao's poetry and writing that he had compiled. But to his surprise, Peng refused to be interviewed. She seemed very nervous, and asked if he was being followed. She also urged him not to make the film, saying it wasn't safe and suggesting that government agents might arrange for him to be struck by a car if he didn't abandon the project. Hu pleaded with her to change her mind, arguing that her sister's story needed to be recorded and shared with the public. When Peng wouldn't budge, Hu lost his temper, jumping out of his seat and raising his voice, declaring that Lin Zhao's story wasn't her family's personal property but part of the national heritage. Eventually, Peng agreed to answer only two questions. Hu asked if she knew anything about an encounter between Mao and her sister. Peng refused to let him film her answer, but replied that when Lin Zhao was home on medical parole in 1962, she heard her tell their mother that Mao had visited the prison and questioned her. Their mother cut her off, and Peng said she never heard her sister speak of it again.

For his second question, Hu asked about a meeting that Ni had told him about between Peng and the doctor at Lin Zhao's prison shortly after the end of the Cultural Revolution. Again, Peng wouldn't let Hu record her answer, but she later published an essay in Hong Kong recounting what the doctor told her:

Doctor X was a small, vigorous man with a nervous expression. . . . He seemed to search his memory of those years: "Lin Zhao stayed at this hospital several times, and most of those times, I was the one who treated her, except for the period when I was deprived of authority, which had something to do with her too. I was always thinking of ways to let her stay a few extra days in the hospital. She was a very excitable, headstrong girl. In the hospital, as soon as she recovered a little, she would start making her political views known again. She was a smooth speaker, and very persuasive. She could write quickly, and as soon as she felt a little better, she would be busy drafting her "memorials to the emperor" and "impeachment scrolls." At first, she came to the hospital mainly because of her hunger strikes. Later, she came several times because she cut herself too deeply while writing letters in blood. . . . I was the one who suggested she be sent to the mental hospital for evaluation, because she often said that other people, including doctors, were plotting against her and wanted her dead. I felt that sometimes she had been tormented to the point that her mental state wasn't normal. Because I "shielded and covered up" for her, I had to undergo labor reform for a year. Of course, my family was very unhappy about it, but I thought it was perhaps the only thing I did in my life that wasn't against my convictions. What I regret is that I didn't have the ability to save her.

The last time she came to the hospital, she was spitting up a lot of blood and so thin that she couldn't have weighed more than seventy pounds. I really couldn't recognize her. Only her eyes still twinkled with radiance. When no one was nearby, I said to her, "Oh, why do you bother?" "Better to be destroyed than give up one's principles!" she said very quietly. I had a bad feeling, and sure enough, that morning, three or four soldiers burst into the hospital ward and forced Lin Zhao out of bed. She was still hooked to a glucose drip at the time, and they shouted, "Incorrigible counter-revolutionary, your judgment day has arrived!" Lin Zhao wasn't afraid at all, and calmly said, "Let me change my clothes." They said, "No!" Right after that, like a hawk seizing a chick, they propped her up to leave. At the door, she said to the nurse, "Please say goodbye to Dr. X." Actually, at the time, I was just in the hospital room next door and could hear very clearly, but I was shaking from head to toe and I didn't dare come out. I've been a prison doctor all my life, but I had never seen any prisoner pulled from a hospital bed and immediately taken to a mass trial and execution. . . .

In the same essay, Peng wrote that Lin Zhao had once been sent to the Shanghai Hospital for the Prevention of Mental Diseases for examination. Later, the director of the hospital, Su Zonghua, a prominent psychiatrist, was accused of trying to protect Lin Zhao by diagnosing her with a mental disorder. After suffering unceasing abuse at the hands of the Red Guards, he committed suicide during the Cultural Revolution in 1970.

Hu eventually tracked down Lin Zhao's prison doctor, the man Peng had described as "Doctor X." He was in his nineties, and living on the fourth floor of a new apartment building in Shanghai. But the man was hard of hearing and nearly senile. He said he couldn't remember anything about Lin Zhao. His wife was there, too, and she recalled only that her husband was once caught with one of Lin Zhao's poems in his pocket. It was frustrating for Hu to finally find the doctor only to learn it was too late, and it served as another reminder that he was running out of time.

Hu wanted to interview other prison officials but he was worried about pushing his luck. Months had passed since he first learned state security agents were asking questions about him, and he was nervous about doing anything that might provoke them. Instead, he asked a friend who did business with the prison to help. The man knew the officials there well and was confident he could persuade them to be interviewed. But when he went to see the old cadres who ran the prison in the 1960s—now retirees who passed the time playing mah-jongg— they immediately said no. Hu's cautious attempts to contact court officials and others who had been in positions of power failed as well.

With the help of another friend, however, Hu did succeed in obtaining one official document from the records room of the Shanghai prosecutor's office. Hu and his friend, a judicial officer from another jurisdiction, simply walked in and requested Lin Zhao's case file. A moment later, the clerk returned with a thin folder containing several typewritten pages that were faded and illegible, and one thirteen-page handwritten report that was readable. It was titled "Excerpt from Materials to Increase Penalty in Lin Zhao Case." Hu skimmed it and quickly recognized its significance. This was the report recommending that Lin Zhao be executed. His friend asked the clerk to photocopy it, and then they rushed out of the office, flush with excitement.

Hu studied the report carefully. It was dated December 5, 1966, and it accused Lin Zhao of "serious crimes" in prison, namely:

1. Insanely attacking, cursing, and slandering our great Chinese Communist Party and our great leader Chairman Mao . . .

2. Regarding the proletarian dictatorship and socialist system with extreme hostility and hatred . . .

3. Publicly shouting reactionary slogans, disrupting prison order, instigating other prisoners to rebel, and broadcasting threats to take revenge on behalf of executed counter-revolutionary criminals . . .

4. Persistently maintaining a reactionary stand, refusing to admit her crimes, resisting discipline and education, and defying reform . . .

The report detailed Lin Zhao's behavior in prison, describing how she cut herself and used her blood to write "extremely reactionary and vicious" letters, essays, and diaries that contained "hundreds of thousands of words," including one work with 180,000 words and another with 200,000. It also said she wrote slogans in blood on the prison walls and on her clothes, smeared blood on photos of Mao, and rallied the other prisoners and led them in shouting slogans of protest. The report concluded, "Labor Reform Bureau opinion: Our opinion is that prisoner Lin should be executed." There was also a notation from a senior Shanghai police official, Wang Jian, dated three days later: "Agree to prosecute to increase penalty. Please consult and research with procuratorate and court, see what opinion they have."

Later, Hu interviewed a man who had been held at the same prison as Lin Zhao and saw her not long before she was executed. He told Hu that everyone in the prison knew her because of her shouting and because the prison's loudspeaker broadcasts often criticized her for resisting reeducation. When he last saw Lin Zhao, she had been moved from the general population to a cell on the building's fifth floor, where she was the only prisoner. Sometimes he was told to take food to her, and he would see her sitting behind the iron bars. Her head was wrapped in a helmet that covered her entire face except her eyes. The prison made her wear it to muffle her voice.

AS HE CONTINUED gathering material, Hu began editing and putting together what he had. He kept only the tapes he was working on at home, hiding the rest with friends and relatives in case the police raided his apartment, and whenever he finished editing a new piece of the film, he made copies and hid those, too. Gradually, the documentary began to take shape. Hu titled the film *Searching for Lin Zhao's Soul*. It was shot in color and opened with footage he took of himself talking about how he had set out to uncover who Lin Zhao was and what had happened to her. He built the movie around his quest and narrated it himself, but he let her friends and classmates do most of the talking. In between these interviews, Hu read excerpts from Lin Zhao's poems, letters, and prison writings, letting the camera linger over her handwriting or on black-and-white photos of her, often with dramatic orchestral music in the background. Hu struggled with the volume of material he had collected and the complexity of the subject, which he suspected much of his audience would know nothing about. In the fall of 2003, he showed an early version to Cui Weiping, a well-known feminist critic and film professor in Beijing, and she liked it enough to invite a small group of scholars and filmmakers to a private screening in her home. It was the first time Hu had shown the film to a group of strangers, and he was nervous. Afterward, the audience discussed the movie. Cui and the historians in the room were impressed and praised it as a breakthrough, the first Chinese-made documentary to confront this hidden period in the nation's past. But the documentary filmmakers in the audience disparaged the movie, saying that it was too emotional and that it wasn't a real documentary. They argued that Hu had lionized Lin Zhao and produced a work of propaganda no better than the government's films.

Hu was encouraged by the feedback, and he took the criticism to heart. He recognized that he was no longer objective about Lin Zhao, that his feelings had evolved from curiosity to obsession to something bordering on worship. When he managed to locate Lin Zhao's ashes in a funeral hall in Shanghai, for example, he took a lock of hair that had not been destroyed in the cremation for safekeeping, because he worried her urn might be lost. Black-and-white snapshots of Lin Zhao decorated his editing studio, and he even painted a small portrait of her. One close friend admonished him, saying he was no longer researching Lin Zhao but falling in love with her, and Hu realized that his friend had a point. He had heard so many stories about Lin Zhao that he felt he knew her, and he could see why so many of the men in her life had fallen for her. He found her fiery personality alluring, and he admired the passion and grace of her writing. But it was more than that. He was also inspired by her courage, and her uncompromising sense of justice. It made him realize how uncommon these qualities were in Chinese society now, and he wondered whether the country was worse off for that.

Hu tried to keep his personal feelings in check as he continued editing his film. He adopted a less sentimental style and a more neutral tone, letting the drama of history speak for itself, and he also added material from new interviews. He was still worried about the state security agents, so he decided to burn the film to disc and begin circulating it. The documentary wasn't done, and he included a disclaimer indicating it was still a work in progress and asking viewers not to distribute it, but he wanted at least some people to see it in case he were arrested. As he continued editing and the secret police still did not come, he distributed additional versions and began to believe he was engaged in a delicate, unspoken negotiation with the authorities. He imagined they had refrained from arresting him because he had not finished the film and formally released it for distribution, by selling it overseas, for example. If they arrested him, he thought, they would be drawing attention to what remained an underground film with a small audience. But if they didn't arrest him, he could keep adding to the documentary and releasing new editions, and slowly he could build a larger audience.

As it happened, *Searching for Lin Zhao's Soul* spread faster than Hu expected. Cui, the film professor, published an essay about it, and then in the spring of 2004, a professor at a university in Guangzhou invited him to screen it for her class as part of a weeklong series of documentaries she was showing. Later, the director of a fine arts museum in the city who attended that screening arranged for Hu to show it in the museum's assembly hall before a crowd of three hundred. Word spread quickly after that, with invitations coming from colleges across the country. A few newspapers found ways to publish articles about the film, too, and then a publisher arranged to distribute the videodiscs along with a new textbook to hundreds of universities. Hu told every audience he spoke to that the film was unfinished, and he meant it, because the more people saw it, the more calls he received with leads to fresh material.

Sometimes, when Hu took questions from audiences, a few college students would challenge him, questioning his loyalty and accusing him of misinterpreting history. But the response was overwhelmingly positive. Older viewers often watched the film in tears and crowded around Hu afterward, thanking him for ensuring their experiences were not forgotten. Younger people also embraced the documentary, saying it opened their eyes to how much they didn't know about their own country's history and forced them to reevaluate everything they had been taught. Students transcribed the text of the film and posted it on the Internet, and there was a flurry of essays and Web sites memorializing Lin Zhao. Her sister returned to Shanghai again and arranged to put the ashes that Hu had located in a cemetery in Suzhou. Hundreds attended the ceremony, and others organized annual pilgrimages to the tomb. After five years of solitary research, Hu realized he had underestimated his nation's willingness to confront the dark chapters of its past.

The state security agents eventually came out of the shadows and knocked on Hu's door. It was 2005, and his film was an underground success. The agents were younger than he expected, and polite, and they said they had come just to talk. One of them said that Hu was quite famous now, and they could no longer "look after" him. The other told him that there were many stories like Lin Zhao's across the country. He said people like Lin Zhao were victims of "an error of the Left" and there was no use talking about them now because no one would ever be held responsible. Then he asked Hu why his films always dwelled on the negative, and why he never made any positive documentaries about China.

Hu replied that he believed it was a documentary filmmaker's duty to look at society critically. He said there were hundreds of television stations in China and they were always broadcasting "positive" stories that glorified "advanced" party members. He asked the agent if he liked to watch those reports. The agent acknowledged that he did not, but pressed Hu again: Didn't he think there had been progress since Lin Zhao's era? Yes, Hu replied. If he had made a film like this during the Cultural Revolution, he would have been shot. If he had done it a decade ago, he might have been followed and arrested. "But now you come to my front door and we can talk to each other like friends," Hu said. "You have been very lenient with me, and this is progress." The agent couldn't help but agree.

A FEW YEARS LATER, I heard Hu Jie was in Beijing again and arranged to meet him at a coffee shop not far from the city's Second Ring Road. He had asked me not to write about him in the *Washington Post;* he was afraid such publicity might anger the authorities. But I was still following his work, because he had agreed to let me tell his story after my assignment in China ended. That afternoon, he arrived at the coffee shop more than a half hour late, looking haggard in a dark t-shirt with a canvas camera bag slung over his shoulder. He mumbled something about the city's traffic, which had grown progressively worse in recent years, and he seemed distracted as he settled into our booth. He said he had been busy with several new documentaries, almost all of which explored politically sensitive subjects, but one project had proved particularly challenging. It was the one that had brought him back to Beijing.

The film was another attempt to illuminate a dark chapter in China's history, he said, but instead of the Anti-Rightist Campaign, its focus was the Cultural Revolution. For more than a year, he had been quietly interviewing an eighty-five-year-old scholar of modern history at the Chinese Academy of Social Sciences named Wang Jingyao. Wang's late wife, Bian Zhongyun, had been a vice principal at one of the city's most prestigious secondary schools, the Girls' Middle School at Beijing Normal University. When the Cultural Revolution began, students at the school had answered Mao's call to root out hidden enemies of socialism and accused Bian of being a counterrevolutionary. Weeks of denunciation meetings followed and ended in tragedy on August 5, 1966, when a group of tenth-grade girls paraded Bian and four other administrators around the school grounds, kicking and beating them with nail-spiked clubs. After hours of torture, Bian collapsed and was dumped in a garbage cart. She was forty-eight, and one of the first people to die in the Cultural Revolution. Devastated by his wife's murder, Wang went to the morgue the next day with a folding camera and photographed her body. In the black-and-white pictures, Bian is laid out on the concrete floor, her face swollen and bruised, her hair tangled and caked in blood, her clothes torn and soiled. In other shots, the clothes have been removed, and bruises are visible all over her body. Wang told Hu he took the photos "to record the truth of history," and he kept them secret for decades. Now he wanted Hu to use them in a film to ensure his wife's death would not be forgotten.

But Hu was having trouble with the documentary. Almost all the former students and teachers he located had refused to talk to him. He tracked down one teacher who had risked persecution after the murder by sending Wang an anonymous condolence letter, but even she refused to be interviewed. She was seventy-five now, and nearly forty years had passed, but she told Hu it was still too soon to discuss what happened. Forced to work with limited material, Hu began building the film around Wang's photos, and he had just screened the latest version for him. But Wang was not satisfied. He wanted Hu to make it even tougher, perhaps by including his suspicion the authorities never fully investigated his wife's death because so many of the girls at the school were the children of senior leaders, including Deng Xiaoping and the former president, Liu Shaoqi. Hu sighed as he discussed the situation. The Cultural Revolution evoked such intense and conflicting emotions. So many people were unwilling to discuss it, which made it difficult for him to gather material, yet Wang was determined to force society to confront his wife's death, and he insisted Hu keep working on the film until it was powerful enough to achieve that goal.

It took Hu another year to finish the documentary, which he titled *Though I Am Gone*. Because he focused tightly on Wang and the story of his wife's death, the movie seemed even more disturbing and emotionally raw than the Lin Zhao film. Hu shot it almost entirely in black and white, and in the most compelling scene, Wang unpacks a suitcase containing the soiled and bloodied clothes that his wife was wearing when she died. Hu was proud of the work, and in the spring of 2007 he submitted it to a prestigious film festival in southwest China. A week before the festival was scheduled to open, though, the government intervened. It didn't just block the documentary from being shown. It canceled the entire film festival.

Hu had better luck at another film festival in Hong Kong a year later. The judges awarded *Though I Am Gone* the festival's top prize.

Cultural Revolution cemetery in Chongqing

4

THE CEMETERY

There are few places in China where people have more reason to forget the past than Chongqing. Built on the mountains where the Jialing River meets the upper Yangtze, the city is one of the fastest-growing in the country, a hulking metropolis of thirteen million shrouded in a thick, perpetual haze of fog and pollution. Once a sleepy treaty port and a wartime capital that endured Japanese bombardment, Chongqing is now the bustling economic hub of southwestern China, a city in the midst of a building frenzy even more dramatic than that of Shanghai downriver to the east. Every year, hundreds of thousands of rural migrants pour into its steamy districts, looking for work in its ever-expanding industrial parks, on the crews building new highways, railroads, and bridges, or in the famed army of *bangbang* porters who haul goods from the docks up the steep mountain slopes. A monorail soars amid the skyscrapers, through cramped tenements and past neon billboards. Construction cranes are everywhere. At night the glow of the multicolored skyline reflects off the muddy Yangtze, and boisterous crowds fill the pungent hot-pot restaurants on the riverfront. Chongqing is a city on the move, as determined to "look to the future" as any in China.

But at the edge of a quiet, leafy park on the city's west side, up a gentle slope from a man-made lake, there is an unusual cemetery enclosed by a stone wall crawling with ivy. The place is set off from Shapingba Park's main pathways and easy to miss behind a grove of pagoda trees; visitors who have been coming to the park for years sometimes never notice it. Those who do and wander through its rusting iron gates find themselves in what may be the only cemetery in all of China dedicated to people killed in the Cultural Revolution. It is a decrepit place, littered with fallen trees and overgrown with vegetation, and when the fog rolls in, as it often does, the atmosphere is downright eerie. The graveyard is fairly large, about thirty yards wide by ninety yards long, but it is the size of the tombstones that visitors notice first. On both sides of a brick path are rows of towering concrete pillars and obelisks, the biggest over thirty feet tall. Each marks the burial site of as many as two dozen people, though erosion has rendered many of the names and inscriptions illegible. Several gravestones are crumbling, and some are almost entirely hidden by dirt, vines, and weeds. But the fact that the cemetery still exists at all is remarkable. In nearly a decade of work and study in China, I never heard of anyplace else like it.

Perhaps no one spends as much time in the cemetery as Zeng Zhong, a teacher who has been trying to identify the people buried there and document how they died. He is a thin, earnest man in his mid-fifties, and at our first meeting, we sat at a stone table under a pavilion in the park not far from the cemetery. It was a cool spring afternoon, and as we sipped tea and chatted, old men were walking backward along the park's asphalt paths, a Chinese form of exercise, and young couples stole kisses on the benches around the lake. Groups of laid-off workers and pensioners were sitting at other tables, drinking, shouting, and playing mah-jongg. Zeng fidgeted in his seat and said he was nervous about speaking to a foreign journalist. But he was also eager to share what he had learned. He said his interest in the cemetery had nothing to do with his job training elementary school teachers, nor were any of his friends or relatives buried there. His research began in the autumn of 2005 after he stumbled upon the graveyard during a stroll in the park. He lived nearby and had heard of the cemetery before, but had never visited it or given it much thought. When he saw it for the first time, he was astonished. For more than an hour, he wandered among the tombstones and monuments in awe. "I never realized the scale of the violence until then," he told me.

"I was completely overwhelmed. The shock sent shivers down my spine."

THE CULTURAL REVOLUTION occupies a special place in China's national consciousness. Too little time has passed since it rocked the nation, and too many people were directly affected by it for it to be completely forgotten. Mao's exploitation of the nation's youth to wage "unending revolution" against the party bureaucracy—and against his rivals in the leadership—touched the lives of almost everyone in China, from the cities to the countryside. If the Anti-Rightist Campaign was a tremor, the Cultural Revolution was an earthquake, with a far greater number of lives ruined and lost. But given the devastating scale of the Cultural Revolution, which began in 1966 and continued until Mao's death in 1976, the party has been remarkably effective at suppressing discussion of what happened—and at presenting what happened as a warning of the chaos that could follow democratic reform instead of a symptom of one-party rule. The party has succeeded in part because people in China have been willing accomplices in the act of forgetting. So many of them were taken in by the Cultural Revolution's frenzied rhetoric, so many of them participated in the violence or stood by in silence, that it has never been very difficult for the party to persuade society to leave that past behind. Families were torn apart as wives divorced husbands who had been accused of political crimes, children condemned parents, and siblings turned against one another. When the Cultural Revolution finally ended, it was easier for many people just to move on than talk about it. Even many of those who suffered were eager to forget, for their hands were rarely entirely clean, either.

Meanwhile, a generation has come of age in China with only the vaguest understanding of the Cultural Revolution. More than half the population today was born after it ended. Many parents choose not to discuss the nightmare with their children, and the party keeps it out of the classrooms. As a result, perhaps the most awful chapter in the party's rule has become the disaster that is dismissed with a nervous laugh, the catastrophe remembered only with the kitsch of a Mao watch or a Red Guard theme restaurant. For those who did not live through it, in China and overseas, it is the absurdity of the Cultural

Revolution that lingers—the images of huge crowds massed in Ti-ananmen Square waving Chairman Mao's little red book, of rampag-ing teenagers shouting idiotic slogans and smashing precious antiques, of teachers forced to wear ridiculous dunce caps and confess to pre-posterous crimes. And of course, the Cultural Revolution was absurd. But it was much more than that. What has been obscured and mini-mized is the horror and evil of what occurred. According to estimates based on the government's own publications, upwards of 36 million people in the countryside were persecuted while about 750,000 to 1.5 million were killed and an equal number permanently injured. The number of casualties in the nation's cities is less certain, but could total in the hundreds of thousands. In Beijing, more than 1,770 were mur-dered in only two months in 1966, according to official reports, and one million were persecuted in Shanghai, with at least 5,000 killed in 1968 alone.

The numbers are staggering enough, but then there are the stories of human brutality behind them—of men and women beaten in the streets or before screaming crowds in stadiums, of children forced to denounce and strike their own parents, of torture so cruel that count-less victims chose to take their own lives, sometimes along with their loved ones. Killing occurred not only at the hands of overzealous Red Guards and in armed street battles between rival rebel factions, but also in organized pogroms carried out by party officials across the countryside. The targets of these mass murders were often former landlords and other class enemies who had already been persecuted for years, as well as their relatives. The executioners sometimes re-fused pleas to show mercy on children because they worried the young would grow up and exact revenge. In Daxin, a rural suburb south of Beijing, 325 people were killed in five bloody days in the summer of 1966, the youngest victim a one-month-old infant. In Daoxian county in Hunan Province, nearly five thousand people were killed in the space of two months after meetings in which names of potential vic-tims were read aloud and votes were taken to decide their fate. People were beaten to death, hanged, shot, and sometimes buried alive or forced to jump off cliffs. In Guangxi Province, there is evidence of cannibalism in at least five counties.

Such violence has not been expunged from the country's collective memory so much as repressed, and repressed memories have a way of surfacing unexpectedly. There have always been voices in China calling on the nation to confront the barbarity of the Cultural Revolution. Only with an honest accounting and thoughtful examination of the era, they argue, can the country come to terms with the legacy of mistrust and moral decay that haunts it today. As early as 1986, the novelist Ba Jin called for the construction of a Cultural Revolution museum and a memorial to its victims. As time passed and wounds healed, the number of people in China willing to face up to the past has grown. But the party has refused to allow a soul-searching national discussion, because it is fearful of the emotions it might unleash and the lessons that might be drawn about the wisdom of one-party rule. In 2006, four decades after the Cultural Revolution began, the party's propaganda ministers issued an edict banning any mention of the anniversary in the media. In 2007, they issued another directive demanding that "vigilance must be increased" against those who would use the Cultural Revolution to discredit Mao, Mao Zedong Thought, and the Communist Party. All accounts of the period, the party reminded its censors, must comply with the official history laid out by the government in 1981.

The party spent more than a year writing that official history, a stilted account laced with ideological jargon and bureaucratic doublespeak, which barely hinted at the violence that ravaged the nation. To be sure, it disavowed the Cultural Revolution, describing it as "responsible for the most severe setback and the heaviest losses suffered by the Party, state, and the people since the founding of the People's Republic." The party blamed Mao's wife, Jiang Qing, and three other radical leaders, vilifying them and labeling them the Gang of Four. But from beginning to end, the Cultural Revolution was really Mao's project. In 1966, at the age of seventy-two, he had grown suspicious of the men around him and the party he had built, and events in Moscow weighed on him. As Khrushchev denounced Stalin and then was ousted himself, Mao worried he, too, might be toppled from power or repudiated by his successors. He believed the Soviets had gone soft on U.S. "imperialism" and abandoned socialism for faster economic growth, and he suspected his colleagues were taking China down the same road. The Cultural Revolution was his response, a mad attempt to revitalize the party by tearing it down while rearing a new generation of revolutionaries in bloody struggle. The party's official history acknowledged that "chief responsibility" for the disaster "does indeed lie with Comrade Mao Zedong." But Deng Xiaoping, the man who succeeded him and was himself a victim of the Cultural Revolution, decided the party could not afford to renounce the Chairman and directed the historians to cast him instead as a tragic hero, "a leader laboring under a misapprehension" who nevertheless remained "a great proletarian revolutionary."

As the official history was being written, Deng also declared that it should "encourage people to close ranks and look to the future." He expressed his hope that after it was released, "common views will be reached and, by and large, debate on the major historical questions will come to an end." In other words, it was a version of history designed to make people forget history. But a single account of the Cultural Revolution, especially one as sanitized as the party's, could never be enough to satisfy a nation that suffered so much and in so many different ways. Inevitably, people have sought to remember what happened on their own.

ZENG ZHONG WAS fourteen and in the seventh grade when the Cultural Revolution began with the mobilization of high school and college students into units of what became known as the Red Guards. He longed to join them, but his father had been a manager in Chongqing's largest bank before the Communist takeover and was labeled a member of the bourgeoisie. Under the party's theory of class struggle, children were destined to behave as their parents did, so only the offspring of workers, peasants, and other members of the proletariat could be true revolutionaries. It made no sense to Zeng, who believed that the best rebels, including Mao himself, had not come from "good class backgrounds." But if he questioned the principle of inherited class consciousness, he never doubted the righteousness of the party. Even after the Red Guards took his father away and put him to work at a local grain depot, even after they ransacked his home and seized everything of value, Zeng wanted to be one of them. One Red Guard unit at his school agreed to accept him, but only as a member of an auxiliary group. "I felt humiliated being identified with a bad family background, but I put up with the disgrace to participate in the revolution," Zeng recalled. A month later, his unit had a change of heart and expelled him. Not long after that, his father returned home on a stretcher. He had suffered a back injury after being forced to carry a two-hundred-pound bag of grain.

Zeng's expulsion from the Red Guards and his father's injury kept him at home as the violence in Chongqing escalated. Workers and other adults began forming Red Guard units, too, and competing factions turned against one another and obtained weapons from the city's munitions factories. Soon the nights were marked by gunfire and artillery blasts, Zeng said. As the fighting raged across the city, the Red Guards pretty much ignored Zeng and his family. The family stayed in their house, kept their heads down, and made it through the worst of the Cultural Revolution unharmed. Zeng knew others were not as fortunate. But it was not until he stepped foot in the cemetery decades later that he began to fathom the extent of the killing and set out to understand what had happened and why.

Zeng took out a notebook and sketched a map of the graveyard for me, dividing it into six sections. He said he had counted fifteen to twenty-five tombs in each section, for a total of 118, and assigned a code to each. Then he began counting the dead. About 350 names or parts of names were visible on about ninety of the pillars and tombstones, but there were more than two dozen tombs with markers that had disappeared or were so eroded the names were no longer legible. Zeng estimated that more than five hundred people were buried in the cemetery altogether. His goal was to identify them all and determine how each had died. He spent as much time as he could in the cemetery, waiting for friends or relatives of the dead to show up and then gently approaching them with questions. In the winter he lurked amid the tombstones for two to three hours at a time, stamping his feet to keep warm, and he stayed longer in the milder seasons. Often, no one would come by. When people did show up, they sometimes refused to talk to him, saying they wanted to forget the Cultural Revolution. But most were willing to help, and gradually Zeng collected information on the deaths of two hundred people buried in the cemetery. "It's like putting together a jigsaw puzzle," he said. "Sometimes, I hear four different versions of the same incident. I write them all down, and save them on my computer at home. If I find someone who witnessed the incident in person, then I give that account primary consideration. That's how history is written."

As we were talking, a park employee rushed up to our table and told Zeng something in the local Chongqing dialect that I couldn't make out. "Would you excuse me?" Zeng said, as he picked up his notebook and stood to leave. "There are people visiting the graveyard." I asked if I could tag along, he agreed, and together we hurried up the path. Zeng explained that he had befriended a few of the workers at the park, and that they quietly supported his research, telephoning him when they noticed people in the graveyard or taking down information when he couldn't get there in time. The park employee who had just tipped him off grinned, and said, "It's all unofficial."

Zeng walked quickly, clearly excited. He said he had been puzzled for a long time by one particular tomb. Most of the tombs were marked with obelisks built in the Soviet style of the Monument to the People's Heroes in Tiananmen Square, often with engravings of hammers, sickles, rifles, torches, and other socialist insignia. But the pillar that marked this one was wider, shorter, and topped with a traditional Chinese roof with round tiles and upswept eaves. It was the only one like it in the cemetery, and Zeng had little information about the five people buried under it. The inscription gave their names but no ages or other identifying details, except that they belonged to a Red Guard unit called the "Set the Prairie Ablaze" Corps. Below the names was the date October 1968, and carved above them were six large characters: "Long Live the Martyrs." Zeng had never seen anyone visit the tomb—until now. As we entered the cemetery and stepped over fallen tree trunks and branches, the park employee pointed out two men and a woman standing next to the tomb.

"Do you know how these people died?" Zeng asked.

"How could I not know?" one of the men replied. He was a stocky fellow in his mid-fifties, and he spoke with a thick Sichuanese drawl. "When Zhu Qingyun was killed, I was in the same bed as him!" Zhu's was one of the five names listed on the pillar.

Zeng checked his notebook. "I heard people from the school at the steel mill did it?"

"It was a guy we called Duo Jian from the steel school."

"Duo Jian from the steel school killed him?"

"Duo Jian didn't do it himself. He led a group of people that did it."

The man said he and Zhu had been classmates and fellow Red Guards at the No. 71 Middle School in Chongqing. On the night of August 16, 1968, they were on the run and hiding in a school from another Red Guard unit that they had clashed with in a dispute over guns. There were more than a dozen of his fellow Red Guards in the school, and because there weren't enough beds, he and Zhu were forced to share one. The next morning, he said, Duo Jian and his comrades burst in and opened fire. The man said he rolled out of the bed and took cover, but Zhu sat up and a bullet struck him in the head. Zeng took down the details, and asked about the unusual design of the tombstone. The man laughed, and said he and his classmates originally planned to build a tall monument like the others in the cemetery. They even forced local residents who were political outcasts—members of the landlord and bourgeoisie classes, as well as Rightists and other criminals—to help them. After two weeks, though, they ran out of material and the corpses were beginning to rot. The stench was overwhelming. Finally, the students decided to just finish the monument by putting a Chinese-style roof on top of what they had built.

Zeng asked about the other names on the tombstone. The man said they were members of the same Red Guard unit but had died in separate incidents. Two of them were ninth-graders and one of them was in the eighth grade, but he couldn't remember how they had been killed. Zeng jotted the information down in his notebook, then thanked the man and gave him a slip of paper with his telephone number. He asked him to call if he wanted to talk more, or if he remembered anything else.

"I always leave my phone number and ask people to call me," Zeng told me after the visitors had left. "But less than a third of them ever do."

At first, Zeng regarded his job as simply the accumulation of raw data—names and places, dates and ages, facts and fates. "I just wanted to collect as much information as possible, and then leave it for future generations to figure out what it meant and draw conclusions," he said. But as he unearthed one tragic story of violence after another, as the enormity of what had happened in Chongqing—and the rest of the country—began to sink in, he could not help but draw conclusions. Sometimes he tracked down the families of the dead and visited them at their homes. He learned of two brothers who were killed in the same battle fighting for rival Red Guard factions; of a group of twenty students who were taken prisoner and executed with a grenade blast when the Red Guards who captured them were forced to retreat; of a young man who was beaten and left to die locked in a hot basement without food or water. And he knew he was just scratching the surface. This was just one cemetery, with some of the casualties from one Red Guard faction in one part of one city. When he asked himself why such violence had occurred, why his contemporaries had been so cruel to one another, he thought of the values the party had taught him as a child—and he worried about what it was teaching children now.

There were once dozens of other graveyards with victims of the Cultural Revolution scattered across Chongqing. The party demolished them all after Mao's death. The cemetery in Shapingba Park has survived, Zeng said, but the government "wants it to erode and deteriorate naturally. It wants people to forget about what happened. But I think it would be a tremendous loss if this history were forgotten, because it was cast in the blood and tears of the Chinese people. Future generations must learn these lessons so tragedies like this don't happen again.

"In the future, when people visit this cemetery, the words on the tombstones won't be visible anymore," he added. "I hope my written record can fill in the blanks."

FOR EVERY TOMBSTONE in the cemetery that is crumbling from erosion, there is another that has been well maintained or restored to good condition. One of them is located near the center of the graveyard, a simple gray obelisk identified on Zeng's map as tomb No. 6 in Section 4. It measures about five feet across the base and stands nearly ten feet tall, and there are no Communist slogans or symbols engraved on it. A single black marble panel graces its eastern face, and nine large characters are inscribed in gold down the center:

Tomb
of
Mother

Huang
Peiying

To the right are three lines of writing in smaller characters:

Born September 24, 1928,
Killed August 24, 1967,
In Maoxian Gully, Chongqing

The names of the woman's five children—four sons and a daughter—
are listed on the left, along with a notation indicating they rebuilt the
tombstone "with filial piety" in 1996, on Qingming Day, the traditional Chinese tomb-sweeping holiday.

Sometimes, early in the morning, a man can be seen standing near
the tombstone, staring at the marble tablet and smoking a cigarette.
He is a burly fellow, not especially tall or short, with a crew cut, metal-
rim glasses, and a fleshy, round face. On these visits to his mother's
grave, Xi Qinsheng often wears a plain black jacket over a dark shirt
and dark pants, and he gives the impression of a man who values his
solitude. When the weather is nice, his wife might accompany him to
the park but she will take a walk around the lake and leave him alone
with his thoughts in the cemetery. He appreciates the seclusion of the
place, the escape from the hubbub of the city, the chirping magpies in
the trees, the distant laughter of children. It gives him a chance to
think, and to remember.

Standing amid the tombs, the memories always come rushing back,
transporting him to Chongqing as it was when these people were buried, the Chongqing of his adolescence. He can feel the rattle of the artillery shelling and the machine-gun fire. He can see the empty,
bullet-marked buildings, and the bodies of the dead scattered on
streets scarred with tank treads. He can smell the smoke and gun-
powder in the air. And he can hear the cries of the men he beat and
tortured as a Red Guard. When he closes his eyes, Xi can picture his
mother's face, too. He remembers the warmth of her love and the
strength of her resolve to protect her children. He remembers her selling her blood to help the family make ends meet, and digging up roots
and vines to feed her children during the famine of the Great Leap
Forward. He thinks of that day when she showed up at his school dur-

ing the Cultural Revolution and dragged him away from the Red Guard unit he had joined. And he pictures her on the ground in the vegetable field, her head in his hands, blood gushing from a bullet wound to her chest, her eyes staring up at him, then rolling backward as her life slipped away.

"I was the oldest of the children, and I was only fifteen when our mother was killed," Xi told me on one of his visits to the tomb. "They say a mother's love is greater than anything. I think those who lose their mothers at an early age value it most. Her death changed everything for our family, so we felt the disaster of the Cultural Revolution on a very personal level."

Few imagined the tragedy that would unfold when Mao launched the Cultural Revolution in May 1966 with a call to "denounce capitalist representatives in the academic, education, news, arts and publishing circles." Party leaders in Chongqing, like others across the country, assumed a movement similar to the Anti-Rightist Campaign was under way, and sent work teams into newspapers, schools, universities, and other "cultural" departments with orders to identify and purge a handful of "capitalist representatives" in the leadership of each institution. But by the end of July, Mao made clear he had more in mind than a routine witch hunt. In Beijing, his agents had quietly encouraged university students to organize themselves into Red Guard units, and when they clashed with the party's work teams, Mao surprised his colleagues by backing the students. "To rebel is justified!" he declared. "Bombard the headquarters!" he commanded. The work teams were withdrawn, and the men who sent them in—top party leaders including the general secretary, Deng Xiaoping, and the president, Liu Shaoqi—came under attack. Egged on by Mao at Nuremberg-style rallies in Tiananmen Square, the Red Guards were given free rein to unmask "revisionists" and "capitalist roaders" hiding in positions of authority.

In Chongqing, students quickly turned against local party officials and their work teams. One source of resentment was the treatment of the popular president of Chongqing University, Zheng Siqun, who had slit his throat after the party denounced him as one of the "capitalist representatives." Local leaders responded to his suicide by expelling him from the party posthumously. Eleven days later, thousands of angry students and teachers from the university surrounded and berated party officials on the campus of a neighboring college. The date of the confrontation, August 15, soon became a rallying cry. Trying to stay in control of the movement, city officials were organizing high school and university students into Red Guard units and directing them to search and loot the homes of landlords, Rightists, and other bourgeoisie elements. But the students at Chongqing University formed their own squad of "August 15" Red Guards and focused their criticism on the local party apparatus. Confusion reigned as Red Guard units proliferated across the city, each pursuing its own agenda in the name of the Revolution.

Xi was fourteen at the time, a spirited, sometimes unruly boy in a school where students spent alternate weeks in classes and on a factory assembly line making shoes. The political turmoil was a welcome interruption from the tedium, and he eagerly enlisted as a Red Guard. After all the stories he had heard about the heroics of the Communists—in textbooks, in movies, in songs—here was a chance to take part in the glorious revolution himself, to do battle with hidden enemies threatening the nation. The young teenager strutted around the neighborhood with his classmates, shouting slogans and waving little books of Mao sayings, a red armband tied over his shirtsleeve. Older students guided the younger ones, distributing handbills, covering buildings with posters, raiding the homes of neighbors with questionable class backgrounds, destroying anything connected to the "old society"—art, antiques, books, even clothing deemed too bourgeois. Street names were changed, and there was a call to rename the city after the title of a socialist novel. Xi watched as students tormented teachers whom they held grudges against and paraded suspected enemies through the city with dunce caps on their heads and blackboards hanging from their necks.

"It was exhilarating. The masses were fully mobilized, marching and protesting and staging sit-ins. Every street in the city was plastered with big-character posters," Xi recalled. "As middle school students, we were so excited about everything, blindly following others and joining organizations. But actually, we didn't understand what was going on. We were just being loyal to Chairman Mao." Mao's cult of personality had reached a fever pitch, approaching religious worship. Students read his words aloud as if they were reciting prayers, sometimes directly addressing his portrait, which was everywhere.

Billions of badges and buttons with his image were manufactured, and people collected them like spiritual amulets. Not everyone bought into the cult. But in that charged environment, dropping a Mao badge on the floor, or making a careless remark about the Chairman, could be a serious offense, enough to be labeled an opponent of the Revolution. So those with doubts kept them hidden.

If the Red Guards in Chongqing were united in their loyalty to Mao, they were nonetheless divided in their opinion of the local party authorities. One camp defended the city's party committee and followed its lead. Established and supported by local officials, these "royalist" Red Guard units dominated the movement at first. But as the weeks passed, the rebel camp critical of the local party establishment began to win support. Members of this "August 15" faction included students and teachers from Chongqing University and other colleges, as well as factory workers, intellectuals, and others alienated and victimized by the party's past policies. As the royalist and rebel Red Guards accused one another of betraying socialism, arguments escalated into scuffles across the city. Young people in China had been raised by the party to believe in ideological absolutes. Compromise was a sin, and if you stood with Mao and socialism, then those who opposed you must certainly be enemies of socialism.

Xi and his classmates were in the August 15 camp, if only because older students from the universities told them they were. He participated in a mass rally and a hunger strike in front of city hall, and he joined a group that said it would march to Beijing to expose the local officials, though he turned back after twenty-five miles. "I was quite muddleheaded, mindlessly following others and just having fun," he said. "But I knew the Chongqing government wanted to maintain the status quo and suppress the students, who were accusing the government of taking a capitalist, reactionary road. The government told us to go back to school, but Chairman Mao said to rebel is justified. We had memorized that, and so we rebelled."

In the fall, public opinion shifted toward the August 15 faction as it became clear Mao was siding with rebel Red Guards against local party committees in other cities. With their support dwindling, the royalists decided to turn against their patrons in the city's party leadership, too. But rather than welcome the reversal, the August 15 faction accused the royalists of hiding their true colors and trying to hijack the Revolution. The rivalry came to a boil on December 4, when the royalists held a mass rally in Chongqing's main sports stadium to denounce city and provincial party leaders. More than one hundred thousand people filled the stadium, including Xi's eleven-year-old brother, Qingchuan, who had also joined a Red Guard unit. The rally had just begun when fighting broke out between the two factions and a riot erupted. "First there was some commotion, and then it was chaos," Qingchuan recalled. "Once the fighting started, it quickly got out of control. They were beating each other with wooden clubs and steel rods, and everyone was trying to get out." Qingchuan escaped unharmed, but hundreds were injured. The clash at the stadium was the first major outburst of violence of the Cultural Revolution in Chongqing. It wouldn't be the last.

Early on, Mao and those closest to him made clear that violence would be permitted, if not encouraged, to achieve the goals of the Cultural Revolution. In disbanding the work teams that other party leaders had sent to the schools to lead the Cultural Revolution, Mao also rejected their efforts to suppress violence. His wife, Jiang Qing, who emerged as a leading voice of the Cultural Revolution, passed on his thoughts to a rally in Beijing: "When good men beat bad men, the bad men get what they deserve." As the violence spread in Beijing and people such as the girls' school vice principal Bian Zhongyun were beaten to death, a few students wrote an appeal urging the party to intervene. Mao responded by complaining that Beijing was still "too civilized." At the first Red Guard rally in Tiananmen, he invited one student to the podium who had publicly assaulted a party official, and he suggested another student change her name from "gentle and refined" to "be martial." But it was his decision to prohibit police from arresting students who were "making revolution" that had the widest impact. Police were encouraged to befriend Red Guards instead. "Don't say it is wrong of them to beat up bad people," the minister of public security advised. "If in anger, they beat someone to death, then so be it. If we say it's wrong, then we'll be supporting bad people. After all, bad people are bad, so if they're beaten to death, it's no big deal."

On his seventy-third birthday, in December 1966, Mao delivered a toast to "the unfolding of nationwide all-round civil war." Within weeks, Red Guards led by his lieutenants seized power from the party committee in Shanghai, and denounced the city's leaders in a mass rally broadcast live on television. Similar power transfers followed elsewhere in China as Mao ordered military authorities in each region to support the rebels. In Chongqing, with the royalists defeated, the August 15 faction took control of the government at the end of January with the blessing of the 54th Army. The city's party leaders surrendered, and were denounced at a rally attended by as many as three hundred thousand people. Like other officials across the country, they were publicly humiliated, forced to wear dunce caps and stand bent over with their heads bowed and their arms raised backward—the notorious "airplane" position. The rebels roughed them up and splashed black ink on their faces, marking them as members of "black gangs." The ranking official in the city, a ruthless Politburo strongman named Li Jingquan, endured several of these public "struggle sessions." His wife was said to have hanged herself. As in other cities, some deposed Chongqing officials—tough men who had no doubt inflicted their share of misery while in power—also chose suicide to escape the torment. Mao and his allies showed little sympathy. After the Yunnan provincial chief took his own life, Premier Zhou Enlai labeled him a "shameless renegade." One senior army general, crippled in a failed attempt to kill himself by jumping from a building, was carried to rallies in a crude basket for further denunciation.

The victory of the Red Guards over local party authorities didn't end the violence. In Chongqing, they began fighting among themselves almost as soon as they took power. Some were upset after being left out of the ruling committee established by the military, while others criticized the August 15 leaders for working with the 54th Army, which they considered part of the old "capitalist" establishment. The military-backed government moved to silence the opposition, arresting hundreds if not thousands of Red Guards in the following months. But at the end of March 1967, Mao concluded that the army was stifling his revolution, not just in Chongqing but in cities across the country. His new deputy, the defense minister Lin Biao, ordered the military to back off and release those who had been detained. As the 54th Army complied, a new Red Guard camp emerged in Chongqing and came to be known as the "Rebel to the End" faction.

Xi said he and his young comrades favored these Rebels, but his parents supported the August 15 faction. His father was a truck driver for a state bookstore; his mother worked in the bookstore's warehouse.

Solid members of the proletariat, they had both been active in the Cultural Revolution, but they seemed to sense the chaos that was coming. One afternoon, as Xi was boasting at school about his performance in a debate with other Red Guards, he turned around and saw his mother standing in the doorway. She grabbed him by his belt and dragged him outside, where his father was waiting with a car. From that day on, he was grounded. His mother stayed home to stop him from going out.

It was a bit of parenting that might have saved his life. The arguments between the two factions in Chongqing quickly escalated into some of the worst violence of the Cultural Revolution anywhere in the nation. The fighting began with scattered clashes in the spring, but on June 5, thousands engaged in a pitched battle in front of the library of a teachers' college that lasted three days. Other major confrontations followed. The Red Guards attacked one another with stones, clubs, and metal rods, then knives, swords, and spears. Soon the focus of the battles turned from schools and colleges to the city's arms factories. Chongqing was a base of weapons production because of its inland location far from the nation's borders, and its factories produced all manner of lethal munitions: semiautomatic weapons, hand grenades, light and heavy machine guns, flamethrowers, howitzers, antiaircraft guns, artillery cannons, tanks, warships—almost everything but fighter jets. Now the rival factions fought to control these factories and distribute the materiel. The Red Guards on both sides established combat bases, fortifying factories, schools, and bridges as well as radio stations, key assets for spreading propaganda.

On July 7, the first shooting deaths occurred, and over the following weeks the city descended into civil war. By late July, the two camps were using grenades, machine guns, and flamethrowers. Tanks and artillery cannons were deployed by early August. And then the fighting spread to the rivers, where Red Guards were raiding ships for food and supplies. On August 8, in perhaps the only naval battle of the Cultural Revolution, three aging gunboats that the Rebels had fitted with artillery cannons clashed with a small fleet of ships manned by August 15 fighters with machine guns. Afterward, at a memorial service for one of the dozens of sailors killed in the battle, a Rebel leader ordered two prisoners executed with the sailor's gun and their bodies dumped in the river as a sacrifice in his honor. A few days later, an August 15 commander ordered five prisoners executed, including a couple expecting a child. The husband begged his captors to spare his wife, or at least delay her execution until after she had given birth. His pleas were ignored.

The numbers of dead and wounded climbed with each battle, some of which involved more than ten thousand combatants and resulted in as many as a thousand casualties. Newspapers published gruesome reports describing how "martyrs" were stabbed, shot, maimed, electrocuted, or found dead in the water, their faces mutilated. Crowds cheered as armored trucks transported fresh-faced Red Guards to battle zones, then looked on with dread as the same vehicles returned carrying the wounded and dead. The city was laid to ruin, with windows shattered everywhere, buildings burned to the ground, and the main harbor destroyed. More than 180,000 people fled the city, seeking refuge in the provincial capital, Chengdu.

At first, Xi was excited by the combat. "Every night, you could hear the gunfire and the artillery explosions. It was amazing! Tanks were moving in the streets! I really wanted to go. I was very interested. I thought participating in the armed fighting was glorious and would be a lot of fun," he recalled. But his parents wouldn't let him leave the house. Later, they took him to see what a neighborhood looked like after a battle, and his enthusiasm was replaced by fear. "It was horrible, a big mess of corpses scattered around. . . . All the buildings were empty shells, and there were burned cars and dead bodies everywhere. I was terrified, and whenever I heard a gunshot, I would hit the deck."

Chongqing wasn't the only city in China to experience such armed warfare in the summer of 1967. Similar spasms of violence occurred in almost every major city in the country. One news bulletin in Beijing reported twenty to thirty armed clashes in the provinces every day in August. But the fighting in Chongqing was perhaps more intense and deadly than anywhere else, because of its concentration of munitions factories. Some of Mao's lieutenants traveled to Chongqing and urged an end to the violence, but the message from the top was muddled. Mao made clear he was not worried about Red Guards obtaining weapons, and called on the military to "arm the left," a phrase that became a slogan across the country. "Why can't we arm the workers and students?" he asked. "I say we should arm them!" Mao's wife,

Jiang Qing, endorsed another slogan: Attack with reason, defend with force. "You cannot be so innocent and naive," she told a group of Red Guards in Henan Province. "When a pinch of people provoke violence, when they attack you with weapons, the revolutionary masses can take up weapons and defend themselves." The editor of a Red Guard newspaper in Chongqing read her remarks and distributed them to his colleagues. "I only said one thing: 'Since even the center doesn't want to control the situation, what are we waiting for?'" he recalled. "Everybody said, then let's fight!"

As the clashes got worse, Xi and his family split up and left their apartment for safer quarters. His three youngest siblings were sent to stay with relatives, while his parents took him and his brother Qingchuan to the distribution center of the bookstore where they worked. They crowded into an office on the ground floor with twenty to thirty others, sleeping on the wood floors and keeping the lights off at night so as not to draw fire. But during the third week of August, a battle erupted that put them in the middle of the crossfire. August 15 forces on a hill to one side of their building were trying to seize control of a mountain held by the Rebels on the other side. Xi watched from the building as tanks and antiaircraft guns began firing at the Rebel position. He could see the shells landing and exploding on the mountain, and the Rebels taking cover. The August 15 fighters climbed slowly up the mountain, occasionally exchanging gunfire with the Rebels. From the distance, they looked like insects making their way up an anthill. Xi watched as they seized the first of the Rebel trenches, but then something happened and they were suddenly scurrying down the mountain, retreating much faster than they had advanced. Rebel reinforcements had arrived with machine guns.

The August 15 forces pulled back to prepare for a Rebel counterattack, and Xi's father, who had done reconnaissance in the battle, went with them. The next morning, Xi's mother decided it would be safer to take her boys to join her other children at a cousin's home. It was Qingchuan's thirteenth birthday, so she prepared a special breakfast of noodles with pickled cabbage for him. Then, they each packed a bag of clothes—Qingchuan packed his pet chicken, too—and headed out on foot, wearing white t-shirts to signal they were unarmed civilians and taking back roads through hilly fields. It was a hot summer morning, and after two hours they stopped at a farmhouse for rest and water. Sitting in the shade, Xi's brother started crying. He was tired of walking, and he didn't want to go any farther. But their mother was anxious to keep moving. She told him they were almost there. Just a few more miles, she said, and they would be reunited with their younger siblings. She stood to leave and Xi got up, too. Qingchuan reluctantly followed, wiping away tears.

They took a road between sorghum and vegetable fields, Xi in front, his mother behind him, and Qingchuan trailing behind, still half crying. Just minutes after they left the farmhouse, a shot rang out. Xi thought he felt the bullet fly over his head, and he hit the ground. Then there was another shot, and he heard his mother cry out. He knew it was bad even before he turned and saw her on the ground, bleeding from her chest. He scrambled toward her.

"I didn't know what to do. I just tore off my shirt and applied it to the wound, but I couldn't stop the bleeding. . . . I was holding her head in my arms, and she was looking at me. I cried out to her. Her eyes were fixed on me, and at that moment, I knew she was clearheaded. Her eyes were fixed firmly on me, and then they rolled backward. I was frantic, and just kept shouting. I shouted out, 'Don't shoot! We're ordinary people!' And then they started firing at us with a machine gun."

Xi got down again. He spotted his brother cowering amid the vegetables. They were both yelling now. "Don't shoot! Don't shoot!" The gunfire was coming from a ridge to their left, and then they heard shots from another direction as well. As the bullets kicked up dirt from the ground, the boys tugged at their mother's body, trying to pull her to safety. Then they heard a man's voice, and saw a peasant beckoning to them from the house where they had just been resting. "Hurry!" he shouted. "Over here!" The boys ran toward him, leaving their dead mother behind, and taking cover inside.

After a while, the shooting stopped. Xi, just fifteen years old, sat dazed, his heart pounding. "The sky seemed to change," he recalled. "It was blue with a few clouds, but it looked pitch-dark to me." Eventually, he mustered the will to crawl back to his mother's body, retrieve her bag, and then take his brother to look for their father. They walked along a highway, dirty and shirtless, passing a checkpoint into August 15 territory and a column of trucks carrying armed men in helmets. Before dusk, they reached their cousin's home, but it was shot up with bullet holes and abandoned. They kept walking, wandering the streets looking for people they recognized. They stopped at a noodle shop, but lost their appetite after a few bites. Then they spotted one of their father's coworkers in a barbershop, and when they rushed over, they found their father inside, too. For the first time since his mother's death, Xi began to cry.

The gunfire had come from the direction of an August 15 position, and it didn't take long for Xi's father to find out who killed his wife. Several people witnessed the incident, and told him the name of the Red Guard responsible, a steelworker in his thirties who had been discharged from the military. The other people on duty had told him not to open fire, because it was obvious the targets were civilians. But the man said that he was going to be leaving the post soon and he wanted to finish his ammunition. No one was firing on him. He just saw some people on the road and wanted to see if he could hit them. Xi's father was furious, and he and his coworkers brandished guns and demanded the man be turned over to them. But it was too late. He had already fled.

That night, the boys accompanied their father and a detachment of fifty armed men to retrieve their mother's body. The next day, it was taken to Chongqing University, where a makeshift morgue had been set up outside the campus stadium. There were dozens of other corpses there, lined up neatly on the ground, and Rebel prisoners captured by the August 15 faction were preparing them for burial. Xi and his brother looked on as the haggard prisoners washed their mother's body, then wrapped it in white silk, covered it with a military uniform, and placed it in a casket. Students and teachers of the university were buried on campus, but most of the other August 15 members were taken to a cemetery located in nearby Shapingba Park. The boys and their father rode there in an armed convoy, then waited as the prisoners dug a grave and lowered the casket. As they covered it with soil and the Red Guards fired their guns into the air in a military-style salute, Xi noticed the cemetery was full of fresh graves, hundreds of them.

XI TOOK A drag on his cigarette and showed me the spot near the edge of the cemetery where his mother was first buried. A year after her death, he said, his father arranged to move her grave to the center of the cemetery, because he thought it might be better protected there.

Xi and his brother built the tomb over the course of a month with the help of laborers from the bookstore where his parents worked. The pillar they erected originally described her as a "martyr" of the bookstore's "combat team" under the command of the "Chongqing Municipal Revolutionary Rebel Headquarters." Three decades later, the family decided she deserved a warmer epitaph, and covered the original inscription with the marble panel dedicated "with filial piety."

Xi and his siblings gather at the cemetery twice a year, on the tomb-sweeping holiday in April and the anniversary of their mother's death in August. He realizes they are fortunate to still have somewhere to go to remember her. He knows other cemeteries from the Cultural Revolution have been bulldozed and covered with highways and buildings and, in the case of the one at Chongqing University, with a fountain in front of a campus hotel. In the mid-1980s, the government built a stone wall around the Shapinga Park cemetery in an attempt to keep the public out. But that didn't stop Xi from visiting his mother's grave. He would just wait until no one was looking, and climb over.

A few years later, Xi learned the government was planning to raze the cemetery to build a theme park featuring replicas of world landmarks such as the Eiffel Tower and the Statue of Liberty. Officials signed a deal with investors from Hong Kong, and construction started in other parts of Shapingba Park. The cemetery, Xi heard, was going to be demolished to make way for cable cars. He was furious, but there were few channels through which to protest. He was just a worker at a state electronics factory, and a letter of complaint might have caused trouble and perhaps cost him his job. So he began making anonymous threats, calling park officials from public phones and telling them that if they touched the graveyard, he would exact revenge.

"I never gave my name. I just told them that I was a relative of one of the dead. I said the Communist Party would be going too far if it left these people without a proper graveyard. I said whoever did this, he and his family would be wiped from the earth. They told me it was wrong for me to talk like that, and then I said I'll kill your entire family. I said you're out in the open and I'm hidden. . . . I used different voices, and made a lot of phone calls like that."

He grew more upset when park officials began charging an admission fee for people to visit the cemetery. It was only five yuan, about

sixty cents, but Xi and his siblings refused to pay. They confronted security guards and demanded to speak to park officials. "We just told
them one thing. If you destroy our ancestor's tomb, we'll take your
heads in return," Xi recalled. Other families objected, too, joining Xi
and his siblings in protests outside the cemetery gate. Once, they
nearly came to blows with the park employees. But the park eventually backed down, and the theme park project was abandoned. Xi
never learned if the decision had anything to do with his anonymous
phone calls and the protests, or if the investors just ran out of money.
In the years since, he said, there have been occasional rumors about
the cemetery being bulldozed for development, but no one has dared
touch it yet.

Sometimes Xi brings a video camera to the cemetery and interviews other people visiting the dead, so there will be a record of the
place and of those to whom it meant something. As the years have
passed, though, fewer people have been coming, and he rarely sees
younger visitors in the graveyard, unless they have stumbled upon it
by accident. They remind him of ignorant tourists, because they know
so little about the Cultural Revolution. "It's pathetic," Xi said. "These
people died meaningless deaths, but they are even more meaningless
if society never reflects upon it. Many people refuse to think about it,
and the party wants to erase people's memories. But the whole nation
should think about what happened. Remembering is painful, but it is
also a kind of responsibility. We have to remember, so the next generation doesn't suffer such pain again."

A FEW WEEKS AFTER Xi's mother was killed, the central government
brokered a cease-fire between the two Red Guard factions in Chongqing. But the political violence in the city and in the rest of China continued as new ruling officials sought to reassert control and organized
one campaign after another to intimidate the public, settle scores, and
eliminate rivals. In the summer of 1968, Mao finally disbanded the
Red Guards, sending millions of urban youths to live and work in the
countryside. Xi was sent to a rural village in 1969, and it was there
that he began to reconsider his loyalty to the Chairman. Seeing the
poverty of the countryside firsthand led him—and countless others of
his generation—to question the party and its lies. Xi's disillusionment

was complete in 1971, when Mao's prominent right-hand man, Lin Biao, died in a plane crash fleeing China, and the party suddenly declared that he had been a traitor from the beginning. As the media rewrote history and heaped abuse on Mao's latest enemy, Xi found himself agreeing with some of the criminal's statements, including a memorable remark suggesting that sending young people to the countryside was a labor sentence in disguise. When Mao died in 1976, Xi was secretly overjoyed.

After Deng Xiaoping took power in 1978 and repudiated the Cultural Revolution, the government set out to rehabilitate those who had been persecuted and punish those who had committed the worst crimes. But Deng's priority was the survival of the Communist Party, so there would be no exhaustive investigation into the events of the past decade, no public debate over degrees of guilt and innocence, no national process of reconciliation. Soul-searching might be good for a society and a nation, but it could have destroyed the party. And so the country was told to get over it and move on. People returned to work alongside those who had tormented them, and the police paid only lip service to justice, punishing killers and torturers in some cases, but looking the other way in others, without ever explaining why. Those who went to prison never had a chance to explain their actions in public, while those who remained free never had to answer for what they had done.

In 1973, even before the end of the Cultural Revolution, the police in Chongqing opened an investigation into the death of Xi's mother, and later informed the family that they had arrested the culprit. But they never told the family whether the arrest was related to her murder, whether the man was ever tried or convicted of any crime, and what kind of sentence he received, if any. After the Cultural Revolution, when the party claimed to be punishing those responsible for the crimes of the past decade, no one contacted Xi's family, and when Xi's father made inquiries, he never received a response. Then one day Xi heard that his mother's killer had been released from prison on medical parole and was receiving treatment in a local hospital. The thought of the man going free infuriated him. He wanted to confront the killer, to force him to face the boys he had tried to shoot that day, and to make him pay for taking their mother away. If the party wouldn't do it, Xi decided, then he would mete out justice himself.

He stole a car, and a policeman's uniform, and he prepared a gar-
rote from steel wire. With his brother Qingchuan, he hatched a plan.
Qingchuan would drive him to the hospital at half past eleven, when
most of the doctors and nurses would be in the cafeteria eating lunch.
Dressed in the uniform, Xi would go inside, introduce himself as an
officer conducting an investigation, and ask the man to accompany
him to the car. The killer would sit in the front passenger seat, and he
would get in the back. They would knock him out, then drive hours
into the mountains, along a route Xi mapped out. If the man came to,
they would tell him that he murdered a woman many years ago. They
would tell him they were her sons come to seek revenge. And then Xi
would strangle him. They would dump the body in the Wu River, and
then drive back to Chongqing. Xi and his brother were no longer boys,
but men in their late twenties and they were serious. They knelt before
their father and told him what they were going to do. Everything was
set. Xi even bought extra gasoline, so they wouldn't run out. The next
day, Qingchuan drove to the hospital as planned, and Xi went inside
to find their mother's killer. But his bed was empty. The doctors said
he had been released just a half hour earlier.

Later, Xi wondered if his father had tipped off the authorities and
arranged for the man to be transferred from the hospital. "I think he
felt this kind of revenge would destroy his two sons, but he never admitted it," Xi told me. "If my father didn't inform on us, then it was
just Heaven's will."

Xi said he and his brother tried for years to find the man again, but
they never did. I asked him if he still wanted to kill him. "These are
different times, and the way I think has also changed," he replied. The
killer, he said, "was a victim, too. It's the system we should take revenge against." But when the subject came up again later, Xi said his
anger toward his mother's killer had not entirely dissipated, and he
was not willing to absolve him of all responsibility. "He brought pain
to my family that words cannot describe," Xi said. "If I didn't kill him,
I'd beat him up. He would be an old man by now, but he would still
deserve the beating."

We were alone in the cemetery, standing by his mother's tomb. It
was nearly noon, but the the sun was still hidden in the thick fog. Xi
lit another cigarette, and walked over to the pillar marking the grave
next to his mother's. Someone had scratched a few words on the side

with a rock. "History is here. They died unjustly." I asked him another question. Was there anything he did during the Cultural Revolution that he particularly regretted? Xi paused a moment before answering.

"After my mother died, I took it out on society. I beat some people. No one cared what I did, and I wanted others to feel the pain I felt."

He said he joined the Red Guards again, and his father couldn't stop him. He was given a gun, and he fired it in several battles. He said he didn't know if he ever hit anyone, but he confessed that he eagerly participated in the violence before he was sent down to the countryside. I asked Xi what the worst thing he did during those years was. He said he tortured prisoners from the other faction, and old men who had been detained because they had bad class backgrounds. "They were held in a small room, and if I was even slightly upset, I would hit them," he said. "We had no humanity. We were young and ignorant, and we would abuse them, and whip them."

Xi tried to explain why he—and so many others—were so cruel during the Cultural Revolution. Part of it, he said, was deep, pent-up frustration with life under Communist rule. The nation had experienced bitter hardship, including a terrible famine, and while people were still loyal to Mao and the party, they resented the local officials who controlled their lives and carried out the party's policies. By targeting the party apparatus, Mao gave the masses an excuse to unleash their anger at these officials. But even more important, Xi said, was his generation's upbringing in what he called "a culture of violent propaganda." The party taught a value system in the schools that encouraged extremism and glorified violence. Children were fed a steady diet of stories that extolled Communist heroes who sacrificed their lives in "class struggle" and that demonized "class enemies" who were hiding and scheming to undo the Communist Revolution. In an essay read by all students, Mao wrote that "revolution is not a dinner party" but an "act of violence in which one class overthrows another." The test of a true revolutionary, he continued, was whether one believed brutality against the enemy was good or bad. Mao said it was "excellent!"

"We were told that we needed to use violence to destroy a class spiritually and physically. That was justification enough for torturing someone," Xi said. "They weren't considered human anymore. If they

were the enemy, they deserved to be strangled to death, and they deserved to be tortured. This was the education we received when we
were young, and the Cultural Revolution developed it to the point
where we were killing each other. . . . The Cultural Revolution
brought out the worst in people, and the worst in the political
system."

Xi said he believed one-party rule was ultimately to blame for the
crimes of the Cultural Revolution, but that individuals—like the man
who killed his mother, and like himself—must also accept responsibility. "How could a ruthless dictatorship thrive in this country? Why
did the nation support it?" he asked.

But when I asked him if he had ever thought about finding the people he had tortured, Xi's answer was as honest as it was revealing. "I
don't want to find them," he said. "I don't want to remember the bad
things I did."

IN THE SPRING of 2007, I met the man who saved the cemetery in
Shapingba Park. Liao Bokang served as the Communist Party chief
in Chongqing in the 1980s as the city was trying to put the Cultural
Revolution behind it. When I visited him, he had been retired for
nearly fourteen years and was living in Chengdu. He was eighty-
three, a jolly type with a bald head and a kindly round face. He welcomed me into the living room of his high-rise apartment, and as we
spoke and sipped tea, he occasionally leaned back in his sofa chair and
smiled, his eyes crinkling up mischievously.

Liao was a native of Chongqing, and he is still remembered in the
city as the target of a vicious political campaign in 1963, when he was
the head of the city's Communist Youth League. Toward the end of
the Great Leap Forward, he had been assigned to investigate conditions in the surrounding countryside and boost agricultural production. The rest of the country was beginning to recover from the famine,
but Liao discovered that people were still starving in his province. In
one village, the entire population had died. The authorities had to
send residents from a neighboring town to bury the dead, but they
were so weak from malnutrition that several of them died while digging the graves. Reporting his findings to Beijing, Liao estimated that
at least ten million people had died in all of Sichuan Province between

1957 and 1960. He blamed the famine on provincial leaders who dictated irrational farm policies, wasted money on showcase projects, and refused grain assistance from the central government. Beijing responded by ordering an investigation. But the powerful Sichuan party boss, Li Jingquan, escaped untouched, and a year later he struck back, purging Liao and sending him to work as a construction laborer. Liao was denounced again at the start of the Cultural Revolution. Then the Red Guards turned against Li Jingquan, and Liao was given a reprieve. He traveled to Beijing to appeal his case, and as a result he escaped the worst of the violence in Chongqing. When he returned, though, he spent four difficult years undergoing "reeducation."

Liao was rehabilitated after the Cultural Revolution, and in 1983 he was appointed to run Chongqing. One of his first jobs was to "bring order out of chaos" and rid the party ranks of factional animosity that still lingered. In speeches to cadres, he often compared the Cultural Revolution to a nightmare. "Since we're awake now, what need is there to recall whether what we did in the dream was right or wrong?" The party had repudiated the Cultural Revolution, he told them, and so you were all wrong.

It was during this campaign to eradicate the ill effects of the Cultural Revolution that the cemetery in Shapingba Park became an issue. The other graveyards for Cultural Revolution victims in the city had been destroyed before Liao took office, but Shapingba Cemetery had survived. It was located in what was then a remote part of the city, and the officials in the neighborhood, most of whom had been members of the August 15 faction, had quietly let it stand. But now there was a push inside the party to get rid of it. Since the government had declared the Cultural Revolution a mistake and was erasing all other traces of the movement, it stood to reason that the cemetery should be eliminated, too. Letting it stand, many officials argued, would send the message that the party believed the August 15 faction was right and that armed battle was justified. Opinion, however, was far from unanimous. The question of what to do with the cemetery reached Liao's desk in 1985.

On a cool day in the spring, Liao and a handful of aides drove out to Shapingba Park and toured the cemetery. There were only a few other visitors, but a small crowd soon gathered as word spread that the city's party secretary had come. Several of Liao's aides, as soon as they saw how big it was, argued for destroying the cemetery. But one aide, a young woman, disagreed and urged him to preserve the cemetery and let it stand as a reminder and a warning to future generations about what had happened in Chongqing. Liao listened to their views and left the park without saying anything himself. But he had already begun to form an opinion.

"When I saw the cemetery, I thought of the many ridiculous things that occurred during the Cultural Revolution, insane things, incomprehensible things," he told me. "These things had all vanished like mist and smoke. But here was something concrete I could preserve. . . . These innocent people who died could be left here to serve as historical evidence, evidence of an insane time and a tumultuous era."

Two things about the cemetery left a lasting impression, he recalled. The first was a tomb for an unnamed fourteen-year-old girl. "She should have been at home, hugging her mother and father or playing with toys in her little bed," Liao said. "But she was sacrificed for nothing and buried there, and no one even knows her name." The other was a sign that described the graveyard as a "Martyrs' Cemetery." Liao found it jarring. "What kind of martyrs were they? A martyr is someone who sacrifices his life for the nation. To die in a mistaken political movement, to die by the guns of your own brothers, you can't use the word 'martyr' for that." Other cities had been torn by armed conflict during the Cultural Revolution but Liao believed that more were wounded and killed in Chongqing than anywhere else. If the cemetery were destroyed, he thought, there would be nothing left to remind people of that tragedy.

A few days after the visit, Liao issued his decision. The cemetery would be preserved. He believed people should reflect on the Cultural Revolution—on what happened and why and what lessons could be learned—instead of simply forgetting it. As the city's party chief, he had the authority to save the cemetery, and he felt there was little political risk for him to do so. But Liao also knew others would disagree with the decision, and to end the debate—to encourage people to "close ranks and look to the future"—he also allocated money to build a wall around the cemetery and ordered it closed to the public. As he described the decision to me, Liao smiled one of his mischievous smiles and added, "Some people say Liao Bokang found a very shrewd way to preserve the cemetery."

I asked him about those who were trying to erase the Cultural Revolution from public memory because they believed it would be better for the party's reputation for it to be forgotten. He smiled again. "You can't eliminate ten years from time and space. . . . Whether good or bad, history exists objectively. People subjectively may want to erase it, but they couldn't erase it even if they tried."

Given his statements about the value of preserving and examining history, I was surprised when Liao told me he agreed with Deng Xiaoping's edict that the history of the Cultural Revolution should be written in "broad strokes" rather than in detail. "People should concentrate on economic construction now," Liao said. "Only when the economy is developed and the country is prosperous will people have the energy and time to research these things. We can't get distracted now." He said something similar when I asked him whether schoolchildren should be taught about the Cultural Revolution. "They should, but how we teach them is something that can be decided later," he said. "Right now, we need to develop productivity and build our country. The past can be discussed in the future. We shouldn't delay what we are doing now because we're always remembering the past. We shouldn't forget it. We should preserve it, but save the discussion for later."

As he spoke, it became clear to me that Liao saw in his rescue of the cemetery an approach for how Chinese society could eventually process the memory of an event as traumatic as the Cultural Revolution. Examining what happened closely, even after forty years, could be too painful, divisive, and perhaps even destructive for society. But erasing it or forgetting it completely would also be dangerous. Perhaps the best thing to do, Liao suggested, was to give it more time. "If people have different opinions, the debate can be put off temporarily," he said. "A wall can be built around history, but without destroying it." After all, he noted, the cemetery in Shapingba Park was now open to the public and no one was complaining. "People can go in and look now," he said. "I think this is progress."

Part II

NO BETTER
THAN THIEVES

A miner carrying coal in Shanxi Province passes a propaganda image of former Communist Party chief Jiang Zemin.

5

ARISE, SLAVES, ARISE!

Long before he led the Communists to victory in war, before he established the People's Republic and came to wield power over nearly a quarter of humanity—before he made himself a tyrant—Mao Zedong was a labor organizer. It was an unlikely calling for a farmer's son in a country with a quarter billion peasants and only the beginnings of an urban working class, a country that had missed the Industrial Revolution. But his family had been prosperous enough to give him a city education, and in the national soul-searching after the fall of the last emperor, Mao had embraced Marxism as the answer to China's humiliation by the Japanese and the Western powers, who had carved the nation into concessions and colonies. He was just a schoolteacher then, a new father not yet thirty years old, and when he joined the Communist Party, it had only a few dozen members nationwide. In those early years, the party sought to imitate the Soviets and mobilize the proletariat, so Mao traveled across his home province of Hunan, helping to set up unions, organize strikes, and agitate for workers' rights. The most famous of the Communist-led strikes took place in 1922 at the Anyuan coal mines on the border of Hunan and Jiangxi provinces, one of the largest concentrations of in-

dustrial workers in China at the time. Mao was only indirectly involved, but the party later exaggerated his role and wove the story of
the strike into its founding mythology. During the Cultural Revolution, a propaganda painting depicted him on a mountain summit near
Anyuan, the wind tousling his hair and sweeping back his scholar's
gown. The government printed more than nine hundred million copies of *Mao Zedong Goes to Anyuan*, enough for every man, woman, and
child in China, making it perhaps the most reproduced painting in the
history of the world.

In 2002, I traveled to Anyuan to attend a ceremony marking the
eightieth anniversary of the miners' strike. On a warm, overcast afternoon, in a plaza near one of the old coal mines, a small crowd gathered as party functionaries unveiled a bronze statue of Mao just as he
had been depicted in the Cultural Revolution portrait. Even by the
standards of the Communist Party, there was something especially
shameless about the event. It wasn't just that these officials were
putting up a new statue of Mao years after most cities had had the
decency to quietly take theirs down. It wasn't just that they were
perpetuating the historical fraud about Mao's role in the Anyuan
strike—a fraud designed to obscure the fact that Mao later persecuted
to death the party men who had done the most to organize the miners.
It was the cynical attempt to present the Communist Party as a cham-
pion of the working class. There was a time when the state seemed
committed to the proletariat, when workers were promised an "iron
rice bowl" of job security and benefits. But a quarter century after
Mao's death, only fools and liars still claimed the party was building a
workers' paradise and looking out for people like the coal miners of
Anyuan.

A day before the statue's unveiling, I spent time with several of the
miners. They were rough, wiry men who lived in cramped, shabby
apartments, and they shared a look of exhaustion on their blackened
faces. Some were descendants of the miners whose strike helped
launched the Communist movement, and they reminded me that after
the 1949 revolution, coal miners were rewarded some of the highest
wages of any occupation. Their nostalgia for that era was tempered by
the memory of the Soviet-style command economy, of the pervasive
poverty and the terror of Mao's misrule. But if the party's version of
socialism had failed the miners of Anyuan, its take on capitalism

brought them only further misery. The government was restructuring the coal industry, and shares of the Anyuan mine, one of the largest in the nation, had been listed on the Shanghai stock exchange. Mass lay-offs had followed, and more were planned. The miners who kept their jobs saw their pay fall precipitously in real terms, even as coal prices and production climbed. Among the worst off were the retirees, old men who suffered lung diseases from a lifetime of digging coal for the glory of the state, and who now complained that officials were looting their pensions and denying them proper health care. Some men spoke of wives working as prostitutes in the big cities to help their families make ends meet.

In the afternoon, a few of the miners fitted me with a set of gear—rubber boots, a suit of rough cloth, a plastic helmet with a small lamp—and showed me where they worked. We began on foot in a large tunnel that sloped downward, then boarded a rickety railcar that took us deeper into the earth at a sharp angle. As we made our descent into the darkness, the miners complained about aging equipment, which made their work more tedious and more dangerous, and one remarked on the rising numbers getting injured on the job, especially among the new workers, who received little training. But when we reached our destination, a cavernous stone hall hundreds of feet underground, I realized that as dismal as the conditions were in Anyuan, they were even worse in most other Chinese mines. A year earlier, I had visited one in Jiangsu Province, a pit known as the No. 5 Coal Mine in Gangzi village. It was one of tens of thousands of smaller mines that local officials and their cronies had opened in the 1980s and '90s as the party embraced market reforms. Anyuan, like most other large mines, was a dinosaur of the old state economy, struggling to survive in the new capitalist economy. The mines like No. 5, however, were private operations, and they were gaining market share by ignoring labor and safety regulations to cut costs. The miners in Gangzi worked long hours, usually six or seven days a week, in cramped shafts thick with coal dust and temperatures as high as ninety-five degrees. In Anyuan, you could walk in the tunnels, but in Gangzi, the miners crawled.

On a rainy summer night a few days before I visited Gangzi, there was an accident at the No. 5 Coal Mine. Dangerous gases in a poorly ventilated shaft ignited, causing an explosion that killed ninety-two

miners. The dead were a cross section of the modern Chinese working class, men who had been laid off by state mines and women struggling to pay their children's school fees. Many were peasants who had
traveled hundreds of miles in search of work. And then there was Gao
Yingru, a skinny sixteen-year-old trying to save enough money to enroll in computer classes. His father, Gao Beiwen, was a coal miner
who had been injured in an earlier explosion, and he told me his wife
had gone to work in the No. 5 Coal Mine to pay his medical bills. He
said his son had started digging coal only recently, after graduating
from cooking school and failing to find a job in a kitchen. "They knew
he was a good worker, so they kept calling and asking my wife to
bring him," Gao said. There were regulations against women and mi-
nors working in coal mines, but in Gangzi no one seemed to care.
Some of the mines hired thirteen-year-old girls to push coal carts.
"They violate safety rules all the time, but where can we complain?"
Gao continued. "We need the jobs, and the owners all have good connections with the local officials." His voice trailed off. The explosion
had killed his wife and his son, and also his younger brother and his
brother's wife. He was forty-six, a lanky man with thinning hair and a
scarred face, and he sat alone on a beat-up couch in the sparsely furnished living room of his simple house. He asked me how he would
support his daughter and his brother's two boys now. When I photographed him for my report in the *Post,* he held in his arms a black-and-
white portrait of his son. His eyes glimmered with a trace of tears, and
in every shot he avoided the camera and cast his gaze on the concrete
floor.

As the party was celebrating the eightieth anniversary of the miners' strike in Anyuan, its statisticians were calculating how bad conditions in the country's coal mines had become. There were the official
figures, of course, the 5,000 to 7,000 deaths in mining accidents reported by the government each year, and that was bad enough. But
everybody knew the reality was even worse, because local officials
and mine bosses covered up accidents. The statisticians tried to figure
out how much worse, and in internal reports and industry journals,
they came up with an estimate: since the economic reforms began two
decades ago, mining accidents had taken the lives of 10,000 to 40,000
coal miners annually. It was a staggering finding, suggesting that
every thirty minutes, on average, a Chinese coal miner perished in

a gas explosion, cave-in, or flooded shaft. In a nation with a free press, such a relentless drumbeat of tragedy might topple a government. In China, it hardly made the news. Even using the official figures, China's coal mines were by far the world's deadliest. For every million tons of coal produced, four to five miners were killed. By comparison, in Russia and India the fatality rate was less than one death per million tons of coal produced, and in the United States and Britain, it was less than 0.05.

When a coal miner dies in an accident in China, the government requires the owners of the mine to pay compensation to his family. At the time I visited Anyuan, the amount ranged from $1,200 to $6,400, the equivalent of a few years of a miner's salary. But coal was the lifeline of the soaring economy, the cheapest and most readily accessible source of energy. It fueled the expansion of industry, powered the mills and the factories, kept the lights and the air-conditioning on in the cities. The ever-rising demand for coal made the officials and businessmen who controlled the mines wealthy, so they pushed output beyond capacity and their miners beyond fatigue. Compared with the flow of profits, the official price placed on the life of a coal miner was a pittance, so it often made more financial sense for a mine boss to let workers die than to invest in safety measures and equipment.

THE COMMUNIST PARTY once condemned such ruthless economic logic as the province of coldhearted capitalists, but now it presided over an economic system in which the abuse of workers was common—and it depended on that system to stay in power. Before Mao's death, the party justified its rule by presenting itself as the "vanguard of the proletariat" leading the nation to a socialist utopia. But the catastrophes of Mao's rule shattered that illusion, and Deng charted a radical new course to rescue the party, gambling that people would overlook the failure of communism as an ideology if Communists could make them richer. He hoped to unleash the power of free markets and private enterprise while preserving the party's monopoly on power, to grant the people economic freedoms while continuing to restrict their political rights. He called it "socialism with Chinese characteristics," but it was really just authoritarian capitalism—and it worked. By the time Deng died in 1997, he had succeeded in remaking China, lifting two hundred million people out of poverty and leaving his nation more prosperous and more stable than it had been in over a century. But in the process, the party adopted a form of capitalism that could be as exploitative as anything Marx—or Mao—ever envisioned. Market forces generated wealth and prosperity, but unrestrained by democratic institutions, they also produced grim work conditions. Barred from setting up trade unions or organizing strikes, coal miners and other workers had little leverage against bosses with access to the world's largest labor pool. Without a free press or independent courts, workers had nowhere to take complaints against employers who refused to pay them or exposed them to health hazards. Without elections, they had no way to remove corrupt officials who colluded with businesses instead of enforcing labor regulations.

No one benefited more from the shift to capitalism than party officials and those with connections to them. The party's betrayal of its founding ideology, the logic-defying contortions that the propagandists used to explain the reversal, the blunt calculus that holding on to power was an end that justified any means—it all bred a cynicism in the party ranks, and access to the riches of the booming economy quickly warped the party-state. As official corruption rose to obscene and unprecedented levels, the party apparatus came to resemble an organized crime network, with its own fiefdoms, factional rivalries, and unwritten rules governing the distribution of spoils. The idealism that once motivated many party officials, however misplaced and misguided, was gone. The party grew addicted to fast economic growth, because it enriched its members and their friends and kept them loyal, but also because it was necessary to sustain the authoritarian system. After the disasters of Mao's reign and the Tiananmen massacre the leadership could point only to their ability to deliver prosperity to placate the public and keep demands for political change at bay. A slowdown could threaten everything.

But maintaining fast growth carried political risks as well. It would require dismantling the bloated state economy—the legacy of decades of irrational central planning—and that would mean shutting down thousands of factories and laying off tens of millions of workers. The state sector employed more than 110 million people in 1995, or nearly two-thirds of the urban workforce, yet it accounted for barely a third of the nation's industrial output. The banks were drowning in bad loans to state firms, loans that would never be repaid but that the banks kept approving because party officials were afraid to let factories go under. It was a precarious moment for the leadership. The privatization of state industry had not proceeded smoothly in Eastern Europe and Russia after the collapse of the Soviet Union, and it promised to be even more difficult in China, where the party still paid lip service to Marxist rhetoric about state ownership of the means of production. But doing nothing could jeopardize growth, so the order went down to get rid of money-losing state firms or find a way to make them profitable. Only the largest enterprises in strategic industries would remain in state hands.

Party leaders were careful never to use the word "privatization" to describe what they were doing. After all, the party had long maintained that workers were "masters of the enterprise," that the factories belonged to them. So how could they be privatized? And who would get the proceeds? Better to avoid such questions, the leadership decided, and just say the factories were undergoing "reform" or "restructuring."

There was no shock therapy, no attempt to force a painful set of reforms through before entrenched interests could stop it. Party leaders moved slowly, hoping to give the flourishing private sector time to expand and absorb the workers losing their jobs. In the late 1990s and into the new century, the government was laying off five million to six million workers every year. By 2002, some forty million jobs had been eliminated, representing more than one out of every three positions in the state sector. Almost all the workers who lost their jobs were unprepared for the new world they faced. Many had never had to look for work before. The state had always assigned them jobs. Their "work units" had always provided housing, health care, and schools for their children, and in exchange for their service on behalf of socialism, they had been promised job security and retirement pensions. Now, suddenly, they were left to fend for themselves.

Party officials meanwhile were more interested in profiting from the process than in helping ordinary workers. Across the country, managers conspired with officials to force factories into bankruptcy and pick up state assets at fire-sale prices. Workers stopped receiving wages and retirees stopped receiving pension payments, sometimes for months or years at a time, as managers embezzled company funds.

It was a volatile mix—mass layoffs and rampant corruption—and it triggered a wave of labor unrest unseen in China since the Communists themselves were fomenting a revolution. In the winter of 2001, I sat with two thousand workers occupying a textile mill in Dafeng, about 150 miles north of Shanghai, because corrupt officials had emptied their pension funds, stolen their factory, and slashed their salaries. Three nights in a row, police tried to expel them, dragging women out by the hair, jabbing others with electric batons. When I visited on the fourth night, management cut off the heat, and as the temperature neared freezing, the workers huddled together and wrapped themselves in thick blankets. "We know this is dangerous," one woman told me. "But it's too late to be scared now." The scene was repeated in cities and towns across the country as millions of desperate workers risked arrest by staging protests and organizing strikes. The number of "mass incidents" recorded annually by the Ministry of Public Security climbed fourfold in the second half of the 1990s, and by 2003 the security forces were trying to contain an average of nearly 160 demonstrations a day. Several took place in Anyuan. Not long after the dedication of the Mao statue, thousands of retired miners blocked traffic around a government building. Another group climbed to the top of a building and threatened to commit suicide.

The party had studied how the Solidarity labor movement in Poland contributed to the fall of the Soviet Union, and its own history was a reminder of the revolutionary potential of worker frustration. So the leadership ordered officials to take these protests seriously and be vigilant against the emergence of any independent labor group. Long ago, Mao and his comrades had demonstrated that the Communists could organize a labor movement. Now, his successors were trying to prove they could crush one.

THE LABOR UNREST reached its climax as a political threat in the spring of 2002. The setting was Liaoyang, an old industrial city in Liaoning Province on the plains to the northeast of Beijing, in the southern part of what was once known as Manchuria. This was China's industrial heartland, an area rich in oil and coal, located near the Korean border with ice-free access to the Yellow Sea. Russian and Japanese occupation at the beginning of the last century resulted in the early development of heavy industry in the province, and after the Communist revolution, state planners made the region the most industrialized and urbanized in the country. In the late 1950s, factories in Liaoning produced more than two-thirds of the nation's iron and more than half of all its steel, and cities like Liaoyang—home to a dozen military manufacturers and a renowned chemical plant—took pride in their prime position in the national economy. But if the stretch of northeastern China from the Great Wall to the Siberian border was once an economic showcase, the region is now the country's rust belt, a place left behind by the boom.

With the advent of capitalism, the state factories that dominated the area were exposed as inefficient money-losers, and as the party pressed ahead with market reforms, the local economy faltered. Unemployment rose to alarming levels, with as much as 30 to 60 percent of all state workers in the rust-belt cities either laid off and unable to find jobs or else clinging to positions in factories that could no longer pay them. The situation in Liaoyang was as bleak as in any city. A string of state enterprises went bankrupt; others teetered on the brink of failure. Miles of empty brick factory buildings lined the streets, the wind whistling through their broken windowpanes. In front of crumbling housing projects, on the sides of dusty roads, clusters of the unemployed gathered in informal labor markets, holding in their hands or hanging on their necks simple handwritten placards advertising their skills: welding, electrical repair, carpentry, cooking, sewing, and so on. They were members of one of the oldest working-class communities in the nation, men and women who had been hailed as proletarians, persuaded of "the superiority of socialism," and promised lifetime job tenure and benefits. Now, just to feed their children and support their aging parents, they were begging for work.

Their frustration erupted on a cold Monday morning in March while the party's national legislature was in session in Beijing. City leaders woke to urgent reports describing thousands of workers massing outside the Liaoyang Ferroalloy Factory, or Liaotie, a large iron alloy producer that had recently been declared bankrupt. As the demonstrators marched up Democracy Road, one of the city's main thoroughfares, thousands of other workers from failing textile, chemical, piston, instruments, leather, and precision tool plants joined them. By the time the crowd reached their first destination, the municipal courthouse, there were as many as thirty thousand protesters. They called for the city's chief judge and chief prosecutor to come out and explain what was being done to fight corruption, and when there was no response they moved down the street to the city's legislature and demanded the resignation of its chairman, one of the most powerful party officials in Liaoyang. By early afternoon the workers were converging in front of city hall. The Liaotie contingent carried white sheets that had been sewn together and hand-painted with slogans in black ink. "We want food! We want work! We don't want bankruptcy!" one declared. "The army of industrial workers must eat!" said another. When the workers carrying the banners arrived at city hall, the crowd let out a loud cheer. Outside the front gate, the protesters asked for a meeting with the mayor or the city's party chief, but the government sent word that only a few low-level officials would see them. The workers refused the offer and instead announced that the protests would continue the next day.

At first glance, party leaders in Beijing might have dismissed the demonstration in Liaoyang as just a routine outbreak of labor unrest, indistinguishable from any of the hundreds of protests nationwide that local officials managed to contain every week. But what happened in Liaoyang on March 11 should have raised alarm bells for several reasons. There was the explicit demand for the resignation of the chairman of the local legislature, whom the protesters accused of corruption, whereas most labor demonstrations focused on economic grievances. There was the fact that workers from at least seven different factories participated in the action, a significant departure from the pattern of single-factory protests that the party was accustomed to handling. And finally, there was a fateful miscalculation by the security services. Worried that the workers were planning to block the trains, the authorities in Liaoyang had deployed police to the railways instead of along the protest route or around city hall. The minimal police presence emboldened the workers the next morning, when they again turned out in large numbers.

There was little doubt the Liaotie workers had the party's attention the second day. When they arrived downtown, they found the government buildings surrounded by riot police, and as they rallied outside city hall again, they received word that a delegation of senior city officials was willing to meet and negotiate with their representatives. For more than an hour the workers debated how to proceed. Some were wary. If they went inside, they would be identifying themselves to the authorities as organizers of the largest labor demonstrations that the city had ever seen—and putting themselves at risk of arrest. But others argued that the time for caution had passed. They had gone without pay for as long as two years and suffered drastic cuts in benefits. They had watched officials steal from their factory and force it into bankruptcy. They had complained to the government and their complaints had been ignored. Now they had discovered they were not alone. Workers from across the city were standing in solidarity with them. If they were ever going to demand change, this was the time to do it. And so, from the cheering crowd assembled in the streets, a dozen men and women emerged, made their way past the cordon of riot police, and disappeared into city hall.

Among the first to step forward was Xiao Yunliang, a tough-talking loading bay worker at Liaotie who played a leading role in organizing the protests. "At the time, we weren't afraid," he recalled years later, after he was arrested and sent to prison. "Of course, we knew we were taking a risk, but we weren't afraid. Rather, we were excited, moved by the vast ranks of workers, by this feeling that we couldn't be stopped."

HE WAS FIFTY-FIVE at the time of the protests, rough-hewn with graying hair, and he had the solid yet weary look of a man who had spent his life doing manual labor. Xiao was neither the most educated nor the most eloquent of the worker leaders—he had never finished elementary school—but he was the kind of person who held a grudge, and his grievances against the party had been building for a long time. As a child growing up in the countryside outside Liaoyang, he suffered through the famine of the Great Leap Forward, eating leaves and grass to survive. As a young man he enlisted in the military and became a party member, but in the Cultural Revolution the state sent him to work at Liaotie. There he found managers more interested in political struggle than iron alloys, and when he questioned their priorities, they put him in a holding cell at the factory for seven months.

Thirteen years later, when the prodemocracy demonstrations erupted in Tiananmen Square, Xiao followed the events in Beijing closely and hoped for a change. After the massacre, he quietly cursed the party.

These feelings of political discontent hardened into more rebellious views as factories in Liaoyang, including Liaotie, began to fail and lay off workers in the 1990s. Critical to the evolution in Xiao's thinking was his friendship with a former steelworker named Yao Fuxin, who lived down the street. Yao was a heavyset man in his late forties, with a round, pudgy face and piercing eyes, and Xiao often saw him walking in the neighborhood with a shortwave radio to his ear, trying to get better reception of foreign news broadcasts such as the Voice of America. Yao's wife had worked at Liaotie until losing her job in the layoffs, and the couple lived in a room behind a tiny convenience store that they owned. In the evenings after work, Xiao would visit them, and they would sit in the store and pick over the problems at Liaotie and other state factories, sometimes talking late into the night. Yao was no intellectual—when the party disbanded the Red Guards, he was among the millions of teenagers sent to the countryside instead of finishing high school or going to college—but he was a clear thinker, and Xiao usually agreed with what he had to say. While other workers grumbled about the transition to capitalism, Yao blamed their troubles on the political system. There was nothing wrong with market reform itself, he argued, but in a one-party state, those with power enjoyed unfair advantages in the economy while ordinary people were more vulnerable to abuse. In a one-party state, there were no checks against the power of government officials, no channels for the public to curb their excesses. In a multiparty system, he said, officials would never get away with what they were doing to the factories in Liaoyang.

In the late 1980s, as the state-owned steel-rolling mill where he worked was faltering, Yao had tried to strike out on his own in the free market. He borrowed money from friends, bought a small truck, and for a while he made a decent income on the side by renting out his services hauling goods around the city. But he and other independent drivers soon found themselves squeezed by local officials who were more interested in collecting taxes and fees than encouraging entrepreneurial activity that threatened the state transport firms they had relationships with. Frustrated, Yao responded by organizing hundreds of truck drivers to converge on city hall in their vehicles and appeal for relief. The government rebuffed them and punished Yao by taking away his job at the steel mill. After his wife lost her job too in 1993, the couple used their savings to start the convenience store.

It was a small shop, less than fifty square feet, located on a main road near Liaotie. As conditions at the factory deteriorated, Xiao invited a few friends to join his talks with Yao at the store, and then other workers began stopping by to share their complaints. Liaotie was just a small smelting operation when it was established in 1949, but the workers had watched it grow into one of the city's largest enterprises, with multiple production lines, schools, a hospital, and as many as seven thousand employees at its peak. Whether it was ever profitable was a matter of some debate in Yao's store, but the workers all agreed that the factory's new manager, Fan Yicheng, was making things worse. He was a tall, handsome party hack about the same age as Xiao, a fast talker who had started as a technician in the factory and climbed his way up the management ranks. The party appointed him to run Liaotie in 1993, and he immediately began "restructuring" the enterprise. He laid off hundreds of workers and forced hundreds more into early retirement. He spun off production lines as independent companies. He surrounded himself with a new team of managers. But instead of improving the factory's performance, Fan ran it into the ground. A year after he took over, Liaotie was struggling to pay its workers on time. Then it fell behind on pension payments to retirees and unemployment benefits to the workers it had laid off. In 1995, it stopped paying the workers' pension and health insurance premiums, and by 1996 supply and cash shortages forced managers to suspend production for long periods at a time.

Xiao and the others who gathered at Yao's store suspected corruption was at the root of the factory's struggles. Demand for the alloys it produced remained high, and the company was cutting costs every year by laying off workers, yet it was starved for funds. Where did the money go? Sitting on folding chairs under the shelves of soda and instant noodles in the convenience store, grumbling about the layoffs and their unpaid wages over beer or tea, the workers thought they knew the answer. They traded stories about how Fan and his managers were prospering, about who was seen driving a new car, or going overseas on a business junket, or sending his children to study abroad.

But it was not until an accountant in the finance department joined them in the store that they understood the scale of the problem: through a variety of complex schemes, she said, Fan and other party officials were transferring millions of dollars in company assets to private companies they owned or controlled. When the accountant tried to report the crime, the police put her in jail for nineteen days. The money trail extended up the party hierarchy, and Fan was protected.

Word of the accountant's disclosures spread quickly among the workers at Liaotie, and the conversations at Yao's store took on a new edge. Xiao was furious. It wasn't enough to just sit around and complain, he felt. They needed to take action. Yao agreed, as did another regular at the store, a truck dispatcher who worked with Xiao named Pang Qingxiang. The three men formed the nucleus of a group of Liaotie employees who set out to demand what was owed them. They drafted a letter outlining the workers' grievances and organized delegations to visit a series of government offices looking for help. The official trade union controlled by the party—the only union allowed under the law—rebuffed them. The labor arbitration bureau refused to accept their case. The state media, the police, the courts, the prosecutors, the party's discipline office—they all turned them away, too. The workers pooled their money and traveled to the provincial capital, Shenyang, and then to Beijing, to lodge complaints, but nothing came of those efforts, either. Some workers even confronted Fan directly, showing him documents outlining government policies prohibiting wage arrears. But the slick hack just brushed them off, saying the documents were worthless because the factory had no money.

In 1998, Yao explored the possibility of finding help for the workers elsewhere. During a brief political thaw before President Clinton's visit to China that year, small groups of dissidents around the country tried to establish an opposition political party. They called it the China Democracy Party, and Xu Wenli, a former electrician and well-known democracy advocate from the late 1970s, was elected chairman of its Beijing branch. Less prominent figures were organizing branches in other cities. It was a bold, perhaps naive endeavor—the dissidents were operating in the open, trying to register the party with the government—but Yao was intrigued, and he traveled to a nearby city to attend a few of the party's meetings. Before long, though, he concluded it could never survive a crackdown, and he declined an offer to join the party and serve as its representative in Liaoyang. His instincts were right. Shortly after Clinton's visit, the security forces arrested Xu, sentenced him to thirteen years in prison, and dismantled the China Democracy Party. In December that year, police in Liaoyang detained Yao for questioning and warned him to stay away from the group. He agreed, signed a statement to that effect, and was released.

By the spring of 2000, the Liaotie workers were angry and desperate. The two thousand workers still on the job had not been paid for as long as two years, and the three to four thousand retirees and laid-off workers that the factory was responsible for had not received benefit payments in three to six months. "Our lives were pitiful," Xiao said. "Workers were living from meal to meal, struggling to feed their children. Elderly workers died in their homes because they had no heat." Meanwhile, disgruntled managers leaked more information about Fan's corrupt dealings. By May the workers had heard enough, and hundreds of them took to the streets, blocking the main highway between Liaoyang and Shenyang and demanding their unpaid wages and pensions. After twelve hours, just past midnight, the authorities ordered antiriot and paramilitary police to break up the demonstration. Dozens of workers were injured in the clash, and Xiao and Pang were arrested. Hoping to prevent further protests, the government let them go the next day. But it was Xiao's first brush with the police, and he would never forget it. "What I saw was the despotism of the Communist Party," he said. "I saw workers begging for food, and the party respond with armed force, with antiriot troops and police. It was just like a fascist dictatorship. On the road that day, there were thousands of soldiers and officers, marching in step, trying to intimidate us."

Workers from other factories were staging similar protests every day across the rust belt. Like the men and women from Liaotie, they had concluded that such acts of desperation and defiance, while risky, were the most effective way to draw attention to their problems in a political system in which the media, courts, and labor unions were controlled by the party. When they sought help through formal channels, the party ignored them. But when they took to the streets, the party snapped to attention. Party officials could be recklessly corrupt, but they were also a nervous and fearful bunch. They understood the depth of discontent with their rule, and they worried that any protest, if handled improperly, could gain momentum and spin out of control. The workers used this fear to their advantage. The bigger and more disruptive the protest, they realized, the quicker the party would respond and the more likely it would be to address their concerns. But if workers were able to win concessions by protesting, the party always gained more than it gave away. It defused demonstrations by dividing workers, paying some while holding out against others, and in doing so, it blunted demands for systemic change, too.

The workers at Liaotie staged more protests. Occasionally, the factory would pay some of what was owed them, but it would always fall behind again. The government promised to look into their allegations of corruption, and it once sent a team of officials to the factory to gather evidence, prompting workers to set off firecrackers in celebration. But nothing came of the investigation. One of the officials privately told the workers that the corruption was much worse than they knew, and suggested that too many senior party officials were involved for investigators to keep digging. Later, the official was transferred. The workers knew that Fan enjoyed good ties with Gong Shangwu, the former mayor and party chief who served as chairman of the local legislature and was said to take lavish trips abroad at the factory's expense. Later, their suspicions also focused on the provincial governor, Zhang Guoguang. In 2001, before being assigned to govern another province, he visited their factory and announced that it was beginning bankruptcy proceedings, the workers said.

The announcement caused immediate alarm. Xiao and his colleagues had seen other state factories driven into bankruptcy, and they knew it would mean a raw deal for them. If Liaotie went bankrupt, they might never recover their unpaid wages. Instead the state would relinquish all welfare obligations, and their years of labor on behalf of socialism would end with a meager severance payment. Meanwhile, the corruption that had crippled their company might never be exposed. The workers believed they had as strong a claim of ownership on the factory as anyone. They were the ones who had built it and made it what it was, and China was supposed to be a workers' state, wasn't it? But if the factory were liquidated, its assets would just be sold behind closed doors at cut-rate prices to party officials and their relatives and friends. A few months after the announcement, a team of men showed up at Liaotie in the middle of the night and began hauling away thousands of tons of valuable iron ore and equipment in a fleet of trucks. Sympathetic security guards woke Xiao, and he rushed to the plant in his pajamas with several other workers. But they were outnumbered, and when they demanded answers, the men just ignored them. The workers staged a protest the next day, demanding an explanation from the government. The government ignored them, too.

Under Chinese law, worker representatives are supposed to vote and approve the bankruptcy of a state enterprise after reviewing a report on its accounts. Liaotie never distributed a report, but it scheduled the bankruptcy vote for a morning in October 2001. As the date approached, Xiao and the others stepped up their protests. "We knew it was a turning point," he said. "It was our last chance to fight for our rights." The day before the vote, more than a thousand workers from Liaotie blocked the highway to Shenyang again. Police detained Xiao and several other worker leaders. The next morning, they also nabbed Yao. Hundreds of riot police were deployed around the factory as a crowd of workers massed outside the front gate. Some worker representatives were blocked from entering, and management split up those it allowed in and forced them to meet in thirteen different locations. Two plainclothes police officers were stationed in each one to make sure the workers voted as they were told. Some of those who attempted to cast opposing votes had their ballots torn up in front of them.

The police released Xiao and the other labor leaders after the vote. A few weeks later, the government formally declared the company bankrupt. Despite the workers' efforts, the Liaoyang Ferroalloy Factory was no more.

THE SPRING FESTIVAL is usually a joyous holiday in China, an occasion for families to come together and mark the start of the lunar year with fireworks, gifts, and homemade dumplings. But in the drab housing estates where the Liaotie workers lived, there was little to celebrate as the Year of the Horse began in February 2002. The only signs of revelry were the elderly workers who occasionally gathered and sang to the neighborhood in frustration. Theirs was a familiar tune, one the workers had all been taught as children, "The Internationale":

Arise, cold and hungry slaves!
Arise, suffering people of the world!
The blood which fills my chest has boiled over,
We must struggle for truth!
The old world shall be destroyed like fallen petals and splashed water,
Arise, slaves, arise!
Do not say that we have nothing,
We shall be the masters of the world!

The workers' circumstances had deteriorated sharply after the bankruptcy. Some workers, including all the managers, were rehired by parts of the plant that resumed production after they were privatized. But most were left unemployed, with months of unpaid wages and benefit payments still owed them. The severance payments that were promised never materialized, and many families could no longer even afford cooking oil and heat. Because so many people had been laid off in the city, the competition for jobs was fierce. Some workers relied on their parents' meager pension payments to support their families, while others tried to make do with monthly welfare subsidies equal to about twelve dollars. Xiao struggled to support his wife and three daughters by picking up odd jobs as a day laborer at construction sites.

But it was not destitution that angered Xiao most. It was the contrast between their lives and those of party officials. He could respect an entrepreneur who made a fortune by relying on hard work and talent, but as far as he could tell, the officials prospered because of the power that they held, not because of their abilities. They were no better than thieves and bandits, he thought, because they stole from factories that ordinary workers had built. Across the city, luxurious saunas, clubs, and karaoke halls opened to serve the new rich, and Xiao burned with frustration as he watched fancy sedans ferrying party officials and their mistresses from one pleasure palace to the next. During the Spring Festival, the Liaotie workers noticed the factory's party officials coming and going from their apartments toting bags full of gifts from their shopping sprees. As far as Xiao was concerned, they weren't just celebrating the holiday. They were celebrating the bankruptcy.

The depth of corruption in the party was evident to the workers as they followed news of a major purge unfolding in nearby Shenyang, the provincial capital and one of the nation's largest cities. The mayor there and more than a hundred other city officials had been detained on corruption charges. While state media presented the case as an example of the party's resolve to keep its cadres honest, the public marveled at the scale of malfeasance and wondered why it went unpunished for so long. At the center of the scandal was a mafia boss, Liu Yong, who sat on the city legislature and ran a crime organization responsible for thirty to forty murders, most of them of people who got in the way of his vast real estate, tobacco, and retail conglomerate. Among his allies was Mayor Mu Suixin, a flamboyant official who rode in a Mercedes and insisted on staying in the presidential suites of five-star hotels when traveling. Mu had once been held up by the party as a role model because of his efforts to "reform" state enterprises. Now it was revealed he had accepted "huge amounts of bribes." When investigators searched his two country homes, they found one hundred and fifty Rolex watches as well as six million dollars in gold bars hidden in the walls. His first wife, second wife, sister, brother, daughter, and chauffeur were said to be on the take, too. Corruption infected almost every agency in Mu's government, from the police to the banks to the construction bureau, and it took many forms: smuggling, extortion, the sale of official positions, the rigging of state contracts, embezzlement, as well as the use of public funds to maintain mistresses. The deputy mayor, Ma Xiangdong, blew nearly five million dollars in city money in gambling sprees in Macao and Las Vegas. Others arrested included the city's chief judge, the chief prosecutor, the head of the tax bureau, and the manager of the state assets agency.

The stories about Shenyang infuriated the Liaotie workers. They were convinced that the situation in Liaoyang was no better than in the provincial capital, and that party officials forced their factory into bankruptcy to cover up similar crimes. They noted that Governor Zhang, who ordered the liquidation of Liaotie, had previously served as the party chief in Shenyang and promoted the mayor and many of the officials now going to prison there. "They're all in it together," Xiao said. "The money that was stolen from our factory wasn't just for Fan himself. He had to pay off city officials, and they had to pay off provincial officials, and they had to pay off national officials." He believed the party itself had become a criminal organization, and he wanted to do something about it.

His wife and children thought it was a foolish impulse, one that would only lead to trouble. His wife especially wanted him to stop. Xiao responded by hiding what he was doing from her. "If I discussed it with her, it would be all over. She would never agree. So I never mentioned it to her," he said. His friend Yao faced similar resistance from his wife. Sometimes she refused to let him out of the house, and he had to communicate instructions to the workers by passing notes to Xiao when he visited the convenience store.

Almost all the labor protests occurring in the rust-belt cities were staged by employees from a single company, in a single city, with narrowly focused financial demands. The demonstrations that Xiao, Yao, and their colleague Pang had organized were no exception. But huddling in the convenience store during the Spring Festival, they discussed the shortcomings of this approach. As long as the political system remained unchanged, they agreed, those with positions of power could always abuse it, and workers could hope only for marginal improvements in their lives. For real progress, they thought democratic reform was necessary, and they believed that most workers supported such a goal. But they also knew that persuading workers to participate in a protest advocating democratic change would be all but impossible. The workers had internalized the lesson of the Tiananmen massacre. Everybody knew that the party would quickly crush a direct challenge to its authority, and nobody wanted to go to prison. People were too afraid.

A better strategy, the three men decided, would be to rally the workers against corruption. Here was a vulnerable spot in the party's armor, an issue that not only inflamed public passions but also hinted at the deeper systemic shortcomings of one-party rule. Most important, it was a problem the party itself acknowledged and claimed to be trying to fight. That made it safer for people to protest against, because the party could not arrest them without hurting its moral authority on the issue and risking a greater backlash. "It was a question of tactics," Xiao said. "We were trying to promote democracy, but we couldn't say it. So we decided to protest against corruption. We wanted to use the corrupt behavior of factory and city officials to motivate people and wake them to the cause."

As Xiao and his comrades prepared to escalate the workers' movement, they shifted the focus of their rhetoric from unpaid wages to official corruption. It was a small adjustment, but the consequences would be dramatic.

ON MARCH 5, party officials from across the country gathered in Beijing for the opening of the annual session of the National People's Congress. On paper the parliament is the highest organ of state power in China, but in reality it is just another tool of the party. Its meetings, held in the Great Hall of the People on Tiananmen Square, are a ritual of Communist politics. Year after year, delegates from the provinces listen patiently to long-winded speeches by government ministers and vote overwhelmingly to approve the party's policies. The exercise is intended to showcase the party's democratic nature to the public and to the world, but the event is carefully staged, and there is rarely any real debate.

On the same day that the Congress convened, more than a hundred workers crowded into a conference room in one of the old buildings of the bankrupt Liaoyang Ferroalloy Factory. On their agenda was a daring plan. While the Congress was in session, the Liaotie workers intended to stage a major demonstration in Liaoyang in an attempt to attract the attention of the party chief, Jiang Zemin, and other national leaders. Some workers believed that party leaders would sympathize with their plight, while others had lost faith in the party and considered the leadership as bad as the party men in Liaoyang. But they all agreed that drawing the central government's attention to their factory would put pressure on city officials to pay them and perhaps prompt an investigation into the bankruptcy. With a show of hands, the workers voted to stage the protest in thirteen days. Then they elected a dozen representatives to negotiate on their behalf with the government. Xiao, Yao, and Pang were among them.

Later in the meeting, Pang stood to speak. A tall, slender man who resembled an elderly professor but had only a high school education, he read to the workers a series of letters that he had written on their behalf and opened the floor to suggestions for improvements. Xiao noticed that Pang had crafted the letters carefully. There was no mention of their dissatisfaction with the political system nor of their support for democratic reform. Instead he positioned the workers as loyal supporters of the party leadership and repeatedly emphasized that their grievances were in line with the party's laws and policies. One letter addressed to Jiang Zemin resorted to flattery, citing the party chief's empty political theories and speeches approvingly and referring to him as a "beloved" leader and "respected elder." Another appealed to a new provincial governor, Bo Xilai, for help, describing him as a "well-known virtuous official and excellent party member." At the same time, the letters attacked Fan and city officials in vivid and unsparing terms:

> With the factory facing the massive challenge of the market and already in trouble, it was Fan Yicheng's duty, in his official position as both managing director and legal representative, to construct a strategy for improving its overall economic performance. It was his responsibility to provide leadership in improving product quality, output performance, and the profitability of the enterprise. . . .
>
> Fan Yicheng did none of this. Following his appointment, he adopted a policy of cronyism in which all those who submitted to his will did well and anyone who resisted was dealt with accordingly. All dissent was outlawed. His close aides, friends and relatives were placed in company positions from which he could directly benefit. . . . These people worked hand in glove as a team to swallow billions of yuan in state funds, resulting in losses of tens of billions of yuan in state property—we have detailed evidence of all of this. . . . The sweat and blood of workers has been used to nurture a colony of parasites. Under the pretext of procuring goods, Fan took holidays abroad and gathered large amounts of foreign exchange to fill his personal coffers to the brim. At the factory, he bullied and intimidated workers, and used hundreds of thousands worth of public funds to refurbish his house and send his two children to study abroad. Fan and his corrupt friends used state funds to eat, drink, gamble, whore, and do anything they wanted. There were no limits to their extravagance. . . .
>
> Liaotie's bankruptcy was not the result of economic restructuring any more than it was brought about by poor sales. It was

the direct result of coordinated embezzlement of national assets and leeching off the workers' sweat and blood by Fan Yicheng and his gang of parasites, with the collusion and support of former mayor Gong Shangwu. . . .

The bankruptcy went through, leaving the workforce in tears and corrupt officials laughing all the way to the bank. Moreover, they are now using the embezzled funds to set up new private enterprises. As if by magic, they have transformed themselves into entrepreneurs, using the workers' sweat and blood as building blocks for their nest of corruption. Illegal activities have produced a legal company, and the government has done its utmost to cover up and collude in this almost perfect crime. Where on earth are we to go to find reason and justice? Is it possible that a Chinese nation under the leadership of the Communist Party can leave no space for workers?

Xiao realized that Pang was trying to drive a wedge between national leaders in Beijing and local officials in Liaoyang. His approach put party leaders on the spot, demanding they live up to their own rhetoric and laws, while also giving them an out, a chance to distance themselves from corrupt behavior that hurt the government's image, even if they condoned such behavior elsewhere or engaged in it themselves. In effect, the letters were asking party leaders to sacrifice their underlings in Liaoyang to bolster the party's reputation and strengthen its grip on power.

But there was also another motive behind Pang's choice of words. He and the other worker leaders understood that their chances of success were limited if they were alone. They had already staged several protests, yet local officials had ignored their demands and the central government had shown no interest in intervening. By focusing on corruption instead of just their economic grievances, they wanted to build a larger movement and draw support from workers suffering similar abuses at other factories. They planned to post the letters in neighborhoods across the city and they hoped to inspire others to join them. They hoped that workers would read about the corruption that shut down Liaotie and think of what had happened to their own enterprises, that they would read about Fan Yicheng and think of the behavior of the party officials who had ruined their lives.

We the working masses have decided that we cannot tolerate these corrupt elements who have imposed an illegal bankruptcy on our factory. We must take back justice and dignity. We will not give up until we get back all welfare payments, unpaid wages, and compensation. . . . Our respected compatriots, brothers and fathers, we are not anti-party, anti-socialism hooligans who harm people's lives and disrupt social order. Our demands are all legal under the constitution and the law. . . . Let us join forces in this action for legal rights and against corruption. Long live the spirit of Liaoyang!

Xiao knew it was a long shot. There were reasons why workers in Liaoyang had not come together before. Conditions at each factory were different, so each workforce had its own grievances. A payment that would satisfy workers at one factory might be dismissed as insignificant at another, and what some workers considered an important complaint others might see as secondary. By focusing on corruption, the Liaotie workers wanted to bridge these divisions. But they were cautious, too. They did not want to alert the authorities, so they reached out only to people they trusted. If a Liaotie worker was married to a worker from another enterprise, they would ask the spouse to spread the word. If they met workers protesting outside a government building, they might ask for their help. But it was difficult to establish the trust necessary to build alliances, especially with distant factories scattered across the city, and so there was no attempt to establish a citywide organization. The Liaotie workers tried to notify other factories of their plans, but it seemed too dangerous to do much more.

The effort might have failed if not for a blunder by one of the workers' enemies. A day or two after the opening of the National People's Congress, Xiao was at home watching television coverage of the event when he saw Gong Shangwu, the city's former mayor and party chief, speaking to a reporter about the city's economic situation. "There are laid-off workers in Liaoyang, but there are no unemployed workers," he declared. "Laid-off workers receive a living stipend of 280 yuan per month." Xiao was stunned. It was a ridiculous statement, and it infuriated workers across the city. How could a senior official, the chairman of their local legislature and a delegate representing them in Beijing, make such a claim with a straight face? The hundreds of thousands who had lost their jobs and were struggling to make ends meet in Liaoyang, a city of two million, were in no mood to hear a portly party boss tell them that they were not really unemployed. The blatant lie about the living stipend was even worse. It was as if Gong expected workers to play along with the fiction, just so he could brag to the nation about what a good job he was doing.

The outrage in the city's working-class neighborhoods was palpable, and the Liaotie worker leaders gathered at Yao's store and decided to move up their protest by a week. That left them just a few days to get organized and mobilize the workforce. Another meeting of the workers at Liaotie was called, and this time more than six hundred people showed up, forcing the group to find a bigger room. The police must have noticed such a large gathering, but the workers didn't care. They were angry, and after all, they said to themselves, what crime was there in holding a meeting? Xiao proposed a new slogan— "Impeach Gong Shangwu, Liberate Liaoyang"—and Pang drafted a new letter with the same title. Committees were set up and tasks were assigned. One group was assigned to make banners. Others were organized to take charge of morale, safety, and emergency medical care during the demonstration.

One of the worker leaders, a stocky carpenter named Chen Dianfan, proposed that they carry a portrait of Mao during the protest. He volunteered to get one and build a large frame for it. Xiao immediately agreed. He considered Mao a disastrous leader, but he knew that some of the old workers, in their nostalgia for socialism and equality among the classes, overlooked the suffering he caused. Xiao was not beyond tapping into such sentiment if it meant drawing more workers into the streets. If the party could use Mao to defend its corrupt ways, he thought, why couldn't the workers use his image to fight back? Marching under Mao's portrait would also help position the workers as loyal citizens, making it easier for those anxious about getting arrested to join them and more difficult for the authorities to suppress the demonstration.

Yao took Pang's letters to a shop to be typed up, printed, and photocopied, along with a notice announcing the date of the protest. In their homes, the workers made paste by boiling a mixture of water and flour, and then, in the middle of the night, they set out on bicycles with stacks of the papers. They worked in pairs in the dark, targeting worker neighborhoods across the city. Xiao was responsible for one not too far from Liaotie. His partner watched out for the police while he pasted the letters on walls and telephone poles. It was cold, and he could see his breath in the air as he hurried, trying to prevent the glue from freezing. He wore plastic bags to protect his hands, and brushed an extra layer of paste over each letter to make it more difficult for police to tear down. By the time they finished, it was 3 A.M.

The workers continued to hold meetings, sometimes in factory buildings, sometimes at Yao's store. Xiao emphasized the need to maintain order in the crowd and prevent tempers from flaring during the protest. Any rash or illegal behavior, he worried, would give the police an excuse to move in. Finally, as the date of the protest approached, the workers discussed a subject that had been nagging at them. What would they do if the police began arresting them? A contingency plan was drafted. The workers considered Xiao, Yao, and Pang their top leaders, but now they made a list of more than forty other workers active in the movement who agreed to take their place if anything happened to them. If police arrested Xiao, Yao, and Pang, another team would take over and lead protests demanding their release. And if those workers were also arrested, another group would step up, and then another and another. At least, that was the way it was supposed to work.

EVERYTHING SEEMED POSSIBLE after the first exhilarating day of the protests. As workers from factories across the city poured into the streets, in numbers greater than he had ever expected, Xiao was seized with excitement. Some of the workers carried banners with the names of their factories, others with slogans denouncing corruption. Xiao saw parents marching with their children and pedicab drivers offering rides to the weak and elderly, and he felt proud to be walking among them. As he stood in front of the crowd, delivering a speech outside the courthouse or reading one of Pang's letters through a bullhorn, he was confident that the long struggle of the workers of the Liaoyang Ferroalloy Factory was nearing a successful conclusion.

Emotions ran high the second day, too. The highlight was a speech that Yao gave in front of city hall. He was standing on a platform, his arm cradling an elderly woman, the widow of a fellow worker. Tears ran down both their faces as Yao raised his voice in anger. "We devoted our youth to the party, but no one supports us in old age!" he cried. "We gave our youth to the party for nothing!" The crowd of tens of thousands was silent, transfixed by his words, and when he finished speaking, it broke into thunderous applause.

After they accepted the government's offer to negotiate, the Liaotie representatives were ushered into a plush conference room on the second floor of city hall. A deputy mayor, the police chief, the chief judge, and ten other municipal officials sat on one side of a table, and the twelve worker leaders sat on the other, Xiao, Yao, and Pang among them. The atmosphere was tense but the discussion cordial. The deputy mayor promised to address the workers' complaints if the protests ended, and the police chief pledged that no one would be arrested. Yao told them that the workers were willing to work with the government and would be satisfied if it kept its promises. Xiao raised the issue of corruption, arguing that if corrupt officials and managers were punished, the city's factories would thrive again. Others discussed the unpaid wages and benefits. At the end of the meeting, the deputy mayor said the government needed more time to respond, because the mayor and party secretary were out of town, presumably attending the Congress in Beijing. But he assured the workers their concerns would be addressed, and their allegations of corruption at Liaotie fully investigated. Encouraged by these conciliatory words, the workers agreed to call off the protests and give the government time to act.

Xiao left the two-hour meeting feeling good about what they had accomplished and optimistic. State media outlets were maintaining a blackout on news of their protests, but foreign news organizations including the Voice of America had reported them, and so Xiao was convinced that party leaders in Beijing were also paying attention. Reviewing the day's events in Yao's store that evening, other worker leaders from Liaotie agreed that a pause in the demonstrations made sense. People were exhausted after two days of marches and protests, after all. But the worker leaders also decided they would not wait indefinitely. At a large meeting the next day, the workers agreed that if the city did not respond within six days, they would take to the streets again—before the end of the parliament session in Beijing.

The first three days passed quietly. On the afternoon of the fourth, one of the Liaotie managers summoned Xiao and told him the deputy mayor wanted to meet with him in private. Xiao did not want to go alone, and instead brought Yao, Pang, and a fourth worker representative with him. A government car whisked them to city hall. The deputy mayor was an older man named Chen Qiang, a tall, bookish bureaucrat with glasses and a dark complexion. He had impressed the workers in the meeting earlier in the week, because he spoke to them without the patronizing, condescending tone most officials used when addressing workers, and he spoke to them again now in a sympathetic voice.

"Old Xiao, I hope you'll put the brakes on this movement as soon as possible," he said. "Don't push it any further. Your problem is already an international one now. Overseas, they're calling you labor leaders."

Xiao understood exactly what he meant. In the mind of a party official, it was not good to be a "labor leader." The party regarded labor leaders as threats.

"I hope you'll stop doing this, because we understand this is serious," Chen continued. City officials were willing to continue meeting with the worker representatives, he said, but the protests needed to stop.

Xiao knew Chen was delivering a message on behalf of the government, but he sensed that the deputy mayor was genuinely concerned. He assumed that meant others in the government were pushing for a crackdown despite the police chief's no-arrests pledge. Perhaps, he thought, the decision had already been made. Still, he could not imagine backing down. The city had not yet taken any action to address their concerns. The next protest was scheduled to take place in two days, and the workers had already begun posting notices around the city. Xiao thanked the deputy mayor, but said to him, "We can't rush out and tell everyone not to protest just because you told us not to."

That night, when Xiao, Yao, and Pang briefed other Liaotie worker leaders about the conversation, they concurred with the decision. Workers from factories across the city had united behind them, and both the foreign media and the party leadership in Beijing were paying attention. It had taken the Liaotie workers years of hard struggle to get to this point, and they wanted to keep the pressure on until the government made real concessions.

The next morning, the government made its move. Yao Fuxin went out early to purchase goods to stock his convenience store and never returned. At first, no one knew what had happened. The police denied they had arrested him, and because party officials had ties to organized crime, his family worried that he had been kidnapped or worse. Xiao raced around the neighborhood, searching for his friend. He found his moped discarded on the side of a road, and a resident told him that he saw three men seize Yao and take him away in a car. None were wearing police uniforms, but Xiao decided the workers needed to act on the assumption Yao had been arrested. As the news spread, people responded with outrage. The worker leaders convened an emergency meeting at Liaotie that night, but there was no need for debate. They all agreed to push ahead with the next day's protest— and make Yao's release their top demand.

Few of the worker leaders went home after the meeting. Most stayed with friends or relatives, because they were worried police would try to break up the protest by rounding up all the organizers. Xiao bundled himself up in a thick cotton coat and hid in one of the factory's abandoned buildings. He found an empty room on the second floor with a broken window that afforded a view of the moonlit street below, then curled up in a corner of the cold, dirty floor. His body ached when he woke at sunrise the next day and set out to lead the protest. "At the time, my mind was clear," he said. "All I could think was I needed to get Yao out, even if it meant risking my own life."

The turnout was even larger than it was the first day, when as many as thirty thousand had marched, and there was a new, angrier edge to the demonstration as throngs of workers demanded the release of one of their own. The protesters hoisted banners denouncing Yao's arrest, and elderly workers wept as they sang "The Internationale" and cursed the party. Xiao and Pang rallied the crowd outside the public security bureau, and Yao's twenty-five-year-old daughter picked up the megaphone and demanded the police come out and tell them where her father was. Antiriot and paramilitary police surrounded city hall again, and in a sign that party leaders in Beijing were worried, a team from the Xinhua news service was sent to the scene with instructions to file internal reports about the demonstration.

The day ended without any response from the government, so the workers resumed the protests the next morning. Xiao spent the night in the abandoned building again, but he knew the police would eventually find him if they wanted. When he returned home after the second day of protests, they did. Instead of arresting him, though, they took him to a meeting room in the local police station. Four men were waiting—the precinct police commander, a security official from Liaotie, and two city officials—and they made an unusual request. They wanted Xiao to take a vacation in Yunnan Province, on the other side of the country. They had already purchased plane tickets for him and his family, and they put them on the table in front of him.

"As long you take the trip and forget about Yao, we'll let bygones be bygones," one of the officials said. "If you're short of money, that's easy to take care of, too."

Xiao told the men his conscience wouldn't let him enjoy a vacation while Yao was in prison. "If you want to find someone else, fine, but I can't," he said.

The official gave him another chance. "We're going to squash you if you don't go. This is the last time we try to change your mind."

Xiao knew that his family didn't support what he had been doing and wanted him to stop. He knew that it would be tough for them to make ends meet if he were arrested. But he stood firm. The entire conversation at the police station lasted less than ten minutes.

It was cold and raining the next morning, and only a few thousand workers showed up for the protest. As they demonstrated outside city hall, a paramilitary police commander used a loudspeaker to declare a curfew under martial law and order them to disperse. Hundreds of armed officers suddenly moved in and split the workers into two groups. Xiao and Pang were in the smaller one. As they marched home, plainclothes officers grabbed Xiao and stuffed him in a car before the workers could react. The police had a tougher time getting Pang. The workers formed a wall around him, trying to protect him, but the police surrounded the group and slowly tightened the circle, picking up workers and tossing them aside like garbage. As the injuries mounted, Pang offered to just turn himself in.

THE DAY AFTER the arrests, the government announced a concession: it would investigate the charges of corruption and begin distributing half of the back pay owed the Liaotie workers. At the same time,

though, it warned that "a tiny minority of people with ulterior motives" would be held responsible for the demonstrations. The Liaotie
workers' movement was at another crossroads. With Xiao, Yao, and
Pang in prison, a second tier of worker organizers was supposed to
take the lead and organize protests to get them out. But it never did.

One of the men who failed to rise to the occasion was Chen Dianfan, the worker who had proposed that the protesters carry the Mao
portrait. A stocky Liaotie employee in his sixties, he had worked
alongside Xiao, Yao, and Pang since the first days of the protests, and
he was considered one of the most enthusiastic and reliable of the labor
organizers. But after the arrests, he disappeared. Months later, workers told me they believed Chen had been paid off by police. He landed
a comfortable job in the cafeteria of one of the Liaotie plants, at a time
when men half his age were struggling to find work and other labor
activists had been blacklisted. Workers treated him as a pariah. Faced
with the prospect of abandoning his family and going to prison, or living with the shame of abandoning his friends and fellow workers, he
appeared to have chosen the latter.

Several months after the protests, I called Chen and tried to arrange an interview with him, but he said that his phone was tapped
and that he couldn't meet me in person because he was under police
surveillance. When I asked if it was true that police had paid him off,
he replied, "I can't answer your questions." Before hanging up, though,
he said he still supported Xiao, Yao, and Pang, but was too frightened
to continue with the protests. "They were candid and straightforward
men, and all they wanted was welfare payments and better treatment
for our workers. They were treated unjustly," he said. "But you have to
understand, I came under intense pressure from above after they were
arrested. I was told I would be sent to prison if I dared do anything
similar."

There were more protests in the weeks and months following the
arrests in Liaoyang, many of them led by Yao's daughter, who succeeded in keeping the case alive in the international news for a while.
But the movement gradually petered out as police moved aggressively
to divide and intimidate the remaining labor leaders. Many of the
workers went into hiding, and some burned their copies of Pang's letters, worried that they might be used as evidence against them. Eventually, police made a list of worker leaders, and visited them one by

one. In each meeting, they made a similar offer: spy on your comrades for us, and your financial problems will go away. The workers I met all told me they refused, but the damage was done. The police had sowed mistrust and mutual suspicion. "For a while, we were united, but there's no worker solidarity now," one of the protest leaders told me. "We don't trust each other. And we probably shouldn't."

As police targeted the worker leaders, the government also tried to assuage the deeper anger that drove the protests. Over the course of a year, it arranged to pay the Liaotie workers much but not all of what they were owed. The party also decided to sacrifice and make an example of Fan Yicheng and seven other factory officials. State media reported that investigators discovered a hundred million yuan unaccounted for at Liaotie, or about $12.5 million, less than half of what the workers alleged had actually disappeared. Fan was convicted of smuggling and fraudulent dereliction of duty and sentenced to thirteen years in prison; three other managers also received jail time. The provincial governor who approved the Liaotie bankruptcy was later implicated in a bribery case and imprisoned. But Gong Shangwu, the party official who was accused of collusion with Fan and bragged about the absence of unemployment in Liaoyang, escaped punishment.

Prosecutors tried Yao and Xiao on charges of subversion in the winter of 2003, after a long delay in which officials made contradictory claims about what crimes the men had committed. In the end, the government settled on an allegation that Yao had joined the China Democracy Party after all, and that Xiao was one of his accomplices. Over the objections of international labor and human rights groups, Yao was sentenced to seven years in prison and Xiao to four years. For a while, the two men spent time in the same prison as Fan Yicheng. Pang was released before trial and died of cancer a few years later.

The party never again faced a threat from laid-off state workers as serious as the Liaoyang labor movement. In the following years, the government finished privatizing the bulk of state industry, shrinking the number of workers in the sector to what it considered a sustainable level. At the same time, it succeeded in riding out a wave of mass layoffs and preventing a national labor movement from emerging despite widespread worker frustration. In effect, the party navigated one of the most difficult political challenges in the transition to a market economy, one that has often tripped up other socialist governments. Key to its success was its tight control of the media, which prevented news of labor protests from spreading from city to city. But also critical was its deft touch at containing unrest, its readiness to take a hard line or offer concessions depending on the circumstances. Party leaders looked the other way and let managers and local officials plunder state industries, providing the incentive that kept privatization from stalling in the bureaucracy. They kept workers divided and distracted by carefully distributing minimal welfare payments. When protests presented a threat, the party moved quickly to intimidate workers by arresting their most outspoken representatives. And if that wasn't enough, it sought to calm the public by arresting a few of its own.

In the years after the Liaoyang demonstrations, the party leadership boosted investment in the rust-belt provinces and set aside more money for welfare payments to laid-off workers across the country. Some workers have managed to adapt to the market economy and prosper. But many, especially in the older generation, continue to live in poverty and remain bitter about how the state has treated them. In Liaoyang, unemployment seems to have fallen somewhat, but the divide between rich and poor is even more obvious, and residents continue to complain about work conditions and corruption. The daughter-in-law of a senior city official is said to have made a fortune with real estate from the Liaotie bankruptcy. And painted on the side of one of the Liaotie factories that has resumed production is a new slogan: "Work hard today, or you'll be working hard looking for a job tomorrow."

When I last saw Xiao, he told me he never regretted turning down the government's final offer to him. "How could I have faced the workers and my neighbors if I had taken the vacation?" he said. "Anyway, I didn't do this for personal gain. I always knew there were risks." Four years of prison had been hard on him and his family, but he remained unbowed. He said he was still pushing for Yao's release and willing to fight for workers' rights. At the same time, though, he seemed torn about what his sacrifice had achieved. "Some people say we failed because we were imprisoned," he said, "but I think we succeeded." He mentioned the payments to the workers at Liaotie, and the increased welfare benefits for laid-off workers nationally. "This is the result of our struggle," he said.

But as we continued to talk, Xiao belittled the payments, saying they helped the government put off demands for more fundamental change, such as the right of workers to organize. "It's nothing but a way to shut workers up," he said. "The workers didn't see their long-term interests. They were paid once, and that was it."

So the party won? I asked. "The party was very successful," he replied.

THE RICH LADY

When the bulldozer pulled up to his house—the house he built brick by brick with his sons, on land his father bought with thirty-six bolts of cloth from a middleman in an old Beijing teahouse—Liu Shiru was standing a good distance away, hiding behind the throng that had gathered to watch the demolition, and trying to avoid being spotted by his brother. It was a cold morning in the winter of 2000, and Liu shivered in a thick cotton coat as he studied the crowd. There were a few city officials, some men from the real estate company, a group of construction workers, and a handful of police officers. Several of his neighbors had bundled up in warm clothes and were also standing outside, but most residents had already packed up and moved out of the neighborhood. Liu's house was one of the last on the street, and by day's end, he knew, it would be gone, too.

Liu was a large, pear-shaped man, not yet fifty years old but almost bald, with only a thin, buzz-cut crop of graying hair. He worked as a salesman at a struggling electrical equipment factory, and he knew he would never be able to afford another home like the one he was about to lose. From the street, it looked like a small, simple structure, with no more than a room or two on each of two floors. But tucked behind the building was a traditional courtyard, with an apple tree and a

Chen Lihua

grapevine trellis and extra rooms on the other side. The location of the house was what made it especially valuable. It sat in the heart of central Beijing, not far from the glitzy Wangfujing shopping district, on a quiet lane steeped in history. The street was a narrow alleyway known as a *hutong*, a Mongolian word imported into Chinese when Kublai Khan rebuilt the city and made it his capital. Liu's particular *hutong* was named Suianbo, after a Ming Dynasty nobleman who lived there in the fourteenth century. More recent, distinguished party and military officials occupied some of the houses on Suianbo Hutong. One of them, Deng Tuo, a prominent writer and a former editor of the *People's Daily*, committed suicide in his courtyard at the start of the Cultural Revolution.

Liu's father purchased the original house at No. 10 Suianbo Hutong a year before the Communists came to power. He was an illiterate repairman at a local hospital who had managed to build a business making medical instruments, and the house was the result of years of sweat and savings. The family moved in soon after Liu, the youngest of five sons, was born. The early years there were difficult. Despite his humble background, Liu's father was persecuted as a capitalist and forced to turn over his business to the state. But Liu clung to more pleasant memories of growing up in the *hutong*—the meals his mother prepared on the festival days, the bag of sand he tied to the branch of a mulberry tree in the courtyard to play at boxing, the warmth of family life before his family fell apart. Liu's brothers got married in the house and moved into different rooms around the courtyard to raise their own children, the oldest of them not much younger than Liu himself. A lifetime later, after his brothers stopped speaking to him, Liu would smile as he recalled how he and his nephews and nieces used to chase one another around, clambering up trees and onto the tiled roofs of the buildings, filling the courtyard with laughter.

The idyll of Liu's childhood ended when the Cultural Revolution began. In the summer of 1966, the party labeled homeowners members of the capitalist class and ordered them to turn in their property deeds to the government. Liu's parents were frightened, and his brothers were busy at their work units, so at age seventeen, Liu submitted the certificates himself. The family began paying the government rent, and the government assigned two other families to live in the house with them. Two of Liu's brothers were forced to move out, and after graduating from high school, Liu was sent away, too. Like many his age, he was sent to the countryside, where he spent the next eight years doing farmwork. As the Cultural Revolution ended, he was assigned a job at a state coal mine. It was not until late 1989, more than two decades after he left, that Liu was allowed to move back to Beijing. By then, everything had changed. His father had passed away, and his mother had had a falling-out with his brothers. The government returned the deed to No. 10 Suianbo Hutong to the family, but there were squabbles over the property. Liu took his mother's side in the family disputes, and before she passed away a few months later, she bequeathed the house to him. Though relations were strained, one of Liu's brothers continued living in rooms on the courtyard's south side, while Liu took over the rooms on the north side with his wife and three sons.

A few years later, Liu and his sons rebuilt the north building, adding a second floor. The original building had been falling apart, but there was another reason for the renovation. Liu was thinking of his two eldest sons, then in high school, and their marriage prospects. Many parents wouldn't let their daughters marry anyone without an apartment. But there was a severe shortage of housing in Beijing, and an affordable place to live, especially near the center of the city, was almost impossible to find. Liu wanted to make sure there was enough room for his sons to stay in the family courtyard after they married. They could raise his grandchildren there, he thought, and maybe the laughter would return to No. 10 Suianbo Hutong.

Liu knew there could be a hitch in his plans. Beijing was changing quickly, and old *hutong* neighborhoods across the city were being demolished to make way for modern office towers, high-end shopping malls, and luxury apartment buildings. Such redevelopment lifted the value of prime downtown real estate. But for homeowners like Liu, that could be a curse as much as a blessing. Rising property prices attracted developers, and they could pay good money for valuable land. Much more often, though, they found a way to take it on the cheap. A year after Liu finished renovating his home, the *hutong* where his sister-in-law lived was slated for demolition to make way for a new complex of office buildings called Financial Street. She and other residents who owned houses in the construction zone never received an offer to buy their properties. Instead they were just evicted and assigned to new apartments on the outskirts of the city worth a fraction of their original homes. Altogether, some four thousand houses were destroyed and more than twelve thousand people were relocated. Liu followed the situation closely, and he worried the same thing might happen to his neighborhood.

Those fears intensified in the fall of 2000 as rumors spread that a massive redevelopment project had been proposed for Suianbo and other nearby *hutong*s. Then, on a cool evening in late October as Liu was watching television, he heard a commotion in the alleyway and stepped out in his nightshirt to see what was going on. His neighbors filled the street, crowding around notices printed on white paper that had been pasted on the walls. Liu made his way to the front of a group gathered around one of the notices. "A Letter to Residents to be Relocated after Demolition," it said at the top, and below was a long body of text that began:

> The Jinbao Avenue Municipal Redevelopment Project Headquarters of the Dongcheng District People's Government of Beijing, as approved by Document No. 0157-2000 of the Beijing Planning Bureau, is carrying out demolition and relocation on Jinbao Avenue and in redevelopment areas on both sides of the street. The construction of Jinbao Avenue and redevelopment of areas on both sides of the street is an important municipal project. This project is key to easing the strained traffic in the Wangfujing shopping area and improving city redevelopment conditions. It is a positive measure that will make the economy of Dongcheng District prosper, and a concrete realization of support for Beijing's application to host the Olympics.

Liu was confused at first, because there was no street named Jinbao Avenue in their neighborhood. But as he continued reading, he realized the city had approved a plan to carve a new boulevard through the community, extending about a half mile from the Wangfujing shopping area to the city's central business district. The letter listed more than two hundred residences—including every house on Suianbo Hutong—that would be demolished to make way for the road and for unspecified new projects alongside it. Demolition work was scheduled to begin the next day and to be completed within a month.

Liu and his neighbors stood on the street, dumbfounded and angry.

Some had lived on the *hutong* all their lives, and now they were being given just a few weeks to move out. The letter said residents could collect the equivalent of about eight hundred dollars in compensation for each square meter of their homes, plus a five-hundred-dollar bonus if they moved out quickly. But there was no distinction drawn between tenants of state-owned housing on the street and residents like Liu who owned their homes. There was no attempt to assess the market value of their property, and no offer to negotiate terms for a sale. Residents stood on the alleyway fuming and cursing until well past 2 A.M. that night. Some tore down the notices in anger. Others vowed to fight the project.

After what happened to his sister-in-law, Liu was determined to protect his property. He owned the house, and if developers wanted to tear it down, they would have to pay a fair price for it. As far as he was concerned, the compensation offer outlined in the letter was nowhere near a fair price. He knew that apartments in downtown Beijing were selling for more than $2,500 per square meter, while the going rate for office space was even higher. His house occupied seventy square meters of land, and if developers built a high-rise over it, the size of the fortune they could make would be multiplied by the number of floors they were given permission to build. So Liu ignored the letter, stayed put, and waited. After a few weeks, when men from the real estate development company finally called on him, Liu told them he objected to the notices they had posted. They asked what he wanted, and Liu told them he wanted them to acknowledge that he owned the house. He refused even to discuss a price until they recognized that simple fact, but they demurred. The conversation lasted only a few minutes.

A few weeks later, the men returned with an offer. They said the developer was willing to treat Liu's family as a hardship case and give him extra money for relocating—about sixty thousand yuan for each member of the household, for a total of three hundred thousand yuan, or about $37,500. But the men wouldn't acknowledge that Liu owned the house, and Liu rejected the offer immediately. It was a large sum of cash, but barely enough to buy an apartment on the outskirts of the city, and nowhere near the market value of his land. In any case, Liu told the men, it wasn't about the money. It was about respecting his rights, about proper procedures. He wanted them to understand that he was not going to roll over. It was his house, and if they wanted it, he said, they should hire someone to conduct an independent appraisal and pay him what it was worth. The conversation was again a brief one.

As the weeks passed, Liu turned out to be the most stubborn of the residents on Suianbo Hutong. His brother wanted him to sell, but Liu refused. At the same time, one after another, his neighbors struck deals with the developer, collected compensation, and moved out. They saw it was the smart thing to do, given that the government had already endorsed the developer's plan and labeled it "an important municipal project." It didn't matter if people owned their houses, or how long they had lived on the street. If the developer had the government's support, it was going to get its way. You could grumble, and you could curse, but in the end, you would have to move. One by one, Liu's neighbors concluded that all they could really do was try to maximize what they got in return. Liu, however, took another approach. He kept insisting that the developer admit he owned the house, a concession that would improve his negotiating leverage and the strength of any lawsuit he might file—and that the developer was unlikely to make. It seemed foolish and reckless, and when I asked him later why he had been so persistent, Liu couldn't really explain what motivated him. "I didn't care about the money," he told me. "It was just a matter of principle."

By early December, the developer had reached agreements with everyone on the street except Liu, and the company applied to the government for permission to forcibly evict him. The government agreed, and a few days before the eviction was to occur, Liu was summoned to a meeting at a temporary office that the developer had set up in one of the courtyard houses in the neighborhood. Two officials from the Dongcheng District's housing bureau sat on the edge of a table, and motioned for Liu to take a seat in front of them. There was no small talk. The men told Liu he had to move. The Jinbao Avenue project had the support of the state, they said, and if he tried to fight it, he would lose. He should turn over his deed, they said, and accept the developer's compensation offer of three hundred thousand yuan. Otherwise, they said, his house would be demolished and he would get nothing. Liu tried to argue with them, but got nowhere. The officials warned Liu that this was his last chance. Liu refused to give in and skulked out.

As he left the office, Liu saw his brother go in. His brother wanted to accept the compensation money and move out, but the developer had refused to pay him. The brother was a tenant on the street like any other, but the developer said he wouldn't get paid until Liu turned over the deed to the property. It was an attempt to split the family, a common tactic used by developers against those holding out, and it worked. That night, as Liu was taking a walk on the *hutong*, his brother and several other men jumped him. Liu cried for help and a police officer appeared, but instead of breaking up the fight, the officer held him in place as the others beat him. Liu lost a tooth in the fight before breaking free and running away. After the assault, Liu stayed away from his house, living with his mother-in-law instead. His two older sons remained at home, though, and they told him when his brother hired a crew of workers and tore down the rooms on the south side of the courtyard. They also told him that his brother was still looking for him, that he had hired thugs and was threatening to pummel him again and force him to turn over the deed. Liu's relationship with his brother had been strained for years, but he never imagined it would come to this.

As he stood in the street on the morning of the demolition, Liu scanned the crowd warily. His brother knew him well enough to know that he would return to watch the demolition, that he needed to see the fight to the end. Liu was sure his brother was somewhere nearby, and he didn't want trouble. Standing at the front of the crowd were his wife, his sons, and his sister-in-law. One of the city officials went up to them, said something, and then shook hands with his wife. Liu realized that the man had just formally ordered them out of the house, and that it all would soon be over.

A crew of workers filed past his family into his home and began loading their belongings onto trucks that were parked outside. A few men were videotaping the proceedings, and the police officers escorted his family away from the house. After the furniture was removed, someone climbed into the bulldozer and started the engine. With a quiet rumble, it moved forward and knocked down one wall, then another, and soon all that was left was a pile of rubble. It happened much faster than Liu expected. As the crowd began to disperse, he stood staring at the cloud of dust that was once his family's house. He felt furious, depressed, helpless, and then numb.

Liu knew the name of the real estate company that was building the Jinbao Avenue project. But it was not until later—after he was relocated into a slum on the outskirts of the city, after plans were announced to build a luxury hotel on the site of his home, after he filed the lawsuits that went nowhere—that he learned who ran the company. Her name was Chen Lihua, and she was the richest woman in China.

WHEN THE WORKERS broke ground on the Jinbao Avenue project, Chen Lihua was already something of a legend in Beijing. Heavyset, with big glasses and a bad perm, she looked like a frumpy aunt who had won the lottery, and residents casually referred to her as the *fupo*, or the Rich Lady. At fifty-nine, she presided over a vast real estate empire, held prominent positions on government advisory bodies, and lived in a ten-story mansion behind a museum she built on the city's east side. She was one of only two women to make *Forbes* magazine's list of China's richest people in 2001, ranking sixth with assets of more than $550 million. State media fawned over her rags-to-riches story and charitable activities, and the public tittered over her marriage to a television star ten years younger than her. Her publicists seemed to work overtime planting sappy features about the couple's romance in the press, perhaps to counter the gossip that he had married her for the money. Almost every time I mentioned Chen's name in conversation, people brought up her marriage first and discussed her wealth later. But it was her wealth, and how she acquired it, that interested me.

There is an assumption in the West that the growing ranks of private entrepreneurs in China represent a force for democratic change in the country. These businesspeople, like businesspeople around the world, prefer a political environment conducive to commerce, and a democratic system serves their interests better than an authoritarian one, or so the argument goes. They favor the predictability of the rule of law over the arbitrary rule of party bosses. They want impartial courts that can enforce contracts, resolve disputes, and protect private property rights. They are frustrated with the government's control of the banks, with their inability to influence economic policy, with the unfair advantages that party officials enjoy in the market.

Some of China's new capitalists fit this description. In 2003, for example, a prominent agricultural tycoon named Sun Dawu was jailed for five months after speaking out against the party. But those counting on the capitalists to lead the charge for democratization in China are likely to be disappointed. China's emerging business elite is a diverse and disparate bunch, and for every entrepreneur who would embrace political reform, there are others who support and depend on the authoritarian system, who believe in one-party rule and owe their success to it. Chen Lihua fits in this latter category, and her story is a reminder that those with the most wealth—and thus the most resources to devote either to maintaining the status quo or promoting change—are also the most likely to be in bed with the party.

Chen's climb into the ranks of the richest of the rich was an exaggerated illustration of how capitalism often worked in China. After living through decades of political turmoil, ambitious men and women like her saw the transition from socialism to capitalism as a once-in-a-lifetime opportunity to make a fortune. New markets were opening every day in the 1980s and '90s as the old planned economy was dismantled, and these entrepreneurs realized that the trick was getting access to these markets first—by obtaining licenses and permits, or special privileges such as the right to buy commodities at subsidized prices, to purchase the assets of a failing state factory, or to build on a prime piece of real estate. The most successful businesspeople, many of them former officials or the children of officials, understood that the best way to secure such advantages was by winning the favor of party bureaucrats. What robber barons like Chen did wasn't necessarily illegal. They bent the rules at a time when the rules were changing quickly, and the Chinese called their crimes "original sins." When the political winds shifted, and their patrons in the party fell from power, some of these new millionaires were prosecuted and ended up in prison on corruption charges. Others, like Chen, managed to outlast the politicians.

Chen Lihua's story has been told many times in the state media, but these tellings are riddled with embellishments and omissions. She is often portrayed as a descendant of Manchu nobility from the Qing Dynasty, or even a distant relative of the last emperor, and she is said to have grown up near the grounds of the Summer Palace. But there is a whiff of mythmaking in these accounts, and Chen says her family destroyed the documents proving her bloodline during the Cultural Revolution to escape persecution, making it impossible to confirm her claim to nobility. Even if true, though, the circumstances of Chen's childhood and early life remain a mystery. The Qing court fell in 1911, three decades before she was born, and none of the published stories about her make any mention of what her parents did after the fall of the dynasty, or how they made a living after the Communists took power. When I first met Chen and asked about this, she repeated that her father had been a Manchu nobleman, and when I pressed her further, she said only that he had an "ordinary job" and declined to elaborate.

There is little doubt, however, that Chen struggled to make ends meet and suffered during the Cultural Revolution because of her family background. She was in her twenties at the time, a young mother who worked as a seamstress and was married to a civil servant. A neighbor told me that Red Guards paraded her through the streets with a placard vilifying her as a woman of loose morals, a common charge leveled against female targets of the political campaigns. None of this appears in the official accounts of Chen's life. Instead, when Chen is quoted talking about the Cultural Revolution, she is usually telling a story about her family's antique furniture. Red Guards seized or destroyed most of it, but she rescued a large, intricate wardrobe made of precious red sandalwood, and she dismantled it and buried it near a pigsty in the countryside. A decade later, after the end of the Cultural Revolution, she returned to the sty, dug up the wardrobe, and reassembled it. To her surprise, it remained in perfect condition. It was then, the story goes, that Chen developed a passion for sandalwood and embarked on her first business venture, running a workshop that restored antique furniture.

The authorized accounts of Chen's life are vague about how she made her first fortune. In the late 1970s and early '80s, she is said to have traveled several times to Southeast Asia in search of supplies of sandalwood, which derives from a rare and endangered species of tree. In several state media reports, she presents herself as a kind of swashbuckling female Indiana Jones, traveling through jungles on donkeys, getting the better of snakes, surviving a vicious attack by poisonous bees. But there are glaring inconsistencies among the reports, as if Chen were trying out different versions of her life story to see which she liked best. In the early 1980s, Chen somehow succeeded in immigrating to and establishing residency in Hong Kong. There are vague references in state media to Chen engaging in "international trade" and making money on a real estate deal there, but no details, and then the official story fast-forwards to 1988, when she returned to Beijing a wealthy woman. At some point along the way, she divorced her first husband, and in 1990 she married the television star.

Behind these ambiguous official accounts, though, was the tale of a sharp businesswoman who recognized early the quickest way to strike it rich in China's freewheeling, transitional economy—ingratiating oneself with party officials. Not long after the Cultural Revolution, according to the explanation I heard most often from people who knew her then, Chen befriended a neighbor who was a party official, and she took care of his daughter when the government sent him to work in Hong Kong. She used that first relationship to move to Hong Kong herself, and later to build a network of connections with increasingly higher-ranked party bureaucrats in Beijing. How she maneuvered herself into such good standing with the party apparatus remains one of the mysteries of her success, but by the late 1980s she had good enough connections to gain access to a state furniture factory on the city's south side that had a warehouse full of antique furniture seized by Red Guards during the Cultural Revolution. According to employees at the factory, Chen visited regularly and was allowed to purchase antiques at a huge discount. These were valuable Qing and Ming dynasty pieces, many of them banned from export under Chinese laws that designated them national treasures. But the factory workers said Chen used her party ties and arranged for much of what she purchased to be exported to Hong Kong. On her visits, the workers said, Chen was always generous with gifts for the warehouse employees, and she once purchased a Soviet-made car for the factory manager. A few years later, the manager was imprisoned on corruption charges. Chen faced no charges. Investigators told workers that she enjoyed the protection of senior party officials.

Chen turned to real estate in the late 1980s, but her inaugural project wasn't an apartment complex, or an office building, or a shopping mall. Instead, she built a private club—the first of its kind in Beijing— and then used it to woo the capital's political and business elite. The ten-story $46 million building boasted fine restaurants, plush lounges with sandalwood furniture, tennis and squash courts, a swimming pool, even a bowling alley, and when it opened in 1995 it quickly became the venue of choice for the city's new rich to hobnob with the party's power brokers. Chen built the Chang'an Club not far from Tiananmen Square and the Forbidden City, on the Avenue of Eternal Peace, the boulevard that runs through the heart of Beijing. The state still dominated the real estate industry at the time, and only the most connected private developers could secure the right to build on such a coveted parcel of government land. When I asked her about the project, Chen told me she spent six years lobbying officials for permission to begin construction, and she hinted at her relationship with city leaders. After one sleepless night worrying about her investment, she recalled, she walked to the site at 2 A.M., picked up a shovel, and began breaking the ground herself. "It was a chilly evening, with a strong wind," she said. "Someone reported me to Vice Mayor Zhang Baifa, and he rushed to the site. When he saw what I was doing, he was worried about me, and pleaded with me to give him the shovel and go inside. He was moved, and he said he would take care of the permits."

The club was a shrewd investment. Even before it was built, Chen recalled, she recognized its potential as "a gold mine." Nearly two decades after Mao's death, the private sector was flourishing and a new class of businessmen had emerged, pragmatic wheeler-dealers who understood the value of access to party officials and were not shy about spending money to impress them. To them, the Chang'an Club was the perfect place to curry favor with a party cadre and strike a deal, and they paid handsomely to use it. But if the club generated a good income for Chen, that was nothing compared with the intangible benefits that flowed from her status as the proprietor. The club gave her a stage to sell herself, an excuse to meet everyone who came in, a chance to hear about every deal going down, a platform to court even the most senior of party officials. It put her closer to the center of the action than any former seamstress might have imagined possible. The vice mayor may have helped her build the club, but Chen was soon linked to Politburo members such as the party chief of Beijing, Chen Xitong, and even a member of the all-powerful Politburo Standing Committee, Li Ruihuan, who was photographed playing tennis at the club with the prime minister of Singapore.

Chen put the headquarters of her company, the Fu Wah International Group, on an upper floor of the Chang'an Club. She served as the chairman of the board, her son as the chief executive officer and her daughter as a board member. In 1999, the company opened its first residential complex, the luxury Lee Garden Service Apartments. Beijing is divided into sixteen districts, each with its own government, and both the club and the apartments were built in Dongcheng District, the downtown area east of Tiananmen Square with a population of more than half a million. Chen cultivated particularly close relationships with the officials in Dongcheng. Some even resigned and joined her company. Such ties at the local level of the party bureaucracy were as important to Chen's success as her access to senior party leaders, and they were critical to her most ambitious project, Jinbao Avenue, which also ran through Dongcheng District. Chen couldn't just pick up her phone and call a Politburo member, but she didn't need to. As long as lower-level officials knew she had clout at the top, she could usually count on getting her way.

On occasion, though, Chen's ventures ran into obstacles. In 2004, as her company was clearing another old neighborhood in Dongcheng District to make way for a new development, a city agency refused to transfer the land-use rights to her. Residents had been complaining about the demolition of their homes, their case had made headlines in the foreign media, and someone in the bureaucracy decided it would be wise to hold off on the project, at least temporarily. Chen wrote to Li Ruihuan, her contact who had served on the Politburo Standing Committee and was thus one of the most powerful men in the country. A few years later, I saw a copy of the letter. It was handwritten on plain white paper, and instead of letterhead, Chen wrote her company's name at the top of the page. The text itself was fairly formal, beginning with an expression of gratitude for Li's support and help over the years, then laying out Chen's complaint in a businesslike tone. She emphasized that she had followed all the procedures and met all the regulations for the land transfer to be approved, and presented the decision to delay the transfer as inexplicable:

Chairman Li, why did this happen? We really cannot understand. After several years of planning, we have invested hundreds of millions of yuan in the Lishan Plaza project . . . spending as much as 60 million yuan on resettlement compensation alone. All the preliminary procedures have been completed. We obtained the approval of the various departments and the project was announced as legitimate early on. Why not conduct the land transfer for us according to regulations? This is also very puzzling. Please find attached the documents regarding the preliminary procedures. This is overwhelmingly urgent. I hope you will please take time from your busy schedule to pay attention to this matter and give instructions to the relevant Beijing departments to resolve it.

The letter had an immediate impact. On the same day she sent the letter, Li forwarded it to his successor on the Politburo Standing Committee with a note, "Comrade Jia Qinglin, please examine and coordinate." Three weeks later, Jia passed the letter on to the mayor of Beijing with an another instruction, "Comrade Qishan, please review and study." The next day, the mayor, Wang Qishan, added his own note and sent the letter to a deputy mayor, "Zhihua, please review and handle." The deputy mayor, Liu Zhihua—a man who would be arrested three years later on Olympics-related corruption charges—then forwarded the letter to another subordinate, "Comrade Jiasheng, please review and handle." Little more than a month after Chen sent the letter, the land transfer was approved and construction began on yet another project that would reshape the city while making her an even wealthier woman.

BEIJING WAS ONCE a marvel of urban design. Positioned on the northern tip of the north China plains, it first served as the national capital nearly one thousand years ago during the Jin Dynasty. But it wasn't until Mongol invaders razed the city in the thirteenth century and Kublai Khan rebuilt it as his capital that the distinctive *hutong*s first appeared. Then, during the Ming Dynasty, the city took its modern shape, with an immense wall surrounding a twenty-five-square-mile expanse of streets, lakes, parks, and temples. For a time it may have been the largest city in the world, with the emperor's palace, the Forbidden City, at the very center. Power and status emanated from the palace along lanes laid out in a nearly symmetrical grid, with the aristocratic elite living closest to the palace, merchants and artisans occupying residences farther out, and most commoners consigned to neighborhoods outside the walls. The majestic design gave the city its form, but it was the *hutong*s that defined life in old Beijing. The quiet alleyways, no more than thirty feet wide and lined with walled court-yard residences, fostered a traditional sense of community, and they survived hundreds of years, outlasting the Ming emperors, their Qing successors, and the short-lived Republican government.

When the Communists seized power in 1949, a new era of urban planning began. The Soviets advised the government to abandon Beijing's "feudal" past, and transform the city into a modern indus-trial capital, with grand boulevards and huge state factories. Some in-tellectuals objected, urging the party to preserve the city wall and the neighborhoods inside, but Mao had little use for the architectural leg-acies of imperial rule. The city wall was torn down in the 1950s, and in the 1960s all but a few of the city's massive gates were destroyed, too. Hundreds of temples were closed, demolished, or converted into offices and factories. The plaza south of the Forbidden City was ex-panded and became Tiananmen Square, the largest city square in the world, flanked on both sides by imposing socialist edifices, the Great Hall of the People, and a museum of revolutionary history. Mao moved the party's headquarters into an imperial compound nearby, and government agencies occupied many of the residences that had once been home to the elite. Over the decades, the city's population mushroomed as outsiders were brought in to work in new factories, but because Mao's production-obsessed economic planners gave hous-ing short shrift, serious overcrowding resulted. Conditions deterio-rated as courtyard houses originally built for one family were subdivided to accommodate as many as a dozen households. For the most part, however, the *hutong*s remained.

It was only after Mao's death that old Beijing was destroyed and replaced with today's congested sprawl of concrete, steel, and glass. Market reforms fueled the frenzy of destruction and construction, but what really made the city's transformation possible was the party's de-cision to strip homeowners of their property rights. In 1982, the state declared for the first time that it owned all urban land, but it quickly backtracked by letting people keep land-use rights. The distinction opened the door to a genuine real estate market, and because of the chronic housing shortages in Beijing and other cities, land values sky-rocketed. Developers sensed a chance to strike it rich. If they could persuade party bureaucrats to sell them land-use rights at a steep discount instead of at market prices, they could make a killing.

More often than not, local officials found a reason to cooperate. Sometimes it was a hefty bribe. Sometimes it was a promise by the developer to build roads, or a municipal building, or apartments for city employees. Sometimes it was just a desire to expedite a project that would look good on their records and help them win promotions. But the most important reason the bureaucrats struck these deals with developers was the desire to privatize the difficult job of evicting and uprooting entire communities. In Beijing, the government held the rights to about two-thirds of the land in the city's central districts. Private homeowners held the rights to the rest. Any major project would be complicated by two tasks—the payment of compensation to residents in public housing who were being evicted despite the socialist promise of an affordable home, and the acquisition of land rights from private homeowners. By inviting developers to step in, local officials passed these burdens on to them.

In the early years of the real estate boom, one industry insider told me, developers could buy land-use rights in central Beijing from the government for about 10 percent of the final value of the projects that they planned to build. The biggest budget outlay for these projects was not the cost of construction but the expense of evicting residents and demolishing their homes. Naturally, developers sought to boost profits by paying the residents they evicted as little as possible in compensation. Private homeowners presented the biggest problem, because they could demand a market price or even refuse to sell. In reality, though, local officials often approved projects and sold land-use rights to developers without going through the trouble of buying or seizing them from homeowners first. Officials then conspired with developers to pressure owners to give up their land. Developers often hired thugs to intimidate residents while police looked the other way, and local authorities sometimes cut off electricity, water, and heat to the holdouts. If necessary, the government intervened on behalf of developers and ordered a forced eviction on questionable legal grounds. Altogether, between 1991 and 2003, more than a half million families in Beijing were evicted by developers. One Chinese scholar estimated that during the 1990s, private homeowners in Beijing lost at least $4.5 billion in land, and tenants of public housing were cheated out of more than $7 billion in compensation that should have been paid them under government regulations. At the same time, if the city had auctioned off land at market prices instead of making sweetheart deals with developers, it could have made at least $5.5 billion more in revenue. Altogether, developers and local officials in Beijing fleeced the public of more than $17 billion in the 1990s—the equivalent of nearly all the city's economic output in 1995.

Such brazen collusion between real estate companies and party officials to deprive homeowners of their property did not go unchallenged. Tens of thousands of residents filed lawsuits in Beijing against the city government and developers, and street protests over evictions became a common occurrence. But the party instructed the courts to dismiss the lawsuits and used police to contain and repress the demonstrations. Sometimes the property clashes had fatal consequences. In February 2006, five security guards employed by a developer beat to death a resident who refused to give up his home in a neighborhood slated to be torn down for a new apartment complex. The same month, another group of thugs attacked the owners of a courtyard house on a doomed *hutong* in western Beijing, killing an elderly woman.

Protests against mass evictions have taken place in almost every major city in China. In Xian, a group of nuns were beaten when they tried to stop developers from seizing a piece of church property. In Nanjing, a desperate homeowner poured gasoline over his body and lit himself on fire inside the eviction office that a developer had set up in his neighborhood. The more stunning the cityscape, the more likely that it was built by developers and party officials who ran roughshod over the rights of ordinary residents. This was the dirty little secret behind the glittering new office towers and apartment buildings that transformed China's big cities. The evictions and demolitions in Beijing set the tone for the nation, but the worst violations occurred in Shanghai, where party leaders and developers built a new skyline that became the defining image of China's booming economy. Shanghai likes to present itself as the most modern of China's cities, but in fact, the authoritarian impulse among officials there is stronger than in much of the rest of the country. The newspapers are on a tighter leash, and the security apparatus is more menacing. More than a million families were evicted in the drive to remake the city, and when large numbers tried to resist, city officials crushed their campaign with little regard for legal niceties. Residents were jailed without charges or committed to mental hospitals. The lawyer who took up the cause of the residents, Zheng Enchong, was sentenced to three years in prison in 2003 for sharing information about the fight with a human rights group in New York. At the same time, party authorities tried to defuse public anger by arresting the city's most prominent developer, Zhou Zhengyi, who ranked eleventh on the *Forbes* list of the nation's richest people. In 2006, Zhou's patron, the powerful Shanghai party chief Chen Liangyu, was toppled in a purge as well.

The Jinbao Avenue project was typical of the real estate deals in Beijing and other cities. Chen Lihua's company obtained the land rights on the cheap from the government in 1998, paying about $250 per square meter. In return for the lower price, she agreed to build the new road and a government building for Dongcheng District, and to cover the cost of evicting four thousand to five thousand families, about a third of whom owned their homes. In total, she pledged to invest about $750 million in the project, which would demolish neighborhoods on fifty-five acres of land in the heart of old Beijing and replace them with office towers, a shopping mall, two hotels, a luxury apartment complex, schools, and other facilities. It was the biggest and most ambitious project Chen had ever undertaken. It was also a nearly risk-free venture. Her initial outlay was minimal, because once she obtained the rights to the land, she used it to secure a substantial loan from a state bank. Later, Chen also persuaded local officials to let her raise the height of several of the planned buildings, doubling the floor space of the project—and her potential profits.

In late 2002, two years after her company broke ground on Jinbao Avenue, the new boulevard opened to traffic. The buildings along the avenue were scheduled to be completed before the 2008 Olympic Games. Chen's company still brags about how smoothly and quickly it was able to oust residents of the old neighborhoods and tear down their homes. "It took us twenty-eight days to demolish the houses of 2,100 families," Wang Shouyuan, a former city official whom Chen hired as the general manager of the project, told me. "This was unprecedented at the time. We finished the demolition and relocation work on the street, and it caused a sensation in Beijing. There were no appeals, no negative reaction at all."

I asked Wang how the company was able to persuade so many people to give up their homes so quickly. "For demolition to proceed quickly, it depends on a combination of strength and force," he replied. "Strength means giving enough money. Force means the backing of the government. That's the key."

OF COURSE, WANG was stretching the truth when he said there had been no negative reaction to the Jinbao Avenue project. Liu Shiru was one of several residents in the demolished neighborhoods who tried to fight back. Many others accepted relocation only reluctantly, because they concluded they couldn't win against someone as wealthy and connected as Chen. The most prominent opponent of the project was Hua Xinmin, a well-known cultural preservationist in Beijing. Her grandfather had been the city's chief engineer during the early years of Communist rule, and her father had served as a senior municipal architect and was among those who tried to persuade Mao to protect the old city. The family fled to France during the Cultural Revolution, but Hua returned to Beijing in the 1990s and took up her father's cause, fighting to prevent developers from tearing down historic courtyard residences and other architectural gems. It was a difficult task, and she lost more battles than she won. Her opposition to the Jinbao Avenue project, however, was more personal: she grew up in a house on one of the *hutong*s that would be destroyed.

Hua had spoken eloquently about the importance of preserving Beijing's cultural heritage, but when she began campaigning to save her family home, she made a different case: she complained that developers were violating the property rights of homeowners. It was a more powerful and politically sensitive argument, one that threatened the business model fueling the redevelopment of China's cities and exposed the hypocrisy of the party's pledge to protect private property rights, which it enshrined in the constitution in 2004. Hua's argument also posed a subtle challenge to the party line that individual sacrifices were necessary for the good of society. She pointed out that ordinary people made the sacrifices in these development projects while people with money and power—people such as Chen Lihua—reaped the benefits.

Over the years, Hua had cultivated relationships at many state media outlets, and a magazine once named her one of the nation's most influential intellectuals. But it was one thing for a journalist to write about cultural preservation, and quite another to question the government's commitment to protecting private property rights. Despite Hua's efforts, few in the state media were willing to take on Chen Lihua or the Jinbao Avenue project. Chen, on the other hand, had no problem finding reporters to file puff pieces. She was known to ply journalists with gifts and cash, and generally it was money well spent. The newspapers were full of stories explaining how Jinbao Avenue would ease traffic downtown and stimulate economic growth. As for the demolition of the old *hutong*s, only residents with the sunniest attitudes about having their homes torn down were ever quoted. "The party and the government are improving living conditions for ordinary people, putting the interests of ordinary people first," one said. Meanwhile, Chen was presented as a patriotic, motherly figure who gave generously to residents so they could move out of "old and dilapidated neighborhoods" and find modern new housing. When she visited the demolition zone, one paper claimed, residents unfurled a banner thanking her and expressed "ecstatic" support for "the Olympics and the renovation of the capital."

On occasion, an editor made the mistake of crossing the Rich Lady. In January 2005, a business newspaper in Shanghai published a tough article asking why Chen was allowed to secure state loans with land that other people still owned. Within days, the paper's editor in chief flew to Beijing and apologized to her. Then the paper published a retraction and a new article singing the praises of the Jinbao Avenue project. Other newspapers that carried similarly critical stories were also pressured into printing retractions. Even newspapers in Hong Kong were not beyond Chen's influence. Reporters at several papers, including the English-language *South China Morning Post*, told me their editors ordered them to stop writing about the Jinbao Avenue story. And then there was the case of the newspaper *Ming Pao*. After writing a story about Hua's campaign against Jinbao Avenue, the paper's Beijing correspondent was accosted at a restaurant by the manager of Chen's demolition company, her lawyer, and a city official. It was late in the evening, the reporter told me, but the three insisted that he accompany them to see the Rich Lady. When he declined, the demolition manager, whom the reporter described as a thuggish fellow, threatened to "adopt other measures" if he didn't "eliminate the influ-

ence" of his article in two days. The reporter retreated to the safety of
Hong Kong the next day. The newspaper refused Chen's demands to
disavow his article and when she threatened to sue, it prepared further stories about her. But before they went to print, the reporter told
me, Chen managed to arrange a truce—by getting the movie star
Jackie Chan to put in a good word for her with the paper's editor.

Chen sometimes displayed unusual foresight in protecting her interests. In 2002, as public anger about mass evictions was building
in Beijing, a few newspapers began publishing essays by a lawyer
named Gao Zhisheng, who objected to the demolitions as a violation
of homeowners' property rights. Gao would later emerge as one of the
country's most prominent and outspoken human rights activists,
someone the party would find it necessary to imprison, but at the time,
he was a newcomer in the capital and little known. Chen, however,
seemed to recognize his potential as a troublemaker, and she tried to
do something about it.

Not long before his arrest, Gao told me about his encounter with
her. It was one of those illuminating behind-the-scenes stories that
helped explain the party's success at defusing opposition, and it said
as much about the relationship between the party and the new rich
who were the beneficiaries of its rule as it did about Chen's personal
style and methods. As Gao was building his law practice in the late
1990s, he recalled, a journalist introduced him to a woman who was
looking for a lawyer to represent a businessman in a corruption case.
The woman worked in the party's United Front department, the bureau responsible for forging alliances with influential figures outside
the party, and over time, as he got to know her, Gao began to consider
her a friend. One afternoon in 2002, after he began writing the essays
protesting the mass evictions in Beijing, she called and told him she
wanted to introduce him to a potential client. Gao had already resolved not to represent real estate developers, but by the time he realized he was being taken to meet Chen Lihua, it was too late to cancel.

Chen's mansion is located in a quiet neighborhood on the outskirts
of Beijing, not far from the home of one of Deng Xiaoping's sons. It
looks more like a grand government building than a residence, and it
sits in a walled compound behind the museum she built to display her
collection of sandalwood furniture. When Gao and his friend arrived,
they were ushered into a second-floor conference room, and he was

seated in a carved wooden chair next to the Rich Lady. She greeted him warmly, and they made small talk for a while, chatting about his background and his work. Then Chen told him she belonged to an association of real estate developers, and that they had noticed his essays. No one was afraid of him, she continued, but because the United Front official was a mutual friend, she wanted to offer him some advice. She told him to think of her as a big sister, because she had much more experience in Beijing than him. "You have no idea how deep the water is," she said. "In the real estate business, you can't succeed without a political patron behind you. So you can't touch them. The only result is that they will hurt you."

Chen asked why Gao had moved his family to Beijing from the western province of Xinjiang. "Wasn't it to make a living and earn money?" she said, before quickly promising: "We can give you whatever you need." At the end of the conversation, Chen made a big show of presenting Gao with a gift, an exquisitely carved sandalwood container for holding calligraphy scrolls and paintings. She boasted that the piece was more valuable than similar ones she had given to members of the Politburo Standing Committee. Gao accepted the present, but Chen refused to let him bring it home himself and ordered her employees to load it into her Mercedes, deliver it to his apartment, and place it wherever he instructed. Riding the elevator down with him as he was leaving, Chen reminded Gao again that she and her industry friends were willing to take care of him. "Listen to me," she whispered. "I can even give you real estate." Then, as she walked Gao to the door, Chen engaged in a last bit of flattery, saying that she usually didn't go downstairs to see off visitors. She was seeing him off, she said, just as she saw off President Jiang Zemin and the premier, Zhu Rongji, when they visited her, but she didn't usually bother for other Politburo members.

Chen's overture was unexpected, because Gao had never mentioned Jinbao Avenue or any of her other projects in his essays. When he continued writing the articles, posting them on the Internet after newspapers stopped publishing them, his friend in the party's United Front department called and insisted on taking him to visit Chen again. This time, Chen offered to pay him three hundred thousand yuan per year to serve as a legal consultant for her company. It was a large sum, almost half Gao's annual income, and Chen added that the amount was negotiable if he thought it wasn't enough. When Gao declined, Chen expressed surprise, telling him that law firms were always trying to persuade her to hire them. Then she summoned her son into the room, and told him that all the lawyers he had hired weren't worth "a dog's fart." Gao was "a real lawyer," she declared, and from now on, he would be the company's chief counsel. Gao refused again, but Chen told him not to rush to a decision. She said they should stay in touch, and she paid him about $1,250 in cash for the two hours he had spent listening to her pitch. Over the next two years, Chen summoned Gao to her home twice more, and she paid him each time. She kept trying to change his mind, telling him she was looking out for him and warning that he would suffer if he didn't heed his big sister's advice. Gao accepted her money—after all, he told me sheepishly, she was taking up billable hours—but he continued writing the essays.

The last time Gao saw Chen was the first time he asked to see her. Hua Xinmin, the preservationist fighting to save her family home, had come to Gao for help, and he had agreed to introduce her to Chen. The meeting didn't last long. Hua appealed to Chen not to demolish her father's house, and Chen listened politely but made no promises. Later, though, the United Front friend told Gao that Chen was offended that he had brought Hua to see her. And he never heard from the Rich Lady again.

ON BOTH OCCASIONS that Chen Lihua agreed to meet with me, she gave me presents. At the end of my interviews with her, she would tell me to turn off my tape recorder and then motion to her secretary, a young, efficient-looking man hovering nearby, and he would scurry over with bags of gifts. The first time, Chen gave me a Chinese-style padded silk jacket and a long cashmere coat, both of which she insisted I try on for size before leaving. The coat cost nearly five hundred dollars, according to a price tag that was still attached to it. The next time, she gave me another silk jacket, and told her secretary to slip a thousand-dollar Hong Kong banknote in the pocket. I objected strenuously both times, telling her that American journalists generally did not accept gifts and that it was against the *Washington Post*'s policies. But the Rich Lady would hear none of it. She said reporters from around the world had interviewed her and accepted her presents, and if I refused, she would take it as a personal insult. Both times, we went back and forth about it for several minutes, and when I finally relented and told her I would take her gifts and donate them to charity, she seemed satisfied that she had gotten her way.

We met in a conference room on the second floor of her mansion, probably the same room where she had wooed Gao. Hanging on the hallway outside were separate photographs of Chen shaking hands with each of the nine men sitting on the Politburo Standing Committee at the time, as well as other photos of her with past party leaders and with foreign dignitaries such as Colin Powell. In person, Chen came across as more down-to-earth than she appeared on television. She was a large woman, and she projected a maternal air. She clearly enjoyed receiving guests, but she also seemed insecure about her limited schooling and humble background. She often mangled her sentences, and she strained to sound more literate by stringing together idioms that made little sense the way she used them. She spoke at length about red sandalwood—its beauty, its history, its scarcity—and at one point, she made me pinch her arm to demonstrate its beneficial health effects. "I'm in my sixties now, but can you tell?" she asked. I politely said no. "I've had diabetes for seventeen years, but can you tell?" she continued. "No, you can't. Red sandalwood is great for my diabetes."

Chen happily repeated the story about the antique wardrobe that she rescued during the Cultural Revolution, and she was eager to tell me about her run-in with the swarm of killer bees in the mountains of Burma. But whenever I asked about how she made her fortune, Chen would get evasive and resort to platitudes. "It was all through hard work," she told me. "Some reporters have asked me where my money came from. They all want to ask this question, and today you've asked it, too. I'll tell you the same thing. Earning money is justified. Spending money is proper. That is, the money I earn, I spend it properly. I feel confident investing in China, and that proves all the money is earned legally. Some things are private, and I don't necessarily want to say too much." I struggled to follow her logic, and I thought my understanding of Mandarin had failed me, but a Chinese colleague who accompanied me to the interview confirmed that Chen was babbling.

Later, I tried a more direct approach. I asked Chen whether she had special access to a factory warehouse full of antique furniture

seized by the Red Guards. She laughed and said she had only purchased a few worthless items from the factory. Then she added that
she never sold any of the antique furniture she collected and restored.
It was a puzzling statement, because she had already told me that she
went into the antique furniture business before going into real estate.
How could she make a living if she didn't sell any furniture? "I had
my savings, and I also have my economic secrets," she replied. "I don't
want to talk about it."

Chen acknowledged the importance of connections in doing business in China, but denied she had any special access to party leaders.
"Connections are very important, but it's different from what you
imagine," she said. "It's not like what people usually say, that connections can overturn the law, that they can trump anything. In my experience, that's not the way it is." Instead, Chen said, her connections
with officials were aboveboard and built on integrity and trust. "You
need credibility to build connections," she said. "You do things according to the regulations and policies. You do whatever they say.
Then they trust you." Once you win their trust, she continued, it is important not to abuse it. "I might never ask favors from friends whom I
have cultivated for decades," she said. "Leaders are leaders of the nation and the people. You can respect them but you can't make requests
of them. If you ask for favors and lean on them like an armchair, it will
cause problems. . . . The leaders will keep a distance from you."

When I asked Chen whether entrepreneurs could succeed without
special access to party officials, she maintained it was possible. All
you needed to do, she said, was "follow the law and the policy of reform and opening, and go to all the departments. Go to the land bureau, and the planning bureau, and the local governments. . . . Go and
have tea and try to understand things." It was as simple as that, she insisted, adding that there was no need to treat officials to fancy meals
or give them big gifts. She said she herself gave them only pieces of
art, such as the sandalwood items her carpenters produced. (It was at
the end of this interview that Chen gave me the thousand Hong Kong
dollars, the equivalent of about $130. Her secretary said I should use it
to buy lunch.)

Chen defended the mass evictions and demolition of Beijing's old
neighborhoods, casting herself as an enlightened developer acting in
the interests of commoners who didn't know what was best for them.

"Some ordinary people don't want to move, and that's understandable. It's hard to leave your native land. Don't say that his house is small. He grew up there, and he's used to it," she said. "If you ask him to leave, he may not be able to understand it at first, but after he leaves and moves into an apartment building, he changes his quality of life, his cultural quality, and his tastes. Then he's very happy." When residents resist demolition, she said, "we try our best to negotiate with them." She claimed she never evicted anyone or demolished a home without reaching a deal. She began telling me about the Jinbao Avenue project and boasting that not one displaced resident complained, but she must have sensed my skepticism, because then she brought up Hua Xinmin, whose name she kept getting wrong. At the time, Chen's company had already torn down Hua's family house and begun building a private club on it.

"I signed a contract with the state. I didn't sign any contract with Hua Jianmin, but Hua Jianmin keeps giving me trouble," Chen said. "She accuses me of occupying her family's land. She's French. She talks like a French person with me, a Chinese businesswoman. . . . I don't care if you're French or what country you're from. I'm going to use local, reasonable, and legal methods to relocate your family. The state gave me permission to do that. . . . She shouldn't be bothering me. She should go to the government."

Again and again, Chen emphasized that she did everything according to the law. She didn't seize private property; she followed the law and bought land-use rights from the government. She didn't court party officials at the Chang'an Club for special privileges; she went to government agencies seeking information and studied their regulations. She didn't use connections to move to Hong Kong; she immigrated legally after "visiting relatives." She didn't bully journalists; she asserted her legal rights and complained when they printed lies. She had an answer or evasion for every question, and she looked flustered only once, when I asked about Gao Zhisheng, who by then had been arrested. When I said his name, Chen seemed stricken and her face blanched. She said she had never heard of him.

Chen also fumbled a bit when I asked what entrepreneurs like her thought of the authoritarian political system. She mumbled something about foreign investment in China before I pressed her to express a preference for a one-party or multiparty system. "I think the one-party system is good for China, because it's always been like this through the generations," she said. "I don't know what will happen in the future, but I hope it's still the one-party system we have now. There are many benefits of the one-party system. It means there will be somebody to rule the country, to give it direction. . . ." I reminded her of the devastation that resulted from one-party rule under Mao, including her own suffering during the Cultural Revolution. "That was before reform and opening. Since reform and opening, things have been quite good," she replied. She paused and smiled blankly. "I'm just a simple person."

THE PARTY BOSS

The residents of Wangying Village woke on the morning of April 3, 1994, to the sound of police sirens and a voice on a crackling loudspeaker ordering them not to leave town. It was not an entirely unexpected development for the villagers, many of whom had been engaged for months in a tax revolt against local officials and had heard a crackdown was imminent. But few were prepared for the sight of the eight military trucks, each mounted with machine guns, that rumbled into their dusty hamlet in Anhui Province, or the battalion of more than one hundred police officers in full riot gear piling out of the vehicles. Even before the police began beating people, most of the peasants grabbed their children and fled in terror, running through their scallion fields toward the nearby provincial border. Those who remained in the village assumed they had nothing to fear because they were elderly or infirm or had not participated in their neighbors' protests against illegal taxes. But they were wrong. When the police left Wangying, an old man lay dying in the dirt and several other residents were bleeding or bruised. About a dozen other men and women, none of whom had been involved in the tax protests, were taken to the local police station, where they were whipped and tortured. Police poured a pot of scalding tea on one man's head, and forced others to run laps around a courtyard while wearing iron shackles around their ankles.

Zhang Xide

Wang Xiangdong, one of the Wangying Village peasant leaders

There was little doubt among the residents of Wangying Village who was behind the raid and what message it was meant to send. The most powerful man in Linquan County, the party secretary, Zhang Xide, was upset with them. A month earlier, a hundred villagers had traveled to the county seat in tractors and trucks and confronted Zhang outside his office, demanding a refund of illegal taxes that his underlings had collected. The villagers had already challenged his authority in late 1993 by going over his head and petitioning for help in Beijing. When the police stormed the village, officers went looking for the men who had led that appeal. All of them had fled, so police ransacked and trashed their homes, taking everything of value and smashing the rest. One of the men returned to find that they had even dumped a stock of rat poison into his grain silo, mixing it in with shovels and rendering a season's harvest worthless.

The party later investigated the events in Wangying Village and confirmed that Zhang ordered the police raid. But one official report after another declared he had acted properly. The party referred to the episode as the "April 2 Incident," because in the official version of events, the police were sent to Wangying to rescue an officer who had been taken captive and lost his gun the night before. "The response to the April 2 Incident was timely and handled correctly," the authorities said in an open letter to residents. "There should be no criticism. This should be fully regarded as positive. The county committee gave careful consideration and acted according to the law. On this subject . . . the provincial and local leadership have all given their full approval."

For years, the residents of Wangying Village lived quietly with this verdict, and few outside the remote and poverty-stricken community heard about the April 2 Incident. As the villagers buried their anger and suppressed their outrage, the police went unpunished and the party boss won a promotion. But in 2003, the story of what happened in Wangying Village was published in a literary magazine, and then in a book. Across the country, people shook their heads in sadness and frustration as they read about Wangying Village and the party boss Zhang Xide. The villagers, it seemed, had gotten the last word.

• • •

A SHORT, SQUAT MAN with a receding hairline and small, narrow eyes, Zhang Xide was working in the party leadership of the city of Fuyang, not far from his old turf of Linquan County, when the story was published in the literary magazine. "You should read it," one of his colleagues told him. "They wrote some terrible things about you." At the time, he was vice chairman of the city's People's Political Consultative Conference, a ceremonial government body that did little more than hold banquets and convene meetings. The job gave Zhang access to a research library, so he ordered the staff to get him a copy of the magazine. At the time, he wasn't very worried. The magazine was printed by a state publishing house, and the censors were pretty good at hiding the party's misdeeds from the public, so how bad could it be?

Zhang had spent almost his entire adult life serving the party in the rural counties around Fuyang where he was born and raised. At the age of fifty-eight, he could look forward to retirement on a government pension and back on a comfortable if unexceptional career in the apparatus. The places where he worked remained poor but he believed he had helped promote economic growth and improved the lives of the peasants in the area. His parents had been illiterate wheat and bean farmers, but he had made something of himself, and now he had a son who was a judge and a daughter who worked in the tax bureau. In many ways, he was a typical party official, one of millions of loyal and anonymous cadres who believed in the one-party state, benefited from it, and helped sustain it.

So Zhang was understandably upset when he saw how he was portrayed in the magazine story, "The Slow Petition Road," which was scheduled to be published as a chapter of the book *An Investigation of China's Peasantry*. Near the start of the piece, the authors wrote that Zhang "bore undeniable responsibility and played an extremely dishonorable role" in the April 2 Incident. Then, it got worse:

> As for Zhang Xide, he was already familiar to everyone in Linquan County from television: He had a "five-short figure"—two short arms, two short legs and a short neck—and he liked to wave his hands when he spoke. The reports and speeches he delivered most certainly were written by his assistants. He could speak pretty well, but as soon as he departed from a prepared

text, he sounded not unlike an uncouth lout. At one meeting, while emphasizing that birth planning workers must not allow births to exceed quotas, Zhang Xide waved his fist and babbled: "I'd rather see seven headstones than one extra head!" When he said this, everybody grimaced. This murderous and bloody sentence spread far and wide, and sent a chill down the spines of all who heard it. . . .

The fact that Wangying Village traveled en masse to petition in Beijing reverberated in Linquan County, and the county party secretary Zhang Xide panicked. His first thought was still not how he might calm the villagers' intense dissatisfaction with their unbearable burden. Instead, he clearly still believed that high pressure or even suppression was the most effective way to put an end to the petitioning.

The article told the story of the villagers' campaign to seek redress against high taxes between 1993 and 1996—and of his efforts to stop them. With each page, Zhang grew angrier. He had no regrets about his tenure as the party chief in Linquan County. He felt he had done a good job, and he considered himself one of the best leaders the county ever had. Now he was being painted as a vulgar tyrant, held up for the nation to mock and condemn, and it was infuriating. He recognized the authors' names. He had had a run-in with one of them before, and he was sure the writer was trying to get back at him. But there was more to his outrage than that. These writers had gone too far, he thought. Their article wasn't just an attack on him, it was an attack on the Communist Party, on the political system that he had devoted his life to and believed had made China a great nation. The way they portrayed the party as incapable of responding to people's concerns, the way they accused local officials of taking advantage of the peasants and covering up one another's crimes, the way they depicted the police as thugs who engaged in torture—to Zhang, it was all an attempt to discredit one-party rule and pander to those who believed China needed democracy.

"The book incites the masses by publicizing all these things," Zhang told me after it was published. "It clearly has an anti-Party tendency. . . . It catered to this kind of thinking, that's why it became so popular. This is all obvious.

"I can't understand it," he continued. "Rationally speaking, during these years of reform and opening, there have been great changes. The planned economy has opened up, and there has been great progress in the environment for speech, in the construction of democracy and rule of law. What I can't understand is why people fall for this book. . . . It's clear that it rejects the Communist Party's leadership."

After reading the article, Zhang flew to Beijing and went to the magazine's offices. He tried to persuade the editors to retract the story. When they resisted, he went to see the editor in chief of the publishing house, and urged him not to release the book, or at least to revise it and edit his name out. He invited the editor to send people to Linquan County and see for himself if the book was accurate. He offered to open up the county's archives and to cooperate fully with their investigation. But a few days later, the editor called him and said he had consulted with the book's authors. They stood by the book and provided evidence to back up the Wangying Village story. And so the publishing house was standing by it, too.

"I listened and was filled with anger," Zhang said. "I told him, 'See you in court.' And then I hung up."

LINQUAN COUNTY SITS on the flatlands of central China between the Yellow and the Yangtze rivers, in the far northwest corner of Anhui Province. A rural backwater afflicted by sandy soil and frequent flooding, it is one of the most populous and impoverished counties in the nation, with nearly two million residents who make on average barely $250 a year, less than a sixth the national average. The villages of Linquan, scattered amid the rice paddies and wheat fields, have a meager, disorderly look, and there is a quiet emptiness about them, because many residents make ends meet by spending part of the year working in cities hundreds of miles away. Yet the rhythms and traditions of rural life seem to resist change. Pearl S. Buck's 1931 novel, *The Good Earth*, was set not far from Linquan, and in much of the county the peasants continue to till the land the way they did in the book—with their hands, simple tools, and the occasional ox.

More than a half century ago, it was the anger and frustration of peasants in places like Linquan that fueled the Communist Revolution and catapulted Mao to power, much more than the party's early efforts to mobilize industrial workers. Yet the party's policies have always favored industry and the cities over agriculture and the countryside, where most Chinese live. When the party did focus on rural issues, Linquan and the other counties of Anhui felt the extremes. As many as eight million people died in Anhui during the Great Leap Forward, almost a quarter of the population. But the peasants in Anhui were also among the first to demand a return to household farming after Mao's death, a change that Deng Xiaoping then endorsed and implemented across the country. By dismantling the communes, leasing land to peasant families, and reintroducing the profit motive, the party sparked an agricultural boom that lifted the national economy and fueled double-digit growth in rural incomes through much of the 1980s. In the 1990s, though, rural growth slowed, and the party's long-standing bias toward the cities again weighed heavily on places like Linquan.

The party has always categorized residents of the countryside as *nongmin*, or peasants, and maintained policies that treat them as second-class citizens. Peasants are forced to sell grain to the state at artificially low prices to keep food costs down in the cities, and their children sometimes must score higher on exams than urban kids to get into college. They make up a majority of the population, but the state invests less in the countryside and spends less on services there— only 20 percent of all health-care funding, for example. At the same time, the government limits the ability of peasants to move to the cities, requiring them to apply for permits and restricting or denying them access to urban schools, health care, and other social services, as well as many jobs. On top of it all, through the 1990s and beyond, peasants have been forced to pay higher taxes. City residents only began paying taxes in 1994, and only if their monthly income exceeded 800 yuan, or about a hundred dollars, but peasants—hardly any of whom earn that much—paid taxes no matter how little they made. During the 1990s, taxes grew faster than incomes across the countryside, and by the year 2000, a peasant paid on average four times more in taxes than an urban resident despite earning six to seven times less.

The rising rural tax burden was the most conspicuous symptom of a political structure in which local officials never had to answer to the public. The party was a parasite, living off the peasants and giving them little in return and no way to fight back. Local officials raised rural taxes to boost their own pay, and in many places they spent the entire budget on salaries and administrative expenses with nothing left over to fund services. As a result, they demanded more fees from peasants who wanted to send their children to "public" schools. Many officials used tax money to finance projects they hoped would impress superiors and lead to promotions. But the projects were often ill conceived and wasteful—factories that never made a profit, palatial government buildings full of empty offices, roads that went nowhere. Even when projects did make sense, peasants were resentful because they had no way to know whether officials were spending their money wisely. In the late 1980s, some officials even began diverting funds meant for grain procurement to their boondoggles and paying peasants with IOUs.

The demand for taxes continued to rise as party officials created new jobs for friends and relatives. The process began in the 1980s, when the nation's 56,000 communes were dismantled and replaced by 96,000 townships, creating an entirely new layer of government between the counties and villages that would have to be financed with money from the peasants. Over the years, every level of the bureaucracy expanded faster than the rural population. At the township level, the ratio of officials to the rural workforce grew tenfold between 1982 and 2000. The rural party apparatus expanded so quickly that often there wasn't enough money left over to pay the salaries of teachers and other civil servants.

As taxation without representation swelled the ranks of local bureaucrats, peasants complained about how these officials ate and drank at public expense. The authors of *An Investigation of China's Peasantry* tell a story in the book about party officials who ran up an enormous tab at a restaurant in Anhui. After several years, the restaurant sued for payment and ended up taking ownership of part of the township government building. It was the third time, the authors discovered, that the township had been forced to sell a public building to cover the restaurant bills of its officials:

> The fact of the matter is the vast countryside of China has become a gourmand's paradise. Like a cloud of locusts, officials with their appetites in tow descend on the countryside and are

infinitely inventive in coming up with excuses to eat and drink: dinners for inspectors, dinners for conferences, dinners for rural poverty relief, dinners for disaster relief; dine if you can afford it, and dine if you can't; dine on credit, dine on loan. . . . To eat free has become a sign of status, an index of position. The quality of a dinner may determine whether or not a project is approved or a deal clinched, or whether a promotion is in the works. It has become part of the political culture.

Nationally, the authors wrote in 2003, government officials spend $10 billion to $13 billion in public money every year on eating and drinking, enough to host four Olympic Games.

Beijing tried to rein in waste by reducing funding for local authorities in the mid-1990s, but rural officials responded by spending villages and townships into debt and squeezing peasants for even more in taxes and fees. I once visited a village named Xiaoeshan in a remote and mountainous part of Sichuan Province, a town so poor it had no paved roads, one telephone, and limited electricity. Peasants there ate most of what they harvested, and by selling the rest, they earned about $25 a year each on average. But local officials demanded about $37 from each resident in annual taxes and fees. The only way to pay the taxes, residents told me, was to supplement their farm income by pulling their children out of school and sending them to find work in the cities.

When peasants resist paying taxes, local authorities send in "shock teams" of officials to collect, and if cash is not forthcoming, the teams confiscate property—livestock, televisions, bicycles—often worth more than the amount owed in taxes. In the 1980s and through the '90s, resentment against the rising tax burden and against the government's demand that couples have no more than one or two children, fueled waves of riots and other violent clashes between peasants and party officials in the countryside. In some villages, peasants fashioned homemade bombs and destroyed the homes of local officials. Alarmed by the unrest, the party leadership tried in 1993 to set a limit on peasant taxes of 5 percent of average local incomes and issued a series of edicts ordering officials to stop levying arbitrary fees, but little changed. Local officials ignored the regulations or found ways around them, sometimes coming up with ingenious new tax schemes. In Lin-

quan County, peasants were required to pay one fee if they slaugh-
tered a pig, and another fee if they didn't. In other counties, there was
even something known as the "attitude tax"—a tax on peasants who
resisted paying their taxes.

WHEN THE WRITER Chen Guidi first met Zhang Xide in the summer
of 1994, he didn't think he was such a bad guy. On the contrary, the
party chief of Linquan County made an excellent impression. He
seemed more open-minded and honest than most party officials Chen
had met in the countryside, more willing to speak frankly without
worrying about the political ramifications or slipping into empty ideological jargon to protect himself. Chen was working for a party
newspaper in Anhui's provincial capital at the time, and he had traveled to Linquan to conduct interviews for an article about a local corruption case involving a businessman who had defrauded the county
and escaped conviction by bribing the province's top prosecutor and
other officials. The story was a blockbuster but also a political mine-
field, and most officials would have been reluctant to discuss the subject. But not only did Zhang cooperate, he arranged for Chen to meet
all the officials in Linquan he wanted.

In some ways, Chen knew, Zhang was acting in his own interests.
It was under his leadership that Linquan County had solved the case
and arrested the crook, and such an accomplishment could boost his
chances for a promotion. But the provincial prosecutor who accepted
the bribe and overturned the case was an official of much higher rank.
By speaking out, Zhang was risking his career. Yet he seemed genuinely unafraid. "He's just the provincial prosecutor!" Zhang told Chen
at a banquet he hosted for the writer. "He's not a big player behind the
scenes at all!" Chen wasn't sure if this was bluster or daring, but he
admired Zhang's guts. He was also impressed that unlike many rural
officials in Anhui, Zhang had attended university in Beijing, earning
a degree in agriculture. Here was a party official with a future, Chen
thought, someone with the confidence to take risks to get things done.
"A lot of officials I met at the time were cowards," Chen told me years
later. "They didn't like to take responsibility for anything. But Zhang
seemed different. . . . I thought he was a very good county party
secretary."

The first hint that all was not as it seemed came the next day, when Chen encountered a crowd of peasants outside the Linquan County courthouse. He asked them what was going on, and they explained they were protesting the arrest of fellow villagers. Then they handed him a stack of papers. It was the summer of 1994, not long after the April 2 Incident, and the peasants were from Wangying Village. The next day, Chen asked Zhang about the protest. The party boss laughed dismissively. "The peasants are running wild," he said, complaining that they were always petitioning the government about one thing or another. Chen made a joke, too, and the conversation moved on. He continued working on the Linquan fraud story, filed away the papers from the villagers, and forgot about them.

A few months later, after the first part of his report on the Linquan corruption case was published, Chen received a late-night phone call from Zhang. The party boss sounded like a different person, nervous and timid. His voice was shaking as he told Chen that people were furious about the article, and that his job was in jeopardy. Even though he had been given an advance copy of the report and cleared it, Zhang pleaded with Chen not to publish the rest of it and to return any evidence that he had signed off on the article. Chen was upset. By backing down, Zhang was leaving him and his newspaper vulnerable to discipline by the propaganda department. "If you take the materials back, that's like kicking me when I'm down," Chen complained. In the end, the newspaper ignored Zhang and published the rest of the report, and Zhang saved his job by denouncing it. Chen concluded that Zhang was an ordinary official after all, more concerned about his career than the truth, and after some time, he forgot about him.

Six years later, in 2000, Chen and his wife, Wu Chuntao, began conducting research for a book about the peasantry. The couple lived in the provincial capital, but both had been born to peasant families. Chen was a native of Anhui, a tall, serious man with sharp features who had once labored on the docks of the Huai River. At fifty-seven, he was the more accomplished writer of the pair, the author of an award-winning book about pollution of the Huai, as well as a few plays and novels. Wu had also distinguished herself as a writer, but primarily in local literary circles. She was twenty years younger than him, a small, affable woman with a youthful face and a gentle manner. They met in a writing class and had been married for nearly a decade when they had a son in March 2000, and saw a young peasant couple in the maternity ward make a devastating decision. The man had brought his wife to the hospital because she was bleeding, but doctors would not deliver their child unless they paid 3,200 yuan, or nearly four hundred dollars, much more than they could afford. Forced to check out, they returned to their village, where it only cost 200 yuan to deliver a boy and 100 yuan for a girl. A few days later, Wu heard an anguished cry in the next room. The woman's bleeding had continued, and she had been rushed back to the hospital, but it was too late. Both she and her baby died, and her husband was banging his fists on the floor in grief. It was then that Chen and Wu resolved to write *An Investigation of China's Peasantry.*

They began to hear stories about Linquan County soon after they started—about the punishing taxes that peasants had to pay, about an official who lived so well he hired nine nannies and maids, about a party boss who drove around in a Mercedes-Benz. Chen recognized the name of the party boss immediately—Zhang Xide—and then he remembered the papers that the peasants had given him outside the courthouse. When he dug them up and finally read them, he was moved by the plight of the residents of Wangying Village, and he realized just how wrong his first impression of Zhang had been.

When the couple finally visited Wangying Village in January 2001, the peasants were reluctant to talk. Though more than six years had passed since the April 2 Incident and Zhang Xide had long since moved on, the villagers were still afraid of provoking the government, and they doubted this couple from the city could do much to help them. But Chen and Wu persisted, slowly winning their trust. When villagers expressed concern about being caught talking to them, the writers drove them to another town and put them up in a hotel. When people important to the story were away working in the cities, the writers tracked them down or arranged to meet them back in the village on other trips. The couple collected a stack of documentary evidence— diaries, official reports, tax receipts. Gradually, over the course of eight visits to Wangying, they pieced together the story of the village's tax revolt.

THE TAX REVOLT began with a television set. In the autumn of 1993, a party "shock team" was collecting taxes in Wangying Village when an elderly woman refused to pay a new seventy-five-cent fee. The officials responded by seizing her television. That year, the villagers made an average of about thirty-four dollars for a year's labor in the fields, less than usual because of a drought. But local officials reported figures four to five times higher to impress their superiors and demanded a total of about twenty-one dollars from each villager in taxes, far above the national limit of 5 percent of the average local income. The incident with the television set was just the latest outrage, and as word of what happened spread, residents began swapping stories about similar abuses and sharing information about their tax burdens. Three young men in the village, all of whom were surnamed Wang, emerged as leaders of a campaign to appeal for help. They began by taking their complaint to the township that governed their village, and when they were brushed off there, they moved up the bureaucracy and tried the government in Linquan County. After they were rebuffed again, the three Wangs decided to bring the village's problem to Beijing.

Chinese use the word *shangfang* to describe the act of petitioning a higher authority for justice. The phrase literally means "upward visit," and the practice has been a part of the nation's political culture for centuries if not millennia. For much of Chinese history, it referred to an appeal to the emperor or one of his ministers to right the wrongs committed by a lower official. Today, *shangfang* continues in slightly modified form. Many Chinese believe they have a better chance of winning redress of grievances by directly petitioning a higher level of the party than by filing a lawsuit because they know the party controls the courts and is above the law. The modern-day version of the imperial appeals bureaucracy is a system of what the party calls "Letters and Visits" offices. Almost every state and party organ in China has one, and the busiest ones are in Beijing. Huge numbers of petitioners from across the country converge on the capital every year clutching sheaves of papers outlining the injustices they have suffered. Many of these people end up living in slums and camping outside the Letters and Visits offices, which are usually located on backstreets away from the gaze of tourists. Their grievances are varied but they share a common hope—that an upright party official will somehow see their complaint and intervene on their behalf. It almost never happens, but that doesn't stop the masses from coming. They stay in Beijing for months, years, even decades, because they refuse to give up or because they feel they have nowhere else to go.

The three Wangs joined the throngs of petitioners in Beijing in the winter of 1993 after the villagers took up a collection to pay for the six-hundred-mile train journey. In the capital, they lodged complaints at the Letters and Visits offices of the Central Committee, the State Council, and the Ministry of Agriculture. At each office, they presented bureaucrats with evidence of the taxes paid in Wangying Village, and the bureaucrats promised they would investigate. The official at the Agriculture Ministry went a step further, giving the men a letter endorsing their complaint to deliver to provincial authorities in Anhui. When the men went to Anhui, officials there read the letter and gave them another one addressed to officials in Linquan County. Armed with the two letters supporting their position, the three Wangs led a group of three hundred villagers back to the government offices in Linquan County, optimistic that their tax problems would soon be resolved. What they didn't realize was that the Letters and Visits offices had little real power and often gave out such letters just to get petitioners to go home. The Linquan County officials who met with them, on the other hand, understood this, and they were noncommittal about the peasants' complaints. One expressed skepticism and said the county wouldn't be able to function if it cut taxes to the levels indicated in the letters. Frustrated, the villagers demanded to see the county party chief and refused to leave until they did.

Hours later, just before dusk, the residents of Wangying Village caught their first glimpse of the most powerful man in the county. They were camped outside the government building when Zhang Xide arrived by car and walked over to them. The peasants quickly surrounded him, and many got down on their knees in supplication. They told him about the illegal taxes in their village exceeding the 5 percent limit, and showed him the letters they had obtained in Beijing and the provincial capital, Hefei. At first, Zhang defended his record, saying he had not raised taxes. But the peasants wouldn't let him leave and pressed him to read the letters, which he did, slowly. He did not look surprised by what he read, nor did he appear nervous about the emotional crowd around him. Finally, Zhang looked up and spoke again. "If the township increased the peasants' tax burden, I'll ask them to return the money to you," he said. The three Wangs asked him to put it in writing, and Zhang scribbled a note for them.

"The masses from Wangying Village have petitioned seeking the return of funds for village administration collected in excess," it said. "Please work diligently, and return all of the funds collected in excess according to the agreed amount in a timely fashion."

The wording was vague, but the villagers were elated. "We believed we had obtained an imperial order from the county party secretary," one of the petition leaders, Wang Xiangdong, recalled. "We thought the money would be returned to us for sure."

Over the following weeks, local officials went through the motions of conducting an audit in Wangying Village. A few tax payments were refunded, and a few village officials were fired. But they refused to return the rest of the money. Then the three Wangs ran into problems. One lost his job in the township land bureau. The other two were jumped by thugs and roughed up after they were summoned to a meeting with township officials. The villagers concluded that township officials were exacting revenge on their representatives and resisting Zhang's order, and about a hundred of them went to see him again, intercepting him on the steps of the county's party headquarters as he was going in for a meeting.

At first, they recalled, Zhang tried to brush aside their complaints, saying he had already directed the township officials to return their money. "If they won't do it, what can I do?" he said. "I can't control them."

But the peasants kept pressing him. Wasn't he the county's party chief? Didn't the township officials report to him? Couldn't he fire them if they refused to return the taxes? The peasants wouldn't let him leave, and suddenly, Zhang lost his temper. "What do you think you're doing?" he said to the group, raising his voice. Then Zhang told them flat out that he wouldn't return the taxes. "I'd rather lose an arm than return the money!" he said.

The peasants were surprised, and some threatened to return to Beijing and file a complaint against him. "If you can make it to Beijing, then go!" Zhang shot back. "If you have the guts to go to Beijing, then go!" The party boss was furious and challenged the peasants to make trouble, saying that would only make it easier for him to punish them. "Come over here!" he shouted. "If you have the guts, come over here!" Zhang took out his cell phone and called his police chief. Within minutes, a large group of officers arrived and forced the peasants out of the party compound.

The violent police raid on Wangying Village that became known as the April 2 Incident occurred just a few weeks later. Over the next year, conditions in the village grew more desperate. Zhang issued arrest warrants for the three Wangs, and two of them were caught after traveling to Beijing again and petitioning for help at one of the Letters and Visits offices. The third continued to lead groups of villagers to Beijing to complain about Zhang's abuses but their appeals were ignored. After all, Zhang was the party's man in Linquan County.

In October 1995, seventy-four residents of Wangying Village and forty-six peasants from elsewhere in Linquan County traveled to Beijing again and staged a public protest by kneeling in Tiananmen Square. That same month, another peasant from Linquan upset about the confiscation of his land to build a police station committed suicide by jumping from the roof of a shelter run by one of the Letters and Visits offices in Beijing. The two incidents finally led national party leaders to order a more impartial investigation into the events in Linquan. This time, the party agreed that the villagers had been forced to pay too much in taxes, and acknowledged that "extreme behavior by a small number" of police officers during the April 2 Incident "hurt the feelings of the masses." The three Wangs were cleared, and some of the tax money was returned. But the party again stood by Zhang Xide, and promoted him to a higher-paying position in the nearby city of Fuyang.

The residents of Wangying Village saw Zhang one last time before he left the county. The news of his imminent departure had spread quickly, and a crowd of as many as five thousand peasants came to settle old scores on one of his last days of work in March 1996. Some were seeking refunds of taxes they had paid, worried that the new party chief would refuse responsibility for Zhang's excesses. Others just wanted to vent their anger, about the torture they had suffered at the hands of the police, or the abuses committed in the name of the one-child policy. When the peasants didn't find Zhang at party headquarters, they forced their way past a security gate into the leafy residential section of the party compound and gathered in front of his five-story building. He lived in a three-bedroom apartment on the top floor, and he must have heard the people assembling below. The crowd shouted for him to come out, and finally, Zhang showed himself.

"I've already resigned," he told the peasants. "Go deal with the other officials."

But the crowd pressed in on him, shouting and cursing. The bravado that the villagers had seen before was gone now. Zhang was alone and surrounded, and he looked smaller than they remembered, almost pitiful. None of his colleagues at party headquarters came to his aid. As Zhang tried to walk away, there was a scuffle. A few of the peasants slapped him, and he fell to the ground. Finally, a team of police officers rushed over and dragged him into another courtyard, locking the gate behind them. The peasants followed, knocking down the wall and rushing in. But Zhang was gone. He had slipped away, out the back.

THE STORY OF Wangying Village was one of several told in *An Investigation of China's Peasantry*, and hardly the most damning. There was also the profile of Ding Zuoming, a peasant who was tortured and beaten to death by police after leading a decade-long campaign against illegal taxes and fees in his village. There was the case of Shen Keli, an idealistic party official devoted to fighting poverty who became a village tyrant. There was the tale of Zhang Guiquan, a corrupt official who murdered four peasants who had tried to audit his accounts. And then there were all the party officials who tried to cover up these crimes. Amid this cast of characters, Zhang Xide came across as only a minor villain. But a few weeks after the book was released, he filed a defamation suit against the authors and their publisher, accusing them of libel and demanding a public apology and about twenty-five thousand dollars in damages.

Published in December 2003, *An Investigation of China's Peasantry* was an immediate hit. Interviews with Chen and Wu appeared in newspapers and magazines across the country, and the authors were booked on the major television talk shows. Their gritty portrayal of rural conditions found an eager audience among city readers, many of whom knew little about the countryside and saw peasants only as an uneducated mass of cheap labor. The book became a bestseller, beating out the sex novels, get-rich-quick guides, and other fluff that dominates Chinese bookstores. The first print run of one hundred thousand copies sold out within a month. The book was a success because Chen and Wu gave readers something they rarely saw—and the censors rarely allowed: an honest look at some of the darkest aspects of party rule, complete with the names of officials and the details of their crimes. The authors were careful to praise the efforts of the party leadership to reduce the rural tax burden and improve the lives of peasants, but they also declared their policies a failure and placed the blame not on economic conditions or natural disasters, as the party often did, but on the political system and its inability to curb the abuse of power by rural officials.

As the book became a media sensation, the propaganda czars decided it was too much. Less than two months after it was released, as another session of the National People's Congress was opening in Beijing, the authorities prohibited any further coverage of the book in the media and ordered the publisher to stop printing new copies. The publisher complied, but the ban came as the book's sales were gaining momentum, and pirates quickly stepped in to satisfy demand, printing and selling as many as seven million more copies across the country. Even party officials wanted to read it; sales were brisk at the hotels in Beijing where delegates to the National People's Congress were staying.

Zhang Xide welcomed the party's decision to ban *An Investigation of China's Peasantry*. He considered it an official endorsement of his view that the book was not only flawed but also subversive. Now that the book was gone, he could claim victory and quietly drop the case. But he didn't. He wanted his day in court.

It was a surprising decision, because party officials almost always dealt with books and articles they objected to behind the scenes, using the hatchet men of the propaganda department to silence their critics. Once they had succeeded in banning a book or recalling a magazine, it was considered bad form to draw further attention to the matter. Doing so would only remind people of whatever it was that the authorities didn't want them to read, as well as the fact that the party still practiced censorship. From this perspective, a lawsuit against two bestselling, blacklisted authors seemed like a bad idea. Media and publishing circles were rife with speculation about Zhang's motives. The book was set almost entirely in Anhui, and some believed Zhang's superiors in the province were using the lawsuit to take revenge on the authors. Others were convinced the propaganda authorities were testing the use of the courts as a new channel for intimidating writers and journalists. But when I asked Zhang if anyone had asked him to file the lawsuit, he said no. Propaganda officials had promised to punish the authors if he prevailed in court, he told me, but the decision to sue was his alone.

When I first met Zhang, he was waiting in a private dining room of the best hotel in Fuyang, a drab three-star establishment with dirty carpets that overenthusiastic proprietors had named Buckingham Palace. He was wearing a white short-sleeved dress shirt and dark pants, and he greeted me as "an old friend" before we even sat down. A younger man, one of his aides, was in the room, too, but Zhang never bothered to introduce him. Instead, he handed me a forty-six-page rebuttal of the Wangying Village story and immediately began bad-mouthing the authors. There was an oily quality about him; he spoke too quickly, and he often got worked up and raised his voice. At one point, he grabbed my copy of *An Investigation of China's Peasantry* and began flipping through the pages, reading sentences aloud and then refuting them in the same breath. He even found it necessary to point out that the peasants of Wangying Village grew only scallions, not cabbage, as the book claimed.

In fact, he denied almost every aspect of the Wangying Village story. "It's all fabricated," he said. "Everything they wrote about me, except my name, was a lie." Zhang said that he kept taxes low, and that when the villagers complained, he immediately conducted an investigation, found some discrepancies, and refunded everything the peasants were owed. He said he paid special attention to the case because of the letters the peasants had obtained in Beijing and the provincial capital, and he denied ever losing his temper or challenging the peasants to go back to Beijing. As for the April 2 Incident, Zhang stuck to the party line and said he ordered the raid to rescue a police officer who had been disarmed and detained by the peasants, not to punish the villagers. He denied any police brutality or torture. An elderly villager died after the raid, he acknowledged, but from a heart attack, not from anything the police did. "I have no regrets about that incident, none at all," he said. "The police had no contact with the masses. There was no clash."

When I asked Zhang why the peasants all told a different story, he asserted that they had been paid off by Chen and he launched into a diatribe against the writer, accusing him of harboring a personal grudge against him, of exaggerating and distorting the truth, of seeking fame, fortune, and "political capital" with the book, and finally, of pandering to and inciting antiparty sentiment. "Chen has fired the first shot in an attempt to overthrow the Communist Party!" he said.

But if conditions were so good in Wangying, why were the villagers petitioning for tax relief? Zhang shifted to another explanation, saying a party official in a rival faction had egged on the peasants to embarrass him. "The tax burden on the peasants isn't heavy here, but there are just some people who are unwilling to pay," he added. Later, when I noted that the party's own investigation concluded the peasants were forced to pay excessive amounts, Zhang offered a third defense, saying that lower-level officials may have demanded too much money and insisting that he was not to blame. If he had been responsible, he argued, the party would have disciplined him instead of giving him a promotion.

Zhang seemed most upset by the book's portrayal of him as a short, inarticulate bully who relied on his aides to write speeches, especially the description of his "five-short figure," or short neck, arms, and legs. "It's insulting. Only soft-shelled turtles have five-short figures," he said. "I'm 165 centimeters tall. No matter what, that's medium height.

"And they said I didn't write my own reports, but that's exactly what I do. That's one of my specialties. Did you know that?" He didn't wait for me to answer. "When I was party secretary of Linquan County, other than the reports used for party conferences and the congress, I never used any prepared texts. I would just write an outline in my notebook and speak. After I went to the People's Political Consultative Conference, I personally wrote several good investigative reports."

He went on for long stretches about himself. He said he had never told a lie in his life. He shared a story about turning down a bribe. He said he always worked late and never turned off his cell phone. While he was the party chief in Linquan County, he said, hundreds of township enterprises were established and tens of thousands of wells were dug. "Wherever I have worked, people always said that I have a good heart, that I'm amiable, and that I have an approachable, democratic working style," he said. "I've worked in ten different places, and they all evaluated me this way."

When I asked about the pressures of governing a county like Linquan, he acknowledged serious financial problems. The county's budget was limited, he said, and it was difficult to pay the salaries of all the people on the payroll. Especially after 1995, he said, townships and villages fell deep into debt as the ranks of officials mushroomed. "You help arrange a job for someone, and they arrange a job for someone else. Add it all up, and it's taking ten minutes to take attendance," he said. But when I asked him why so many officials were necessary, he replied, "Generally speaking, it's to develop the economy, to make ordinary people rich."

Zhang said one of the most difficult challenges was enforcing the one-child policy. If too many children were born in excess of state quotas, he said, a party official's career would be in jeopardy. But that never happened to him. On the contrary, Zhang said he handled his birth planning duties so well he was named a model worker and elected director of the provincial birth planning association. "I was very strict, and I established my own set of methods," he said. What kind of methods? "I mainly relied on propaganda work, letting cadres take the lead," he said. "I didn't use coercive measures." Then he told me how he handled a mother of two who was six months pregnant with a third child:

Someone had informed on her, and she fled to her mother's house. Her car was slow, and ours was fast, so we arrived as she got there. We just worked on her, and we wouldn't stop until we finished the work. There was a deep river nearby, and that day she was in her father's room. I sat on a stone near the front door. I sat there the whole day. She thought she would wait until I left, so it would be easier to run away. I couldn't force my way into the house to grab her, so I just waited into the afternoon. Finally, she came out, but as soon as she came outside, she jumped into the river.

Zhang started laughing, adding that the woman wasn't wearing any underwear. I asked him to continue. He said the woman's father pulled her out of the water, and eventually, as other relatives were summoned to put pressure on her, she agreed to an abortion. "Later, I talked to her and I said, 'You already have two boys. The burden is heavy enough. How many more do you want?' I said, 'When your life gets better, you won't curse me. You'll thank me.' We went to the hospital, and I waited there. She said she would have the shot the next day, but I said no. You're already here today. Have the shot today."

Zhang said he traveled to the United States in the early 1990s on an inspection trip arranged by the Ministry of Construction. The delegation visited several cities, but he was most impressed when he saw a group of Somali protesters outside the White House. "Public order was excellent. Shout for a while, sit down and rest, drink some water. The police weren't even there, and order was great," he said. In China, he said, you couldn't do that. "People here have insufficient awareness of the law. If they do anything forcefully, they will break the law." As an example, he cited the behavior of peasants such as those from Wangying Village who petition the county over grievances. "It's our job as officials to solve their problems. On the other hand, we can see that even after the masses developed the beginnings of democratic awareness, they still lack awareness of law. For example, they block the roads. They block the gate. They curse at people," he said. "Our problem is their awareness of law isn't strong enough. They can't use the law to restrain themselves."

This was one reason, he argued, why China wasn't suited for a multiparty democracy. "China has China's conditions," he said. "The leadership of the Communist Party developed over a long period of time, and it has the public's trust. If it were overthrown, the masses wouldn't accept it. Free elections would lead to great disorder, because the masses are already used to the current system.

"I'm an intellectual, and I've always believed in the Communist Party. There's no doubt that some of our superstructure needs reform, but we must maintain the stability of the nation," he added. "If there was chaos in the nation, no one would be able to endure it."

I suggested that some people believed the one-party system might be incapable of restraining officials and protecting the rights of peasants. Zhang shook his head. "It's actually the opposite," he said. "Only under this system, with China under the leadership of the Communist Party, can the interests of the peasants be guaranteed. Look how satisfied the peasants are now."

Part III

STRUGGLE
SESSIONS

Jiang Yanyong

8

THE HONEST
DOCTOR

The men who ran the Communist Party had good reason to be pleased with themselves as they celebrated the arrival of the Year of the Goat in February 2003. They presided over the world's most dynamic economy, which had recorded more than a decade of uninterrupted breakneck growth. They had put down the worker protests in the rust belt and survived the worst of the labor unrest caused by the dismantling of state industry. They were enjoying new influence in international affairs and making good progress with preparations for the 2008 Summer Olympics. And they were halfway through a delicate leadership transition. The general secretary who took power after the Tiananmen massacre, Jiang Zemin, surrendered the party's top job in November to Hu Jintao, the colorless bureaucrat who had been his heir apparent for more than a decade. In March, Jiang was scheduled to step down as the nation's president, too. It was an important milestone—the most orderly and peaceful transfer of power in the history of modern China—and it meant the party had avoided the kind of destructive succession fight that often plagued authoritarian governments.

For many in China, the smooth transition was fresh evidence that the Communists had found a way to address the shortcomings of their autocratic political system without adopting democratic reforms or giving up power. They had already demonstrated that capitalism and authoritarianism could make a powerful combination: the party relied on its monopoly on power to push through painful economic reforms and used the prosperity generated by those reforms to strengthen its rule. The party's experiment in grafting market-oriented policies onto the Leninist model of government had proved a smashing success, and in capitals around the world, politicians and pundits spoke of the Chinese model with awe, envy, and sometimes fear. Foreign investors and multinational corporations, meanwhile, flocked to the mainland in what seemed like the first gold rush of the twenty-first century.

But if the Communists had shown they could deliver economic growth at rates rivaling those of any democracy, it was still unclear how well they could meet other expectations of an increasingly complex and demanding society. Could their profit-driven model of authoritarianism stop the coal mine accidents? Could it deliver clean air and water? If the party maintained its stranglehold on civil society—its obsessive effort to control churches, charities, advocacy groups, labor unions—could it narrow the gap between rich and poor, or build an effective social safety net? Without a free press or independent courts, could it curb corruption or the abuse of power? The party had made many people wealthier but could it count on their support in hard times or inspire their loyalty?

An example of the limits of the Chinese political structure was the shameful AIDS crisis unfolding in central Henan Province. In the early 1990s, hundreds of thousands of impoverished farmers there contracted HIV by selling blood at state hospitals and private clinics run by local officials and their friends. These facilities often used unsanitary methods, including a process in which blood from several donors was mixed in a centrifuge to remove valuable plasma and then reinjected into them so they could recover faster and sell more blood. Such practices caused AIDS to spread quickly, and by the beginning of 2003, the disease had devastated villages across the Henan countryside. Bold leadership, grassroots activism, and the free flow of information are critical to stopping the spread of AIDS, but China's rigid political system has never tolerated much of any of the three. Instead, the party's instinctive response was to protect the officials who had profited from the blood trade—and to hide the outbreak. The police harassed and arrested activists who challenged the government to take action, and the censors restricted reporting on AIDS in the state media. The nation's top leaders remained silent and devoted few resources to educating the public about the disease. In August 2003, I visited one village in Henan where desperate residents had staged a protest demanding better medical care. Local officials reacted by sending not doctors but riot police, who stormed through town and beat up sickly villagers.

Despite such stories, which the foreign media and a few brave Chinese journalists had begun to expose, the AIDS epidemic in Henan barely registered a blip on the radar of the party leadership at the start of 2003. In a nation of 1.3 billion, outbreaks of deadly illnesses were a common occurrence, and the Ministry of Health received reports about them from the provinces every day. But career-minded local officials preferred to handle problems themselves rather than admit they needed help, and if they briefed Beijing on the diseases they were seeing, they were more inclined to downplay outbreaks than sound an alarm. Generally, the central authorities took notice only if a disease caused a serious public panic or represented a threat to political stability. And so, as the government prepared to convene the National People's Congress in early March—an important session because Jiang Zemin would be passing the presidency to Hu Jintao— the leadership paid little attention to the AIDS crisis in central China, or, for that matter, to reports of another deadly disease that had made its debut in southern China a few months earlier. In party documents passing through internal channels, this other disease was described as an "atypical pneumonia." Within weeks, the world would know it as severe acute respiratory syndrome, or SARS.

THE FIRST REPORT of the illness to reach Beijing came in January. A chef at a restaurant that cooked wild animals to order in Shenzhen, the freewheeling metropolis across the border from Hong Kong, had come down with a fever and checked into a hospital in his hometown of Heyuan, another city in the southern province of Guangdong. The man was diagnosed with a serious case of pneumonia, but within days, several doctors and nurses at the hospital had also fallen ill. By the first week of January, provincial authorities had sent a team of medical experts to investigate. By the third week, a more serious outbreak had been reported in the city of Zhongshan near the provincial capital of Guangzhou—nearly thirty patients in three hospitals—and a secret bulletin had been sent to the Ministry of Health in Beijing. In their report, the medical experts described a mysterious respiratory ailment, warned that it was "highly infectious," and recommended that medical workers isolate patients and take precautions to protect themselves, by wearing masks and goggles, for example. It was a report that could have stopped SARS before it became a global epidemic, but the party's knee-jerk secrecy ensured that it was never widely distributed among the nation's hospitals. Instead, Beijing sent a team of its own experts to Guangdong, and they returned with reassurances from provincial officials that everything was under control. "We thought it was just high fevers, pneumonia, and a few deaths," recalled Bi Shengli, a senior virologist in the central government's Center for Disease Control and Prevention. "We figured they could handle it. We trusted them in Guangdong, because it's a relatively advanced province."

Provincial officials immediately imposed a blackout on news about the disease. The day after the medical experts visited Heyuan, the local paper published the world's first story about SARS under a headline that read "Epidemic Is Only a Rumor." Officials later acknowledged that their primary concern was the provincial economy. The weeklong Spring Festival holiday was scheduled to begin on February 1, and local businesses were counting on people to spend money. "The most important vacation in the life of Chinese people, the Spring Festival, was coming. We didn't want to spoil everyone's happy time," Feng Shaomin, director of foreign affairs for the Guangdong health department, told my colleague John Pomfret. "You can imagine how people would have reacted if we had told them about the disease. They wouldn't eat out, nor would they go shopping or get together with family members and friends. If we had done it earlier, it would definitely have caused chaos."

But if party officials didn't want to tell the public about the disease before the Spring Festival, they were even less eager to do so after the holiday. On February 10, the Guangdong government announced that three hundred people had been diagnosed with "atypical pneumonia" and five patients had died, but officials assured the world the disease was under control. It was a lie, but all provincial newspapers were ordered to publish it. With the National People's Congress only weeks away, no one wanted to be blamed for spoiling the picture-perfect ceremonies installing Hu Jintao with headlines about a fast-spreading illness of unknown origin. Even after the congress, the cover-up continued. Now officials were worried about the impact on tourism during the next national holiday, the May Day vacation. It seemed like a bad joke: When is the best time for the party to break bad news to the public? Never.

The Communist Party devotes tremendous resources to the collection and control of information, and the care with which it guards its secrets has been critical to its ability to stay in power. But its institutional obsession with secrecy can also leave it vulnerable. As party officials withheld information about the "atypical pneumonia," the disease was spreading. And unlike AIDS, it moved at a frightening pace. Doctors and nurses, kept in the dark about the illness and how contagious it was, continued treating people without protecting themselves or other patients. People who developed symptoms didn't realize how sick they were and didn't know how easily they could infect loved ones, coworkers, or fellow travelers. During the Spring Festival, millions of migrant workers packed into trains and streamed out of Guangdong. By late February, the virus had struck at least five provinces and crossed into Hong Kong, a travel hub with more than six hundred international flights daily. By the end of the month, it had reached Vietnam and Singapore, and jumped across the Pacific Ocean to Canada.

IN CHINESE, THEY called them Poison Kings. In English, they were known as "super-spreaders." It is one of the lingering mysteries of the 2003 epidemic of SARS that certain individuals were prone to accelerate the transmission of the disease, infecting many more people than others who carried the virus. Scientists never figured out exactly why. But by tracking these Poison Kings, you could trace the progress of the epidemic, following the path of the virus from its initial appearance in the cities of Guangdong Province to the rest of China and then the world. One of the first super-spreaders to be identified was a twenty-seven-year-old businesswoman whom I caught up with in May, a few months after the epidemic became a national crisis. She was a frail, slender woman with long black hair, and she asked that I identify her only by her surname, Yu. I met her at night, in a car parked in front of her apartment compound, with her husband, whose surname was Chen, seated at her side. Her eyes were slightly puffy, perhaps from tears, and she wore on the sleeve of her white blouse a black button with a Chinese character, a traditional symbol of mourning.

She lived in Taiyuan, the dreary capital of Shanxi Province, an industrial region in north-central China best known for its abundant coal deposits and mining operations. The city was an epicenter of the SARS epidemic, with more infections than any other in China besides Guangzhou and Beijing, and Yu was an important reason why. In mid-February, she had traveled to Guangdong on a buying trip for the small business she ran trading in jade and jewelry. Before going, she had heard that a strange illness was spreading through the province. Because of the news blackout and the absence of good information, rumors of a "weird sickness" were circulating there and had led to panicked buying of vinegar, herbal medicine, and other items believed effective in warding it off. But Yu's mother, a Taiyuan journalist, had called a few colleagues in the region and was told there was nothing to worry about. The provincial government, after all, had assured the public that the atypical pneumonia was under control. A few days into Yu's visit, though, on February 22, she began to feel feverish on a bus ride from Shenzhen to Guangzhou. She thought about going to a hospital, but her husband persuaded her to fly home the next day instead.

Back in Taiyuan, Yu visited one hospital after another, telling doctors that she might have been infected with the atypical pneumonia reported in Guangdong. The doctors had received no information about the disease, and were naturally skeptical. None of them protected themselves when they asked her to cough and listened to her lungs. "They thought it was a cold and gave her normal antibiotics," Chen told me. "They didn't have the information about SARS." Meanwhile, Yu's fever was getting worse. After a few days, it was up to 104 degrees, and she was too weak to eat. The city's best doctors were stumped. On February 27, the director of the respiratory department at the Shanxi Provincial People's Hospital finally moved her into a special ward and ordered staff to wear masks when treating her. By then, though, Yu had already infected at least a dozen people in Taiyuan, probably more, setting off a chain reaction that would hobble the city.

The next day, Chen decided to take his wife to Beijing. It was an easy decision, because the capital was only 250 miles to the northeast and the nation's best hospitals were there. He and a friend rode with Yu in an ambulance, while her mother and the doctor followed in another vehicle. The trip took nine hours, including a delay caused by a flat tire. Neither Yu nor any of her companions wore masks or other protective gear. They arrived after midnight on March 1 and checked into the People's Liberation Army No. 301 Hospital, a well-known military facility that had a special ward for senior government officials. Deng Xiaoping himself had received treatment there in his final years. If a new illness was spreading through China, Chen thought, surely the doctors at this hospital would know about it. But he was wrong. The staff at the No. 301 Hospital was as unprepared as those at the hospitals in Taiyuan. The hospital admitted Yu to a general ward with other patients, and the doctors and nurses took no special precautions while examining her. Three days later they transferred her to a private room in the respiratory ward. By then, both of Yu's parents had come down with fevers. They had tried to hide it, hoping not to upset their daughter, but on March 4, Yu's mother was admitted to the hospital. Her father flew in from Taiyuan and checked himself in, too.

The next day, Yu and her parents were moved to the People's Liberation Army No. 302 Hospital, which specializes in infectious diseases. But Chen was upset because the ambulance driver and medical staff failed to take any infection-control measures during the transfer. When he returned to his hotel room, he phoned a newspaper in Guangzhou with a reputation for investigative reporting, hoping to raise an alarm. "This disease is very dangerous and infectious," he told the reporter who took his call, pleading with her to warn the public. But she told him the newspaper already knew about the disease and that there was nothing it could do. She suggested he contact the local health department instead. What the reporter didn't say was that the annual session of the National People's Congress had just opened in Beijing and negative news reports had been forbidden. As the party's senior leaders were congratulating themselves across town, Yu watched her father and mother, both in their early fifties, grow weaker at the No. 302 Hospital. It became so difficult for her father to breathe, he was forced to sleep sitting upright to avoid violent fits of coughing. On March 6, a team of doctors tried to save him by performing a tracheotomy. He died the next day. Later, the epidemiologists would identify him as the first SARS fatality in Beijing.

Chen came down with a fever next, and friends who had accompanied the couple to the capital also got sick. Then came terrifying news from Taiyuan: their one-year-old boy also had developed a fever, as had Yu's brother and her brother's wife. The three of them flew to Beijing and were admitted to the same hospital. Yu and Chen were placed in rooms on opposite sides of a hallway, and they communicated by shouting from their beds. On television, they watched government officials continue to downplay the epidemic.

After a week, Yu and her child began to show signs of recovery, and doctors said they wanted to transfer them back to Taiyuan. The family resisted, arguing that they should be moved only if they had fully recovered. But the hospital insisted, saying it needed the beds for other patients. Chen wondered if they were forcing his wife to leave because they were scared, or because they wanted to reduce the number of cases of the new disease in Beijing for propaganda purposes. By then the virus was already spreading among the hospital's staff. Several of the doctors who had performed the tracheotomy on Yu's father fell ill. On March 11, the chief of one of the respiratory wards collapsed.

Thus did SARS make its way from the southern province of Guangdong to the nation's capital. By the end of May, the virus would infect more than 2,500 people in Beijing and kill 175 of them—only Hong Kong suffered a greater death toll. It is unclear how many people Yu infected in Beijing, or how many cases in the city were indirectly linked to her. At least two other super-spreaders accelerated the transmission of the disease in Beijing in those early weeks, but Yu was the first of the Poison Kings to arrive in the capital, and serious outbreaks were reported in both hospitals where she was treated. By the end of March, thirty of the forty doctors and nurses in the respiratory wards of the No. 302 Hospital would be diagnosed with SARS. At the same time, one of Yu's uncles checked into another hospital in Beijing and infected at least a dozen doctors and nurses there, including a visiting physician from the province of Inner Mongolia who then carried the virus home, causing another outbreak that sickened as many as one hundred people.

It was snowing on March 15 when the No. 302 Hospital decided to send Yu and her son to a hospital in Taiyuan. The roads between Beijing and Taiyuan were sure to be treacherous, but the hospital refused to extend their stay. Yu and her son left at about 4 P.M. Because of the weather, they didn't make it to Taiyuan until six the next morning. While Yu's ambulance was making its way along the mountain roads that night, her mother died in Beijing.

On the same day, the World Health Organization issued its first global alert about SARS. At the time, the WHO had received reports of about 150 cases of the disease, including four deaths. The alert provided numbers and details of cases in Vietnam, Singapore, Hong Kong, Thailand, Canada, and the Philippines. But there was no information from China. Only two sentences addressed the glaring omission: "An epidemic of atypical pneumonia had previously been reported by the Chinese government starting in November 2002 in Guangdong Province. This epidemic is reported to be under control."

As the carefully choreographed rituals of the National People's Congress session played out, the party stood by the Guangdong government's February announcement that the outbreak had been contained. Even after the parliament finished installing Hu Jintao and adjourned on March 18, the party said nothing about the worsening epidemic. By then, the cover-up was no longer a local matter. As soon as people started getting sick and dying in Beijing, the party's top leaders had to be briefed. But if the new members of the Politburo Standing Committee were alarmed by what was happening or had any inclination to come clean with the public, they didn't act on it. Instead, nearly four weeks after Yu checked into the No. 301 Hospital, party leaders broke their silence by issuing a feel-good statement about a mysterious disease they knew to be highly contagious and frequently lethal.

"Beijing Effectively Controls Imported Atypical Pneumonia" read the headline carried by state news wires on March 26. The story said eight patients from Shanxi and Hong Kong had been transferred to hospitals in Beijing for treatment. Three of them had died, it said, but the others had "basically completely recovered." Two medical workers had developed symptoms, but they were quickly isolated and the disease had not spread to the general public. A spokesman added that the city "has already established a perfect disease monitoring network, set up a special team and lab for investigating and handling the disease, and trained relevant medical and nursing personnel." The government, he said, was "capable of responding to the epidemic and guaranteeing the health of the people of the capital."

It was the first of what would be a series of stunning lies uttered by officials in Beijing as SARS began to tear through the city of fifteen million. Far from the reassuring picture of calm and competence the article presented, the hospitals of Beijing were woefully unprepared and quickly overwhelmed with patients in respiratory distress running fevers. Doctors and nurses who were never warned to protect themselves contracted the disease in large numbers, and many of them later unwittingly infected their families and patients. As medical workers became patients in their own hospitals, fear and exhaustion haunted those who remained on the job. Meanwhile, the government research labs assigned to figure out what was happening and find a cure were struggling to make progress, slowed by professional rivalries, bureaucratic feuding, and the party's limits on information sharing. Researchers in the Center for Disease Control and Prevention, for example, couldn't get access to good tissue samples from their counterparts in Guangdong until late March, in part because the central government's Ministry of Health couldn't give orders to the Guangdong government, whose leaders ranked higher in the party hierarchy. Senior officials wasted time holding a series of "coordination meetings" instead.

As the cover-up continued, many doctors were too busy treating patients, or too accustomed to bad news going unreported, to ask why the government was hiding the disaster unfolding around them. Decades of party control and corruption, under both socialism and capitalism, had corroded the medical profession and its values. In its mildest form, this meant physicians accepting bribes from patients or prescribing unnecessary drugs to boost profits. At its worst, it meant the trade in organs from executed prisoners, the forced abortion of pregnancies violating the one-child policy, the psychiatric commitment of dissidents, even the euthanasia of infants born with severe disabilities. Doctors in China were trained as technicians to serve the state, to do their work and leave questions of ethics and public policy to others. Yet many on the front lines of the SARS epidemic privately questioned the wisdom of keeping the outbreak secret. Some were afraid to speak out and risk losing their jobs, or concluded there was little they could do because the government controlled the news media. Others complained to their superiors or sent urgent messages through internal channels recommending that the authorities go public with everything they knew about the disease. Only then, they argued, would the public and the hospitals have a fighting chance against it. But their appeals were met with silence.

AMONG THE DOCTORS who were uneasy about the cover-up was a semiretired military surgeon at the No. 301 Hospital named Jiang Yanyong. He was seventy-one, tall and distinguished-looking, with a long, crinkled face and a head of hair that he dyed black in the manner popular among aging intellectuals and party officials. If it was a cynical time to be a doctor in China, Jiang had come to the profession in a more hopeful era. Born to a wealthy Shanghai banking family, he studied medicine at Peking University just as the Communists were taking power and he trained at Peking Union Medical College, the nation's most prestigious medical school. He eagerly joined the party and enlisted in the People's Liberation Army even before graduating. He decided to specialize in surgery because he was inspired by the example of Norman Bethune, the Canadian battlefield surgeon who joined the Red Army and was eulogized by Mao as a martyr after his death in the Sino-Japanese War.

Jiang's idealism was shattered not long after he was assigned to the staff of the No. 301 Hospital in 1957. His brothers were persecuted in the Anti-Rightist Campaign, and he came under attack himself in the Cultural Revolution. Imprisoned in the hospital, he endured beatings and public condemnations because of his privileged family background. Once, when he managed to escape, his sister betrayed him and turned him in. Later, he spent five lonely years on a prison farm in the remote deserts of Qinghai Province in western China, separated from his wife and children. Mao's rule shook his faith in the party, but Jiang was the kind of man who needed to believe in something, and when he finally returned to Beijing and the No. 301 Hospital, he committed himself to the values of his profession. If he could not change society, he decided, he could at least do right by his patients. By the time of the Tiananmen demonstrations in 1989, Jiang had developed a reputation as one of the nation's finest surgeons. He served as the hospital's chief of general surgery, held a rank equivalent to that of a major-general and counted senior party officials and their relatives as former patients. After the massacre, the party asked him to express support for the suppression of the student-led democracy movement. He was a senior military official and a veteran party member, but Jiang resisted. The hospital responded by denying him a promotion and easing him into retirement. Others more willing to toe the party line moved up instead.

After his retirement, the No. 301 Hospital retained Jiang as a member of its experts' committee and continued to call on him to perform operations and consult on difficult cases. It was in that role that he heard about the woman from Taiyuan whose parents died after they were transferred to the No. 302 Hospital. The cases were unusual—his colleagues said the diagnosis was atypical pneumonia—but what really caught Jiang's attention was the fact that so many doctors and nurses became severely ill after treating them. Later, he learned that the president of his hospital, and those of all the hospitals in Beijing, had been summoned to a meeting at the Ministry of Health. They were told that a serious infectious disease had arrived in the capital, and that information about the outbreak was to be kept strictly confidential to ensure the success of the National People's Congress session. "I heard about the meeting soon after it happened," Jiang told me. "I thought it was wrong to handle the situation this way. But at the time, I didn't realize that this disease SARS was so serious and dangerous. So I didn't do anything."

Soon, though, Jiang heard that a patient awaiting gall bladder surgery in his hospital had come down with a fever and was having trouble breathing. The patient was transferred to the PLA's No. 309 Hospital, where he passed away. Several of the medical workers who treated him got sick and had to be hospitalized, and the gall bladder surgery department was forced to shut down. Other patients in the respiratory and neurology departments began showing symptoms, too, followed by doctors and nurses in those departments. It became clear to Jiang that this "atypical pneumonia" was the same disease that had struck hospitals around the world and that the WHO was calling SARS. Then, near the end of March, an old medical school classmate of Jiang's, the chief of the No. 301 Hospital's neurology department, was diagnosed with lung cancer. While waiting for an operation, he developed a high fever and doctors identified him as another suspected case of SARS. Because of his relationship with the patient, Jiang was invited to consult with the team of doctors assigned to treat him. It was then, Jiang told me, that he finally realized "this infectious disease was anything but ordinary, and we should be paying closer attention to it."

Over the next few weeks, Jiang began following news reports from around the world about the SARS epidemic. He spent most of his time in his apartment watching Hong Kong news programs or reading articles on the Internet. On the afternoon of April 3, he was watching television in his living room when a live broadcast of a news conference with the Chinese minister of health, Zhang Wenkang, came on. Zhang was a soft-spoken man in his early sixties with wire-frame glasses and slightly graying hair. At first glance, Jiang had a lot in common with him. Zhang was younger, but he too was a Shanghai native and a doctor who had spent his career in the ranks of the military. In the early 1990s, he had served as deputy chief of the PLA's health department, making him one of Jiang's superiors. But if Jiang considered medicine a calling, Zhang was as much a smooth-talking politician as a physician, and everybody knew it. In 1998, when he was appointed health minister, many whispered that he won the job because he had developed a friendship with President Jiang Zemin while supervising his medical care. Now he was on television, telling the world that the SARS epidemic in China "was effectively under control."

"Through the hard work of the central and local health departments, the number of people infected has fallen sharply," he declared. "Mainland China is stable, and people are going about their lives and work as usual." Zhang said 1,190 cases of SARS had been reported in China, but almost all of them were in Guangdong Province, and nearly 80 percent of those patients had recovered. In Beijing, he said there were only twelve cases. Addressing a journalist wearing a surgical mask, Zhang added, "I can tell you all responsibly that it is safe to work, live, and travel in China. Each one of you seated here, I believe you are safe, whether you are wearing a mask or not."

As he watched Zhang's performance on television, Jiang grew furious, and the intensity of his outrage surprised him a bit. He had been a party member long enough to understand how common it was for government officials to lie to the public. But this was somehow worse. Jiang knew that SARS was a dangerous disease, and that a major epidemic could be in the works in Beijing. He had watched enough of his colleagues get sick to understand that doctors and nurses in the city were unprepared. Beijing's long winter was giving way to spring, and tourists from around the world, reassured by Zhang's pronouncements, would soon converge on the ancient capital. Jiang worried that if just a few of them contracted SARS, they could infect fellow airline passengers and carry the virus to their home countries. The consequences could be catastrophic. Perhaps what upset him most, though, was the fact that it was a fellow doctor—a man who had taken an oath to his patients—who was trying to conceal the outbreak. A doctor, he thought, should know better.

Jiang was just one surgeon, at one hospital, but he had already seen enough patients to know that Zhang's claim that there were only twelve cases of SARS in Beijing was untrue. After the news conference, he called colleagues at the No. 302 and No. 309 hospitals to discuss the situation—and to gather hard numbers. One of the doctors whom Jiang contacted recalled that he sounded extremely agitated on the phone. Jiang urged him to tell the hospital president that the health minister's numbers were wrong, and demanded the president's home phone number so he could call him, too. But the doctor was worried that Jiang "was getting himself into trouble" and refused to give him the number. Another colleague recalled the urgency with which Jiang tried to gather information about the outbreak. "I would tell him what I knew, and he would tell me what he knew," he said. "We were quite worried at the time, because there had already been large-scale outbreaks in Guangdong and Hong Kong. If it wasn't handled well, it would explode in Beijing as well. We thought some of what was being done was wrong, but we were frustrated and could only talk about it privately. At the time, I had no idea what Jiang was going to do."

Jiang himself wasn't sure, either, but he kept collecting information. He quickly discovered there were forty patients diagnosed with SARS at the No. 302 Hospital and sixty patients at the No. 309 Hospital. The health minister had said that only three people had died of

SARS in all of Beijing, but Jiang was told that nine had died in those two hospitals alone. The next morning, he learned there were forty-six more SARS cases in his own hospital. He sought out hospital officials, and asked them to report to their superiors that Zhang's figures were incorrect. "But they told me their superiors had issued regulations," Jiang recalled. "As members of the military, we couldn't report this problem." In the afternoon, Jiang ran into two of the army's former health chiefs, and he asked them what they thought of Zhang's news conference. Both said they believed that what he had said was wrong. One told Jiang he had heard there were already more than forty SARS cases in the army's general logistics department. The health minister had served as a deputy to one of the men, and Jiang asked him sarcastically how he could have trained a liar.

It was possible the health minister didn't have accurate data about SARS. Party bureaucrats often tried to hide bad news from senior officials to avoid blame. But it seemed more likely to Jiang that the minister was fully informed and simply concealing the truth from the public. He could be following orders from the party leadership, of course, but even if Hu Jintao himself had approved the cover-up, Jiang believed it was wrong. Sitting in front of his computer that night, he began writing an indignant e-mail.

Yesterday, the Chinese minister of health said at a news conference that the Chinese government has already fully and conscientiously dealt with the SARS problem, and that this disease is under control. But after seeing the numbers he provided, that there were 12 cases of SARS in Beijing and three deaths, I simply can't believe it. Zhang Wenkang is a doctor who graduated from the People's Liberation Army No. 2 Medical University, but he has set aside a doctor's most basic ethical standards. . . .

The health minister, he wrote, appeared to be a student of Lin Biao, the military leader who was Mao's second-in-command during the Cultural Revolution and who once declared that "without telling lies, one cannot accomplish great things."

"Today, I went to the hospital wards," Jiang continued, "and all the doctors and nurses who saw yesterday's news conference were very angry." He explained how the parents of the woman from Taiyuan had died, and how ten doctors and nurses at the No. 302 Hospital were infected while treating them. He described how SARS had spread through his hospital, and how some departments were forced to shut down. Finally, he said he had called colleagues at the No. 309 Hospital, which had been designated by the military to handle its SARS cases. "They said that Zhang was just talking nonsense," he wrote, "that the No. 309 Hospital had already admitted close to 40 SARS patients. As of yesterday, six had already died.

"The material I am providing has been verified, and I accept full responsibility for it," he concluded. After signing his name, Jiang looked up two e-mail addresses and typed them in—one for the international news channel of the national broadcaster, China Central Television, and the other for the newsroom of Phoenix Satellite Television, a government-friendly station in Hong Kong with permission to broadcast in the mainland. Then he hit the send button.

Years later, when I asked him why he decided to speak out, Jiang said it wasn't an easy decision. He knew the cover-up depended on the silence of countless people like himself, and he knew the cost of breaking ranks could be severe. He knew he could be accused of violating military discipline or disclosing state secrets. He knew he could lose his pension or even face arrest. But Jiang said he also reminded himself that he really wasn't doing anything wrong. He was just telling the truth and expressing his opinion, and those were rights guaranteed to all citizens by the constitution. "Of course, it was possible, very possible, that it would mean trouble," he told me. "I was prepared for that." In the end, he said, he was driven to act by a sense of responsibility as a doctor. "This disease wasn't something invincible," he said. "As long as you confronted it properly, it could be contained. But if there was incorrect information out there, then it would be difficult. If everyone believed it was already under control, then people would relax, they wouldn't work hard at it, and that would lead to a disaster, not just for China but also for the world. So as a doctor, I felt I had a duty to tell the truth. I felt I should tell the public everything I knew about the situation. If doctors didn't tell the truth, more people would die, and the nation would suffer."

JIANG WAITED ANXIOUSLY for a response to his e-mail. At first, nothing happened. There was no reply, no phone call, not even a knock on the door. Instead, the government's denials continued. A pamphlet titled "Atypical Pneumonia Is Nothing to Be Afraid Of" was published and the national tourism bureau convened a meeting of foreign airline and travel agents to reassure them the epidemic was over. "A well-organized holiday, with millions of people traveling around this vast country, will show the world that tourism in China is safe and healthy," one official, Sun Gang, told the *People's Daily* of the upcoming May Day vacation. A few days later, the government held a news conference to disclose that a Finnish diplomat employed by the International Labor Organization in Beijing had died of SARS. But a city official claimed he had been infected overseas, and reiterated that "the problem of SARS spreading in Beijing does not exist."

Jiang didn't know whether his e-mail had been lost or ignored, but he grew impatient. Every day that passed with the epidemic hidden from the public was a day the virus was moving unchecked through the city and its hospitals. Frustrated, Jiang forwarded his e-mail to a few friends, hoping one of them could get it to someone in the leadership, or perhaps the foreign media. Soon the *Wall Street Journal* was calling him, and then *Time* magazine. It was one thing to send a letter to the state-owned China Central Television or to reporters at the party-sanctioned Phoenix Satellite Television, but it would be quite another to give an interview to an American journalist. Throughout Chinese officialdom, there is a taboo about speaking to foreign reporters, who are regarded as hostile elements determined to weaken China. The unspoken rule is that loyal Chinese should never say anything to an outsider that would make the motherland look bad. In the military especially, doing so would be seen as an act of betrayal or even treason. But Jiang had tried going through official channels, and he had tried going to the domestic press, and nothing had changed. So he told the American reporters what he knew.

The *Journal* was the first to obtain a copy of Jiang's e-mail, but the correspondent from *Time,* Susan Jakes, moved on it faster. She arranged to meet with Jiang, and she offered to withhold his name from her article to protect him. But Jiang insisted that she identify him. Information from an anonymous source, he said, would be much less credible.

Jiang was far from the only doctor to recognize that a cover-up was under way, but he was the first to muster the courage to challenge it openly. In a political system that relied on self-censorship, the impact of his disclosure was breathtaking. Almost immediately, the fiction that the party had sustained began to come apart. The international media seized on the *Time* article as soon as it was published on the magazine's Web site, and reporters from around the world flooded Jiang with calls. He answered as many as he could before his stunned superiors at the hospital figured out what to do. The hospital's party chief and its political commissar visited Jiang at home that evening and asked him to stop talking, saying he was violating military regulations that prohibited contact with the foreign press without permission. Jiang agreed but also chastised the men for remaining silent when the health minister lied to the press. "Our nation has suffered enough in the past because of lying," he told them. "I hope from now on you will try your best to tell the truth." Later, Jiang sent a letter through internal channels offering to accept punishment if the numbers he had made public were incorrect. But if he was right, he said, the health minister should resign and the government should move quickly to implement infection-control measures.

For several days, the party struggled to maintain the cover-up, but it seemed to move in slow motion as news of Jiang's e-mail raced across China on Internet bulletin boards and in cell phone text messages. Party officials couldn't even keep their lies straight. Beijing health officials held another news conference, saying there were twenty-seven cases of SARS in the city, but the same day, the city's mayor told a visiting dignitary that there were just twenty-two. It really didn't matter, though, because by then no one believed the government anymore—not the press, not the team from the World Health Organization that had arrived in Beijing to examine the situation, not the people of the city. Soon the party's efforts to deny the truth began to reflect its desperation. Several hospitals were ordered to hide SARS cases from the WHO team by physically moving frail patients into different wards or even into hotels. At one hospital, doctors and nurses loaded patients into ambulances and rode around in circles with them until the WHO team left. Word of such outrages quickly filtered back to Jiang, whose classmates, students, and friends worked in hospitals across the city. Infuriated, he defied his superiors by writing a letter describing the hide-and-seek tactics and arranging for it to be delivered to *Time* and the WHO team. Another wave of damaging headlines followed.

And then, almost without warning, the party caved. One day it was saying there were only thirty-seven cases of SARS in Beijing. The next, it was suddenly acknowledging 339 confirmed cases and 402 suspected ones. One day health minister Zhang and his deputies were assuring the world it was safe to travel in China. The next, the health minister was abruptly dismissed, along with the mayor of Beijing, Meng Xuenong. And all this was less than two weeks after Jiang stepped forward with the truth. Faced with condemnation abroad and growing skepticism at home, not to mention an epidemic that showed no signs of slowing, the new president and party leader, Hu Jintao, had decided the cover-up was no longer tenable and ordered an end to the lies. It was a remarkable turnaround and political gamble, and in the highest ranks of the party it was greeted with caution. For several days, Hu and the new premier, Wen Jiabao, appeared alone on state television, promising honest and open government and calling for an all-out campaign against SARS. Their colleagues on the Politburo Standing Committee—many of them allies of the former president, Jiang Zemin—were nowhere to be found. They seemed wary of the new strategy, for it went against the party's instincts to admit wrongdoing. After all, the health minister and the Beijing mayor had hardly been alone in approving the cover-up. Could the leadership really get away with pinning the blame on them alone? And what if SARS could not be contained? Would an angry and panicked populace demand more dismissals, a full accounting of the government's blunders, or worse yet, fundamental political reforms? The safe move was to let Hu and Wen take the lead in the SARS fight, because if their approach failed and caused problems for the party, the political error would be theirs alone.

Fortunately for the new party leaders, SARS proved a less formidable opponent than feared. Jiang Yanyong was right: the disease was no match for a government willing to confront it openly and honestly. Under Hu's leadership, the party mobilized the full power of the state to contain the epidemic, setting up infection-control checkpoints, opening fever wards, ordering mass quarantines, even setting up temporary hospitals. Three months later, after infecting more than eight thousand people in twenty-nine countries and taking the lives of 774, including 349 in China, the virus was gone. But the party's victory had come at a price. The government had been forced to admit it lied about a pressing matter of public health, and the shine on the Chinese model of authoritarianism was tarnished. Perhaps as important, the SARS epidemic showed the public that one man with the courage of his convictions could challenge the party-state and not just survive but prevail.

SUDDENLY, JIANG YANYONG was a national hero. State media portrayed him as the honest doctor who dared to speak when others were silent, the man who stood up to the party bosses and saved lives around the world. His wizened face appeared on the cover of *Sanlian Shenghuo*, the popular weekly newsmagazine published by Xinhua, and producers at China Central Television invited him to appear on one of the nation's top news shows. Even the staid *People's Daily* posted a flattering article about him on its Web site. The censors, meanwhile, didn't know what to do. The leadership had abandoned the cover-up so abruptly, the rank and file in the party apparatus were stunned and confused. Did Hu and Wen really mean it when they declared that lies—the stock and trade of the party hacks—would no longer be tolerated? Were they planning political reforms and proposing greater freedom for the press, or just distancing themselves from the cover-up and the old guard that had just retired? The propaganda department wasn't sure, and journalists eager for change sensed the hesitation. Emboldened by the reversal of the cover-up, encouraged by the talk of openness coming from the party's new leaders, they seized on the chance to tell the world about Jiang.

He was just an elderly surgeon, but he presented a dilemma for the government. Punishing him while the nation and the world were watching would undermine its attempt to put the cover-up behind it and bring the epidemic under control. But the propaganda czars were accustomed to handpicking the nation's heroes and celebrities—even its film stars—and they were uncomfortable when someone won the public's respect on his own, especially if the person in question had an independent streak. Fame, they knew, could mean influence, and they worried when someone they couldn't control had influence. Jiang presented a particularly troublesome case because, despite his party and military credentials, he had already demonstrated an ability to think for himself and a willingness to challenge the government. So as the campaign against SARS began to show results, the party began to rewrite history. In a news conference on national television in late May, a deputy health minister, Gao Qiang, denied the government had ever tried to conceal the epidemic, and when a reporter asked about Jiang, he feigned exasperation and said he didn't know why people were interested in him. "We have six million doctors and health-care workers," the minister said. "Jiang Yanyong is one of them." It was an unconvincing performance, but it served its purpose. The censors snapped into action, the state media fell into line, and the doctor's run of good press came to an end. Persuading the public to forget him, though, would not be as easy.

Jiang wasn't surprised when the state media stopped writing about him. He had been told by the military he needed permission to speak to the press, and he had referred countless reporters to hospital officials, who always rejected the interview requests. Many of these reporters had gone ahead and written stories anyway, but Jiang never expected the coverage to continue for long, and in any case, it wasn't that important to him. He had not spoken out about SARS to bring attention to himself but to force the government to openly confront the disease, and by that measure, he could feel good about what he had accomplished. He had called on the health minister to resign, and the health minister had been dismissed. He had recommended infection-control measures, and they had been implemented across the country. He had urged the party to share what it knew about the disease, and a propaganda campaign had been launched.

But even as the government contained the epidemic, Jiang felt a pang of guilt. The SARS cover-up was not the first time he had to decide whether to submit to party authority and keep quiet about wrongdoing. He had confronted a similar choice after the Tiananmen massacre. At the time, he believed he had acted honorably. He had accepted retirement rather than endorse the crackdown, and for years he felt that his conscience was clear. Occasionally, he told friends in private what he saw in the emergency room on the night of June 3, 1989, but he never became a public critic of the government. He sympathized with the families of those who were killed, but he knew that speaking out would cost him his job, perhaps his pension and apartment as well, and it would certainly make life more difficult for his wife and children. And what would it accomplish? Like millions of others angered by the massacre and disappointed in the path that China took after it, Jiang had chosen to live in silence.

As the years passed, though, the decision began to weigh on him. Had he really done enough? Could he have done more? Now, as the public praised his integrity and hailed him as the "honest doctor" who exposed the SARS cover-up, those feelings of shame and remorse were stronger than ever. If one person speaking truth to power could force the party to admit its crimes and change history, as he had shown in the SARS crisis, then why had he remained quiet for so long about the Tiananmen massacre? Had he been too quick to compromise, too willing to play it safe all those years? These were difficult questions for the elderly surgeon to consider as he looked back on his life, and Jiang wrestled with them for months. Then, as the party celebrated its victory against SARS and did its best to persuade the public to forget him, Jiang quietly decided he would speak out again. He had gained a measure of fame and political capital in the SARS crisis, and he resolved to use it on behalf of the victims of Tiananmen and their families.

Jiang sat down to write, to record what he had seen that night so many years ago and share it with the party's new leaders. The words came easily, in a flood of suppressed memory and emotion. "I am a surgeon at the PLA No. 301 Hospital," he wrote. "I was chief of the department of general surgery on June 4, 1989."

On the night of June 3, I heard repeated broadcasts urging people to stay off the streets. At about 10 P.M., I was in my apartment when I heard the sound of continuous gunfire from the north. Several minutes later, my pager beeped. It was the emergency room calling me, and I rushed over. What I found was unimaginable—on the floor and the tables of the emergency room were seven young people, their faces and bodies covered with blood. Two of them were later confirmed dead by EKG. My head buzzed and I nearly passed out. I had been a surgeon for more than 30 years. I had treated wounded soldiers before, while on the medical team of the PLA railway corps that built the Chengdu-Kunming Railway. But their injuries resulted from unavoidable accidents during the construction process, while before my eyes, in Beijing, the magnificent capital of China, lying in front of me, were our own people, killed by our people's army, with weapons supplied by the people.

I didn't have time to dwell on it. After the sound of another round of gunfire, ordinary residents using wooden boards and pull carts brought more injured young people to the emergency room. As I examined the wounded, I asked the staff to tell other surgeons and nurses to hurry to the operating rooms. Our hospital had a total of 18 operating rooms, and all of them were put to use saving lives. I was in the emergency room, doing triage and emergency care. In the two hours between 10 P.M. and midnight, our hospital's emergency room admitted 89 patients with gunshot wounds. Seven of them later died because efforts to save them were ineffective. In the hospital's 18 operating rooms, three groups of doctors worked late into the night, saving all who could be saved.

I will never forget some of those who died. There was a young man in his 20s, whose parents were retired officials from the Seventh Ministry of Machine Building across from our hospital. . . . There were shots outside, and this young man—the youngest of the family, who had picked up his marriage license earlier that day—ran out with his fiancée. Just before they reached the Wukesong intersection, they were strafed by gunfire. The young woman turned and ran, and she yelled at her boyfriend to run too. She had not gone far when she realized he hadn't followed her, so she went back. After a short while, she found him lying on the side of the road in a pool of blood. She screamed at him, but he didn't respond. She tugged him, but he didn't move. People nearby quickly gathered around, and four or five of them pulled him up and dragged him to our emergency room. The nurses tried to take his blood pressure and found none. They hooked him to a cardiograph, and it showed a flat line. . . .

His girlfriend begged us to save him, but there was really nothing we could do, because the flat line meant his heart had stopped beating. I believe the bullet struck his heart. The girl sobbed frantically, but quickly ran home to get her boyfriend's mother. After arriving, the mother stood over his body, checking it over again and again, but she found only one bullet wound.

Then she came over and threw herself at my feet, clasping my legs in her arms and crying out for me to save her son. My face was wet with tears; there was nothing I could say. I squatted down next to this grief-stricken mother, and told her the facts, that her son's heart had been shattered, that there was no way to save him. Then, after calming down a bit, this mother wept and cursed: "I joined the military when I was very young. I joined the party, and fought with the Communist Party against Japan and Chiang Kai-shek. Now, our People's Liberation Army has killed my dearest son. . . ."

Jiang wrote about how he had struggled to save a young athlete who died on his operating table because the hospital didn't have enough blood. He recalled his conversation with an army major who had been shot but counted himself lucky because an elderly man and a young child standing next to him were killed. He reported that tiny bullet fragments had shredded the organs of several patients and suggested soldiers had used special ammunition that shattered to cause more harm. The students he treated that night were innocent civilians, Jiang wrote, young men and women who were peacefully protesting corruption and demanding honest government. His fellow soldiers in Beijing understood this and they refused to use violence to suppress the demonstrations, he wrote, but "a small number of leaders who supported corruption acted in a frenzied manner" and summoned reinforcements from the provinces, troops who were kept in the dark about the student movement and told to open fire on a "counter-revolutionary rebellion."

On page after page, over a period of months, Jiang poured his heart into the letter. He had been thinking about breaking his silence on Tiananmen for a long time, and over the years, he had discussed the subject with friends, many of whom had also been pushed into retirement after refusing to adopt a "correct attitude" toward the crackdown. Now, he shared drafts of his letter with them and asked their permission to write about them. In some ways, they had inspired him to act, and he felt as if he was writing for them as much as for himself. One classmate he wrote about, Tang Peixuan, a ranking official in the Academy of Military Sciences, lost his job in the purge that followed the massacre. When party officials pressured him to endorse the crackdown, Tang reminded them that as a young man he had participated in Communist-backed student protests against the Nationalist government. The Nationalists had used fire hoses to break up the demonstrations, he said, so how could the party that overthrew them resort to machine guns and tanks? Another acquaintance, the famed playwright Wu Zuguang, spoke out against the massacre at a meeting of prominent writers and artists on a party advisory committee. None of the other committee members—some of the nation's brightest talents—had the courage to stand and support him. Their silence disappointed Wu and weighed on him in his final years, Jiang wrote. Not long before his death, Wu told him that a person's mouth was only good for eating and speaking, and if it could not be used for speaking the truth, then it was only good for eating and that wasn't much. "My conversations with Wu taught me a lot," Jiang wrote. "People should speak out, and speak the truth."

Jiang also wrote about the wife of one of his patients, Ding Zilin, a historian whose seventeen-year-old son died in the massacre. She was the leader of the Tiananmen Mothers, a group of parents and others working to record the names and stories of all those who were killed or injured in the crackdown, and Jiang had recently read a book she published in Hong Kong about the group's efforts. "She and other family members of the victims have located and contacted the families of nearly 200 of the dead and injured, and in various ways, they have expressed their hope—their demand that the government earnestly and responsibly explain the killing of their innocent relatives," Jiang wrote. "This is a completely fair and reasonable request. Who doesn't have a father, a mother, children, or siblings? Anybody whose loved ones have been murdered like this would make the same request. As Communist Party members, as Chinese citizens, as human beings, we should all support their righteous demand with the knowledge that justice is on our side." Every year, Jiang wrote, the Tiananmen Mothers appealed to the National People's Congress for redress, and every year they were ignored.

The party worried that acknowledging the massacre would cause "instability," he argued, but its obsession with stability only stirred greater resentment and disaffection. Every spring, as the anniversary of the massacre approached, the party became nervous and mobilized to prevent any attempt to memorialize the victims. It wanted people to forget about Tiananmen and move on. It spun the massacre into a "political disturbance" and then just an "incident," and it hoped the truth of what happened would fade with time. But people had not forgotten, Jiang wrote. They had been bullied into silence, but with each passing year, their anger and frustration grew—and the party's anxiety climbed, too. Jiang urged the new leaders to take a new approach. They should admit the party was wrong to send troops into the square and order them to fire on unarmed civilians. They should address the pain of those who lost their loved ones in the massacre, and acknowledge, at long last, that the protesters were not "thugs" or "counter-revolutionaries" but patriots calling for a better and more honest government. Simply put, Jiang asked them to end the lies. Only if the party corrected its mistakes, he argued, could it count on the support of the people—the source of real stability.

It was February 2004 by the time Jiang finished showing drafts of his letter to friends and making the final changes to the document. Nearly a year had passed since he exposed the SARS cover-up, and the National People's Congress was preparing to convene again. The fifteenth anniversary of the Tiananmen Square massacre was just months away. From Jiang's perspective, the timing was perfect. "I have considered the various consequences I might encounter after writing this letter, but I have decided nevertheless to tell you my views truthfully," he wrote. "If the leadership feels it is necessary, please make time to speak with me." Jiang made eighty copies of the letter and prepared a list of the nation's top officials, including the leaders of the National People's Congress. He sent most of the letters by express mail from his local post office. He asked a few well-connected friends to hand-deliver others. Finally, he gave several copies to his superiors at the hospital and asked them to pass them up through official channels. Then he went home to wait for a response.

THE HOSPITAL'S PRESIDENT, Zhu Shijun, and its political commissar, Guo Xuheng, visited Jiang at home two days later. They were career military officials, loyal party men who had won promotions after the Tiananmen massacre and climbed the ranks by never questioning orders. Zhu, a self-important official in his early sixties with narrow eyes and pale lips, spoke first. All citizens had the right to send a letter to the National People's Congress, he told Jiang, but the party's position on the "June 4th Incident" was decided long ago, and as a party member, he must "maintain consistency" with that position. "I hope you can improve your understanding," he said, "and recognize that what you did was not right." Guo was less polite. "By doing this, you have committed a serious political mistake!" he declared. Jiang argued with the men for a while, but when they warned him not to give his letter to the media, he promised he wouldn't. He reminded them that he had distributed his letter through proper channels, and said he would neither contact reporters nor post the letter on the Internet. It was an easy promise to make. Jiang had sent the letter to so many people, he knew it was only a matter of time before a copy leaked out.

Four days later, it did. The National People's Congress had just opened its annual session, but the foreign journalists gathered in the capital ended up writing and asking questions about Jiang's letter instead. It was a dramatic story: the elderly surgeon who exposed the SARS cover-up was now challenging the party to come clean on the Tiananmen massacre. The full text of the letter was published on Internet sites overseas, and copies circulated throughout Beijing, where some people began selling them in the city's underground book markets. Jiang was inundated with phone calls again, from reporters but also ordinary citizens who had seen his letter. He was careful to refer the journalists to his superiors, but he told everyone who called that yes, he had written a letter to the leadership about the Tiananmen massacre. He added that he had not posted it online, and did not know how it had gotten out.

Once again, Jiang had put the authorities in a difficult position, and at first they responded with restraint. No one came to put him under house arrest, or drag him to prison in handcuffs, as the police sometimes did to those who spoke out about the Tiananmen massacre. Instead, the military sent a party historian to speak to Jiang; the middle-aged man lectured the doctor about how Mao had overcome internal rivals with "incorrect thoughts," united the party, and led it to victory in the Communist Revolution. Deng Xiaoping, he argued, had done the same in 1989 with the Tiananmen crackdown, triumphing against officials with "incorrect thoughts" and leading the party into a new era of stability and prosperity. But when the historian finished speaking, Jiang peppered him with questions—about Mao's persecution of the Rightists; about the famine caused by the Great Leap Forward; about the violence of the Cultural Revolution. Jiang asked, Why didn't anyone stand up to Mao? What kind of lessons should we draw from such a painful history? The historian mumbled something about continuing the discussion another time and left. He never came back.

Instead, the party sent others. Zhu and Guo returned, and more senior officials from the military's general logistics department also visited Jiang or summoned him to meetings at the hospital. They urged him again and again to admit he was wrong to send the letter, but he refused. Gradually, they stepped up the pressure. Zhu denounced Jiang at a hospital staff meeting, saying the foreign media had made a big deal of his letter and that he had caused great harm to the nation, the party, the military, and the hospital. "We must repudiate his mistake," he said. But Jiang stood and challenged him, telling everyone that he had only written the truth and that he had sent the letter to the leadership through proper channels. If Zhu really believed it should be condemned, he added, he should distribute copies to the hospital staff so they could see what he had written. The room erupted, with some doctors and nurses cheering him and others trying to shout him down.

Jiang thought the men trying to silence him were a nervous bunch. He knew he had angered the old guard in power, and he expected he would eventually be made to suffer the consequences. But these men behaved as if they were the ones in trouble. When Jiang arranged to travel to western China to oversee an operation on an old patient, they assigned an official to accompany him, and then at the airport, they suddenly tried to stop him from leaving before he boarded the plane. When he made plans to attend a literary conference in Beijing, a half dozen of them showed up at his home and tried to persuade him not to go, and when he insisted, they told him he couldn't use the hospital's car service. He hailed a cab and went anyway. These men were nervous not just because Jiang's actions reflected poorly on their ability to keep subordinates in line. They were also worried, Jiang realized, because the Tiananmen massacre was a subject that could still divide the party, and because his letter had come amid uncertainty caused by the leadership transition. Hu Jintao was the new president and party chief, but his predecessor, Jiang Zemin, retained influence and remained head of the People's Liberation Army. Jiang Zemin owed his job to the Tiananmen massacre; Deng had appointed him party chief after Zhao Ziyang was purged. Hu Jintao's career, on the other hand, had not been tarnished by the massacre, and some held out hope that the new general secretary, who had moved so boldly to end the SARS cover-up, might actually consider the doctor's appeal.

In late March, three senior officials in the military's discipline department began meeting with Jiang Yanyong and questioning him at length about his letter. They focused first on a passage in which he described a meeting with Yang Shangkun, the military leader who had served as Deng's deputy and China's president when Deng ordered the assault on the Tiananmen protesters. The encounter took place in 1998. Jiang had just returned from a visit to Taiwan, where he had met with a distant relative who worked in the government there, and he had been given a chance to brief Yang about the meeting. Afterward, the doctor asked the retired party leader if he would be interested in hearing him describe what he saw at his hospital on the night of the massacre, and Yang agreed. Jiang spoke for several minutes, he recalled, and when he finished, Yang sighed and told him that Tiananmen was the biggest mistake the party had ever made. The former president said there was nothing he could do to correct it, but added that he believed the party would eventually have to make amends. It was a remarkable admission, and Jiang included it in his letter because it strengthened his case for a reevaluation of the events of June 4. If someone as high-ranking and deeply involved in the crackdown as Yang could acknowledge the massacre was wrong, certainly the party's new leaders could do so as well. But the discipline officials challenged Jiang's account, asking him how he could prove the conversation took place as he described it, given that Yang passed away later that year. Jiang replied that he had told several people about it at the time. When the officials asked him to identify them, he demurred, saying he didn't think that was necessary.

The officials challenged Jiang to prove other parts of the letter, too—his estimate that hundreds of people were killed in the massacre, his claim that soldiers fired bullets that fragmented and shredded organs. The doctor told them that if the number of deaths was in question, they could check with city hospitals and come up with a more accurate figure. As for the bullets, he acknowledged he was not a weapons specialist, and he offered to issue a clarification saying that he could only confirm that tiny metal fragments were discovered in the wounds of several patients, and that photos and X-rays taken at the time would back him up. The officials also pressed Jiang for names. They wanted to know if anyone had helped him write the letter and who had seen drafts of it in advance. They wanted to know what he did with every copy he made of it. Jiang answered carefully, to avoid inadvertently implicating friends, and he went out of his way to point out that everyone he consulted urged him not to send the letter, including his own wife. The questioning continued for six or seven sessions, as the officials picked over the letter sentence by sentence and reviewed Jiang's answers again and again. Finally, after about two weeks, the men showed Jiang a lengthy printout of their interview notes. He read through it carefully, made a few corrections, and signed his name.

THE NEXT SEVERAL weeks passed uneventfully, and Jiang began to wonder if the party had decided not to take action against him after all. Every summer, he and his wife traveled to the United States to visit their daughter and grandson in California, and he applied to his military superiors for permission to go again as usual. The officials at the hospital were noncommittal, and told him they would pass his request up the chain of command. Jiang told them he would make travel arrangements, and they voiced no objections as he reserved tickets on a flight in mid-June and applied for a visa at the U.S. Embassy. Then, in late May, as the fifteenth anniversary of the Tiananmen massacre approached, his nervous superiors began trying to persuade him to leave Beijing and "recuperate" outside the city somewhere. Every year, the police forced prominent dissidents to leave the capital and spend the anniversary of the massacre elsewhere, and Jiang assumed that he had now made that list of "troublemakers." He told his superiors there was no need for them to worry about him. He guaranteed he would do nothing to embarrass them on June 4. He felt he had already done enough by sending the letter, and he didn't want to risk being denied the chance to visit his daughter. At the same time, he told his superiors that if the leadership didn't want him to make the trip, he wouldn't go. They told him they had heard nothing to indicate that was the case. On May 31, though, they summoned Jiang again and urged him once more to leave Beijing to "recuperate," arguing that "anti-China forces at home and abroad" might try to "take advantage" of him. He insisted there was no need for him to leave, adding that there would be plenty of time for him to "recuperate" in California.

Jiang and his wife were scheduled to visit the U.S. Embassy the next morning for their visa interviews. The first sign something was wrong came when the young soldier assigned by the hospital to drive them showed up with a small van instead of the regular car, which he said was being repaired. Then, after they boarded the van, he drove toward a rear gate of their apartment compound, telling them there was too much traffic at the main gate. Suddenly, he stopped short, the doors flung open, and eight large soldiers rushed in and pinned Jiang and his wife to their seats. Jiang shouted, demanding to know what was happening and why he was being abducted. His wife was terrified and shouting, too. The hospital's propaganda chief climbed into the front passenger seat, and he eventually told the soldiers to ease up. Then he told the couple that they would reach their destination shortly, and their questions would be answered then.

A half hour later, the van arrived at a military guesthouse on the western outskirts of Beijing, and the soldiers escorted Jiang and his wife to a conference room on the third floor. Several officials were waiting there, including Zhu, the hospital president, and Guo, the political commissar. This time, Guo spoke first. "We have invited you here for your own safety," he said. "June fourth is approaching, and there will be various people outside looking for you, which would be harmful for your security. Here, you can rest, study, and improve your understanding."

Jiang was furious. "After abducting us like this, how can you say that we were invited?" he asked. His wife, Hua Zhongwei, a medical researcher, also challenged the men. "This is clearly a kidnapping!" she said. "Why are you calling it an invitation? How can you invite somebody this way?"

Wen Degong, an official with the army's general logistics department, tried to calm them. "We hope you can understand that the leadership is concerned for you. It is very disorderly outside. Here, you can rest and study in peace."

"The leadership is doing this for your own good," Zhu added. "This arrangement is for you to rest. We hope you can understand."

Jiang demanded to see a formal document approving his detention.

The officials said they did not have one but promised to show him one soon. "You haven't even received formal approval, but you can arrest people?" Jiang asked. "What's the use of the constitution then?" He demanded pen and paper, and quickly scribbled out two letters. The first was a letter of protest addressed to Hu Jintao, accusing the men who had detained him of acting without regard to the law or the party's policies. The second was a letter expressing his desire to resign from the military. When he finished writing, he asked the men to pass both letters up the chain of command. They agreed, and then they left.

Jiang and his wife waited in the conference room, and when they were offered food, they refused to eat, in protest. At about 1 A.M., they were taken to a guest room on the first floor and told to rest. Four burly soldiers stood guard in the room and wouldn't leave. Whenever Jiang or his wife used the bathroom, the soldiers insisted the bathroom door remain open. The couple complained they couldn't sleep under such conditions, but the soldiers ignored them. "They claimed that we had been invited to rest," Jiang recalled, "but in reality, we had been illegally imprisoned."

The next morning, doctors were summoned to examine Jiang and his wife. The stress, the sleepless night, the refusal to eat—it had clearly taken a toll on the elderly couple. Both recorded a spike in blood pressure, and Hua's heartbeat also showed some irregularities. A decision was made to transfer them to a hospital. Jiang asked which hospital, and a colonel promised they were going back to the No. 301 Hospital. But Jiang sensed the man was lying, and he refused to go unless he put it in writing. The colonel wouldn't do it, and he instead ordered soldiers to force Jiang and his wife into a car. As the car headed to the northwest, away from the No. 301 Hospital, Jiang and his wife huddled in the backseat, whispering about where they might be going. At first they worried the soldiers were taking them to be committed to a mental hospital they knew was in that direction. Later, they realized their destination was the army's No. 309 Hospital, where the majority of the military's SARS cases had been sent a year earlier. Jiang and his wife were taken under armed guard into a special ward and placed in separate rooms. Eight soldiers were assigned to watch each room.

The next night, Guo and several other officials visited Jiang and read him a military order placing him under "administrative detention" until June 7. Jiang asked to see the regulations governing such detentions, and the officials promised to bring them to him the next day. Jiang argued that his wife should be allowed to go home, since the order didn't cover her, but the officials told him not to worry about her. Over the next few days, the couple studied the volumes of military regulations that the officials provided them. They learned that "administrative detention" could be imposed on soldiers who disobeyed orders, created a public disturbance, engaged in drunken behavior, or threatened superiors with guns, as well as those suspected of planning to desert, murder someone, or commit suicide—none of the conditions applied to them. They also read that the detention of any military official of Jiang's rank required the approval of the chairman of the Central Military Commission. In other words, Jiang Zemin himself must have approved the arrest.

The doctor assumed at first that he had been detained as part of the government's regular security sweep before the June 4 anniversary and that he would be released soon afterward. But as the anniversary came and went and he remained in custody, Jiang realized something else was happening. His days were divided into "rest time" and "study time," and during the "study sessions," military officials grilled him about his letter and tried to pressure him into retracting it and admitting he had been wrong to call for a reevaluation of the Tiananmen massacre. Jiang resisted, and he continued his hunger strike, refusing solid foods until June 6, the night before he was supposed to be released. The next day, Guo and Wen announced that his detention had been extended another week. Guo told Jiang that his hunger strike was an act of "serious resistance against the organization," and as punishment barred him from seeing his wife. Later, after Jiang made it clear he would eat, he was allowed to see her during meals.

After Jiang spent another week under "administrative detention," Guo and Wen returned and told him he was now being detained under party regulations that allowed him to be held indefinitely. His wife could go home, they said, but he would have to stay until he "changed his thinking" and "improved his understanding." Soldiers moved him to another military facility where he remained under twenty-four-hour guard, and the "study sessions" continued. Jiang had survived the Cultural Revolution, so he was familiar with the party's indoc-

trination methods—the lengthy interrogations, the ideological ha-
rangues, the daily requests for him to think about what he had done
and submit written statements so officials could scrutinize them for
errors and push him to admit he was wrong. The pressure was intense, but Jiang refused to acquiesce. Day after day, he stood by his
letter. Some of the officials berated him and tried to scare him into
backing down. Others adopted a softer approach, gently urging him
to consider the party's point of view. He was even forced to watch a
long film that blamed the Tiananmen protests on a handful of intellectuals who wanted to overthrow the party and a rift in the leadership
caused by the fallen party chief, Zhao Ziyang. Deng was hailed in the
film as a hero, the man who decided that no sacrifice would be too
great to save the party from collapse, who ensured that the Communist martyrs who fought the Japanese and the imperialists to establish the People's Republic of China had not died in vain.

The process, Jiang knew, was aimed at breaking his will and ex-
tracting a confession that could be used to undermine his public
standing. At the same time, the officials wanted information that could
be used to implicate others. They wanted to know how his letter had
leaked, and they wanted Jiang to accept that it was a "serious political
mistake" for him to write it in the first place. Jiang, of course, refused
to play along. He told them he had sent the letter to so many officials,
that any of their secretaries, relatives, or friends might have posted it
online. He didn't know who leaked it, he said, so it was pointless for
them to keep asking him. When Deng Xiaoping passed away in 1997,
he reminded them, the BBC broadcast the news before Xinhua could,
and no one ever figured out how it leaked. The officials, though, insisted Jiang accept the blame for the letter getting out. If he had not
written it, they said, it couldn't have been leaked, so he must take responsibility for the "losses" suffered by the nation as a result. Jiang
generally kept his cool in the face of such circular reasoning, but the
questioning sometimes tried his patience. One senior military official
asked him where he bought the paper he printed the letters on, how
many pieces he purchased, and what he paid for it, and then followed
up by also asking where he bought the envelopes and how much he
paid for those. Jiang blew up, stormed out of the room, and refused to
speak to him. "They never asked me questions like that again," he
said.

As the weeks passed, Jiang began searching for a way to persuade the authorities to release him. In late June, he wrote a forty-page letter to Hu Jintao urging him to allow him to return home and continue his "study sessions" under house arrest. His indefinite detention, he argued, could be used against the party by prodemocracy forces abroad. He also considered using more agreeable language in the statements he wrote. Jiang could never bring himself to condone the Tiananmen massacre, but he wanted to go home, and he needed to write something to appease the men who had imprisoned him. Finally, while insisting that he shouldn't be held responsible for the actions of others, he conceded that some people might have used his letter to attack the party. He also settled on a medical metaphor to illustrate his "improved understanding" of the Tiananmen massacre. There were costs and benefits to using troops to suppress the student protests, he wrote. If the benefits outweighed the costs, then one might take such action. "The situation could be likened to that of a patient with rectal cancer," he continued.

> With surgery, he might live and that would be a benefit, but the colostomy would make life inconvenient and that would be a cost. Comparing the major benefit of living with the minor cost of a colostomy, the benefits still outweigh the costs, so the surgery should take place. We often talk things over with patients like this, to persuade them to undergo surgery. On June 4th, hundreds of students and ordinary people were killed. This was an extremely high cost to pay. But in the end, the Communist Party was not toppled, the People's Republic was not overthrown, and this was also a significant benefit. I should improve my understanding in this way.

That was as far as Jiang was willing to go. He hoped the authorities would focus on his conciliatory tone instead of his refusal to endorse the massacre. He hoped they would overlook the fact that he had just compared the party to a dying cancer patient who could no longer have normal bowel movements and was likely to suffer impotence and incontinence. He knew that even with surgery, the survival rates for rectal cancer were very low. But he didn't think the men deciding his fate knew that.

• • •

SEVEN WEEKS AFTER Jiang was detained, the authorities suddenly sent him home. He had to stay in his apartment, accept restrictions on his ability to see and talk to people, stop using e-mail, and disconnect his Internet line. But at least he was home. Jiang never learned why he was released. His more conciliatory statement might have been a factor. The officials assigned to reeducate him might have concluded that that was the closest they would ever get to an admission of guilt from such a stubborn old man. Or maybe the party's leaders recognized the risk they were taking by arresting a man who had become a hero at home and abroad for exposing the SARS cover-up. If they had not released him, he would have become the nation's most famous political prisoner. The case would have drawn attention again to the Tiananmen massacre, and it could have triggered a public backlash or divided the party. The *Washington Post* had published my article about Jiang's detention as the lead story on the front page, and a commentator on Hong Kong's Phoenix television had discussed the article on a show broadcast into millions of homes in China. Jiang and the soldiers guarding him saw the show, too. Within days, the authorities agreed to discuss his proposal to be held under house arrest, and less than two weeks later, they took him home.

The party's investigation into Jiang's letter dragged on for another eight months. The government never charged him with a crime, and he was finally released from house arrest in March 2005. Afterward, though, Jiang disappeared from public view. When I last visited him, he turned up the volume on his television set because he believed his apartment might be bugged and he whispered that he was trying to avoid provoking the government. He said he still wanted to visit his daughter and grandson in California, and he believed that if he behaved, the authorities would give him permission to go. As I listened to him speak, I couldn't help but feel a pang of disappointment. The state had been unable to break Jiang, but it had succeeded in silencing him.

After I left his apartment, though, I decided it was unfair to expect the elderly doctor to continue standing up to the party. He had already achieved more than most and paid a price for it. I doubted the government would ever let him visit his daughter and grandson, but how could anyone expect him to give up that hope? There was only so much one man could do, and only so much a nation could ask of him.

9

THE
NEWSPAPERMAN

During that critical National People's Congress session in 2003, when the party was still trying to keep the SARS epidemic under wraps, only one newspaper in China dared publish anything about the disease, a gutsy tabloid in Guangdong Province named the *Southern Metropolis Daily*. Like all newspapers in China, the *Daily* was owned by the state and the party appointed its editors, and like every major paper in Guangdong, it had been ordered to publish word for word the government's statement before the Congress that the disease was under control. Like most journalists in the province with any experience, the paper's editors knew when they put the story on the front page that it wasn't true. It pained them to participate in such deceit, but that was not what set them apart from their peers in the propaganda apparatus. Many men and women in the nation's newsrooms aspired to do more than repeat the party's lies. What distinguished the editors of the *Southern Metropolis Daily* — a thick paper known for its populist style and color photos — was their refusal to drop the story, and their willingness to take matters a step further.

After reporting that SARS had been contained, the newspaper's editors began looking for a way to publish a more truthful story about

Cheng Yizhong

the outbreak that had originated in their circulation area. They wanted to make up for what they had done and get even with the bureaucrats who had forced them to lie. Their chance came a few weeks later. On the opening day of the Congress in Beijing, one of the paper's reporters assigned to cover the session managed to stop a deputy health minister between meetings and ask a few questions. The minister's answers, though carefully worded, gave the editors an opening. On the front page the next day, the paper broke the censors' blackout on news about SARS with a headline noting that international experts had been invited to help conduct research into the epidemic. It was a minor development, chosen by the editors for the front page to soften the impact of their decision to defy the censors, but readers who opened to the article inside found a full page of coverage that directly challenged the government's position on SARS. The deputy minister was quoted acknowledging that the illness could not be considered "under control" because no one knew what caused it or how best to treat it. The paper also quoted him saying officials should provide more information to the public about future outbreaks, to prevent the spread of rumors like those that had caused panicked hoarding of vinegar and other folk remedies in Guangdong.

The health official erred by wandering off message, but it was the newspaper the party blamed. As far as the propaganda czars were concerned, the editors should have known better than to practice real journalism and print what the minister said. They should have known to stick to the script of the Congress and keep SARS out of the news. Zhang Dejiang, the party chief of Guangdong, in particular, was furious. A thick-faced politician with a degree from a university in North Korea, he lost his temper at a meeting in Beijing with journalists from his province. He shouted at the *Daily*'s reporter and complained that the press in Guangdong had grown too independent and needed to be reined in. The *Daily* had embarrassed him while he was in Beijing attending one of the most important party events of the year, and now he demanded that it be punished. The paper was ordered to bring home the reporters assigned to cover the Congress and prepare for a shake-up.

But this was not the first time that the *Southern Metropolis Daily* had angered its superiors in the party, and the editors knew what they needed to do to survive. They quickly submitted a report confessing to a grave mistake and outlining the steps they had taken to make sure it wouldn't happen again. The reporter who wrote the SARS story had been fired, they said, and the editor who put it on the front page was suspended. Ultimate responsibility, they said, lay with the editor in chief, a rising star named Cheng Yizhong, and he had been demoted. The sternly worded report appeared to satisfy the party bosses. None of them seemed to notice that the fired reporter continued writing for the newspaper under a different byline, or that the suspended editor continued to show up for work, only on a different shift, or that Cheng was still running the newspaper, even if he no longer held the chief editor's title. Then, a few weeks later, when the SARS cover-up finally unraveled, it was as if the *Southern Metropolis Daily* had been right all along. The new president, Hu Jintao, condemned the lies and promised greater government openness. The party's censors never lifted their ban on coverage of SARS, but everyone in the media knew the political winds had shifted and the epidemic was fair game again. It was a huge story, and Cheng marshaled his staff to fill the paper with the articles he couldn't publish earlier. Even as he put SARS back on the front page, though, Cheng was getting ready to publish an even bigger story, one that would make the paper's earlier transgression look insignificant—and push the party's relationship with its journalists to the breaking point.

HE WAS A slim, compact man, with piercing eyes, handsome features, and the sly, confident smile of a smart aleck. He dressed casually at the office, usually in jeans and plain collar shirts, and he looked younger than he really was, which was young enough. At thirty-seven, Cheng Yizhong was probably the youngest editor running a major newspaper in China. And yet when strangers visited the newsroom of the *Southern Metropolis Daily,* they rarely mistook him for one of the reporters on his staff. Despite his slight frame and youthful appearance, there was an intensity and a natural air of authority about him that commanded respect even from older and more experienced journalists.

From the day he was hired out of college by the Southern Newspaper Group, the state media firm that later launched the *Daily,* Cheng stood out among his peers. In a room full of city folk, he was a son of peasants from Anhui. (He often pointed out that Chen Duxiu, one of the founders of the Communist Party, was born in the same rural county.) He was also the only new employee who admitted participating in the 1989 prodemocracy protests. Cheng had escaped the countryside to the Chinese literature department at Zhongshan University, the most prestigious college in Guangzhou, and in his senior year, students there and in cities across the country marched in support of the movement in Tiananmen Square. Unlike most of his classmates, who later denied taking part in the demonstrations, Cheng admitted his involvement when the Southern Newspaper Group vetted his job application. At the time, the men who ran the Group could boast to party superiors that none of the company's employees had participated in the Tiananmen movement. The claim was true only on paper, but it gave them a bit of political protection in the crackdown that followed the massacre. If they hired Cheng, they would lose that deniability. After some deliberation, they hired him anyway.

It was not an entirely surprising decision. The Southern Newspaper Group was an oasis of open-minded thinking in the state's hidebound media empire, and it was known for pushing the limits within the propaganda apparatus. Its most daring publication, a paper based in Guangzhou named the *Southern Weekend*, was winning readers and inspiring journalists across the country by showing how aggressive reporting and elegant writing could be possible despite censorship. On the Communist organization charts, the Group was part of the propaganda bureaucracy, but it also occupied a special place in the informal web of interest groups that made up the party. Ideologically, it was a camp for the party's liberal wing. The editors of its newspapers were heirs to a tradition that began in 1957 during the Hundred Flowers Movement, when their predecessors launched a paper that gave voice to opinions that differed from the party line. One of the founders of that paper, the *Yangcheng Evening News*, argued that even if political conditions made it impossible for journalists to always write the truth, they should at least refuse to publish lies. Generation after generation, the editors of the Southern Newspaper Group tried to live up to that standard.

The Group was also an arm of the party apparatus in Guangdong, the vast manufacturing region on the nation's southeast coast that used to be known as Canton. With one hundred million people, the province is China's most populous, its wealthiest, and, other than the ethnic regions such as Tibet and Xinjiang, its most independent-minded. Ever since Mao, the central government has tried to keep a rein on the Cantonese, who often take their cues from neighboring Hong Kong instead of faraway Beijing. In part because of its long history of interaction with the outside world—foreign traders colonized its ports while waves of Cantonese immigrants settled across Asia and the West—party ideologues have viewed Guangdong with suspicion, and the leadership has made a point of naming outsiders to senior positions in the province. But the locals take pride in their distinct identity and remain a political force to be reckoned with. In the 1980s, Guangdong helped pioneer the market reforms, sometimes pushing ahead with policy changes before they had been approved in Beijing.

For a college student like Cheng, who spent his summers working the family rice fields in Anhui, the Southern Newspaper Group was a new world. Cheng was drawn to the Group because of its reputation, but also because he wanted to stay in Guangzhou, the vibrant boomtown on the Pearl River that was the provincial capital. He was assigned a job as an editor for a literary supplement to the *Southern Daily*, the staid party mouthpiece that was the Group's flagship publication. His college sweetheart, whom he would later marry, landed a position in another section of the paper. After a year, the newspaper sent him to work as a reporter in Zhanjiang, a port city in the province that served as headquarters of the navy's South China Sea fleet. He quickly built a reputation as one of the staff's most prolific and aggressive writers. He filed reports on social problems such as conflicts between rural clans, as well as on public corruption, detailing the crimes of local officials caught taking bribes and building themselves lavish new homes. Occasionally, he wrote articles that his editors felt were too sensitive to publish. They would transmit these pieces for party officials to read in internal publications or kill them entirely. Cheng told himself that such disappointments came with the job. He was not yet the idealistic newsman he would become, and he took comfort in the fact that his newspaper was better than most, and that conditions for journalists seemed to be improving. After the assignment in Zhanjiang, the paper brought him back to headquarters and gave him a job editing one of its feature sections. He was ambitious and hardworking, and he joined the party and tried to make a good impression. He always got to the newsroom before anyone else, so he could put stories and thermoses of hot water on the desks of the senior editors before they arrived.

By the mid-1990s, the Southern Newspaper Group faced a business crisis. Market reforms had stalled after the Tiananmen massacre as hard-line conservatives gained power, but Deng Xiaoping rescued his capitalist economic program in 1992 with a tour of southern China that included several stops in Guangdong. State media companies such as the Southern Newspaper Group were told they could no longer rely on government subsidies and had to finance their own operations. The Group tried expanding into real estate and other ventures, but after a string of bad investments, the men in charge decided to focus on the business they knew best—newspapers.

Their main product, the *Southern Daily*, was a money-loser, and they knew it would be impossible to turn it around. The paper was the mouthpiece of the provincial party committee, and like all official party newspapers, it was constrained by a rigid set of traditions and customs. In the 1980s, the party chief Zhao Ziyang had urged these papers to begin publishing stories that used "the language of humans" instead of the "language of officials," but when he was purged and placed under house arrest, the party all but abandoned that effort. Papers like the *Southern Daily* were still required to carry front-page stories on tedious party meetings and the empty pronouncements of party officials. They were still barred from leading with articles the censors considered too downbeat or critical. And they still had to measure the photos of party leaders before publishing them, to avoid giving offense or sending incorrect signals about each leader's political standing. The editors of the Southern Newspaper Group tried to make the *Southern Daily* better, injecting more real journalism into the mix, but they could only tinker with the old formula, not rewrite it. If they wanted to turn a profit, they needed to start from scratch and launch a newspaper that could break free from the old rules. The state would still own the new paper, and the party would still control it, but it would not be a dedicated mouthpiece. Instead, it would be a newspaper people wanted to read. If it succeeded, the editors reasoned, advertisers and profits would follow, and the party would have a new, more effective vehicle for influencing public opinion.

Cheng was only twenty-nine, but the Group asked him to help start the experimental new paper. Management wanted someone young involved, and he was well regarded by the senior editors, who considered him not only talented but also, equally important, likeable. It was a big promotion—he was one of only three people appointed to the committee that would set up the paper—and Cheng hardly felt prepared, but he threw himself into the project, studying newspapers across the country and around the world. The Group decided early on that the new paper would be a tabloid named the *Southern Metropolis Daily*, and Cheng focused on the handful of market-oriented tabloids that had been established by party newspapers in other provinces. Then he wrote a ten-thousand word plan of action to make the *Southern Metropolis Daily* better than all of them. Cheng even designed the new paper's red-and-yellow masthead. The traditional approach was to use the calligraphy of a party leader—the masthead of the *People's Daily*, for example, was penned by Mao—but Cheng didn't want the newspaper associated with any official or party faction. Instead, he chose calligraphy used on monuments during the fifth-century Northern Wei Dynasty. That was how he thought of the newspaper he was creating: as a monument, something that would endure through history and remind future generations of the past.

The paper hit the newsstands in January 1997, with Cheng as the deputy editor. Its first issue had only sixteen pages. There were fewer than a hundred reporters and editors on the staff then, and Cheng put in long hours, editing and laying out several pages himself every night. He found it exciting and rewarding work. He felt as if he was on the ground floor of something special, something that could further the ideals he had fought for as a student in the 1989 demonstrations and fulfill his traditional duty as an intellectual to serve the nation. He had seen a bootleg copy of the Watergate film *All the President's Men*, and he imagined he was building an independent newspaper like the *Washington Post*, one that could serve as a watchdog against the abuses of the powerful. He lived nearby in an apartment provided by the Newspaper Group, but he often slept in the office. His wife complained that she would sometimes go days without seeing him. The couple had a baby boy, but it was the newspaper he doted on.

"I loved my job," Cheng told me. "It was a good fit with my ideals and my values, and I felt I was doing something big and important."

The *Southern Metropolis Daily* lost money in the beginning. In its first year, it ran a deficit of more than a million dollars, and some of the Group's leaders expressed doubts about the project. But Cheng was confident, almost arrogantly so. In one meeting, he predicted the tabloid would emerge as the top-selling newspaper in Guangzhou, and officials laughed at what seemed at the time an outlandish claim. Their skepticism only seemed to fuel Cheng's determination, though, and he kept pushing to improve the paper. The *Southern Metropolis Daily* broke one taboo after another, printing stories that never would have appeared in other papers, stories that people actually wanted to read. It put international news on the front page, which the traditional party newspapers never did. When Princess Diana died in a car crash in Paris, other papers ran short articles but Cheng stunned the media establishment by filling a quarter of his tabloid's pages with coverage. When the Starr Report on President Bill Clinton's affair with White House intern Monica Lewinsky was released, the *Southern Metropolis Daily* published ten pages of excerpts. The censors expressed disapproval, calling the material "vulgar," but Cheng wanted readers to draw a comparison at home, where party officials who did far worse went unpunished. At other times, though, the paper served the party's propaganda purposes. When NATO bombed the Chinese Embassy in Belgrade, it ran twelve pages of stories and photos on the attack and the anti-U.S. protests that erupted in cities across China.

Cheng's formula was simple. He asked himself what he wanted to read, and then he ordered up the stories. The paper was the first in China to offer daily consumer sections—automobiles on Monday, real estate on Thursday. It broke new ground with blowout coverage of the World Cup finals in 1998, publishing eight pages a day for forty-three consecutive days to the delight of a soccer-crazed nation. Cheng himself helped pioneer a new genre of journalism in China. A movie buff since college, he wrote reviews of the foreign films that were widely available on video CDs. His favorite was the prison movie *The Shawshank Redemption*.

But if he filled the pages of the paper with sports and entertainment, Cheng also saw to it that he provided readers with another scarce commodity they craved—journalism that challenged the government. There was certainly a market incentive to do so, but Cheng was motivated by principles as much as profits. At weekly staff meetings, he reminded his reporters that they worked for the public, and he urged them to act as a check against government officials and others with power. When reporters asked him whether a story might be too sensitive to publish, he expressed exasperation. It was bad enough that he and other editors had to act as censors. He wanted reporters who would push the limits, not censor themselves. Under his guidance, the *Daily* began to distinguish itself with critical reporting on social problems such as crime and corruption. In one memo, he criticized an article that picked on the city's prostitutes, arguing the paper should speak for the weak and "supervise" the powerful. Other newspapers in China played it safe and avoided angering local officials by muckraking only outside their home provinces, but Cheng focused on hard-hitting reporting in Guangzhou and the rest of Guangdong, because that's where his readers were. Early on, the paper caused a sensation with an investigative report detailing how restaurants in the city were using cooking oil extracted from kitchen waste. Local officials were furious and complained to the propaganda authorities that the *Daily* had hurt the city's image. But Cheng coolly defended the report, telling the authorities that the officials were really angry because the paper had exposed their failure to enforce the city's health and sanitation codes.

The mix of soft and hard news that the *Southern Metropolis Daily* offered was a hit with readers. Circulation climbed from 80,000 at the end of the first year to nearly 400,000 at the end of the next. In 1999, it rose past 600,000, and as the advertising money began rolling in, the paper eked out its first profit. By 2000, the tabloid was both the thickest and the most expensive daily newspaper in China, charging about twelve cents for seventy-two pages. Circulation soon hit the one million mark, and Cheng was promoted to editor in chief. A close friend, a talented ad salesman named Yu Huafeng, became a top deputy and the paper's general manager. The two men were young, but the paper's staff was even younger. The average age of its 2,200 employees was twenty-seven. The average age of its senior editors was just thirty-three.

It was a heady time for Cheng and his colleagues. The *Daily* leapt from one success to another, and it emerged as one of the most profitable and widely read newspapers in the country. Other party newspapers launched similar market-oriented tabloids and attempted to duplicate the *Daily*'s success. "It was exhilarating," Cheng told me of those early years. "Sitting in my office, I could hear the sound of the newspaper growing. You would assign an article on some subject, publish it, and newsstand sales would go up. You knew that readers were embracing your newspaper, and you could sense your newspaper was getting bigger and better. That was the most satisfying feeling." The paper published more photos, bought new color presses, and moved into a bigger, more modern headquarters in downtown Guangzhou. One of the few sources of frustration for Cheng was a bureaucratic holdup preventing him from putting the newspaper's name in neon lights on the roof of the new building.

The paper's success gave it more clout, and Cheng pushed his reporters to be more aggressive. "In the newspaper business, we have already learned to be without power," he told them. "Now, we must learn to act like a newspaper with power." But as the *Southern Metropolis Daily* asserted itself, it also made enemies. In Cheng's first year as editor in chief, the nearby city of Shenzhen attempted to banish the tabloid from its newsstands. Not only was its brand of critical coverage unwelcome, the *Daily* was also winning advertising and readers from Shenzhen's own papers. Cheng fought back, sending a team of twenty reporters into Shenzhen and hiring a thousand people to distribute tens of thousands of copies of the newspaper there for free. "Someone in Shenzhen Shamelessly Shut Out This Newspaper" read a front-page headline the next day. But Cheng was careful to focus his paper's criticism on the officials who controlled the city's newsstands instead of the city's top leaders, and he published several flattering stories about Shenzhen as well. A month and a half later, the ban was lifted.

To read the *Southern Metropolis Daily* in those years was to read a newspaper with an attitude. When most papers in China reported on crime, the articles were edited to leave readers with the impression that police were doing a good job and that lawbreakers were always caught and punished. The *Daily*, however, published stories that suggested the opposite and pointed out problems with the administration of justice in China. One article that infuriated officials in Guangzhou, for example, told the story of a woman who was abducted and forced into prostitution in a neighborhood that the city had recently pronounced safe. "All of our negative reports had the same theme—that unchecked power is harmful to society," Cheng said. "It was just common sense, but our reporting led readers to ask why our system was like this, and why it had so many flaws."

The tabloid enjoyed a bureaucratic advantage when it angered party officials in Guangzhou, Shenzhen, and other cities. The Southern Newspaper Group was part of the provincial apparatus, and thus outranked city officials in the party hierarchy. When an article in the *Daily* upset a local official, he couldn't punish the newspaper directly. Instead he had to complain to the provincial propaganda department. Depending on the severity of the transgression, the provincial propaganda department might reprimand the Southern Newspaper Group and demand it take appropriate action against the *Daily*. Cheng had to respond in writing to each reprimand with a "self-criticism" that owned up to mistakes and explained what was being done to address them. There was an art to writing these memos that involved evaluating just how upset officials were and how much clout they had, and then proposing a punishment that would satisfy them. More than once, propaganda officials rebuked Cheng for treating their complaints too lightly and demanded he adopt more severe sanctions. Sometimes, the pressure on the paper was so great that Cheng was forced to print a retraction or an apology. He hated doing that, but he knew it was a small price to pay to continue publishing.

The Group did its best to protect the paper, but as the number and intensity of the complaints grew, Cheng devised a creative strategy for handling them. He hired an expert, a former propaganda official from a small city in Guangdong, to write the self-criticisms for him. The man understood exactly what the authorities wanted to hear. He knew when to fight, and, more important, when and how to retreat. Depending on his assessment of the situation, the newspaper would tell the authorities that it had launched an investigation, or required an editor to write a self-criticism, or punished people by docking their bonuses, suspending them or firing them. What he wrote for the benefit of the propaganda officials, though, rarely bore any relation to the reality in the newsroom. If the *Daily* had actually carried out the sanctions he proposed, some reporters would have been fired multiple times, and some editors would have lost three years' worth of bonuses in a single year.

Cheng pushed the limits, but he recognized that some stories would always be out of bounds. He knew better than to ever directly challenge one-party rule or to broach taboo subjects such as the Tiananmen massacre. What infuriated him, though, was that party officials tried to keep a host of other stories out of the news, too, almost always for selfish, personal reasons. They wanted to protect their own reputations, not the party's, and they were more worried about advancing their careers than about the injustices the paper exposed. "You can oppose the party," Cheng sometimes joked, "but you can't oppose party officials."

Once, after the *Daily* received a string of reprimands over several critical articles published in a short period of time, a provincial propaganda chief, Zhang Yangsheng, summoned Cheng and his senior editors to his office to berate them. Cheng had little respect for old-school bureaucrats like Zhang, but he held his tongue through the three-hour session. After the meeting, though, he vented to his colleagues over lunch, unleashing a stream of vitriol about Zhang and his mother. Then, in the afternoon, one of Zhang's deputies called and took him to task for cursing the propaganda chief. Cheng realized that one of his newspaper colleagues had reported his lunchtime tirade. He could have lost his job, but he didn't. Cheng assumed that the deputy never shared his off-color remarks with the propaganda chief. But the episode drove home to him the risks of running a newspaper in a one-party state. In his own words, he was "walking a high wire."

Yet when he had the chance to break the news blackout about SARS, he didn't hesitate. The government had forced him to demean his newspaper by publishing a story he knew wasn't true—a violation of the old editor's adage about refusing to lie even if telling the truth wasn't possible—and he wanted to get even. The *Southern Metropolis Daily* was established now, and he didn't think party officials would shut it down over the SARS report. He figured the worst they could do was fire him, and he decided the risk was worth it. He felt the SARS epidemic was exactly the kind of story that a good newspaper should pursue. He felt the same way about the story that editors put on his desk a few weeks later.

THE INITIAL TIP came in a message posted on an Internet bulletin board. Chen Feng, the reporter who received it, was a newcomer to the *Southern Metropolis Daily* but also, at age thirty-one, one of the most experienced journalists on the staff. A pudgy, good-humored fellow with close-cropped hair and round glasses, he had been a reporter at *Caijing*, the nation's premier business magazine, and a top editor at a newspaper he helped start in Henan. The *Daily* had recruited him to join its in-depth reporting team, a group of about a dozen veteran journalists responsible for producing longer, investigative articles. A few days after he started work, a college student he had met online left him a note—she had a story for him. She said a friend of a friend had died in Guangzhou after being detained in a *shourong* station, a facility used for holding vagrants and others lacking proper residency permits. The details were sketchy, but she knew the victim was a recent college graduate named Sun Zhigang.

Chen saw the potential of the story immediately. The *shourong*, or "custody and repatriation," system was notorious, a shadowy network of detention centers that the authorities used to enforce an internal passport policy and keep undesirables, usually peasants, out of the nation's cities. Almost everybody knew someone who had had an unpleasant run-in with the *shourong* process, which let police stop people on the street, demand to see their papers and take them away if anything was amiss. There were few safeguards against abuses, and officers often hauled people in without any real legal justification. Those detained were supposed to be sent back to their hometowns, but the *shourong* facilities usually demanded exorbitant fees before releasing anyone. If detainees didn't have the money, and no one came to bail them out, they were forced to work in prison farms or factories to earn their freedom.

Depending on the circumstances, Chen realized, the death of a university graduate in a *shourong* station could be an explosive story, but it was also a politically sensitive one. He wasn't sure the *Daily* could publish anything on the subject. He knew from experience that most publications steered clear of any critical reporting on the criminal justice system. The police, the courts, the prisons—they were all considered off-limits. But when Chen told his editor about Sun's death, she gave him permission to investigate without even hesitating. He was impressed. This was why he had moved to Guangzhou—to work for a newspaper with the courage and clout to do journalism that mattered.

It didn't take long for Chen to track down Sun's family. Two weeks after Sun's death, his father was still in Guangzhou, trying to get answers. He was a peasant from rural Hubei Province, about five hundred miles to the north, and officials had treated him dismissively. They told him only that his son had died suddenly from a heart condition. But Sun had been in good health, the father insisted, and he was only twenty-seven. What happened to him in the *shourong* station? Why were the police holding him there anyway? Sun had just moved to Guangzhou and taken a job as a graphic designer, and his papers were in order, his father said. Chen advised him to find a lawyer and to hire a medical examiner who could perform an autopsy and provide a legal opinion.

Later, Chen asked a colleague to help him with the reporting. Wang Lei was his physical opposite, tall and thin, with long hair and a goatee, but he shared Chen's passion for chasing a good story. Both reporters agreed there was little they could write without determining the cause of Sun's death. When Sun's father called and said none of the lawyers in Guangzhou were willing to take the case, they encouraged him to keep trying and emphasized the importance of the autopsy. Without it, they said, the newspaper wouldn't be able to help him. In the meantime, they began gathering evidence—police records, hospital records, everything the authorities would let Sun's father copy, none of it very helpful. Then, in mid-April, about three weeks after he first began working on the story, Chen got a call from Wang. Sun's former classmates had raised the money for an autopsy, and the family had given him a copy of the medical examiner's report. The young graphic designer had been beaten to death.

Chen rushed back to the newsroom, and huddled over the report with Wang. It took some time to work through the medical terminology, but the conclusion was clear. Sun had suffered blunt trauma over large areas of his body, including his arms, legs, ribs, and back. The trauma was so severe it had sent him into shock, causing organ failure and death. The two reporters went to one of the paper's top editors, Yang Bin, with what they had learned. He immediately told them to keep working on the story, and issued specific instructions. First, he told them to take extra care to get every detail right. There was no room for even a small error in a story this sensitive. Second, he told them to finish their investigation quickly, before propaganda officials learned about the incident and barred reporting on it. The *Daily* could get away with publishing as much as it did because the party didn't have an army of censors who read every story before publication. Instead it relied on journalists to censor themselves and issued regular directives banning coverage of specific subjects. It would be risky to defy such a directive, but if the newspaper acted before the authorities imposed a ban, it could claim it hadn't intentionally broken any rules.

Yang never discussed with the two reporters the possibility their story might be too sensitive to publish. But later that day, he met with Cheng Yizhong over lunch and briefed him on what they had uncovered. He was concerned because the newspaper had already made enemies of the police and other law enforcement agencies in Guangzhou. These were dangerous and powerful institutions, and so far they had retaliated only through proper channels, by applying pressure through propaganda officials. But a hard-hitting article about the *shourong* system could put them over the edge and prompt a more forceful response. The timing of the piece could also be problematic. Cheng and the newspaper were already on thin ice with the authorities for violating the SARS blackout. Technically, he wasn't even the editor in chief. But Cheng thought the story was too important to ignore, and he told Yang to get it into the paper.

The reporters moved quickly, splitting up the remaining interviews. Chen Feng met with the medical examiner, who nervously explained that Sun must have been brutally beaten to have the injuries he discovered and estimated that the assault occurred within seventy-two hours of death. Wang pretended to be one of Sun's relatives and went to the *shourong* station's hospital ward, where he questioned the staff and recorded their evasions. The reporters interviewed Sun's family and friends, his roommate and his employer, and they pieced together a timeline of the last days of his life. He had arrived in Guangzhou less than a month earlier, and he was working for a clothing company and living with a friend. At about 11 P.M. on the night he was detained, he called his roommate and told him he had been stopped by two police officers while walking to an Internet cafe. Because he couldn't produce any identification, they had taken him to the local precinct station. The roommate rushed over with Sun's ID and money to bail him out, but the officers refused to let him go, even as they released others who had been detained. One of the officers declared that they had the right to decide whom to hold and whom to release. Later the roommate spotted Sun in the station and quietly asked him if he had done anything to upset the police. Sun said he had exchanged a few words with the officers but nothing serious. The next day another friend received a phone call from Sun, who sounded scared now and said he had been taken to a *shourong* station. The friend called Sun's boss, who went to the station to vouch for him and try to get him out, but he was turned away, too. On the third day, Sun's friends learned that he had been transferred to the *shourong* station's hospital ward, and they tried to visit him. The doctors refused, and told them only Sun's family could bail him out. When Sun's friends called the hospital on the fourth day of his detention, they were told he was dead.

Chen and Wang saved the interviews with the police for last. They visited the precinct house, the *shourong* station, and the hospital ward, as well as police headquarters, but no one would talk to them. The only government official who spoke to them was a bureaucrat in the city agency responsible for managing the *shourong* system. Chen showed up at his office without making an appointment and found him playing solitaire on his computer. He agreed to interrupt his game for an interview, but he said only that he was "ninety-nine percent certain" Sun had not been attacked in the *shourong* station. There were video cameras installed both at the station and its hospital ward, he said, and supervisors would have spotted and stopped any assault. When Chen asked to see the videotapes, though, the official said that would be impossible.

It was past 5 P.M. by the time Chen and Wang returned to the office, and they were planning to write their story the next day. By coincidence, though, they ran into Yang Bin, the senior editor, and when he asked how the reporting was going, they mentioned that they had tried to interview the police that morning. The editor's face dropped, and he got worked up. He told the reporters they should have waited until the last minute to contact the police, in case officials called the propaganda authorities and tried to squash the story. Then he told them to sit down and start writing immediately. He wanted to publish the story that night.

Chen and Wang skipped dinner, wrote quickly, and finished the article by 9:30 P.M. They recounted the efforts of Sun's friends to bail him out. They catalogued in clinical detail the injuries that caused his death. And they raised the question of whether it was right for police to hold him in the *shourong* station. Only the homeless, the unemployed, and those without a national identification card were subject to *shourong*, they pointed out, but Sun's friends had provided the police with his ID card and demonstrated that he had both an apartment and a job. It was an impressive piece of journalism, at once dramatic and restrained. Only at the very end of their story did Chen and Wang quote friends and family describing what kind of person Sun was—artistic, hardworking, stubborn. They closed with an image of Sun's family traveling to Guangzhou from their little village in Hubei, and showing reporters copies of the awards he had won as a young student. "He was the first person to go to university from our hometown," they quoted Sun's father saying. But if he had not studied so hard, the father continued, maybe he wouldn't have been so stubborn, and maybe he wouldn't have been killed.

Yang splashed the article across two pages inside the tabloid, and put a large headline near the bottom of the front page: "The Death of *Shourong* Detainee Sun Zhigang." A smaller one beneath it added "University Graduate, 27, Dies Three Days After Being Detained on Guangzhou Street, Autopsy Shows Violent Beating Before Death."

The presses were scheduled to begin publishing the next day's paper in a few hours. When the night editor read the Sun Zhigang story, though, he hesitated to send it on. Yang told him that Cheng had read the piece and approved it, but the night editor wanted to give the editor in chief one last chance to reconsider. There was still time to pull the story if he changed his mind. When the night editor reached him at home, though, Cheng gave the order to publish.

CHENG KNEW THE story was a blockbuster, and he slept restlessly in anticipation of its publication. He was certain people across the country would be talking about it. Before leaving the office, he had reminded his staff to send a copy to the editors of the nation's top Web sites, Sina and Sohu. The two portals attracted more readers than any newspaper or magazine in China, and because private firms ran them, they had a little more room to maneuver against the censors. Though they were barred from producing news stories themselves, the Web sites could link to the best articles in publications across the country.

Their huge national readership allowed them to draw attention to stories, influence opinions, and set the public agenda in a way no party media outlet could. The rise of papers like the *Daily* had already transformed the nation's media landscape, but the Internet was accelerating the process. Cheng recognized the potential of the Web early on and cultivated a partnership with Sina and Sohu, making it standard practice to send the *Daily's* best pieces to their editors at about 2 A.M. every morning. When they highlighted the *Daily's* stories on their home pages, the number of people who saw them jumped exponentially. The Web sites magnified the paper's influence and impact, and by distributing its stories, they made it more difficult for the propaganda officials to censor them. When the report on Sun Zhigang's death appeared on the Web, Cheng knew, it would no longer be just a local story that local officials could hush up. It would be a national story, with a national audience and national implications. And he was looking forward to it.

The *Southern Metropolis Daily* had published other big stories, but the response to the Sun Zhigang report was unlike anything Cheng had ever seen. The story spread across the Internet in e-mails and instant messages, and copies proliferated in the nation's most popular Web forums. The newspaper was overwhelmed with phone calls and faxes from readers who wanted to express their outrage or share their own stories of abuse in the *shourong* system. Tens of thousands of people posted messages on Sina and Sohu. Sitting in his office, watching the message count on the two sites climb, Cheng realized something remarkable was happening, and his newspaper was in the middle of it. It had tapped into a deep well of public resentment against the *shourong* system, and people were acting on their frustration and speaking out. The newsroom was buzzing as reporters began following up on the phone calls and faxes. Chen Feng and Wang Lei wrote a follow-up story based on an interview with Sun's father. But late in the afternoon, an official from the provincial propaganda department called and ordered the paper not to publish anything else about the case.

Cheng wasn't surprised by the call. He had been waiting all day for a response from the authorities, and their silence had been making him nervous. He had worried it might mean they were preparing to take severe action against him or the paper. Now he knew where he and the paper stood. He called his editors and reporters into a meeting, and he told Chen and Wang to keep following the Sun story, even if the paper couldn't publish their articles. He said the propaganda department's ban was a temporary setback, and he vowed to find a way around it. If the party prohibited the *Daily* from writing about the Sun case, then they would write about other *shourong* cases. If it blocked the paper from reporting on other cases, they would write about the *shourong* system itself. The paper should continue to question and challenge the *shourong* system, he said, because a good newspaper should promote progress in society. If the *Daily* did its job, *shourong* could be abolished. That, he argued, was the paper's ultimate goal.

Chen and Wang looked at each other. The idea of the government abandoning *shourong* was so far-fetched, they thought their editor in chief had lost his mind.

But as the weeks passed, it began to seem possible. The party's new leaders had just ended the SARS cover-up, and hopes for political reform were running high. All the talk of honesty and openness in government had knocked the censors off their game. The propaganda officials in Guangdong had blocked reporting on the Sun case, but their counterparts in Beijing had not done the same, and newspapers there picked up the coverage where the *Daily* left off. Even the first follow-up story that Chen and Wang wrote, and that the censors prevented the *Daily* from publishing, appeared in a Beijing newspaper. Chen had sent it to a friend who was an editor there, and she had published it under a pseudonym.

Reporters across the country began digging into the *shourong* system, and editors reassigned stories on the subject that they had buried in the past. The picture that emerged was not flattering. Laws the party said were intended to help runaways and vagrants in the cities return to their rural villages were being used by police to "clean up" neighborhoods and generate income. Officers were arresting as many as two million people every year, holding them in a network of seven hundred detention camps, and demanding cash in exchange for their freedom. The newspapers—and the Internet—were full of stories of abuse, of men and women who were picked up for no good reason and not only shaken down but also roughed up. There was a middle school student who was taken to a *shourong* station after getting lost in the city of Nanning; he returned home in a daze four days later, bruised, stripped of his belongings, and babbling incoherently. There were the two thirteen-year-old girls who were forced into prostitution in Beijing after a pimp "purchased" them at a *shourong* station in Jiangsu Province. There was the young woman who presented her residency permit to a police officer only to watch him tear it up and detain her anyway; in the *shourong* station, she was raped.

Cheng tried to keep the *Southern Metropolis Daily* on top of the story. The government announced a high-profile investigation into Sun's death, and he put reporters up in the hotel where Sun's family was staying so they could monitor developments more closely. He assigned others to interview legal scholars about regulations limiting the use of *shourong*, then ran an article pointing out that a senior city official had arbitrarily expanded the categories of people who could be detained. The *Daily* also published a series of hard-hitting editorials. In effect, the newspaper was on a crusade. This was no time for objectivity, Cheng felt. Too much was at stake. The institutions that supported *shourong* were too strong and the forces fighting for justice were too weak for the newspaper to hold back and not take sides.

Cheng's sources in the party apparatus told him the provincial party committee had convened an emergency meeting to discuss the Sun case. During the meeting, party officials watched the video of Sun's beating that had been captured by closed-circuit cameras in the *shourong* station's hospital ward. It was brutal footage. A gang of men covered Sun with a blanket and beat and kicked him for several minutes. The party officials were also told that the ward had been open for less than a year, and in that time, nearly one thousand people had been admitted and close to one hundred of them had ended up dead. Cheng pressed Chen Feng and Wang Lei to find out what happened to the others who died in the ward. If they could get a copy of the video, that would be even better.

The two reporters tried their best, but had no luck. None of the officials in Guangzhou wanted to talk to the *Southern Metropolis Daily* anymore. But Chen did write another remarkable investigative report detailing the operations of a *shourong* station in Hunan Province that paid police in Guangdong a bounty of about thirteen dollars for each prisoner they transferred there. The station wasn't collecting enough money from the people that local police brought them and had resorted to "buying" prisoners from other areas. It would then charge the prisoners a higher fee to be released. Those who couldn't raise the money were forced to work on the prison farm, hired out as slave laborers, or "sold" to still other *shourong* stations. Over the course of five years, Chen wrote, the station made a profit of nearly half a million dollars.

It wasn't just the press that was campaigning against the *shourong* system. Three young legal scholars in Beijing caused a sensation by petitioning the National People's Congress to review the constitutionality of the *shourong* regulations and strike them down. They had discovered an obscure law that gave citizens the right to make such requests and were apparently the first to ever take advantage of it. A week later, five well-known law professors endorsed their interpretation of the law and submitted their own request for a constitutional review. Meanwhile, public outrage continued to build on the Internet, where Sun's friends and classmates set up a site to memorialize him. There was even talk of organizing a protest vigil in Guangzhou.

Throughout it all, the party's new leaders maintained a public silence on the subject. If they acted on the calls to abolish the *shourong* system, they would be following their reversal of the SARS cover-up with another bold reform and further distancing themselves from their predecessors and the party's old ways. They appeared to be giving the decision serious consideration, but no one knew for sure and no one expected them to act quickly. Even the *Southern Metropolis Daily* dared not speculate about the leadership's secret deliberations. Then one evening at about 9 P.M., less than two months after the *Daily* published its report on Sun's death, the official Xinhua news agency moved an item: the new premier, Wen Jiabao, had convened a meeting of his cabinet and abolished the *shourong* regulations, effective immediately. The system's seven hundred detention centers were going to be shut down. In the newsroom of the *Daily*, someone rushed a copy of the Xinhua article to Cheng Yizhong. He was stunned. He turned to one of his colleagues and expressed wonder at how the leadership had acted so quickly. Never before had any newspaper in China influenced national policy in such a dramatic fashion. The front page for the next day's paper was already set, but Cheng ordered his staff to add one more headline. He assigned a writer to compose a quick editorial. And then he went out to celebrate.

• • •

MANY INSIDE THE party celebrated the newspaper's victory, too. They saw the *Daily*'s reporting on the Sun Zhigang case as a textbook example of how a more assertive press could help the party fight corruption and improve governance. But it was clear early on that not everyone was happy with the newspaper, and that some believed losing control of the media would be hazardous to their hold on power. Just days after the original article was published, the party chief of Guangzhou, a tough operator named Lin Shusen, pulled aside one of the *Daily*'s reporters at a news conference and threatened to take the paper to court if he found any inaccuracies in the report. Later, an old college classmate of Cheng's passed on a private message from another senior city official warning him to back off. The provincial government made a show of launching a special investigation into Sun's death, but it was obvious it wanted to put the case behind it as quickly as possible. A month later, it announced the arrest and conviction of eighteen people, including eight prisoners accused of beating Sun and five security guards who encouraged or condoned the assault. The police officer who first detained Sun was also jailed. Tough sentences were handed down, including the death penalty for one of the prisoners implicated in the beating. But their trials were closed to the public, and the government never provided a full accounting of the events that led to Sun's death. Only a few reporters were permitted in the courtroom, and they were barred from taking notes and told to publish only an official press release. When the sentences in the case were announced, the censors ordered Web sites to restrict public commentary.

Cheng understood from the start that the *Daily*'s crusade would make enemies of powerful people and institutions. The end of the *shourong* system deprived police across the country of both a convenient tool and a lucrative source of income, and the Sun Zhigang case had embarrassed party leaders in Guangzhou and damaged the careers of a host of officials. Publicly, more than twenty officials were formally disciplined, including the city's deputy police chief, but Cheng's contacts told him that members of the Politburo had also rebuked the city leadership through internal channels, an action that could derail promotions for many other cadres. Later, word filtered back to Cheng that party officials in the city were determined to exact revenge on the *Southern Metropolis Daily*. If the propaganda authorities could not act, then they would find another way.

The first sign of trouble came just weeks after the decision to abolish the *shourong* system. Cheng and the paper's general manager, Yu Huafeng, were in Shanghai on business when Cheng received a phone call from an executive with Kodak, one of the tabloid's top advertisers. She told him that police in Guangzhou had visited her office and questioned her about her interaction with the *Daily*'s top senior officials. In particular, she said, they wanted to know about any potentially improper exchanges of gifts or cash. Later, Cheng received a similar call from the president of one of the province's largest advertising firms. By mid-July, almost all the major companies that advertised in the *Daily* had been questioned. The Guangzhou party boss, Lin Shusen, had apparently ordered a criminal probe into the *Daily*'s finances in an attempt to find evidence of corruption at the newspaper. Cheng wasn't worried at first. He knew he and his colleagues ran a clean business. He also felt confident the *Daily* enjoyed more support in the party than its enemies. When police detained Yu for questioning in late July, they were forced to release him a day later after the Southern Newspaper Group persuaded a senior provincial official to intervene.

Except for the corruption investigation, the *Daily* was riding high in the aftermath of its victory in the Sun Zhigang case. Cheng continued to push the boundaries of permissible journalism, running a number of tough articles on police scandals in Guangdong, and the paper won several of the nation's top journalism honors. Circulation climbed past 1.4 million readers for the first time, and profits for the year approached twenty million dollars. Cheng and Yu envisioned further growth and made plans to expand into other cities. In a major breakthrough, the party's central propaganda department approved a proposal in October for the *Daily* to establish a partnership with a state newspaper in Beijing and launch a new tabloid in the capital. It would be called the *Beijing News* and adopt the *Daily*'s feisty brand of journalism. The party appointed Cheng the editor in chief, a job he would hold while continuing to run the *Daily*, and Yu was named the general manager.

Back in Guangzhou, though, the police continued to step up the pressure on the *Southern Metropolis Daily*. Advertisers were warned to stop buying ads from the paper, and some reported being threatened with prosecution if they did not provide evidence against the men who ran the *Daily*. Investigators seized several boxes of documents from the newspaper and scoured expense reports and insurance claims, searching for any irregularity. Then, in December, police showed up at the newsroom and detained Yu again. This time, even after the Southern Newspaper Group appealed to provincial leaders, the police didn't release him. Cheng was upset but he believed his friend's detention would be temporary. He worked to mobilize support within the party for Yu, drafting letters to senior officials and reaching out to influential party elders. He was nervous, but told himself the *Daily* would again prevail against its enemies.

Ten days after Yu's arrest, one of the *Daily*'s reporters returned to the newsroom with a terrific scoop. Provincial health authorities had diagnosed a suspected case of SARS in a Guangzhou hospital. It was the first case of the disease in China in several months, raising fears the virus could be making a comeback. Cheng was in Beijing at the time, running the new tabloid, but one of his deputies called and asked if the *Daily* should publish the information. Yu was still in prison, his fate uncertain, and the story was sure to anger the authorities. But Cheng was focused on the next day's front page—there were no other strong stories lined up for it. So he gave the go-ahead.

Years later, when I asked him about the decision, Cheng told me it had not been difficult. Yes, he acknowledged, it would have been "logical" to exercise caution after Yu's arrest. "We considered it," he said, "but we didn't think there was enough reason for us to sacrifice freedom of the press or compromise our values." The *Daily* had been complicit in the provincial government's first cover-up of SARS, and he didn't want to put the paper in that position again. In addition, he said, it wasn't clear at the time how much trouble Yu was in or whether softening the *Daily*'s coverage would help him. Even if the paper published eight pages of stories complimenting the police and the party bosses, Cheng argued, it might not have made a difference. Men like that, he believed, had already made up their minds about the paper.

But printing the SARS article certainly didn't help, either. The next day, Zhang Dejiang, the provincial party chief, convened an emergency meeting to share the news of the SARS case with the province's top officials. He was embarrassed to discover that everyone in the room had already seen the news in the morning paper, which he alone apparently had not read. He was furious, and those determined to punish the *Southern Metropolis Daily* now had an important new ally— the most powerful man in Guangdong, the same man the *Daily* angered a year earlier by reporting on SARS during the National People's Congress. The corruption probe immediately intensified. During the first two weeks of January, prosecutors interrogated more than twenty editors and advertising executives at the newspaper. Cheng was escorted out of the newsroom by police and questioned for nearly seven hours. Then police arrested the Southern Newspaper Group official responsible for overseeing the *Daily*, Li Mingyi.

It was during this time that Cheng was contacted by a man who introduced himself as one of the officers assigned to guard Yu. They met at a local restaurant because Cheng was worried his office might be bugged. In the busy dining room, over a lunch of spicy cuisine from Hubei Province, the guard told Cheng that Yu was being held in a hotel outside the province that the police used as a secret detention facility. There, the guard said, police had beaten him so badly that he had tried to kill himself by slamming his head against a wall. Suddenly, Cheng felt sick. He and Yu had built the *Daily* together, and he considered him one of his closest friends. Now his friend was being tortured because of stories that he had decided to publish. Yu was a businessman, not a journalist, and though Cheng knew his friend shared his editorial vision for the paper and had always been willing to take risks for it, he still felt guilty that it was Yu suffering and not him. What made it worse was that he was free, a star editor running two of the nation's best newspapers, yet apparently powerless to help his friend. "I felt I was responsible for his suffering," Cheng told me. "The pain was like a knife twisting in my heart. It was guilt and outrage at the same time. And it intensified my hatred of the system."

Cheng's relationship with Yu's wife was already strained, and when he told her what he had learned, it only got worse. She blamed him for her husband's arrest, and she sometimes accused him of not doing enough to save him. Her anger weighed on him, but he sympathized with her. She was alone, worried, emotional, trying to help her husband while also protecting her son, a little boy who believed his father was just away on a business trip. She had hired lawyers, but neither she nor the lawyers had been allowed to see Yu. Cheng told her he was working hard to get him out, but he knew that wouldn't be enough for her. Only when the police came for him, too, he thought, would she understand that they were all victims in this.

Cheng assumed that he was the real target of the investigation, that police were trying to force Yu to implicate him. He concluded it was only a matter of time before they arrested him as well. The focus of the investigation had shifted to the bonuses that the *Daily* awarded its top editors and managers every year. Prosecutors were trying to characterize the payments as embezzled funds, and they were putting pressure on people to return the money and admit wrongdoing. It was a ridiculous charge, but the authorities were threatening prison and, one by one, the senior editors and managers of the *Daily* gave in to save themselves. Only Cheng refused. Unlike the others, a confession was unlikely to save him. It would only be used against him, and perhaps also against his jailed colleagues. As a journalist, Cheng had never been naive about the capacity of the party's security services for brutality, yet he still found it hard to believe they were doing this. It was just so foolish, he thought, because there was certain to be a public backlash. People would see the arrests for the politically motivated frame-up jobs they were.

At the end of January, the authorities turned the screws tighter. At a large gathering of party discipline officials, the provincial party chief, Zhang Dejiang, asked sarcastically whether the party still owned the *Southern Metropolis Daily*. Then he declared that the media couldn't just monitor others; someone had to monitor them, too. One of Zhang's deputies, the official responsible for the police and the courts, then took the microphone and accused the *Daily*'s executives of stealing state funds, essentially convicting Yu and Li before trial.

The remarks angered Cheng, and a few days later he delivered a defiant speech to the senior staff of the newspaper. He wrote it out in advance, because he expected it to be a farewell address. Sitting at the head of a conference table in a room with more than a hundred people, Cheng began with a nod to Yu by quoting a line of ancient poetry about a brother who is missed at a family reunion. Then he addressed what he called the "dark night" facing the newspaper. Ever since the Sun Zhigang report was published, he said, it had been an "open secret" that a few powerful individuals in Guangzhou were "sharpening their weapons" and plotting to punish the *Daily*. "This storm was bound to come sooner or later," he said. "We are already prepared. For the progress of the nation, the development of society and the happiness of the people, it is worth suffering some inconvenience and misery. . . ."

When the Heavens assign you a great task, they also impart great suffering and difficulties. Since we have chosen excellence, we have no reason to refuse setbacks. . . . Our sense of responsibility is what made us excellent. Our excellence is the source of our success and also the source of our suffering. The wind always knocks down the tallest tree in the woods. . . .

Whatever happens, we must not give up the values and beliefs of the *Southern Metropolis Daily*. We have reason to be proud. The *Southern Metropolis Daily* is a newspaper that can endure history's test and that deserves to survive. The values of the *Southern Metropolis Daily* are the values of mainstream society. The path of the *Southern Metropolis Daily* is the path that this nation's newspapers should take. . . . People have built a monument for the *Southern Metropolis Daily* in their hearts, and they have high expectations of the *Southern Metropolis Daily*. The existence of the *Southern Metropolis Daily* is a sign that this society is healthier and more civilized, and it guarantees that this society is more reasonable and fair. To tolerate the *Southern Metropolis Daily* is the most basic attitude of an open society and democratic politics. . . .

Colleagues and comrades-in-arms, I must tell you that the situation we face is very serious. The reality is cruel and cold. Our cause faces an unprecedented test. The *Southern Metropolis Daily* is going through a baptism of blood and fire. We cannot guarantee that every warrior who goes out will be able to return. . . .

Nevertheless, Cheng said, he hoped reporters would not leave the newspaper while it was down, but instead continue fighting until it had been restored to glory. "There are no dark nights that we cannot suffer through," he declared. "There are no dawns that we cannot wait for."

In early March, party officials in the propaganda apparatus forced Cheng to step down as editor in chief of the *Beijing News*. He took that as a sign that the party's new leaders in Beijing—the same men who ended the SARS cover-up and abolished the *shourong* system—were about to let their subordinates in Guangzhou go ahead and arrest him. In meetings over the next few days, he told his supervisors at the Southern Newspaper Group that no matter what happened, they should know that he had never broken the law or done anything to bring shame to the Group. In a final memo, he urged his colleagues at the *Daily* to stick together and defend the newspaper. He said good-bye to his son, and he went for a long walk with his wife. As they strolled through his neighborhood, away from any listening devices that might have been installed in his home, he told her what she should tell reporters after he was arrested—that he was innocent, that he had been imprisoned because the *Southern Metropolis Daily* had angered local officials, that he was willing to sacrifice his freedom for the progress of journalism in China, and that history would vindicate him and he would be released.

Several days later, Yu was tried, convicted, and sentenced to twelve years in prison. Li received an eleven-year sentence. The next day, police arrested Cheng. His initial reaction was relief.

IT IS ONE of the sad ironies of the Sun Zhigang story that the editor who published the exposé of the young graphic designer's death now found he was one of the beneficiaries of the reforms it prompted. Outside Cheng's jail cell was a poster that declared the party was conducting a "rectification campaign" and encouraged detainees to report guards and bullies who abused them. Cheng's cellmates told him conditions in the Guangzhou No. 1 Detention Center had been far worse before his newspaper's report on Sun's murder. They were in a position to know. Some of them had been jailed there for as long as six years awaiting trial or sentencing. Cheng made a mental note to assign a reporter to the subject if he had the chance again.

About twenty men shared the cell with Cheng. The boss appeared to be a Hong Kong gangster, a large, muscular inmate covered with tattoos who was awaiting a death sentence. When Cheng first arrived, the man demanded that he "register" with him. But before Cheng could find out what that meant, a prison guard called the inmate over and whispered something in his ear. When he returned, the gangster was much friendlier and offered to show Cheng around the small cell. He assigned a handsome young inmate to be Cheng's "servant," some-one who would wash his clothes, and fetch water and take away garbage for him, and then he invited Cheng to share a cup of tea and a bag of peanuts with him. Cheng never learned what the prison guard told the cell boss, but he assumed that the prison authorities wanted to make sure he was treated well in case he was released and decided to write anything about his experience. Later, as word of his identity spread in the detention center, other inmates looked out for him because they considered him an ally. Anybody who dared stand up to the police was all right by them.

Prosecutors came to interrogate Cheng every day in the beginning. They still wanted him to "confess" that the annual bonuses he accepted were illegal payments. On some days, they harangued and threatened him. On others, they tried simple persuasion. Early on, they tried to demoralize him by telling him that one of his editors, a young man he considered a protégé, had betrayed and condemned him. Later they ratcheted up the pressure by withholding food, keeping the lights on to make it hard for him to sleep, and dumping cold water over his body or pulling his hair as soon as he did fall asleep. But Cheng refused to give in. No matter what happened, he told himself, he would not confess. No matter what promises they made, he reminded himself, a confession would only result in a prison term. If he wanted to preserve any chance of getting out, he had to maintain his innocence. It was the truth, after all. Cheng told the prosecutors again and again: If the bonuses were really illegal payments, as they charged, then they didn't really need a confession to convict him.

Time seemed to stop in the Guangzhou No. 1 Detention Center. There were no windows, no sunsets or sunrises. There was no passing of the seasons. None of his family and friends were allowed to visit him. At times, Cheng looked forward to the visits from the prosecutors, because at least he could look at their clothing and try to figure out what the weather was like outside. He could only imagine what else was happening out there. He could only hope that people were fighting for his release. If there was a public outcry over his arrest, he thought, then perhaps party leaders were having second thoughts about imprisoning him. If that were the case, then it would be critical that he refuse to give in to the prosecutors' demands. A confession could be just what his enemies needed to win permission to convict him.

The prosecutors wore uniforms and worked in shifts, and the interrogations usually stretched overnight. But one morning they showed up refreshed, with new haircuts and in plainclothes. They told Cheng to relax. It was sunny out, they said, and they were going to take him to their offices. Cheng was wary. It was his birthday, and he suspected the prosecutors were going to try to use that against him. They escorted him out of the detention center and drove him to their headquarters, where he was taken to a conference room. Today, the prosecutors said, there would be no talk of his crimes. Instead, they had arranged for him to chat with several of their recent hires, young graduates of Peking University who were fans of his newspaper. Several young men and women entered the room. The women were especially pretty, Cheng noted, and they sat next to him and began asking him questions about life and literature and idealism. They said they worshipped him, and one of them read him poetry. Cheng played along, answering their questions and drinking tea. At lunchtime, waitresses brought in baskets of dishes from his native Anhui Province—crispy wok fish, Yellow Mountain stone chicken—and served bowls of noodles. After Cheng finished eating, one of the prosecutors made a signal, and then a woman brought in the biggest birthday cake he had ever seen.

"Editor Cheng, today is your thirty-ninth birthday," the prosecutor said. "It is still uncertain where you will be on your fortieth birthday. We hope the road to your fortieth birthday will be a pleasant one."

Then they gave Cheng a knife and asked him to make a wish and serve the cake. Some of the men and women in the room had taken out cameras. For a moment Cheng thought of his family and was on the verge of tears. And then he realized that was what they wanted. They wanted him to break down and then capture it on film, for the documentaries with the corrupt officials crying and confessing their crimes that state television often broadcast.

One of the prosecutors spoke again. He pointed out that the headquarters of the *Southern Metropolis Daily* was just across the street. He asked Cheng to imagine what a great birthday celebration he could be having over there. There was no need for him to stay in prison, he said. It was just stupid for him to be so stubborn. While others celebrated their birthdays with their families, he was alone and his wife and son were living in shame. The man asked Cheng if he understood what it meant for an eight-year-old boy to be without his father. He asked if he knew how much his family missed him. And then he asked if he wanted to see them. They were right in the next room, he said. Cheng could go see them, and maybe even go home with them that night. It was entirely up to him. Then the prosecutor showed him a bag of clothes. He said Cheng's wife and son had brought it that morning. They had been kneeling outside the gate, begging the guard to let them see him. The prosecutor took out a snapshot of Cheng's family and waved it in front of him. He looked at Cheng, anticipating a reaction. But Cheng had had enough. He stood up and said he didn't want to see his family. He wanted to go back to his cell.

It was nearly dark out when Cheng boarded the police sedan that would take him back to the detention center. The car pulled out and stopped at a red light. Through the window, he looked up at the headquarters of his newspaper. He could see the window of his office on the fifth floor. Then, suddenly, there was a flicker and five large characters appeared in red neon on the roof of the building. *Southern Metropolis Daily*. While he was in jail, his staff had finally managed to put up the sign he wanted. Cheng began to tear up. He realized that he might never work at the newspaper again. Then the light changed, and the car pulled away.

WHILE CHENG SAT in prison, his colleagues at the *Southern Metropolis Daily* launched a campaign to win his freedom. They appealed to the party leadership, and then to the public on the Internet. Some of them, like the reporter Chen Feng, issued open letters on the editor's behalf. Others quietly contacted me and other foreign journalists and fed us information. News of the arrests at the *Daily* spread quickly, and soon journalists across the country were signing petitions. Many of those who had campaigned against the *shourong* system now took up the cause of the three jailed newspaper executives. Xu Zhiyong, one of the young scholars who had requested the constitutional review of *shourong*, volunteered to help with their legal defense and called a news conference in Beijing. Behind the scenes, the Southern Newspaper Group mobilized the party's liberal faction, and several influential figures, including three retired provincial party chiefs, called for a review of the case. Cheng never found out exactly what turned the tide, but the public outcry had an impact. About five months after his arrest, party leaders in Guangdong reversed themselves and released him. Yu and Li remained in prison, though their sentences were reduced and Li was later released, too.

I last saw Cheng in late 2007. We had lunch in a private room at an upscale Shanghainese restaurant in Beijing, and he spoke proudly, even defiantly, of his experiences. Yu was scheduled to complete his four-year sentence in a few months' time, and Cheng planned to be there to greet him when he walked out of prison. He said he was still struggling with survivor's guilt. "It makes no sense that he's in prison and not me," he told me. "The prosecutors said I was the chief culprit and he was the accomplice. So how could they release me but keep him in prison?"

Cheng still looked young, and he seemed as confident and intense as ever. He had not been allowed to return to the *Southern Metropolis Daily* or the *Beijing News*, and it clearly saddened him. More than once he told me he believed the two tabloids were the only publications in China that deserved to be called great newspapers. Both were flourishing and continuing to push the limits of press freedom under the leadership of editors he had trained. He, however, had taken a job editing the Chinese edition of *Sports Illustrated*.

After we finished our meal, Cheng told me he once believed that the Communist Party could reform itself and that journalists could help it do so by speaking out for the weak and exposing the abuses of the powerful. But prison had changed him, and now he considered the party's rule irredeemably corrupt. That judgment, however, left him with few options as a citizen and a journalist, and he was restless. "The worst thing that happened to me," he said, "was that I lost all hope in the system."

Chen Guidi and Wu Chuntao outside the courthouse in Fuyang

10

THE PEOPLE'S TRIAL

On the day that Cheng Yizhong was released from prison in Guangzhou in August 2004, I was watching another battle over freedom of speech unfold in the city of Fuyang, nearly seven hundred miles to the north on the wheat plains of Anhui Province. Cheng's fate had been decided by party leaders who weighed the political costs and benefits of his imprisonment and judged that letting him go would better serve their interests. Legally, it was a decision for the courts to make, but the Communist Party exercises firm control over the judiciary and the word of a party boss trumps that of any law, judge, or prosecutor. There seemed to be little doubt, then, who would prevail in the libel trial that opened the same week in the Fuyang Intermediate People's Court. At the plaintiff's table sat Zhang Xide, former party chief of Linquan County and member of Fuyang's party leadership. On the other side of the room was the couple he had sued, Chen Guidi and Wu Chuntao, authors of the banned bestseller, *An Investigation of China's Peasantry*. Given Zhang's clout in the city—his son was a judge in the same courthouse—and the attention that his lawsuit had received, it appeared that a show trial was in the making.

There were reasons, though, to suspect the proceedings in Fuyang might prove more interesting. By the summer of 2004, hopes that Hu Jintao's government would usher in real political change had already begun to fade. More than a year had passed since the party's new leaders ended the SARS cover-up and abolished the *shourong* detention system, and there was no sign they planned to do much more. On the contrary, the evidence suggested they were as obsessed with challenges to the party's rule as their predecessors. In November 2003, a group of residents in Hubei Province led by a schoolteacher and election reformer named Yao Lifa had attempted to run in local legislative elections, only to be subjected to a campaign of harassment, intimidation, and voter fraud that ensured, as usual, only the party's candidates won. Yao's appeals to the leadership were ignored. The crackdown at the *Southern Metropolis Daily* came soon afterward, sending a chill through the state media and dimming the optimism of journalists across the country. Then, in June 2004, the authorities detained the SARS whistle-blower Jiang Yanyong and suppressed attempts to commemorate the fifteenth anniversary of the Tiananmen massacre.

If political reform was off the table, though, Hu and his premier, Wen Jiabao, seemed determined to address rising discontent among those left behind by the economic boom. They had sent more welfare funds to the industrial northeast, helping to tamp down worker protests in the rust-belt cities, but they still faced an explosive situation in the countryside, where taxes and fees levied by rural party officials were chipping away at peasant incomes. One of Hu's first initiatives had been a plan to begin phasing out all rural taxes, and in a symbolic gesture, he celebrated the Lunar New Year with a peasant family, sharing dumplings with them on national television. Nearly two years later, though, rural conditions seemed to be getting worse. Rural officials in many places continued to demand exorbitant taxes, and a decision to relax investment controls to boost the economy after the SARS epidemic led to a rush of real estate and industrial projects in the countryside that required land—land that officials were seizing from peasants and selling to developers. The confiscation of farmland soon became a leading cause of rural conflict, as families accused officials of pocketing profits from the sale of their plots and demanded compensation. Meanwhile, Hu's populist rhetoric only raised expectations among peasants, who were emboldened to resist local officials they believed were violating his policies. Unrest was on the rise, with po-

lice struggling to contain an average of two hundred "mass distur-
bances" every day in 2004, some of them violent clashes. Given the
challenges in the countryside that the leadership faced, it was easy to
imagine the trial in Fuyang sending the wrong signal to the public. In
effect, Hu had staked his reputation on reining in the abuses of rural
officials. Yet here was one of those officials trying to punish two writers who had dared expose his record.

The trial in Fuyang also opened against the background of a surge
in legal activism around the country, the result of a profound shift in
public attitudes toward the law. For centuries, the Chinese have regarded the law as an instrument of state control, a way for those in
power to regulate the behavior of their subjects and punish those who
step out of line. The Communist Party shared the same view, adding
the Marxist notion that the law should be a weapon used by the proletariat in class struggle. But after Mao's death, the party began building a modern legal system suitable for a market economy, and soon a
competing vision of the law emerged. People began to think of the law
as a check on the power of government officials and a guardian of individual rights. They started to believe that judges should rule impar-
tially instead of just following the party's orders. They began to expect
that everyone, even government leaders, could be held accountable in
court. In an authoritarian state, these were subversive ideas, yet the
party itself helped foster this rising legal consciousness. Ever since the
chaos of the Cultural Revolution, it had bombarded the public with
propaganda proclaiming its commitment to the rule of law. Now, in
courtrooms across the nation, citizens were insisting that it live up to
that commitment.

Leading the charge, naturally, were the lawyers. They were a diverse, unruly bunch, men and women—mostly men—who were essentially establishing a new profession and figuring out how as they went
along. Some were educated in the nation's best universities. Others
taught themselves the law and passed the bar on their own. Only a
fraction took on the hard cases that challenged party officials or their
cronies, cases that would be difficult to win and even more difficult to
make money on. The risks were substantial. A vigorous defense of a
jailed client or an aggressive lawsuit against entrenched interests
could land a lawyer in prison. But there were rewards, too—prestige,
self-respect, the satisfaction of fighting for justice. In the year before

the Fuyang libel trial, these lawyers—some called themselves *weiquan* or "rights defense" lawyers—were beginning to come together, emerging as a diffuse yet significant political force. Some had organized to support a prominent colleague, Zheng Enchong, who was jailed in Shanghai for his work representing residents evicted by a corrupt developer. A few worked together to defend a well-known entrepreneur, Sun Dawu, who had angered the authorities with his criticism of the political system. So when the authors of *An Investigation of China's Peasantry* were sued, there was a community of lawyers willing to help. One of those who volunteered was a lawyer named Pu Zhiqiang.

A TALL, BRAWNY MAN with a square jaw and a crew cut, Pu looked more like a lumberjack than a lawyer, and when I met him, I was struck by how he sprinkled his sentences with both street profanities and classical Chinese, a mix that could confound even a native speaker of the language. Gregarious and garrulous, he was in many ways an example of the modern Chinese success story. Born in an impoverished village in Hebei Province, the youngest son of illiterate corn and potato farmers, he was now, at age thirty-nine, a partner in a successful Beijing law firm, enjoying a comfortable life in the middle class, complete with a high-rise apartment and a Volkswagen.

Pu's journey out of the countryside began when he was three months old. His parents entrusted him to an uncle and aunt to raise, because the couple had no children of their own and they lived closer to the county seat. Pu's parents hoped that he would get a better education there, and as it turned out, he was among the first in his village to go to college, enrolling in the history department at Nankai University in Tianjin, the big port city east of Beijing. He was a good student and popular among his classmates, and the party tried to recruit him. But it was 1984, during the political thaw after the Cultural Revolution, and campuses across the country were buzzing with an intellectual fervor not seen since the Hundred Flowers Movement. Bookstores were full of works that had once been banned, the truth of the past was beginning to emerge, and Pu found himself questioning much of what he had been taught in school. Many of his classmates joined the party without hesitation, because party membership meant better jobs and valuable connections, but Pu spent a week in the

Pu Zhiqiang speaking to peasants outside the courthouse during a break in the libel trial

library reading about history and politics. Then he turned the party down. Communism, he decided, was a sham, and he didn't want any part of it.

After graduating, Pu taught at a small college in Hebei, then enrolled in graduate school at the China University of Political Science and Law in Beijing, where he studied ancient Chinese literature and legal texts. Like many of his classmates, his dissatisfaction with the party's rule continued to grow. Inflation was spinning out of control and corruption seemed to be getting worse. Pu looked up to scholars who advocated democratic reform, such as the physicist Fang Lizhi, and with each attempt by the government to censor and suppress "spiritual pollution" and "bourgeois liberalization"—code words for the liberal ideas that threatened the one-party system—he grew more disgusted. Then, in the spring of 1989, a former party chief, Hu Yaobang, who had been ousted for being too soft on dissent, suffered a fatal heart attack during a Politburo meeting. Two days later, Pu joined tens of thousands of students who marched through Beijing to mourn his death. It was the start of the Tiananmen Square democracy movement.

The movement was a turning point in Pu's life. He was twenty-four, older than and respected by many of the undergraduates, and he emerged as one of the many leaders of the demonstrations. He helped organize the marches and the boycott of classes. He participated in the hunger strike. He delivered speeches and gave interviews to foreign reporters. It was an emotional time, and one of his teachers recalled that Pu struck his head with a bullhorn in frustration when party leaders refused to receive three students who knelt four hours on the steps of the Great Hall of the People with a petition. Pu spent weeks camped in the square, and he was there on the night of June 3, huddled with a few thousand others near the Monument to the People's Heroes, when the army began shooting protesters as it entered Beijing. Fires around the city gave the sky an eerie glow, and loudspeakers in the square repeated the government's martial law warnings again and again. Pu could hear the crackle of gunfire, dull and distant at first, then sharper and closer. He decided it would be safer to stay in the square than try to leave, and he was right. The bloodshed took place on the streets outside Tiananmen. On the morning of June 4, when soldiers occupied the square and ordered the tearful students to clear out, Pu was among the last to leave but he was unharmed.

The party conducted investigations at every university afterward, but many officials sympathized with the students and there was a perfunctory quality to the process. It might have been possible for Pu to escape punishment by going through the motions of criticizing the protests, voicing support for the government and condemning the party leaders who were purged. But he couldn't bring himself to do it. "I have a stubborn disposition, and I didn't think I had done anything wrong," he wrote in an essay published overseas more than a decade later.

> At the same time, it occurred to me that millions of people around the country had participated in the movement, and I didn't think it would be appropriate if the majority all examined their thinking and raised their understanding, and it was as if Zhao Ziyang had tricked everyone. Some people had to take responsibility. I was just a student, and of course, I didn't have the status or influence to take any responsibility. But if I loudly declared that the Communist Party was right and I was wrong, when I hadn't come around to that, I would have let down my conscience. It also would have easily sent the Communist Party the wrong signal. So, in the end, I couldn't give those above me a conclusion that would satisfy them. . . . I didn't see a problem, much less any need to hang my head and admit a mistake. We weren't the ones who should be admitting mistakes, at least not primarily us.

As graduation approached, university officials pressed Pu to submit a self-criticism. He responded with an essay he sarcastically titled "Baring One's Heart to the Party," in which he defended his activities during the demonstrations, arguing that he had acted with good intentions. "At the time, I thought the government was ridiculous," he wrote of his participation in the hunger strike. "We were nearly starving to death, but you were still so devoid of human sympathy. As a result, my attitude hardened. I believe my thinking was the same as others. We were all trying to help the Communist Party and the government correct their mistakes." One of the professors assigned to Pu's case asked why he couldn't include just a few boilerplate sentences endorsing Deng Xiaoping's "Four Cardinal Principles," the ideological underpinning for one-party rule. Pu replied that he opposed the principles, and said he would say so in the essay if the professor insisted. The professor just shook his head and told him to leave the essay the way it was.

Considering his refusal to toe the party line, the university could have expelled him, but instead it let Pu graduate with a "serious administrative warning" in his file. The warning ended his dream of a career in academia, because it meant no university or government agency would hire him. "Thinking about it today," Pu wrote later, "maybe the Communist Party didn't really want people to examine their thinking and sincerely submit. Maybe from the start, it wanted to make people hang their heads just superficially, to make everyone despise themselves and face that reality. I didn't do it, and my mind has always been at ease. Although I lost many opportunities over the years, I never regretted it."

For years, Pu drifted from one job to another, working as a salesman, a secretary, even at an agricultural market. Then, in 1993, a friend urged him to try a career in law, because his master's degree was technically a law degree. Pu began studying for the bar and took the exam twice before managing to guess enough answers to pass. He was not enthusiastic about his new profession, but he was almost thirty, married, and the father of a two-year-old boy. "I didn't do it because I thought it would be interesting. I did it because I had nothing better to do," he told me. "I had to make a living, and with June fourth on my record, I couldn't get a better job."

The legal profession was still in its infancy in China when Pu began practicing. Mao had all but dismantled the nation's courts during the Cultural Revolution, and the government was essentially starting from scratch when it began rebuilding the judicial system in the 1980s. It took time, but gradually lawyers shed their traditional role as civil servants loyal to the state and became independent advocates devoted to their clients. The first private law firms opened in 1992, and Pu started taking on cases just a few years later. He helped companies declare bankruptcy and settle business disputes, and studied the law as he went along. But he quickly learned that a lawyer's connections were more important than his skills. Connections brought in clients, and connections helped win cases. It wasn't that evidence and knowledge of the law never mattered, just that they didn't always matter. Judicial corruption was common. There were late-night mah-jongg games, where lawyers were expected to lose hundreds of thousands of dollars to judges. They also gave judges extravagant gifts, or simply paid them cash bribes.

Pu found the legal environment depressing, but he prospered. In four years of college and three years of graduate school, he had culti- vated a network of acquaintances who could help him find clients. "I had a lot of friends, and to be a good lawyer in China, you had to have friends," he said. Soon he was handling twenty to thirty cases a year, earning a big portion of his firm's profits and taking home a comfort- able salary. At the same time, though, he struggled with his conscience. "If I told my clients I wouldn't use my connections, they would never agree. So when they ask me if I have connections, I always say yes," he told me. Pu tried to set limits. He resolved never to ask a friend to break the law or do anything dishonorable. He tried never to give bribes. If a client asked him to subvert the legal process, he would reply that the best he could do was slow it down. Still, sometimes he did things he wasn't proud of. "Sometimes, I had no other choice," he said.

Pu didn't handle criminal cases, but once, early in his career, he agreed to represent a peasant woman from a village on the outskirts of Beijing who wanted to sue the local police. Officers there had been running an extortion scheme, arresting women and forcing them to confess to prostitution, pay hefty fines, and implicate men who could then be shaken down, too. Pu's client had been beaten badly for refus- ing to go along. When he accepted the case, pro bono, he believed that he was finally doing something good with his law license—seeking justice on behalf of an ordinary citizen. The local court, however, re- fused even to accept his lawsuit, and the police retaliated by framing and arresting his client's brother-in-law. Pu was powerless to help, and the experience left him with tough questions: Did he take the case to make himself feel better about his job, or because he believed he could actually make a difference? Did his involvement only make the situation worse for his client? Afterward, Pu decided he would never again raise clients' hopes if he didn't think he could really help them.

Six years passed before Pu accepted another case that tapped into his idealism about a lawyer's ability to make a difference. In 2003, he agreed to defend a literary critic who had been sued for defamation by one of China's most famous authors, Yu Qiuyu. While preparing for trial, he read about *New York Times Co. v. Sullivan*, the landmark 1964

Supreme Court decision on freedom of the press. The decision protected the publication of all statements, even false ones, about public officials except those published with reckless disregard for the truth. By setting such a high burden of proof for defamation, Pu read, the Court made it possible for American news organizations to report on civil rights infringements in the South without fear of being sued. He thought the case was an inspiring example of the power of the law to move a society, and he incorporated the decision's reasoning into his defense. Uninhibited discussion of public issues was so important to society, he argued, that public figures should not be allowed to use the law to intimidate their critics. The judge never addressed his argument, but Pu won the case.

Suddenly, Pu began to feel better about being a lawyer. He had found a legal principle he wanted to fight for—freedom of speech— and he began to believe that a good lawyer who picked the right cases could make a difference. Over the next year, he took on four more defamation cases, defending two magazines, a newspaper, and a scholar from lawsuits filed by companies and business tycoons. In a nation where censorship is standard and criticizing a party leader can result in a prison sentence, Pu was carving out a niche for himself as a free-speech lawyer.

The four cases were still pending when Pu heard about a fifth, Zhang Xide's lawsuit against the authors of *An Investigation of China's Peasantry*. The case was different from the others, because Zhang was a public official. Pu purchased a copy of the book, pirated editions of which were widely available despite the government's decision to ban it. "I read the book carefully," he recalled, "and it made me furious." It reminded him of his own experiences in the countryside; only a decade earlier, rural officials enforcing the one-child policy had forced his sister-in-law to abort a pregnancy in the ninth month. The authors Chen Guidi and Wu Chuntao already had an attorney, but Pu contacted them and offered his services for free. He told them he wanted to turn the case into China's version of *New York Times Co. v. Sullivan* and argue that the nation would be better served if the courts protected the public's right to criticize party officials. He also faxed them a copy of the argument he filed in the case he won a year earlier. The authors were impressed. A few weeks later, in a meeting in Pu's office in Beijing, they invited him to join their defense team.

• • •

ON AUGUST 22, two days before the trial was scheduled to open, I met
Pu on the platform at Beijing's mammoth western rail station and we
boarded an overnight train to Fuyang. There are more than a hundred
cities in China with populations over one million, and many Chinese
have probably never heard of most of them. Fuyang, however, a gritty
railway hub that calls itself the nation's Liquor Capital, had been in
the news lately. A few months earlier, authorities discovered that factories there were producing fake baby formula that had caused dozens
of infants to starve to death and left more than two hundred others
severely malnourished. Local officials were accused of taking kick-
backs and looking the other way. It was not the first scandal to hit the
city. A huge airport sits unused outside Fuyang, the vanity project of a
former mayor who wanted to make it easier for himself to jet off to
Beijing and Shanghai. He was later implicated in a massive bribery
case and executed. The party was so worried about corruption in
Fuyang that afterward it distributed a photo of his corpse to city officials as a warning.

It was a nine-hour journey from Beijing to Fuyang, and when Pu
wasn't sleeping in his bunk, he sat hunched over a stack of court papers, working on his defense under the dim lights of the train car.
Given the city's reputation for corruption, it seemed doubtful he had
much of a chance of winning the case, and I asked him why he was
even bothering. He laughed, and acknowledged he didn't expect to
win. "I still have to do a good job," he explained. "That's my obligation
to my clients." But there was more to it than that. The party claimed to
govern by the rule of law. It debated legislation, set up courts, hired
judges, held trials—it wrapped itself in the trappings of the law, because doing so conferred an aura of legitimacy on it. It was a charade,
of course. The party spent three times more on its riot control police
than it did on courts and prosecutors, and when push came to shove, it
believed it had the authority to do whatever it wanted, legal or not. Pu
understood this as well as anyone. But he believed the legal charade
offered an opportunity. Using the courtroom as a stage, he intended
to present a convincing case to the public. If he did a good job, the
party could still rule against him, but it would have to drop the charade, expose its commitment to the law as a fraud, and pay a price in

damage to its image. The stronger the case he presented, Pu believed, the higher that price would be, and if it were high enough, party leaders might think twice about putting themselves above the legal system. In that moment of hesitation, something remarkable could happen. The charade could become a reality—the party could be constrained by its own sham laws.

It was a long shot, of course, and Pu knew it. He had been to Fuyang three times already for pretrial hearings and had seen little to give him hope. The plaintiff and defendants had been summoned to exchange evidence in advance of the trial, in the equivalent of the discovery process in an American civil suit, but the sessions were haphazard and neither side was required to produce witnesses for depositions. The attorney representing Zhang Xide even resisted giving Pu a copy of the documents he planned to introduce at trial, complaining that it would cost too much to photocopy. After all, he seemed to be saying, why waste the money when it was obvious how the trial would end? But Pu insisted and offered to cover the cost himself. Eventually, the judge intervened and ordered Zhang's lawyer to make the copies. It was the smallest of victories, and Pu knew it didn't mean much. Even if the judge sympathized with the defendants, he had little real power. Judges are appointed by the party and required to carry out the party's orders. They preside over cases but generally don't have the authority to decide them. Instead, they make a recommendation to a party committee, and the party committee determines the verdict. The bottom line was that local party officials controlled local courts. In one survey, less than 5 percent of Chinese judges said they would rule according to the law if it conflicted with the instructions of their party bosses. Since Zhang was one of those bosses in Fuyang, Pu's only real hope was the intervention of more senior party leaders. For that to happen, the trial would have to attract a great deal of public attention, and that seemed unlikely because propaganda officials in Beijing had not only banned *An Investigation of China's Peasantry*, they had also prohibited media coverage of it.

A few weeks before the trial, though, one journalist did manage to break the news blackout and publish an article about the case. It was really just a transcript of an interview with Zhang, but he came across as a buffoon and it put the lawsuit back in the news. Wang Heyan, a tough-as-nails investigative reporter for a business newspaper in Beijing, had persuaded her editors to run it by arguing that the censors had barred coverage of the book but not specifically the lawsuit. By just reporting Zhang's answers to her questions, instead of writing a full article about the case, she also made it more difficult for the censors to punish her paper. After all, shouldn't a party newspaper give a party official such as Zhang a chance to address the public? When Sina, one of the nation's top Web sites, picked up the interview, it received national attention, and many readers who saw it were outraged by Zhang's attempt to use the courts to punish the authors. Pu thought the report was terrific, a clever bit of journalistic maneuvering that worked to his clients' advantage.

But another lawyer on the defense team reacted differently. Wu Ge, a clean-cut, bespectacled man who looked like a nervous history teacher, was one of the more prominent public interest lawyers in Beijing. At age thirty-seven, he was the director of a constitutional law and civil rights center at Tsinghua, the nation's most prestigious university after Beida, and he had helped represent the family of Sun Zhigang, the college student whose death in police custody in Guangzhou led to the abolition of the *shourong* detention system. Like Pu, he was a hustler and a believer in the power of the law to change society. But while Pu was an outsider and a political outcast, Wu's position at Tsinghua made him an insider, someone who could work with the party's legal establishment. At first, he had asked simply to observe the case for research purposes, but the authors Chen Guidi and Wu Chuntao later invited him to join their defense, because they believed his connections could be useful. He had also said he could get funding to help cover the trial costs, primarily the expense of bringing witnesses to Fuyang.

When Wu saw the Zhang interview, it gave him an idea. He met with Chen and Wu and proposed a countersuit. Zhang, he argued, had slandered them in the interview by accusing them of making up the stories about him in their book. The newspaper and Sina were guilty as well because they published his interview. But most important, Wu said, if the authors filed a countersuit, they could do so in a court in Beijing, because both the newspaper and Sina were based there. Zhang Xide might be able to control the courts in Fuyang, but in Beijing his influence would be limited and it would be easier to attract media coverage and the attention of party leaders. In Beijing the authors would have a chance.

Chen Guidi liked the idea immediately. He had been upset by

Zhang's interview. It angered him that Zhang had been allowed to vent at length in the newspaper while the censors prohibited reporters from quoting him and his wife at all. He was also thinking ahead to the trial. Zhang was almost certainly going to win, and the court could then order them to apologize and pay the entire twenty-five thousand dollars he had demanded in damages. If they were going to lose in Fuyang, then it made sense to him to try to fight back in Beijing. He believed that he and his wife needed to defend their reputations. And at the very least, a countersuit would give them some leverage in settlement discussions.

Pu was furious when he heard about the plan. He told Chen that a countersuit was a terrible idea, that Zhang had just as much a right to criticize the book as Chen and his wife had to write it. He argued that they should be thanking Sina and the newspaper, not suing them. After all, no one had dared write about the lawsuit after the book was banned until Wang came up with the idea of publishing the interview with Zhang. Both her newspaper and Sina had risked punishment from the propaganda authorities, and they had focused public attention on the trial again—attention that was critical if the authors were to have any chance of winning. Chen was unconvinced at first. He kept arguing that it wasn't fair that Zhang's accusations could be published while he and his wife had been silenced. If Wang Heyan had only published a few sentences on his behalf, he said, it would have been different. Wu Ge defended his proposed countersuit, too. But Pu retorted that he was the specialist on defamation cases, and he reminded the authors why they had retained him. He had successfully defended a literary critic who had been sued by one of China's most famous writers. If they sued the newspaper and Sina, Pu said, they would lose in court, just as that famous writer lost. But most important, he said, they would be giving up the moral high ground and undermining their own best defense—that the law should be used to protect speech, not suppress it.

In the end, the authors took Pu's advice and decided against the countersuit. But the fight placed a strain on the defense team that lingered as we arrived in Fuyang. Pu and Wu Ge were barely on speaking terms, and it was clear neither man liked the other very much. What little respect they did have for each other dissolved on the eve of the trial in a last-minute dispute over who would serve as the authors' lead attorney. Pu had been involved in the case longer, but Wu attempted to take the job from him. Both lawyers lost their temper and threatened to quit. The authors couldn't decide what to do and considered firing both lawyers and representing themselves in court the next morning. It was not until well past midnight that they finally decided to keep Pu as their main attorney.

"We had to make a choice, and in a place like Fuyang, we needed somebody like Pu," Wu Chuntao told me. "We knew we needed a cannon."

ROOM NO. 2 at the Fuyang municipal courthouse had that drab, functional, wood-paneled look of courtrooms around the world. Three judges in black robes presided from the bench, with the red-and-gold emblem of the People's Republic of China on the wall behind them. A stenographer sat in front of them, hunched over a desk next to the witness stand. To the left, at the plaintiff's table, sat Zhang Xide and his two attorneys, one of whom also wore a black robe, signaling his status as a former prosecutor. Facing them on the right were the defendants and their lawyers. Pu and Chen sat in front, along with an older woman, Lei Yanping, a lawyer from the provincial capital whom the authors had hired before Pu joined the team. Wu Ge, who never carried out his threat to quit, sat at a table behind them, next to Chen's wife and Lu Zhimin, a lawyer who represented the authors' publisher.

More than a dozen police officers stood guard around the courtroom, and everybody had to show a ticket to get in. The court had given the authors twenty-five tickets, and they distributed most of them to peasants who had traveled to Fuyang from Linquan County to watch the trial. They gave me one, too, and I dressed as a peasant and sat in a row near the back of the gallery, trying to blend in and avoid the gaze of the police. A handful of Chinese reporters had also come, though most on their own time to show support for Pu and the authors, because their editors had already told them it would be impossible to publish anything about the trial. Sitting on the plaintiff's side of the room were some of Zhang's supporters, including several young toughs in crew cuts who appeared to be his bodyguards. Though there were plenty of empty seats in the gallery, hundreds of peasants from Linquan County were refused entry and forced to wait outside. They milled about in front of the courthouse, crowding together every once in a while when someone emerged from the building during a break and gave them a blow-by-blow of the proceedings.

The presiding judge, Qian Weiguang, a slim, middle-aged man who wore plain glasses and an impatient scowl, did all of the talking for the court. The other two judges—a younger man and an even younger woman—sat silently on either side of him, and sometimes appeared to be dozing off. None of them had a law degree, but that was not unusual for judges even in a city of 1.7 million. More than a quarter century after reopening the courts, the party was still struggling to find qualified people to staff them. In many jurisdictions, judges had little more than an elementary school education. Others were demobilized soldiers for whom the party needed to find jobs. Judge Qian's résumé was about average. He had been appointed to the bench after working his way up from a position as a courthouse clerk.

Zhang's lead attorney, the one in the robe, delivered the first opening statement. He spoke with a local accent and read from a prepared text. He said Chen Guidi and Wu Chuntao fabricated the material in their book about Zhang and libeled the party boss twenty-three times by lying about his appearance and his job performance. Zhang did not speak like an "uncouth lout," as the authors wrote, he said, nor did he have a "five-short figure," the phrase they used to describe his short arms, legs, and neck. The lawyer also denied that Zhang had imposed excessive taxes on the peasants of Linquan County or ordered police to beat the residents of Wangying Village after they traveled to Beijing to complain. "As a senior party member and a qualified cadre who has made no mistakes . . . Zhang Xide is using the weapon of the law to demand justice," he declared. He asked the court to seize the publisher's profits from the book and order the authors to apologize and pay about twenty-five thousand dollars in damages.

The four defense lawyers took turns responding. Lei Yanping, the lawyer from the provincial capital, spoke first and set a defiant tone for the team. "If a party secretary can't take criticism without considering it defamation," she said, "I suggest he quit and go home." But it was Pu who laid out the bulk of the case. Wearing a silver tie and a gray short-sleeved shirt, he spoke quickly and forcefully, only occasionally referring to his papers. He noted that *An Investigation of China's*

Peasantry was a work of "reportage literature," a popular Chinese genre in which writers sometimes embellish the facts for literary effect. The authors, therefore, should not be held responsible for minor inaccuracies, only for serious and malicious falsehoods. On that score, Pu said, they stood by their book. The chapter on Zhang was based on extensive research, he said, including internal party reports and countless interviews with the residents of Linquan County. To prove defamation under Chinese law, Zhang would have to demonstrate that the book had damaged his reputation, but Pu argued that his reputation was in tatters long before the authors began their research in Linquan County. It was not the book that damaged his reputation, Pu said, but his own misconduct in office.

Finally, Pu made the *New York Times Co. v. Sullivan* argument. He urged the court to set a higher burden of proof for a public official to prove defamation. Government officials wield so much power that people are naturally afraid to say anything bad about them, but public scrutiny and discussion are essential to reducing corruption and improving governance, Pu argued. Officials should not be allowed to use the law to suppress criticism of their job performance, he said. On the contrary, the law should encourage and protect public criticism of government officials. Judge Qian, however, was not persuaded, and he dismissed Pu's request to allow debate on the issue, ruling that the trial should focus on the narrow question raised by Zhang's complaint—did the book insult Zhang and damage his reputation? Pu stared dumbfounded at the judge and slapped his forehead in frustration.

The trial began with Zhang's lawyers entering documents into evidence, mainly party reports that praised him and witness statements that supported his version of events. These were the documents that Pu had insisted on receiving copies of in advance, so he was ready with a rebuttal for each one. He asked why some of the reports had portions blacked out, and challenged the accuracy of others. He mocked the fulsome praise of Zhang offered by his subordinates, and he drew attention to facts in the reports that supported the authors' story. Lu Zhimin, the publisher's attorney, was also well prepared, picking at inconsistencies in the documents and ridiculing statements from Zhang's colleagues about how the book had harmed his mental health. As effective as their rebuttals were, though, the defense law-

yers seemed to be fighting a losing battle. The dynamic of the trial remained the same. The party official had the upper hand, and everybody
knew it.

But on the second day of the trial, when Zhang's lawyers began
calling witnesses to testify on his behalf, the mood in the room
changed. The experience of the first witness was typical. Han Yong-
zhong, a tall, lanky man who had served as one of Zhang's subordinates in Linquan County, strode confidently to the witness stand and
began reading from a prepared text, explaining how the residents of
Wangying Village had never been levied illegal taxes and praising
Zhang's leadership skills. Before he could finish, though, Pu interrupted, pointing out that the defense was entitled to a copy of Han's
text if he planned to read it into the record. Judge Qian sighed, and
told the witness to put the text away. Han looked stunned, did as he
was told, and fumbled through the rest of his testimony, with the help
of softball questions from Zhang's lawyers. But when it was the defense side's turn to question him, he got flustered. At one point, after
being asked about the tax rate in the county, he hesitated and tried to
steal a glance at his text again. The defense objected loudly, and the
judge instructed the clerk to take it away from him. He looked like an
overgrown schoolboy whose teacher had just seized his cheat sheet.
Then Zhang tried to whisper the answer to the official, and the defense objected again. Judge Qian could barely hide his exasperation
as he agreed to move the witness stand farther from the plaintiff's
table.

Han's squirming continued as Pu began asking him about material
he had discovered in the reports that had been entered into evidence.
Pu read from one passage that indicated Han had collected illegal
fines from residents who violated the one-child policy, embezzled
funds that were supposed to be used to compensate peasants, and
killed a person while driving drunk. "How did you get away with it?"
Pu asked, prompting laughter from the gallery. The official bristled
and snapped at Pu, saying his record had nothing to do with the case.

"This is slandering our witness!" Zhang's lawyer objected. "The
witness is here to provide evidence! The witness is not a criminal!"

Judge Qian admonished Pu: "Defense attorney, we cannot treat
the witness as a criminal."

"Yes, yes," Pu replied, raising his voice. "But I just want to know,

how could someone who has clearly committed a crime not only escape any punishment but then receive a promotion? If Secretary
Zhang can interfere with the law—" But the judge cut him off.

By the time Pu finished his cross-examination, though, the mood in
the courtroom had begun to shift. Now it seemed as if Zhang and his
cronies were on trial, not the authors. Zhang's lawyers called more
than a dozen witnesses, almost all of them party officials who must
have expected the trial to be just a formality. One after another, they
took the stand and backed Zhang's version of events. And one after
another, they faltered under cross-examination, losing their temper
and generally making fools of themselves. A senior police official denied that his officers had beat villagers, but when Pu pressed him, he
shot back that his men "controlled" residents if they got in the way.
Another official backed Zhang's explanation that a rival party leader
had encouraged the peasants to complain about taxes in an attempt to
embarrass and undermine him. But when Pu challenged him to identify this rival leader, the official refused, saying it was "inconvenient"
for him to say because it would hurt "party solidarity."

Often the witnesses stammered in anger and just refused to answer
Pu's questions. They were men with power who were clearly unaccus-
tomed to being challenged, much less being put on the spot and grilled
about their work. Sometimes Judge Qian would intervene and direct
them to answer a question, but they would ignore him, too. The
highest-ranking official to testify, a haughty, gray-haired county
leader named Li Pinzheng, demanded to know Pu's name when he
started quizzing him. He also answered his cell phone while on the
stand. Later, when Lu Zhimin asked the official to pay attention,
the man blew up. "You're telling me to pay attention?" he shouted.
"You're the one who needs to watch out!"

As the defense pressed the witnesses, some revealed damaging details. The authors had described how officials in Linquan County
punished peasants for violating the one-child policy by demolishing
their homes and seizing their livestock, but one official who took the
stand admitted the government had also forced couples to be sterilized, requiring it of women even if their husbands had already undergone surgery. The disclosure caused a stir in the gallery, and Pu spoke
at length about how the policy violated not only the government's own
regulations but also universal human rights. Zhang's lawyers denied

it had ever been carried out. The issue came up in dramatic fashion during the testimony of Zhang's last witness, a peasant named Dai Junming, who had agreed to speak up for the party boss.

Pu asked him how many children he had.

"Three," he said.

"Have you taken birth planning measures?" Pu asked. "There was a policy in Linquan County in 1993. If you were under the age of forty-five, and you had two children or more, even if the man was sterilized, the woman was also required to be sterilized. Ten years ago, you were about forty years old. Were you forced to undergo birth planning measures?"

The room hushed. Dai stared blankly at the lawyer.

"I object!" Zhang shouted.

"This is a matter of the witness's personal privacy!" his lawyer added. "Whether he has been sterilized, that's private. You can't ask the witness if he's been sterilized."

But Pu lowered his voice and addressed the witness again. "Have birth planning measures been taken against you?" he said softly. "Please answer. I sympathize with you."

Everyone in the room was waiting for an answer, and Judge Qian seemed interested in learning the truth, too. "Witness, answer the question," he said, surprising Zhang and his lawyers. There was another awkward silence. "Witness, answer the question," the judge said again. "Have birth planning measures been taken against you?" When Dai refused again to say anything, the judge told the stenographer to record that the witness did not answer.

Finally, Pu asked Dai another question. "Do you think Zhang Xide was a good party secretary in Linquan County?" He didn't answer that one, either.

ON THE THIRD day of the trial, the defense began calling their own witnesses, all of them peasants from Linquan County. Pu's cross-examinations had put Zhang on the defensive, and now he seemed like a prosecutor building a case against him. One after another, the peasants took the stand and recalled the abuses described in the book in damning detail: the exorbitant taxes and fees that local officials had demanded from them; the one-child crackdown in which Zhang had declared it would be better to end seven pregnancies than to allow an extra child to be born; the appeals for help that took them all the way to Beijing, where they had knelt in protest in Tiananmen Square. One witness said Zhang's minions had offered before the trial to pay him if he would testify on behalf of the party chief. Another said he had been sentenced to three years in a labor camp after getting in a scuffle with Zhang during one of the protests against him. While in custody, he said, the prison guards beat him while asking how he could dare hit a party secretary. When he was released, he said, he discovered that his elderly father had passed away while he was in prison and had been denied a chance to visit him.

"Allow me to express my sympathies to you," Pu told the witness, his eyes tearing up. "It was your misfortune to be born in Linquan County."

The most vivid testimony concerned the police raid on Wangying Village that the party had dubbed the "April 2 Incident." More than a decade had passed since the authorities hushed up the raid, but now, at long last, the peasants were getting their day in court. One after another, they took the stand, spoke into the microphone, and described how the police had stormed the village in retaliation for their tax protests and beat anyone they found outside. "It was worse than when the Japanese devils invaded," recalled Wang Yongliang, a white-haired farmer who looked old enough to remember the Japanese occupation. Another elderly resident, Wang Hongyan, testified that police grabbed him and dragged him away even though he had not been involved in the tax protests. They held him for seven days, poured hot tea on his head, and forced him to run laps in a courtyard with his wrists cuffed and his legs in shackles.

"Had you been impeding the police when they arrested you?" Pu asked.

"No, I was just pulling weeds!" Wang answered. "Why would I hinder the police?"

Two of the peasant leaders also described being tortured by police. "Every officer hit me, and they kept asking, 'Are you tired of living yet?' " said Wang Xiangdong, a rugged-faced man wearing a mechanic's shirt. "They would grab my hair and slam my head against the wall."

The other leader, Wang Hongchao, said the police handcuffed his wrists tightly behind his back for an entire month, forcing him to eat and piss "like a dog." His hands swelled up and when the officers finally unbound him, the cuffs tore away his flesh. "I would like to pay special tribute to Secretary Zhang," he said angrily. "Thank you, Secretary Zhang!"

The last witness was a frail sixty-nine-year-old woman in a flower-print blouse, Zhang Xiuying. She recalled how her husband had shouted for help when police seized him during the April 2 Incident, then suddenly collapsed. The officers left him lying in the dirt unconscious. "He was just standing near the door when the three officers grabbed him," she testified. "I went to see what was happening, and I heard him shouting, 'Why are you arresting me? Why are you arresting me?' After he fell to the ground, I rushed to find help, but everyone in the village had run away." One neighbor was hiding in the fields, she recalled, but he was too scared to come out to help her.

"My husband died the next day!" she said, breaking down and sobbing on the stand. As she wept, I could see several of the peasants in the gallery were wiping away tears, too, as were Pu and Lu Zhimin. But Judge Qian seemed oblivious. "Witness, control your emotions!" he barked. "You are in a courtroom!" Then, after she finished testifying, the woman suddenly knelt down on the floor and cried out, "May the honorable judges render justice to my family!" Judge Qian shouted again for order, but another woman in the audience also knelt and pleaded for justice. The gallery erupted, and when the police moved to escort the women from the room, the peasants jumped to their feet, furious. Pu stood up as well, and calmed the crowd.

Zhang Xide, however, appeared amused by the scene. He had been sitting quietly at the plaintiff's table through much of the trial, sipping tea from a steel thermos and excusing himself occasionally to use the restroom. He let his lawyers do most of the talking. But as the proceeding began spinning out of his control, he smiled less and spoke up more. "That's a lie!" he blurted out occasionally, drawing rebukes from the judge and laughter from the gallery. For the most part, though, he stayed cool and casually dismissed the peasants' testimony. From the plaintiff's table, he said the party had long ago concluded that the police raid was justified and handled properly, and he rejected the corruption allegations against him as "just a few trifles." Addressing the one-child crackdown, he maintained that "only twenty or so families had their homes torn down," as if that were nothing to be concerned about. He also defended his use of county funds to buy a Mercedes-Benz. "I didn't buy it for myself, but for anyone who needed the car for work," he said. When Pu brought it up again, he retorted: "This has nothing to do with this case. I have my human rights!"

From beginning to end, Zhang maintained that the book was trouble for the party. "This book doesn't encourage people to obey the law or work hard, but glorifies crime and violations of discipline," he testified. "It incites the peasants to protest in large groups, launch surprise attacks on police, steal guns, insult county party secretaries, and so on. . . . If nine hundred million peasants are guided like this, what kind of result will there be for China?" When the defense noted that the book had been critically acclaimed, he smugly reminded them that it had been banned. "Why haven't domestic newspapers and media said anything about it since March?" he asked, before answering his own question. The book, he said proudly, had been "strangled" by the party.

When it came time for Pu to question Zhang, he asked only one question. "I've been willing to believe you originally didn't know the facts," he said slowly. "But today, facing the suffering of these people, including suffering at the hands of your subordinates, do you have any regrets or remorse or a feeling you let these peasants down?"

Without even hesitating, Zhang replied, "No."

THERE WERE MOMENTS in the trial of *Zhang v. Chen, Wu, and the People's Literature Publishing House* when I felt like I was watching history unfold. As I sat in the courtroom, scribbling notes on scraps of paper whenever the police seemed to be looking away and then hiding them in my socks, I wondered if years from now, people in China would look back and remember the case as a milestone, the moment when a team of lawyers representing two blacklisted writers made a stand for freedom of speech in a small city courthouse and prevailed. As the trial drew to a close, though, it occurred to me that something even more remarkable had happened. After four days of testimony, the original defamation suit had all but been forgotten. Pu and the other defense lawyers had presented such a powerful case that now it seemed as if Zhang, and the Communist Party itself, were the ones on trial.

In his closing statement, Pu repeated his argument that the law protected criticism of a government official's job performance. Article 35 of the Chinese constitution, he pointed out, guaranteed freedom of speech for citizens. Article 47 guaranteed their literary and artistic freedom. Article 41 gave them the right to criticize and offer suggestions to the government. "As the masters of the nation, the masses have the right—and a responsibility—to criticize the government and its personnel," Pu said. "Writers and intellectuals should be spokesmen for the masses. It is the writer's duty to reflect the reality of society, so what the authors did was not illegal."

But Pu also broadened his rhetoric, suggesting the trial had shown that not only Zhang but also other party leaders could be held accountable under the law, no matter how old their crimes. "From this case, we have had the chance to reexamine what happened during the reign of Secretary Zhang a decade ago," he said.

> I am forty years old, and if I had been born in Linquan County, I might have had two children. I might have been sterilized. My house might have been torn down, and my appeals for justice might have been suppressed. . . . Under the leadership of Secretary Zhang, the excessive tax burden on the peasants of Linquan was a problem. Many people appealed to the higher authorities, and some of their representatives were arrested and cruelly suppressed. Those are the facts. . . .
>
> Each of these statements could mean a history of misery for a family. The silent majority, whether they have rights or not, whether they can speak out or not, will remember this kind of history, and justice will eventually prevail. . . . We hope this case will make clear to hundreds of thousands of officials that they should not abuse their power and oppress the people. Everything comes out with time. . . .

Pu ended with a subtle plea to the judges to defy their party superiors. "The civil suit procedure is meant to protect an individual's legal rights," he said. "It is not a tool or a method for certain officials to attack or exact revenge. Regardless of whether the legal system accepts this now, some day we believe it will be true. . . ."

> Honorable judges, the noble nature of your profession gives you the power to establish rules for all of society. . . . Obviously, there is room for you to be creative. If you are appropriately cre-

ative, your efforts and morals will lead society toward the further development of civilization and democracy. Your names will go down in history. Your verdict can show that our society can tolerate criticism and scrutiny. Your verdict will demonstrate whether the conduct of public figures can be a subject of public discussion and independent examination. Finally, your verdict will also demonstrate whether the Chinese judiciary, surrounded by layers of money, power, and local influence, can shoulder its historical responsibility to act on its conscience and promote the progress of society.

It was dark outside when the lawyers finished making their closing statements. Judge Qian adjourned the trial without indicating when he might issue a verdict. Zhang Xide left the courthouse first, in a shuttle bus with a police escort, and the crowd of peasants from Linquan County waiting outside watched him drive off into the night. Then Pu and the defense team emerged with the authors, and the peasants quickly surrounded them to learn what had happened on the last day of the trial. They would be talking about it for years.

Chen Guangcheng

11

BLIND JUSTICE

I n a small farmhouse in Dongshigu Village, on the rural plains south of where the Yellow River empties into the Bohai Sea in Shandong Province, a blind man prepared for a long and dangerous journey. Chen Guangcheng was in his mid-thirties, a slim, handsome fellow with a thick mop of hair and a smile that could dazzle. He wore dark sunglasses, and in a different setting he might have been mistaken for a hip young musician or a Hong Kong film star. On this night in the summer of 2005, though, he was a prisoner planning an escape.

Chen shuffled across a dimly lit room and gathered some papers, which he folded and stuffed in his pockets along with a digital voice recorder and a few other items. He would have to move quickly to elude the thugs who had been posted around his house, and he couldn't afford to be slowed down by carrying a bag. A few days earlier, he had consulted the Book of Changes, an ancient oracle text, and determined the most auspicious time to run: August 25, between 9 and 11 P.M. If everything went according to plan, his nephew would be waiting on the outskirts of the village, ready to take him to a car and put him on a train to Beijing. He just had to get past the thugs.

It was a warm, breezeless night, and as he waited Chen could feel a bead of sweat forming on the back of his neck. He stood by the door and listened intently, but heard only a dog barking in the distance and his own nervous breathing. For a moment he wondered if the government's men were still out there. But of course they were. They had been a constant presence for weeks, preventing him from leaving his house and blocking anyone from visiting him.

As the hour approached, Chen's wife helped him take off his shoes and put on a pair of sneakers. Yuan Weijing was a tough, sturdy woman, and a co-conspirator in Chen's plot to escape. They had met four years earlier, just after she graduated from college. Chen had heard her on a call-in radio show, a sad, soft voice from a village in the next county talking about how hard it was to find a good job, and he had called her to cheer her up. He reminded her how fortunate she was compared with most peasants in the area, and teased her about how much more difficult it was for a disabled person to find work. His words touched her and, with his encouragement, she found a job as a teacher. A romance quickly blossomed, on the phone at first, then in person. Her parents objected strenuously. She wasn't pretty, they told her, but she was tall and healthy and had a good job, so there was "no need" for her to marry a blind man. At one point they locked her in the house to prevent her from seeing him. But she escaped and eloped with Chen, and soon afterward they had a boy and then a second child, a girl.

From the start, Yuan had tried to persuade her husband to take a quiet job at a local hospital practicing traditional medicine and massage, one of the few careers available to the blind in China. But Chen had never been one to let his disability constrain him. The youngest of five peasant brothers, he had lost his sight as an infant, the result of a high fever and the awful state of rural medical care during the Cultural Revolution. He couldn't go to school until he was seventeen, and he was twenty before he finished elementary school. But then instead of attending a vocational school, where he would only learn massage, Chen convinced his parents to send him to an academy for the blind in the port city of Qingdao so he could continue his education. It was there that he learned about a new law protecting the rights of people with disabilities. When he returned to his village, he told local officials the law required them to reduce or waive taxes on the disabled, and when they ignored him, he made the four-hundred-mile trip to Beijing to complain and won a refund for his family. The money helped his parents send him to a university in Nanjing, where he studied traditional medicine, the only department open to the blind besides music. On the side, though, Chen took a few classes in the subject that really interested him: the law. Discrimination against the blind and others with disabilities was common in China, and he believed he could use his legal knowledge to fight it.

Even before graduating, Chen began to develop a reputation back home as someone who understood the law and wasn't afraid to stand up to the government. The fact that he was blind only enhanced people's respect for him. They understood the difficulties faced by the disabled, especially in backward and impoverished villages like Dongshigu, and they admired Chen for making something of himself despite these challenges. At first he was known as a legal advocate for people with disabilities. If officials could not provide better services for the disabled, he argued in court again and again, they should at least stop collecting taxes from them. Judges sympathized with his cause, handing him victories in three cases. But then the party bosses instructed the courts to stop accepting any more of his lawsuits; apparently, they were worried about the loss of tax revenues.

Word of Chen's success spread, though, and residents began seeking his legal advice on other matters. In 2002, he helped organize dozens of villages in a petition campaign to shut down a paper mill that was dumping black noxious wastewater into a local river, destroying crops, killing fish and turtles, and making residents sick. When the government refused to act, because a party official owned the mill, Chen found another solution, persuading a British aid agency to fund the construction of a new well, complete with pipelines for irrigation and drinking water. A year later, Chen and his wife traveled to the United States on an exchange program run by the State Department. After he returned, he won another big lawsuit, forcing the Beijing subway system to waive fares for the handicapped.

Yuan objected to her husband's crusades at first. She told him there were too many problems in the countryside, and he couldn't solve them all. But Chen insisted he should try his best. He argued that victories even in small cases could be life-changing for the families involved. Eventually, Yuan came to support him in his battles with the authorities, but she never stopped worrying he was too much of a dreamer. He wanted to set up a legal aid group for people with disabilities in the countryside; she doubted the government would ever let him. The party required nongovernmental organizations to register with a state sponsor, and the state only sponsored groups it could control. The closest Chen came was an offer to let him start his center under a party-run organization—as long as he agreed to pay a huge annual kickback. Yuan feared for her husband's safety, too. She knew he had angered and embarrassed local officials. Helping him get around, she was painfully aware how vulnerable he was and how easy it would be for someone to hire a few of the local bullies to rough him up. But she also knew her husband wouldn't change. When villagers came to him asking for help, he just couldn't ignore them.

The latest trouble began about five months earlier, while Chen was in Beijing trying to find support for the legal aid group he wanted to start. A man from Dongshigu had called and told him that officials were visiting every couple in the village with more than one child and taking either the mother or father away to be sterilized. The caller wanted to know if what they were doing was legal. Chen told him that it wasn't, and he rushed back to find out what was going on. One of his neighbors, a woman named Du Dehong, was waiting in tears at his home when he returned. She said a group of officials had stormed into her house and demanded she accompany them to the local clinic to be sterilized. When she refused, they dragged her outside and stuffed her into a van as her two children watched. At the clinic, one of the officials grabbed her hand, pressed her thumb on an inkpad, and then forced her to leave a print on a consent form. She tried arguing with them, but it was no use. A doctor finished the procedure in less than five minutes.

The story infuriated Chen, but it was just the beginning. Over the next several days, other neighbors came to him with similar stories, and worse. Mothers pregnant with a third child, some more than eight months along, described being forced to have abortions, weeping as they explained how doctors injected poisons into their wombs. Relatives of couples who went into hiding told of being tortured and held by local officials until they persuaded missing family members to turn themselves in and submit to the operations. Many residents said they were held for days in makeshift jails packed with dozens of people, including small children.

One after another, the villagers came to Chen and asked for his help. He had never taken on anything as sensitive as the one-child policy, which was a pillar of the state's development strategy and considered off-limits for public debate. He knew the government had outlawed forced sterilization and abortions years ago but that officials in many parts of the country continued to use such methods. To Chen, it was another maddening example of the party ignoring its own laws, and when his neighbors asked him what they should do, he suggested a class-action lawsuit against local officials. In the quarter century since the party adopted the one-child policy, no one had ever attempted a mass legal challenge against the state's power to compel sterilization and abortion, and Chen knew the odds were against him. But he held on to the hope that party leaders, once confronted with the abuses committed in their name in his village, would step in and punish those responsible.

As word of Chen's plan spread, residents of other villages across the county began visiting him to share their own horror stories. Then peasants from neighboring counties started calling him. Before long, Chen realized that party officials in the nearby city of Linyi had ordered a crackdown on "unplanned births" in the entire region, home to about ten million people. He started collecting evidence, traveling from one village to another and taking depositions from residents using his digital voice recorder. In his farmhouse, Yuan and other volunteers transcribed the testimony on an old computer. Then Chen traveled to Beijing and tried to find journalists who would expose the abuses. All of the reporters he contacted said there was nothing they could do. The one-child policy remained a forbidden zone for the state media, too risky for even the most daring newspapers like the *Southern Metropolis Daily* to broach. But Chen did persuade a blogger and a few foreign journalists, including me, to visit Linyi and write about the crackdown. He also found several lawyers who were willing to come back with him and help, including one of the legal scholars who had called for a constitutional review of the *shourong* detention system. The lawyers traveled to Linyi and filed several lawsuits to pave the way for a class-action case, and the scholar authored a lengthy, powerful report that he posted on the Web. The abuses committed in Linyi were now international news, and on the Internet at least, a subject of national discussion and condemnation.

For officials in Linyi, the scrutiny was decidedly unwelcome, and they tried to silence Chen. Three times they visited the blind man and urged him to persuade the villagers to withdraw the lawsuits. Three times he refused. When they told him their birth planning crackdown was over, Chen said people still needed to be held accountable. When they warned him that people might seek revenge against him if they lost their jobs because of his lawsuits, Chen ignored them and concluded he had rattled them. Not long after the lawyers and reporters left, the officials confined Chen to his home and stationed thirty men in his village with orders to prevent anyone else from visiting him. Chen had no idea how long they were going to hold him, but he didn't intend to find out. He had heard that government officials in Beijing sympathetic to his cause were already planning an investigation. If he could just get to the capital, he thought, he would be able to go to the lawyers and the media for help again.

Chen and his wife made their move just before 11 P.M., stepping quietly out their front door. "Seven guards," Yuan whispered in Chen's ear. "About twenty feet away." Chen knelt down and grabbed a fistful of sand and pebbles. Then he took a deep breath and started walking briskly, his wife holding his arm and guiding him. After a few minutes, he heard the men following them, and getting closer. When he sensed they had almost caught up, he tossed the sand and pebbles over his shoulder. The men cursed, and fell back.

The couple picked up the pace, making one sharp turn after another on the village's muddy lanes. Then they stepped into the fields and began running through the rows of high cornstalks. When they reached the intersection where Chen's nephew was waiting, they were out of breath. The sound of barking dogs seemed to be coming from every direction. The government's men were closing in. Chen knew it was best to split up and try to confuse them. There was hardly time for a good-bye. Yuan ran west, deliberately making more noise and trying to lead the men away. Chen and his nephew slipped into the cornfields again, heading east.

The plan seemed to work. Hiking through the fields, a half-moon in the sky, Chen and his nephew reached another village after about an hour. But men were patrolling that village too and spotted them. Chen and his nephew fled into a thick wooded area. The government's men were forced to abandon their motorcycles and cars and pursue them on foot. Because Chen was accustomed to feeling his way through the pitch dark, he moved faster than they did, leading his nephew swiftly through the trees. After an hour, they finally stopped to rest. The men were gone.

It was past 3 A.M. Chen's nephew called a friend with a car. When the driver arrived, Chen hugged his nephew and got in. He would make the rest of the journey on his own.

THE ONE-CHILD POLICY may be at once the best known and the most overlooked of the Communist Party's many efforts to transform Chinese society: best known because it ranks among the most ambitious experiments in social engineering ever attempted anywhere in the world; most overlooked because it almost never figures in scholarly studies of China's reform era, and the suffering it has caused is rarely mentioned alongside the great tragedies of Maoist rule.

Launched in 1979, the program was breathtaking in its audacity. With few exceptions, all couples were told they could have just one child, while local officials were given the power to decide when women could conceive and what kind of contraception they should use after giving birth. In effect, the state claimed the authority to regulate the most personal and private behavior of its citizens. Given the scale of the project, the confidence with which the party embraced it is remarkable. Party leaders were convinced not only that the one-child policy was justified, but also that it was enforceable in a nation of nearly one billion people, the vast majority of them peasants who could be expected to resist for cultural and economic reasons. Perhaps the most striking aspect of the program is its longevity. The communes of the Great Leap Forward lasted only a few years and the Cultural Revolution a decade, but nearly thirty years after it was first adopted, the one-child policy—or at least its most basic components— remains an enduring fixture in Chinese life.

It is easy to forget that this program was launched not by Mao but by his successors, at a time when the party was generally withdrawing from people's lives. Mao himself had been ambivalent about population control. At first, he stood by Marxist and Soviet orthodoxy against limiting population growth, but he later changed his mind and endorsed birth control and "birth planning." During the Hundred Flowers Movement, the president of Peking University, an economist named Ma Yinchu, won Mao's praise by arguing that strong measures were needed to prevent the nation's fast-growing population from slowing economic development. But the economist came under withering attack in the Anti-Rightist Campaign, and on the eve of the Great Leap Forward, Mao suggested that a larger population was good for China because it meant more workers. His flip-flops resulted in a pair of baby booms in the 1950s and '60s that swelled the Chinese population. It wasn't until the 1970s that Premier Zhou Enlai managed to outmaneuver the leftists who opposed population control and launch a national "birth planning" program rooted in the socialist planned economy. For the first time, the production of children, like the production of grain or steel, was subject to the targets and quotas of the government's Five-Year Plan. Couples were told to marry later, limited to two or three children, and required to wait three to four years between births.

After Mao's death, this relatively moderate approach to slowing population growth was ditched in favor of the far more radical one-child policy. The sudden shift came as Deng Xiaoping was rolling out his market economic reforms, and it seemed to run counter to his effort to lead the party away from disruptive mass campaigns and toward more pragmatic policy making. But if Deng was abandoning doctrinaire socialism, he was replacing it with a new ruling ideology, a belief in the power of "science" and "scientific decision making" to solve the nation's problems.

For more than a century, the Chinese have used the word "science" to refer not just to the study of the natural world but also to a way of thinking that is supposed to be rational, objective, and modern. In a nation disillusioned by Mao's utopian fantasies, Deng's emphasis on science as the party's new touchstone was a political masterstroke. But as the anthropologist Susan Greenhalgh has shown, the leadership's blind faith in science led it to adopt an extreme solution to a problem that, while serious, could have been managed in other ways. At the center of the process was a group of eminent rocket scientists, men who had been sheltered from Mao's campaigns, who had access to computers and international journals, and who were supremely confident in their own abilities. Chief among them was the cyberneticist Song Jian, who later served as minister of science and technology. These men viewed the population as a machine to be fine-tuned by engineers like themselves, not a society of humans with rights, values, and preferences. In 1979, they made the mistake of accepting as mainstream science the most alarmist theories of overpopulation and ecological crisis then circulating in the West. They used weak data, plugged them into formulas adapted from their missile optimization work, and created population models and forecasts that gave the illusion of fact. Then, over the objections of other scholars, they used these "scientific" results to persuade the leadership that China faced a grave crisis and that immediate implementation of a one-child program was the "only way" to avoid environmental disaster and meet Deng's economic goals.

What followed was a mass campaign not unlike those that Mao had unleashed on the public. All the familiar elements were there: the intense propaganda, the colorful slogans, the struggle sessions against offenders, the shock teams of party activists. By the mid-1980s, the campaign had basically succeeded in the nation's cities. Because the state still controlled almost all urban jobs and social services, the consequences of having more than one child could be severe, and given the party's extensive surveillance network in city neighborhoods and workplaces, unauthorized pregnancies were easily detected. As a result, few in the cities were willing to defy the authorities. In rural villages, however, the party encountered widespread resistance. Peasants depended on their children, especially sons, to help work the fields and support them in old age. But under the one-child policy, a family's future might rest entirely on the talent and health of a single son—a risk few wanted to take. With a daughter, the situation would be even worse, because she would be married off and required by tradition to support not her own parents but her husband's. And, of course, only a son could carry on the family line.

Despite open hostility across the countryside, the party pushed ahead with the one-child program, resorting to what became known as the "five procedures" to deter and punish violators—seizing grain, livestock, and furniture, demolishing houses, and putting people in prison. When that wasn't enough, it launched a mass campaign of forced sterilization and abortion in 1983. By the government's own count, birth planning officials performed nearly twenty-one million tubal ligations and vasectomies that year and more than fourteen million abortions. But the abuses strained the party's relationship with the peasants and resulted in a backlash that sometimes turned violent.

Reformers in the party leadership responded by issuing a new directive in 1984 prohibiting the use of coercion to enforce the one-child
policy. By 1988, the party had scaled back the program to allow most
rural couples whose first child was a girl to have a second baby—in
effect, to try again for a son. But after the Tiananmen massacre, birth
planning hard-liners staged a comeback and signaled again that coercive tactics would be tolerated to reach population targets. There was
another crackdown, another wave of violence and abuse, another
surge in abortions and sterilization. For the first time, the party made
the ability to meet birth planning targets a key criterion in evaluating
apparatchiks. No matter how good a job they did in other areas, no
matter how well the economy performed under their watch, local officials would now be denied bonuses and promotions if they missed
their birth planning goals. For the party's rural officials, many of
whom were not fans of the one-child policy, this was powerful incentive to do whatever was necessary to keep births down. By the year
2000, the total fertility rate in China had fallen to a historic low of 1.6
births per woman, well under the natural replacement rate and nearly
comparable to levels in the industrialized nations of the West.

There is reason to believe, however, that a similar decline could
have been achieved without the one-child policy. What neither the
missile scientists who devised the program nor their critics anticipated
at the time was the phenomenal performance of the economy under
Deng's market reforms. The rapid growth far exceeded expectations,
rendering the limited impact of the one-child policy on population size
almost irrelevant. At the same time, rising living standards caused a
historic shift in childbearing preferences, with growing numbers of
couples marrying later and choosing on their own to have fewer children. Fertility rates were already falling quickly in the 1970s under
the more moderate program launched by Zhou Enlai, from just under
6 births per woman at the beginning of the decade to 2.7 births when
the one-child program was launched—one of the fastest declines in
modern history. Nearly three decades of the one-child policy reduced
the rate further by only about 1 more birth per woman, and even the
government attributes half of that reduction to the impact of rising
living standards. The government takes credit for the other half but
could that modest decline have been achieved by just enforcing a later
marriage age or wider spacing of births? Could it have been achieved

by following the experience of other developing countries and focusing on education and facilitating contraception? If just a fraction of the energy and money devoted over the past thirty years to enforcing the one-child policy had been invested instead in rural education, the government could have put hundreds of millions of rural women through high school—and women with high school degrees in China have fewer children than those without them. Such an investment in education would almost certainly also have led to economic gains—the reason Deng launched the one-child policy in the first place.

The true costs of the one-child program, however, go well beyond the wasted effort and money. The campaign cast a pall of violence and fear across the countryside that has not been fully appreciated even by many urban Chinese, and those who suffered most were society's weakest—rural women and infant girls. Unborn babies, many aborted in the last months of pregnancy, could be considered victims as well. As early as 1981, the party began receiving disturbing reports of a spike in female infanticide, baby abandonment, and domestic violence against women who gave birth to daughters—all examples of what happened when the traditional demand for sons collided with the one-child policy. Even the *People's Daily* reported the drowning of forty infant girls in one rural Anhui county during a two-year period in the early 1980s. The high rate of suicide among rural women, a resurgence of baby trafficking and the higher infant mortality among girls could be linked to the one-child program as well. At the same time, the state carried out more than a half billion sterilization operations, abortions, and IUD insertions in the name of the program, and the health impact is believed to be staggering, given that many birth planning personnel received limited training and worked under rushed conditions with cheap equipment. Women bore the brunt of botched operations, because the IUD was the party's preferred choice of contraception and because husbands often volunteered their wives to be sterilized rather than submit themselves. Women made up nearly three-quarters of the 151 million people sterilized in China between 1971 and 2001, even though vasectomies are easier to perform and pose fewer complications.

During that same thirty-year period, the government conducted 264 million abortions, many of them repeat and late-term abortions, which carry greater health risks. Women often waited into the second

trimester to determine the gender of their child and terminated pregnancies again and again until they were sure to have a son. These sex-
selective abortions skewed the gender ratio of China's children—about
120 males to every 100 females born in 1999—and as a result, the full
impact of the one-child policy may not be known until later in the century, when these baby boys become unmarriageable young men. At
about the same time, the nation may confront a serious aging crisis,
with an explosion in the number of senior citizens and a much smaller
working-age population left to support them.

By the late 1990s, a consensus had emerged among many demogra-
phers and birth planning officials that the human, social, and political
costs of continuing to enforce the one-child program were too high,
especially given the evidence it wasn't doing much good. At the start
of the next decade, the government began shifting the birth planning
program toward a more voluntary system involving financial rewards
and penalties, as well as improved medical services and counseling. It
issued new directives prohibiting the use of coercive methods to enforce birth planning, and adopted a new law guaranteeing citizens the
right to an "informed choice" in reproductive matters. Reformers
drafted proposals to begin allowing all couples to have two children.
But neither the party chief, Jiang Zemin, nor his successor, Hu Jintao, was willing to abandon the one-child policy. The government had
insisted for nearly three decades that it was justified, necessary, and
worth the sacrifice, and neither man wanted to take the political risk
of overturning it. Any party leader who scrapped the one-child policy
would be vulnerable to attack if birth rates then climbed. The political system rewarded caution, not risk taking, and it was almost always safer to stick with the status quo than to try to change it.

The result has been a patchwork of policy approaches. In some
areas, local officials have made "informed choice" a reality, allowing
couples more freedom to plan their own families and collecting only
modest fines when they choose to have more than one child. But in
others, the old, violent methods still prevail. Population control targets continue to be distributed to provincial leaders, and local officials
who fail to meet their targets continue to be judged harshly and denied promotions regardless of their job performance in other areas.
The system has resulted in a perverse set of incentives, not unlike
those that lead officials to pursue economic growth regardless of the

cost to the environment. It didn't matter what happened to the air or the water, or even what happened to people's health: as long as an official reported solid growth numbers, he would thrive in the apparatus. In birth planning, it didn't matter if birth rates were too low, only if they were too high, and lower population figures had the added bonus of juicing the per capita economic numbers. To make matters worse, provincial leaders often played it safe, handing down tougher goals to the city and county officials under them, just in case some failed to keep births in check. Those officials then did the same thing, issuing even more stringent birth quotas to district and village officials that could be nearly impossible to meet—impossible, that is, without the use of brute force.

The precise sequence of events that resulted in the crackdown in Linyi is unknown, but birth planning officials told me that local officials were no doubt trying to meet unreasonable targets. Shandong Province already boasted one of the lowest fertility rates in the nation, and apparently that was not enough for provincial leaders. Any slip, after all, could derail their careers. Linyi was one of several cities in the western part of the province with slightly higher fertility rates than the rest of the province, and it came under pressure to do better. The burden fell on the Linyi party chief, Li Qun, an up-and-coming politician in his early forties who was being considered for a promotion to a provincial leadership post. The party had selected Li for a special training program in 2000, and he had spent six months in the United States taking public administration classes and serving in an internship as a special assistant to the mayor of New Haven, Connecticut. When he returned to China, he was named Linyi's mayor, and then two years later its party chief. An internal report he submitted about his U.S. experience was said to have received good reviews in the leadership, and he later published a popular book titled *I Was an Assistant to an American Mayor*, in which he wrote that Chinese officials could learn a lot from their American counterparts about how to improve governance. The national media presented him as a face of the future, an open-minded and savvy reformer.

But if Li were to continue his rise through party ranks, he would have to meet population targets like everyone else. In the summer of 2004, he issued a directive calling on his subordinates to "strengthen population and birth planning work in a new age." Given the government's softer and more voluntary approach to birth planning, he said, the task of population control faced "new situations and problems" and "severe challenges."

> The thinking, job understanding, and work methods of some comrades do not suit the demands of the new situation. They are uncertain what to do, flinch at difficulties, and handle phenomena reactively. There are also problems of complacence, blind optimism, and slackening vigilance. Population and birth planning work has reached a key moment where it must move forward or it will fall behind.

Li's directive went on to set a goal of limiting population growth to under 6 percent and guaranteeing more than 97 percent of births satisfied the one-child policy. It reminded officials to obey the law and respect the "informed choice" of residents, but the emphasis was on getting the job done, and it outlined rewards and penalties for officials in the three urban districts and nine rural counties under Linyi's jurisdiction. Seven months later, Li followed up with another directive on the subject. This one was not publicized, but I was told it adopted a much tougher tone. The peasants weren't educated enough to respect the law, it said, so legal procedures would not be enough to enforce compliance with birth planning targets. Instead, "the old methods" had to be used. It was this document that resulted in the violent crackdown in Linyi during the spring of 2005. Within the first few months, one county alone reported completing seven thousand sterilization operations. Teng Biao, the legal scholar who traveled to Linyi to investigate, estimated that 130,000 people had been detained, beaten, and held hostage by officials trying to compel relatives or neighbors to abort pregnancies or submit to sterilization.

It wasn't until a blind man forced the nation, and the world, to look at what was happening in Linyi that the crackdown was suspended. When I traveled to Linyi, Chen Guangcheng took me from village to village, introducing me to women who had been dragged away like animals to be spayed and men who still bore bruises from being beaten and whipped. Villagers described midnight raids on their homes involving as many as thirty officials and hired thugs. Others recalled being packed into small rooms with as many as seventy others and released only after paying exorbitant fees. One woman could barely walk because of a botched tubal ligation. When the doctor told her what had happened, he didn't apologize; he just told her she needed to come back in a month so he could try again. Another woman told me she was seven months pregnant and in hiding when officials detained all her aunts, uncles, cousins, and in-laws, as well as her pregnant sister. Every day her family called her, begging her to turn herself in so the beatings would end. Finally, she did and gave in to the government's demand she have an abortion. At each village we visited, the peasants crowded around and greeted Chen like a returning hero. He recorded their stories, and told them not to give up.

Local officials confined Chen to his farmhouse not long after my article and others like it were published. But within weeks, the National Population and Family Planning Commission, the government ministry that administers the birth planning program in Beijing, announced it was opening an investigation and sending officials to Linyi. By then, though, Chen had escaped and was making his way to the capital.

EVEN BEFORE CHEN'S train arrived in Beijing, the goons from Linyi were waiting for him at the station. One of his lawyer friends had gone to pick him up and noticed several men outside speaking with Shandong accents about how to spot him. The lawyer called Chen's cell phone, then arranged to meet him on the train. Together they disembarked and doubled back through a tunnel onto another platform. Then they slipped out a cargo exit on the other side of the station. But the next day, the men from Linyi managed to track him down again. Chen and the lawyer were about to enter a subway station when someone tapped him on the shoulder.

"Let's go home, brother. You've made me come so far. You're killing me!"

Chen recognized the weary voice immediately. It was Zhu Hongguo, a portly rural official he often dealt with back home. "I'm not going home," he told the official.

But then there was another voice: "We're from the Linyi Public Security Bureau."

"So what?" Chen said. "Have we broken the law?"

"No."

"Then why are you following me? The police must conduct their business according to the law!"

"We want to have a word with you."

At this point the men began trying to separate Chen from his companion. There were about six of them, and they kept telling the lawyer that they were old friends of Chen's. "Who says we're friends?" Chen shot back. Addressing Zhu, he said, "If you had come by yourself, we could talk, but you've brought so many police and thugs with you." The lawyer began shouting that hoodlums from Shandong had come to Beijing to bully a blind man, and a crowd of passersby started gathering around them. Chen called a friend on his cell phone, telling him to come to the subway station with a camera and take pictures. The men from Linyi backed off a distance, apparently worried about causing a scene.

But when Chen and the lawyers entered the station, they followed. Chen knew they wouldn't try to grab him in such a public place, but he didn't want them following him, either. So he took the lawyer's hand and began leading him briskly toward the subway line. He knew the station well. After all, he had sued the subway system just a few years earlier. The men from Linyi had fallen behind while paying their fares, but they caught up in time to follow Chen onto the subway. Chen moved through the car, pushing his way past the other passengers, dragging the lawyer along, and then suddenly he got off the car at the other end just as it was about to leave. The Linyi men were caught off guard and scrambled to get off, too, but only one or two of them managed to make it before the doors closed. Chen kept moving, heading through the crowd down the platform toward another line in the station, his lawyer friend trying to keep up. He boarded another train, and the remaining Linyi men followed him on. When he got off again, they got off. But then he and the lawyer jumped back on. The doors closed before the Linyi men could follow. The subway pulled out of the station.

I saw Chen that night at a restaurant on the north side of Beijing, and he was his usual charming self, regaling a roomful of friends with the story of his adventure in the subway system and his earlier escape through the cornfields of his village. More than once, a listener interrupted to express wonderment that a blind man could outmaneuver the state's agents. "I wasn't leading Guangcheng around. Guangcheng was leading me around!" exclaimed Jiang Tianyong, the lawyer he had dragged through the subway station, and everybody laughed. Later, I asked Chen what his plans were. "We need to prepare the case and talk about bringing it to court," he said. "I can't collect any more material. If I go back now, many, many people will be waiting for me. . . . We could get more evidence, but I want to get started on the case and collect material later. We need to file the lawsuits, go to the media."

Over the next several days, Chen said, he planned to meet with more lawyers and try to persuade them to join the case. About a half dozen of those who had already agreed to help were at the table with us, among them an attorney named Li Heping, whom I had met years earlier. Li had handled the defense of Yang Zili, a computer programmer jailed in 2001 on subversion charges for setting up a study group to discuss political reform. At the time, Li had struck me as a particularly nervous and frightened man. (When I showed up at his office to ask about that case, he had started sweating and refused to talk to me.) But he was a different person now. He had converted to Christianity and become one of the more prominent *weiquan,* or "rights defense," lawyers in Beijing. His firm had already filed several of the lawsuits on behalf of Linyi residents. He told me it would be nearly impossible to persuade the courts to allow a class-action or collective case. That's why Chen needed to recruit more lawyers—to help file more individual lawsuits. Chen himself hadn't given up on the idea of a class-action case, but he agreed he needed more legal help. Li and his colleagues were working pro bono, and they could only do so much.

I asked Chen if he had considered seeking help from the National Population and Family Planning Commission, the agency that had announced an investigation into the Linyi crackdown. He replied that he would try but that he was unsure how to get in touch with officials there and worried he might end up getting arrested outside their offices. He still believed the courts were his best option for seeking justice. He had had some success in the legal system, after all, and he was familiar with the process. "Everyone has to be held accountable under the law," he told me. "These officials broke the law, and they have to take responsibility."

Four days later, the men from Linyi caught up with Chen again, ambushing him outside the apartment building where he was staying. Chen tried to resist, shouting for help as they dragged him across a parking lot and bundled him headfirst into an unmarked car. A friend who was with Chen at the time called me and I rushed over from the other side of the city. By the time I arrived, a crowd of Beijing residents, upset at seeing such rough treatment of a blind man, had surrounded the car and were preventing it from driving away. Behind dark-tinted windows, I saw two beefy men in the rear of the sedan but no sign of Chen. The people in the crowd told me to look again, and I pressed my nose on the window. Then I realized Chen was indeed in the car. The two men had pinned him facedown to the floor of the vehicle, and I could hear muffled screaming. Some of the angry onlookers said the men had hit him a few times. Residents called the Beijing police, and eventually two uniformed officers arrived. They consulted with the Linyi men, and then cleared a way through the crowd for the car to leave.

As I watched them drive off, I was reminded of something Chen had said while we were in Linyi a few weeks earlier. I had asked one of the villagers we were interviewing whether she was afraid that local officials might punish her for speaking out about the abuses. Chen interrupted and said the authorities wouldn't do anything to the villagers. "If anything," he said, "they'll go after me."

IN THE TWO years since the *Southern Metropolis Daily* published its report about the death of Sun Zhigang, prompting the party to abolish the *shourong* detention system, a loose collection of lawyers, journalists, and activists had coalesced around the *weiquan,* or "rights defense," concept—the idea that citizens could bring about gradual political change by fighting for legal rights one case at a time, without directly challenging the authoritarian system. But the fledgling movement was divided from the start over what to do about Chen Guangcheng and the abuses he exposed in Linyi. The journalists were on the defensive after the arrests at the *Daily* and unwilling to break the long-standing taboo against coverage of the negative effects of the one-child policy. The lawyers were in a stronger position but also hesitant. Among the most prominent of them were Xu Zhiyong and Teng

Biao, the young scholars who had called for a constitutional review of the *shourong* regulations. Former classmates at Beida and now lecturers at different universities in Beijing, the pair had set up a legal institute to take on cases they believed had the potential to highlight wider problems and promote change. They had helped defend the newspaper executives at the *Daily*, tried to stop the closure of a popular Internet bulletin board site, and represented private entrepreneurs who ran afoul of party bosses. When the two men heard about the crackdown in Linyi, though, they had reacted differently. Teng had agreed to help Chen, but Xu was worried the one-child policy was still too sensitive to take on in court.

The dynamic changed after Chen's public abduction in Beijing. The image of hoodlums from Linyi coming to the capital and snatching a blind person off the streets—along with later reports that they had beaten him—galvanized the community. Xu and other *weiquan* lawyers who had been reluctant to get involved now rallied to Chen's defense. Chen didn't have a law degree and he wasn't a lawyer, but the *weiquan* attorneys considered him one of their own—a rights defender. The big Internet firms Sina and Sohu were ordered by censors to keep news about Chen off their sites, but the lawyers and others posted a flurry of open letters condemning the Linyi officials elsewhere on the Web. Meanwhile, officials confined Chen to his farmhouse again, and the government investigation into the abuses in Linyi seemed stalled. The birth planning agency confirmed it had found misconduct, but provincial authorities closed ranks around the Linyi officials and no specific punishments were announced. A series of *weiquan* lawyers and activists traveled to Dongshigu and tried to visit Chen, but local officials and their enforcers blocked the entrance to the village and roughed up those who insisted on trying to get in.

After a while, the lawyers backed off. Chen had not yet been charged with a crime, and they didn't want to escalate the conflict with the Linyi officials and force their hand. At the same time, the movement had turned its attention to a series of clashes in the countryside between peasants and local officials who had seized farmland from them for development. The case that attracted the most attention involved an attempt by residents of Taishi Village in Guangdong Province to impeach their local leaders. But as *weiquan* lawyers and activists traveled to Taishi and other villages to provide the peasants with legal services, a disturbing trend emerged. With increasing frequency, local party bosses resorted to the use of violence against them, often hiring thugs like the men posted around Chen's village to do their dirty work. The violence put the "rights defense" movement in a difficult position. These lawyers wanted to force the government to live up to its own laws, one case at a time, without directly challenging the party's authority. Each case that they won would bring China a step closer to the rule of law, and each case that they lost would damage the party's reputation. But violence was an outcome they had not fully contemplated, and it left them divided about how to respond. Some said they should back down, arguing that by resorting to violence, the party had already exposed the nature of its political system and damaged itself. Refusing to retreat would change nothing and only get more people hurt. But other lawyers were uncomfortable abandoning the people they were trying to help, and argued that they should stand their ground. They believed in nonviolent resistance, even if it meant that local officials had forced them into a more direct confrontation.

The debate would eventually focus on one of the lawyers who spoke out in Chen's defense, Gao Zhisheng. A former soldier who passed the bar after taking night classes and studying on his own, Gao first made a name for himself protesting the mass evictions of homeowners in Beijing and other cities by corrupt officials and private developers who refused to pay market rates for land they seized. He was enough of a concern that China's richest woman, Chen Lihua, tried to buy his silence. He later emerged as one of the most outspoken of the *weiquan* lawyers, and he was the first of them to agree to defend victims of the party's brutal crackdown on Falun Gong, the popular spiritual movement that the party had banned as a political threat. The government retaliated by shutting down Gao's law firm in late 2005. A few months later, as the attacks on *weiquan* lawyers grew, Gao launched a "relay hunger strike to oppose violence." The plan was for individuals across the country to refuse food for one day at a time and share their views online. It immediately attracted support among a diverse collection of people with grievances against the state, from Falun Gong practitioners to residents in Shanghai who had lost their homes to corrupt developers.

The hunger strike seemed relatively harmless, but it split the group campaigning on Chen's behalf as well as the larger community of people working for political change. The critics argued that Gao was politicizing the "rights defense" movement because the hunger strike amounted to a direct challenge to the party's authority. The most visible proponent of this view was Ding Zilin, the historian who had lost a son in the Tiananmen massacre and organized the families of other victims to demand redress. She posted an open letter to Gao on the Internet arguing that the party was bound to overreact to his hunger strike just as it did to the 1989 democracy movement. The security services had already begun arresting and beating participants in the strike, and she blamed Gao, saying he shouldn't have encouraged others to participate in the strike if he couldn't protect them. Other critics were less strident, but agreed with Ding's basic point: the hunger strike could provoke a backlash from party hard-liners, jeopardizing the entire "rights defense" movement and the gains it had achieved. Without coverage in the mainstream media and with only limited support from the general public, the strike would have no impact on the party's willingness to use violence. On the other hand, they hoped, a steady, moderate approach to "rights defense" would foster civil society and build momentum for gradual political change, both inside and outside the party.

The activists who supported Gao, though, argued that he and the others participating in the hunger strike were doing nothing illegal. They were merely protesting injustice, and doing so in a quiet, nonviolent fashion. Among those who sympathized with Gao's cause was a network of Christian lawyers, including Li Heping, who worshipped in underground churches and made up a growing wing of the "rights defense" movement. They likened the hunger strike to the nonviolent campaigns led by Martin Luther King, Jr., and Mohandas Gandhi, and argued that it was unfair to blame Gao for the government's response, just as it was unfair to blame the students for the Tiananmen massacre.

The dispute spilled into Chen's case after Gao declared that one of his days of fasting was intended to protest Chen's treatment at the hands of the Linyi officials. Chen reciprocated while under house arrest, announcing in late February that he had joined the relay hunger strike for a day. He fasted another day in support of the hunger strike in early March. Just days later, after months of simply holding him in his farmhouse, the police suddenly decided to take Chen into custody. He was later charged with disturbing public order and disrupting traffic.

The key figures in the "rights defense" movement quickly met to discuss Chen's case. The room was divided roughly into two camps: pragmatists and purists. The pragmatists believed the only way to help Chen was to persuade party leaders in Beijing to intervene on his behalf. The best way to do that, they argued, was to rally public opinion against the Linyi officials and show the leadership that the interests of the Communist Party would be better served if it sided with Chen instead of its local apparatchiks. In the party's flawed legal system, the men on the Politburo Standing Committee were the ultimate judges and jurors, they said, and local officials were no doubt trying to present Chen to them as a subversive troublemaker, perhaps someone allied with "overseas, anti-China forces" because of the interviews he had given to foreign journalists. It was critical, they said, not to do anything that would alienate the leadership or allow Linyi officials to cast Chen in a negative light. They pointed to the timing of his arrest and argued that these officials had been emboldened by his participation in Gao's hunger strike. But the purists were skeptical. They argued that it was useless to speculate about the party's internal politics and foolish to count on a benevolent leader to step in and help them. That kind of thinking would not promote rule of law but instead further entrench the rule of party officials. The better approach, they said, was to stick to the law and take any action permitted by law to help Chen. It was more important to stand up for justice, they argued, than to be worrying all the time about offending party leaders.

The debate stretched on for hours, but eventually a rough consensus emerged. "Localize and depoliticize" was the motto coined by Xu Zhiyong, the young legal scholar. The campaign would focus its attacks on local officials in Linyi, not the one-child policy, party leaders, or the political system. Xu would coordinate the effort, and his colleague Teng Biao would be responsible for disseminating information. A veteran AIDS activist in the room, Wan Yanhai, agreed to help mobilize nongovernmental organizations. As for Gao, the lawyers decided that he should stay out of Chen's case.

Chen's actual courtroom defense was left to a "rights defense" lawyer named Li Jinsong. A soft-spoken, mild-mannered man, Li once worked as a tax official in his native Jiangxi Province, and he had originally obtained his law license as a way to expand his accounting practice. Like many others in the "rights defense" movement, he was a

Christian, but he had come to his religion much earlier than most of the others, and he worshipped in a state-sanctioned church, not an underground one. In the 1990s, he gained notoriety by filing lawsuits against government agencies in Guangdong Province, suing a local labor bureau for failing to protect a worker's rights, for example, and a state transportation company for raising ticket prices before the Spring Festival holiday. Once, he even sued a local court, accusing it of failing to pay overtime to one of its security guards. The court put him in jail for fifteen days.

Li had met Chen only once, the day before he was abducted in Beijing. Chen had asked him to help with the Linyi lawsuits, and he had declined. Given the sensitivity of the one-child policy, he thought the cases would be too difficult to pursue without stronger evidence of the abuses, such as video or audio recordings. But he had been impressed enough by Chen to promise to defend him if the police attempted to prosecute him. Now he was keeping that promise.

On his first trip to Linyi, Li was harassed by thugs, threatened with arrest, and blocked from visiting Chen's wife. Some of the lawyers who accompanied him were beaten. Li was allowed to see Chen in prison, but the guards refused to let them even discuss the case. Other attempts to collect evidence in Linyi were equally fruitless, and with each visit the authorities ratcheted up the violence against the lawyers. On one trip, the thugs overturned Li's car and rolled it into a ditch while he was still in it.

As the trial date approached, the public campaign on Chen's behalf was also faltering. All of the lawyers believed public opinion was critical to saving Chen, and they agreed it was necessary to shine a light on his case, exposing injustice and putting pressure on the leadership to respond. But the mere act of speaking out on Chen's behalf could be viewed as a challenge to the party, or presented as such by the Linyi officials, and even the pragmatists disagreed among themselves about how to handle that problem. The lawyers tried to hold a press conference about Chen's case, but police in Beijing shut it down, and some of the pragmatists argued that it had been a mistake to try at all. Others objected when Chen's supporters printed t-shirts and buttons with photos of him on them, saying that would anger party leaders, and they complained that the near-daily reports that Li wrote about the case and posted on the Internet were counterproductive. Still others objected when activists who directly challenged the party leadership, including dissidents overseas, issued statements to support Chen. The problem for the pragmatist camp was that it was impossible to know for certain what kind of advocacy would help Chen, and what kind of advocacy might be used by the Linyi officials against him. At the same time, it was easy to disagree and criticize one another.

Tensions over these questions came to a head in late July, when the courts abruptly postponed Chen's trial a day before it was scheduled to open. Gao Zhisheng and a crowd of activists, villagers, and people with disabilities showed up outside the courthouse anyway, many of them wearing the t-shirts with Chen's photo. Local thugs quickly attacked them, injuring several people and scattering the crowd. After the clash, the split in the "rights defense" movement widened further. The purists defended Gao and the others, saying they had done nothing illegal and were just trying to show their support for Chen. The pragmatist were furious. They argued that the incident had given local officials the excuse they needed to persuade the leadership to imprison Chen. A few suggested that some of those who had gone to the courthouse were sacrificing Chen to further their own political agendas. Chen's lawyer, Li Jinsong, was stuck in the middle, awkwardly arguing that he didn't support such aggressive campaigning for his client while also insisting that he was powerless to stop it and defending the flood of statements he himself had issued about the case.

Another trial date was set a few weeks later. The legal scholar Xu Zhiyong planned to represent Chen in court, but on the eve of the trial, police in Linyi detained him on trumped-up theft charges. Li then refused to attend the trial, in protest. None of the "rights defense" lawyers were in the courtroom when Chen was tried, convicted, and sentenced to four years in prison.

Less than a year later, the party quietly rewarded the man behind the birth planning crackdown in Linyi. Li Qun, the party chief who once served as an assistant to an American mayor, was promoted and named the provincial director of propaganda.

EPILOGUE

Not long after I left China in December 2007, police arrested a young dissident in Beijing named Hu Jia. He had been involved in the campaign to free Chen Guangcheng, but he was an unlikely enemy of the state—a scrawny thirty-four-year-old vegetarian computer wiz who wore baggy t-shirts and was either unwilling or unable to hold down a regular job. I first met Hu nearly seven years earlier, while working on a story about environmentalists who refused to use disposable chopsticks because of the damage they caused the nation's forests. Hu brought his own chopsticks to restaurants instead, carrying them in a little cloth bag. At the time, he struck me as an ordinary fellow, perhaps more civic-minded than most college graduates, but over the years I watched him evolve into one of the nation's most outspoken human rights advocates. His efforts on behalf of the endangered Tibetan antelope had led him to speak out for Tibetan rights, and later, he became one of the country's first AIDS activists. When the "rights defense," or *weiquan* movement began, Hu served as a one-man clearinghouse for news about government abuses. He was fearless, issuing statements and sending cell phone messages while others hesitated. When I last saw him in the summer of 2007, he was sheltering Chen's wife in his apartment and trying to help her draw more attention to her husband's plight.

In the debate between the purists and the pragmatists, Hu was one of the purists. Some people thought he was too much of a self-promoter, too willing to confront and provoke the authorities. When police put him under surveillance, he filmed the officers assigned to keep an eye on him and posted a documentary about his experience online. When they put him under house arrest, he used his Webcam to testify in a European parliamentary hearing on human rights. But if he sometimes behaved recklessly, he also never backed down. Xu Zhiyong, the pragmatic legal scholar who led the campaign to free Chen, disagreed with Hu's tactics but called him "modern China's conscience." Hu's stubborn insistence on speaking out against wrongdoing finally got him arrested two days after Christmas. Officers dragged him away as his wife was giving their two-month-old daughter a bath in another room. Not long before his arrest, Hu had written an essay challenging the government to improve its human rights record before the Olympics opened in Beijing the coming summer. Police charged him with incitement to subversion, and a court later sentenced him to three and a half years in prison.

Hu's arrest was part of a broad government crackdown on dissent ahead of the 2008 Summer Games—a crackdown that continues to unfold as I write. The party wants to use the Olympics to highlight its achievements over the past three decades and appears determined to stop people like Hu from spoiling the celebration, even if it means breaking the promises it made to win the honor of hosting the Games. In the early 1990s, Beijing had lost to Sydney in the competition for the Games because of Western criticism of its human rights record, and the government had reacted indignantly, denouncing its detractors for interfering with China's "internal affairs." But when it applied again in 2001, it made a new pitch: Our human rights record has improved. Give us the Olympics, and we will do even better. "Eight years is a long time," Liu Jingmin, the deputy mayor responsible for the Olympic bid, told me at the time. "If people have a target like the Olympics to strive for, it will help us establish a more just and harmonious society, a more democratic society, and help integrate China into the world." The argument seemed to resonate, and Beijing was awarded the Games a few months later. Then, as now, people wanted to believe that prosperity and engagement with the international community would soften China's authoritarian political system.

China has changed in remarkable and often unexpected ways since celebrating its winning bid to host the Olympics. The government has largely withdrawn from the workplace as well as from the personal lives of its citizens, and rising incomes have given people more control over their lives. The labor camps of the *shourong* detention system, which had been singled out by critics of China's Olympic bid, have been shut down. Newspapers, magazines, and television and radio stations have won more freedom from the censors, and some nongovernmental organizations in fields such as environmental protection have managed to flourish despite the party's controls. Widespread access to the Internet has opened up new channels for citizens to obtain news and information, to express themselves, and to build civil society. Conditions have even improved for foreign correspondents. I asked Deputy Mayor Liu in 2001 about regulations that made it illegal for foreign journalists to travel and interview people without the government's permission. He said he didn't believe they would still be in place in 2008, and he was right. The government has suspended the regulations for the Olympics.

Still, the arrests of individuals like Hu Jia and Chen Guangcheng are a reminder of how much remains the same. The Communist Party continues to enjoy a monopoly on power, refusing to tolerate any organized opposition. Independent labor unions and churches are still illegal, and the party still exercises firm control over the courts. The *shourong* system is gone, but police have found other ways to detain people arbitrarily and force undesirables out of the cities, including the use of extralegal "black jails" to hold the seemingly endless stream of peasants traveling to Beijing with grievances against local officials. The vast propaganda apparatus of censors remains in place, working overtime to sanitize the Internet as well as mainstream media, and officials continue to harass and bully journalists, both domestic and foreign. It is one of the paradoxes of living and working in China that the country can feel one moment as if it is changing almost too quickly to comprehend, and another moment as though it is running in place. Society is racing forward, emerging from decades of violence and turmoil, but the political system is stuck in the past, with party officials struggling to preserve their power and privileges.

The libel case filed by the rural party boss Zhang Xide against the authors of the banned bestseller *An Investigation of China's Peasantry* is an example of this disconnect. Nearly three years after that remarkable trial in the courthouse in Fuyang, the judges have yet to issue a verdict. They probably never will. A ruling in Zhang's favor would have angered the public and sent the wrong signal to corrupt local officials, but a decision for the authors would have encouraged further challenges to the party's authority. Party leaders decided to solve the problem by just doing nothing. The stalemate is a victory for the authors and their lawyer Pu Zhiqiang, because everyone expected a swift verdict against them, but it is far from a resounding triumph. Pu continues to thrive as a lawyer, but Zhang has retired with a full pension, and the authors remain blacklisted. Meanwhile, much of the countryside remains a powder keg. The party has nearly succeeded in eliminating the agricultural taxes that fueled peasant resentment for so long, but the gap between rich and poor continues to widen and the seizure of farmland for development by local officials has emerged as a new source of conflict. In Wangying Village, residents also complain that officials have tried to make up for lost taxes by collecting even more punishing fines for violations of the one-child policy.

Chen Guangcheng, who led the legal crusade against abuses of the one-child policy in Linyi, remains in prison and is not scheduled to be released until late 2010. The lawyers who rallied to defend him are a demoralized and divided bunch, and the greater *weiquan* movement is foundering and on the verge of collapse. The optimism that followed the successful campaign to abolish the *shourong* detention system has been replaced with a profound sense of despair over the arrest of activists such as Chen, Hu Jia, and the lawyer Gao Zhisheng. The authorities continue to hire thugs and criminals for the dirty work of assaulting and intimidating lawyers, and the lawyers and their allies have been unable to agree on an effective response. Despite its promises and the public's rising expectations, the party remains above the law.

Journalists, on the other hand, are making progress in their fight for greater freedoms. Despite the censors' best efforts and crackdowns such as the one at the *Southern Metropolis Daily*, state newspapers and magazines continue to find ways to expand the boundaries of what they can report. The commercialization of the industry has resulted in more gossip and entertainment—and more reporters accepting bribes in exchange for positive coverage—but also more serious journalism that speaks truth to power. The exploding popularity of the Internet, too, has transformed the media landscape. Since the *Southern Metropolis Daily's* investigative report about Sun Zhigang's death ricocheted across Chinese cyberspace, the Internet has acted again and again as a catalyst that amplifies voices and accelerates events. More people are online now in China than in the United States, and the Web has become the leading source of news for most of them, eclipsing the party's propaganda outlets. When editors refuse to print their stories, reporters post them on the Web. When journalists tire of the censors or lose their jobs in state media, they launch blogs or take new positions at Internet companies. At the same time, the Internet has emerged as an important venue for people with shared interests—or grievances—to gather, talk, and organize. The government is investing in new software and building new bureaucracies to rein in the Internet, but increasingly, information—about history as well as current events—is available to people who look for it.

The hard truth, however, is that many people aren't looking and that the Communist Party is winning the battle for the nation's future. Its propaganda efforts and its "patriotic education" classes in the schools have dulled the public's curiosity, and its attempts to filter the Web are just effective enough to discourage people from trying to get around them. The government has grown expert at manipulating public opinion, especially at rallying nationalist sentiment to its side. The party's most important advantage, of course, is the wave of prosperity that it has been riding for more than a quarter century, and that has lifted average incomes threefold in the past eight years. The extended boom has enhanced the party's reputation and filled its coffers with resources that can be used to buy support and defuse opposition. Because party officials can often determine who succeeds and fails in the new capitalist economy, they wield tremendous leverage over the emerging class of private businessmen and entrepreneurs that might otherwise support political change. The wealthiest and most influential tycoons, people such as Chen Lihua, are the most likely to owe their wealth to the one-party system and the least likely to challenge it. Meanwhile, funding for the People's Armed Police, the paramilitary force used to suppress domestic protest, has climbed sharply, far

exceeding budget outlays for courts and prosecutors. Given the resources and determination of the government, given the temptations
and distractions of the booming economy, given a half century of
Communist rule in which people have been taught that the consequences of challenging the state can be severe, it is no wonder that
many in China choose not to concern themselves with politics.

What is surprising—and inspiring—is that so many others continue
to push for political change, in so many different ways, despite these
circumstances. If prosperity has helped the Communist Party forestall democratization, it has also made it more corrupt and warped its
values. The fusion of capitalism and authoritarianism has resulted in a
government that can resemble a Mafia organization and a political
system obsessed with profits at the expense of other social goals—
public health, environmental protection, economic justice. The Chinese people want and deserve better. With rising incomes and national
pride have come higher expectations. People have seen how other
countries are governed, they have greater access to information about
their own nation, and they have more time and money to devote to
civic affairs. Prosperity has also given them more to defend and fight
for. When their lives are touched by the state—when judges refuse to
protect their property, when factories spew pollutants into the air and
water, when police restrict their right to worship, when corrupt officials squeeze them for taxes and bribes—they manage to find a way to
express their discontent and demand change despite the risks. In the
months before the Summer Games, residents in the seaport city of
Xiamen were marching in the streets against a proposed chemical
plant. In Shanghai, they were campaigning against the extension of a
high-speed magnetic rail line. In Lhasa, they were rioting against the
government's hard-line colonial policies in Tibet. In Guangdong, they
were facing off against police with an illegal strike against exploitative conditions at a wood-processing factory. And in rural communities across Heilongjiang, Jiangsu, and Shaanxi provinces, tens of
thousands of peasants were fighting to take ownership of the land they
till and block local officials from seizing and selling their farms to
developers.

I often hear people say that political change is inevitable in China.
When incomes rise above a certain level, they argue, the nation will
follow Taiwan, South Korea, and other authoritarian countries that

evolved into democracies as their capitalist economies developed. But rarely have people anywhere in the world gained political freedom without pain and sacrifice, and the Chinese Communist Party has shown it will not surrender power without a fight. It held on after the disasters of Mao's rule, and it outlasted its brethren in the Soviet Union and Eastern Europe after the Tiananmen massacre. In the years since, it has demonstrated its resilience again and again, nimbly adapting to new challenges and reasserting itself as a rising world power. What progress has been made in recent years—what freedom the Chinese people now enjoy—has come only because individuals have demanded and fought for it, and because the party has retreated in the face of such pressure. What the leadership doesn't seem to understand is that it is not a zero-sum battle and that these concessions strengthen the nation and, at least in the short term, also the party's rule. The more democratic and responsive they make the political system, after all, the more effectively they will be able to govern. But the party's aging technocrats are more worried about losing their privileged place in the one-party system than governing well, and they tell themselves that democratic reform only weakens China.

The Chinese Communist Party could make a strong case for the advantages of authoritarian rule. It could point to the nation's stunning economic achievements and argue explicitly that none of it would have been possible in a messy, multiparty system. But instead of proudly defending its record and its political system, it denies its autocratic nature and tries to argue that it, too, leads a democracy. "Democracy doesn't belong just to the Western world," the *People's Daily* intoned in an editorial in advance of the Olympics, complaining in all seriousness of "a narrowed definition of democracy" imposed by the Western media that excludes China and other countries. It is not unusual for authoritarian states, especially Communist ones, to try to hide their true colors. But rarely has a government had a better case for authoritarianism than this one. By refusing to make it, the party has in effect conceded that, in the struggle for China's future, it is on the wrong side of the fight.

When I visited Linyi with Chen Guangcheng before his arrest, the blind legal advocate asked me how long I thought the Communist Party could survive. The sun had set, and we were sitting in a car, driving in the pitch dark along a country road toward a village where we had received reports of forced abortions and other birth planning abuses. I told him that when I was studying Chinese in Beijing in the early 1990s, I honestly thought the party's fall from power might be imminent, perhaps after the death of Deng Xiaoping, who was aging and in poor health at the time. I was reluctant to leave the country at the end of the semester because I didn't want to miss it, I recalled. But now I felt foolish for being so naive and told Chen that I believed the party could hold on for quite some time and that I planned to leave Beijing as scheduled before the Olympics. Chen smiled and joked that I was abandoning the Chinese people, but agreed it made no sense for me to wait. He had his digital voice recorder in his hand, and he was still wearing his dark sunglasses. It had been a long day and I could tell he was tired. After a moment, Chen turned toward me and said, "I hope it happens in our lifetime." He said it almost cheerfully, without a hint of sadness.

NOTE ON SOURCES

The main sources of information for this book were interviews that I conducted and documents that I obtained while working in China between late 2000 and early 2008. Because many of those interviewed speak for themselves in the text and many others have requested anonymity to protect themselves, I have not listed them here. I also drew on my own reports in the *Washington Post* and those of my colleague John Pomfret. The following notes highlight other important sources that may not be apparent in the text.

CHAPTER 1
In addition to interviewing Wang Junxiu and several other participants, I attended Zhao Ziyang's funeral myself, staying for more than an hour before police identified me and forced me to leave. The account of the negotiations over his funeral arrangements is based on interviews with members of Zhao's family and information from other sources close to the family. In describing Zhao's career, I drew on interviews with several former aides, the two volumes of commemorative essays published in Hong Kong after his death, interviews he gave to others while under house arrest, and other materials.

Gorbachev, Mikhail, *Memoirs*, Doubleday, 1996.

Jin Ren, *Ruhe zai zhongguo shixing minzhu zhengzhi—Zhao Ziyang wannian tanhualu*, published in *Ming Pao Monthly*, May 2005.

Wang Yangsheng, *Kouwen fuqiang hutong liuhao—Zhao Ziyang shengqian fangtanlu*, posted online January 2005.

Wu Guoguang, Zhang Weiguo, and Bao Pu, eds., *Ziyang qiangu—Zhao Ziyang jinian wenji* (Zhao Lives: A Collection of Commemorative Essays), Pacific Century Press, 2005.

Wu Guoguang, Zhang Weiguo, and Bao Pu, eds., *Ziyang qiangu—Zhao Ziyang jinian wenji xubian* (Zhao Lives: An Additional Collection of Commemorative Essays and Poems), Pacific Century Press, 2006.

Yang Jisheng, *Zhongguo gaige shiqi de zhengzhi douzheng*, Excellent Culture Press, 2004.

Zong Fengming, *Zhao Ziyang nuanjin Zhong de tanhua* (Zhao Ziyang: Captive Conversations), Open Books, 2007.

CHAPTERS 2–3

Hu Jie generously shared his research materials with me. I also drew on the collections of remembrances written by Lin Zhao's classmates and her sister that were edited by Xu Juemin. Throughout this book, I relied heavily on Philip Short's authoritative biography of Mao and Roderick MacFarquhar's extensive research into his political campaigns. I gathered additional details on how the Hundred Flowers and Anti-Rightist campaigns unfolded at Peking University from Goldman's eyewitness account and the materials translated by Doolin. Schoenhals helped me understand the party's use of language. For the Mencius quote that Hu recalled on his bicycle ride, I used the David Hinton translation on page 230 of *Mencius*, published by Counterpoint in 1999.

Doolin, Dennis, *Communist China: The Politics of Student Opposition*, Hoover Institution Studies, 1964.

Goldman, René, "The Rectification Campaign at Peking University: May–June 1957," *China Quarterly*, Oct.–Dec. 1962, pp. 138–53.

MacFarquhar, Roderick, *The Hundred Flowers Campaign and the Chinese Intellectuals*, Octagon Books, 1974.

———. *The Origins of the Cultural Revolution: Contradictions Among the People, 1956–1957*, Columbia University Press, 1973.

Mu Qing, Guo Chaoren, Lu Fuwei, *Lishi de shenpan*, published in the *People's Daily*, January 27, 1981.

Peng Lingfan, interview on Radio Free Asia, February 28, 2005.

———. *Wode jiejie Lin Zhao—2004 xinzuo*, published in *Kaifang*, May 19, 2004.

Schoenhals, Michael, *Doing Things with Words in Chinese Politics: Five Studies*, RoutledgeCurzon, 1995.

Short, Philip, *Mao: A Life*, Henry Holt & Co., 2000.

Wu Fei, *Hu Jie: Yong jingtou jishi yi yingxiang sixiang*, published in *China Youth Daily*, November 22, 2004.

Xu Juemin, ed., *Zhuixun Lin Zhao*, Changjiang Literature and Art Press, 2000.

———. ed., *Zoujin Lin Zhao*, Ming Pao Publishing House, 2006.

Yue Daiyun and Carolyn Wakeman, *To the Storm: The Odyssey of a Revolutionary Chinese Woman*, University of California Press, 1987.

Zhang Yuanxun, *Beida wangshi yu Lin Zhao zhisi*, first published in *Jinri Mingliu*, February 2000.

CHAPTER 4

The history of the Cultural Revolution by MacFarquhar and Schoenhals is the best so far, and I draw on it for details, chronology, and interpretation. My account of how the Cultural Revolution unfolded in Chongqing relies on the work of He Shu, a scholar and editor in the city, who generously shared his unpublished research with me, as well as on memoirs written by former Red Guards there. Other amateur historians in Chongqing who helped me include Chen Xiaowen and Han Pingzao.

Chen Xiaowen, *Chongqing Shaping gongyuan hongweibing muyuan beiwen jilu*, unpublished.

Esherick, Joseph, Paul Pickowicz, and Andrew Walders, eds., *The Chinese Cultural Revolution As History*, Stanford University Press, 2005.

He Shu, *Chongqing wenge wudou dashiji*, unpublished.

———. *Lun zaofanpai*, unpublished.

———. *Wenge shouli daguimo wudou buzai Shanghai zai Chongqing*, unpublished.

Li Musen and He Shu, *Qinli Chongqing dawudou—Chongqing fandaodipai yihao qinwuyuan zishu*, unpublished.

Liao Bokang, *Lishi changheli de yige xuanwo—Sichuan Xiao Li Liao shijian huimou,* Sichuan People's Publishing House, 2005.

Liu Zhiming, *Chongqing hongweibing muqun chaiqian fengbo,* published in *Phoenix Weekly,* January 19, 2006.

MacFarquhar, Roderick and Michael Schoenhals, *Mao's Last Revolution,* Belknap Press, 2006.

Morning Sun, documentary film produced and directed by Carma Hinton, Geremie Barmé, and Richard Gordon, Long Bow Group, 2003.

Wang Youqin, *Wenge Shounanzhe,* Open Magazine Publishing, 2004.

Yu Liuwen and Han Pingzao, *Qingchun mudi maizang Chongqing wenge wudou,* published in *Southern Weekend,* April 29, 2001.

Zhou Ziren, *Duanyi Chongqing wudou,* unpublished.

———. *Hongweibing xiaobao zhubian zishu,* Fellows Press of America, 2006.

———. *Zheng Siqun zhisi he Chongqing bayiwu yundong,* unpublished.

CHAPTER 5

In addition to Xiao Yunliang, I interviewed several of the worker leaders as well as Yao Fuxin's daughter and wife over a period of years. For information on Mao's brief career as a labor organizer, I consulted the Short biography as well as the earlier work of Lynda Shaffer. During my research into labor issues in China, I often crossed paths with Ching Kwan Lee, whose excellent academic treatment of the protests in Liaoyang was helpful. The state sector employment figures are drawn from the government's statistical yearbooks, and the numbers of "mass incidents" are taken from statements by Chinese public security officials. Details of the Shenyang corruption scandal are drawn from state media reports as well as articles published in Hong Kong. The best English accounts of the scandal were written by John Pomfret in the *Washington Post* and James Kynge in the *Financial Times.*

Human Rights Watch, *Paying the Price: Worker Unrest in Northeast China,* July 2002.

Lee, Ching Kwan, *Against the Law: Labor Protests in China's Rustbelt and Sunbelt,* University of California Press, 2007.

Shaffer, Lynda, "Mao Ze-dong and the October 1922 Changsha Construction Workers' Strike: Marxism in Preindustrial China," *Modern China* 4, no. 4, October 1978, pp. 379–418.

———. *Mao and the Workers: The Hunan Labor Movement, 1920–1923*, M. E. Sharpe, 1982.

Yu Jianrong, *Zhongguo gongren jieji zhuangkuang—Anyuan shilu*, Mirror Books, 2006.

CHAPTER 6

Glowing reports about Chen Lihua and the Jinbao Avenue project are easy to find in the state media, so I have not listed them here. Instead, I have included a few pieces that took a more critical approach. The best research into the demolition of the neighborhoods of old Beijing and the role of developers and local officials in the process is by the urban planning scholar Fang Ke, who is profiled in Johnson's book.

Chen Yongjie, *Gangshang Beijing chai hutong beikong jin kaiting*, and related articles, published in *Ming Pao*, March 31, 2005.

———. *Wei hutong dizheng daodi*, published in *Ming Pao Monthly*, April 19, 2005.

Fang Ke, *Dangdai Beijing jiucheng gengxin—diaocha, yanjiu, tansuo*, China Architectural Industry Publishing House, 2000.

Fang Ke and Zhang Yan, "Plan and Market Mismatch: Urban Redevelopment in Beijing During a Period of Transition," *Asia Pacific Viewpoint* 44, no. 2, 2003, pp. 149–62.

Fang Yu, *Yige hutong baoweizhe de shuangzhong jie*, published in *Economic Observer*, January 27, 2006.

Johnson, Ian, *Wild Grass: Three Portraits of Change in Modern China*, Vintage, 2005.

Liu Chunqiu and Xu Huiying, *Siya yezhu zuchan kaifashang beichai zhi gongtang*, published in *No. 1 Financial Times*, January 7, 2005.

Wang Jun, *Zouchu chaiqian jingji moshi*, published in *Oriental Outlook Weekly*, October 25, 2006.

Xie Guangfei, *1380 yi nali qule? Zhuanye renshi jisuan tudi pizu heidong*, published in *China Economic Times*, October 15, 2003.

Zhang Tingwei, "Urban Development and a Socialist Pro-Growth Coalition in Shanghai," *Urban Affairs Review* 37, no. 4, 2002, pp. 475–99.

Zhang Yan and Fang Ke, "Is History Repeating Itself? From Urban Renewal in the United States to Inner-City Redevelopment in China," *Journal of Planning Education and Research* 23, no. 3, 2004, pp. 286–98.

Zhang Yan and Fang Ke, "Politics of Housing Redevelopment in China: The Rise and Fall of the Ju'er Hutong Project in Inner-City Beijing," *Journal of Housing and Built Environment* 18, 2003, pp. 75–87.

CHAPTER 7

I visited Wangying Village and interviewed the three Wangs as well as several others who participated in the tax revolt. In quoting from *An Investigation of China's Peasantry,* I used my own translation in some places and that of the abridged English edition, *Will the Boat Sink the Water? The Life of China's Peasants,* in other places.

Chen Guidi and Wu Chuntao, *Zhongguo nongmin diaocha* (An Investigation of China's Peasantry), People's Literature Publishing House, 2003.

———. *Will the Boat Sink the Water? The Life of China's Peasants,* Public Affairs, 2006.

Wang Heyan, *Wo weishenme gao zhongguo nongmin diaocha,* published in *China Business Herald,* July 20, 2004.

CHAPTER 8

In addition to my interviews with doctors, virologists, and disease control officials, I obtained from a third party a copy of Jiang Yanyong's diary notes and consulted the excellent reporting in *Caijing* during the epidemic. Greenfeld also tracks the development of the epidemic well.

Greenfeld, Karl Taro, *China Syndrome: The True Story of the 21st Century's First Great Epidemic,* HarperCollins, 2006.

Jiang zhenhua de Jiang Yanyong, published in *Caijing,* June 3, 2003.

Li Jing, *Jiang Yanyong: Renmin liyi gaoyu yique,* published in *Sanlian Shenghuo Zhoukan,* June 9, 2003.

Li Ya, *Jiang Yanyong tan pilu zhongguo yinman SARS zhenxiang guocheng,* Voice of America, April 9, 2003.

Wu Xiaoling, *SARS quanguo chuanbolian,* published in *Caijing,* May 6, 2003.

Chapter 9

The development of the *Southern Metropolis Daily* can be observed in the pages of the newspaper itself, including its coverage of the death of Sun Zhigang and its campaign against the *shourong* system. After the arrest of Cheng Yizhong and his two colleagues, I interviewed family members as well as many of the newspaper's reporters, editors, and advertisers, a few of its political patrons, and other sources in the propaganda apparatus. I also collected the open letters and petitions that were written on behalf of Cheng.

Dong Fanyuan, *Baoye fengyun—Nanfang dushi bao jingying shilu,* China Finance and Economy Publishing House, 2002.

Lin Wei, *Shui zhizaole canjue renhuan de lunjianan,* published in *China Youth Daily,* July 26, 2000.

Tang Jianguang, *Sun Zhigang siwang zhenxiang,* published in *China Newsweek,* June 12, 2003.

Chapter 10

In addition to my notes on the trial and interviews with those involved, I obtained audio recordings of all four days of the court proceedings. Pu Zhiqiang provided copies of two essays he wrote that helped explain the development of his thinking: *Xiangdang jiaoxin,* his statement to the authorities; and *Guanyu Hebei sheng Gaobeidian shi gonganju zhifa qingkuang de huibao,* his thoughts on the failure of his first attempt to defend the civil rights of a client.

Wang Dan, ed., *Liusi canjiazhe huiyilu,* Mirror Books, 2004.

Chapter 11

I drew on the pathbreaking scholarship of Susan Greenhalgh and Tyrene White for history and analysis of the one-child policy. In addition to my interviews with the key players involved in Chen Guangcheng's defense, I also relied on news coverage of the case by Maureen Fan in the *Washington Post* and Joseph Kahn in the *New York Times.* The Pils paper also helped shape my thinking about the *weiquan* movement.

Greenhalgh, Susan, *Just One Child: Science and Policy in Deng's China,* University of California Press, 2008.

Greenhalgh, Susan and Edwin A. Winckler, *Governing China's Population: From Leninist to Neoliberal Biopolitics,* Stanford University Press, 2005.

Pils, Eva, "Asking the Tiger for His Skin: Rights Activism in China," *Fordham International Law Journal* 30, April 2007, pp. 1209–87.

Teng Biao, *Linyi jihua shengyu diaocha shouji,* posted online September 2005.

White, Tyrene, *China's Longest Campaign: Birth Planning in the People's Republic, 1949–2005,* Cornell University Press, 2006.

ACKNOWLEDGMENTS

This book would not have been possible without the help of countless people across China who let me into their lives during the past seven years. They include the main characters and their families, of course, all of whom were generous with their time and patience, but also hundreds of others who shared their experiences and insights with me, sometimes at significant personal and professional risk and often for no reason other than a desire to explain their nation to the world. I am especially grateful to friends and colleagues in the Chinese press, journalists laboring under difficult conditions who routinely reminded me of the nobility of my profession. Given the political situation in China, it would be unwise to identify those who helped me most. My hope is that circumstances will some day allow me to thank them all individually and publicly.

I owe a special debt to the *Washington Post*, one of the few American newspapers still committed to covering the world. Don Graham, Len Downie, and Phil Bennett gave me one of the best jobs in journalism by sending me to China and also graciously granted me time off to write this book. David Hoffman, the paper's superb foreign editor, never failed to improve my work and went beyond the call of duty by reading the manuscript and showing me how to make it better. Ed

Cody introduced me to foreign correspondence both as an editor in Washington and as a colleague in Beijing. I was particularly lucky to spend many of my years in Beijing working alongside John Pomfret, the best correspondent in China. John was the ideal bureau chief and he taught me more about reporting in China than anyone else. He was also kind enough to read the manuscript and offer smart advice.

A succession of talented researchers assisted me in China. Wen Haijing, an outstanding journalist and translator, worked tirelessly on the book and demonstrated a remarkable ability to find people and track down information. Greg Distelhorst provided critical support early in the project, and Cui Weiyuan ably took up Greg's duties when he turned to academia. Jiang Fei introduced me to Hu Jie and joined my interviews with him. In the Beijing bureau, Chen Hong, Zhao Wei, Zhang Jing, Jin Ling, and Zhang Wei shared their friendship and wisdom, joined me on my travels, and assisted with articles that later inspired several chapters of the book. Jin Ling, especially, helped make the chapters on Zhang Xide and his lawsuit possible.

At Simon & Schuster, I am grateful to the indomitable Alice Mayhew and her colleague Roger Labrie for their patience and guidance. Chris Klein and Ann Mah were among the first in Beijing to encourage me to write this book. They also introduced me to my agent, Kathy Robbins, who helped transform my early musings into a book proposal. Her wise counsel shaped the project, and her steady support helped get me through it. In the Robbins Office, Kate Rizzo expertly managed the foreign rights, and Rachelle Bergstein offered helpful notes on a difficult chapter.

Julian E. Barnes has been editing my copy since college and he read this book as I wrote it. His suggestions and encouragement kept me going during the long months of writing and revisions. Another college friend, Tom Scocca, showed up in Beijing to write his own book, and when my son, Mookie, was born, Tom and his wife Christina Ho happened to be in the same hospital with their new baby. In between our conversations about fatherhood, Tom helped solve a structural problem in Chapter 4. Andrew Yeh also read the chapter and shared his thoughts from the perspective of a Chongqing resident.

I also want to thank my friends in the press corps in Beijing, one of the most talented and collegial groups of reporters in the world. Special thanks to Audra Ang, Jonathan Ansfield, Henry Chu, Grady

Epstein, Maureen Fan, Ed Gargan, Peter Goodman, Joseph Kahn, Ben Lim, Melinda Liu, Mark Magnier, Paul Mooney, Ching-Ching Ni, Evan Osnos, John Ruwitch, and Jim Yardley.

I learned a great deal from the larger community of China specialists and scholars, especially the accomplished members of the Chinapol listserv who allowed me to listen in on their debates. At Harvard, Ed Steinfeld and Rod MacFarquhar introduced me to Chinese politics and got me hooked.

I received wonderful moral support from my parents and my brother Michael. My brother Vincent also took time from his busy life to read the manuscript and provide helpful comments.

My greatest thanks are to Sarah. Every day, I marvel that I was able to persuade someone as beautiful and intelligent as she is to move to Beijing and marry me. She learned Chinese and wrote for *Newsweek* magazine, and even when pregnant or getting by without sleep as a new mother, she was the manuscript's most devoted and skillful editor. She believed in the book even when I had my doubts, and I couldn't have written it without her.

INDEX

ABOUT THE AUTHOR

Philip P. Pan is a foreign correspondent for the *Washington Post* and the newspaper's former Beijing bureau chief. During his tour in China from 2000 to 2007, he won the Livingston Award for Young Journalists in international reporting, the Overseas Press Club's Bob Considine Award for best newspaper interpretation of international affairs, and the Asia Society's Osborn Elliott Prize for excellence in journalism about Asia. He is a graduate of Harvard College and studied Chinese at Peking University. He lives with his wife and son in New York and will begin a new assignment for the *Post* in Moscow in 2008.